W9-APU-546

MARITAL CONFLICT AND CHILDREN

The Guilford Series on Social and Emotional Development
Claire B. Kopp and Steven R. Asher, Editors

Children and Marital Conflict:
The Impact of Family Dispute and Resolution
E. Mark Cummings and Patrick T. Davies

Emotional Development in Young Children
Susanne Denham

The Development of Emotional Competence
Carolyn Saarni

The Social Context of Cognitive Development
Mary Gauvain

Social Aggression among Girls
Marion K. Underwood

Peer Rejection:
Developmental Processes and Intervention Strategies
Karen L. Bierman

Marital Conflict and Children:
An Emotional Security Perspective
E. Mark Cummings and Patrick T. Davies

MARITAL CONFLICT
and CHILDREN

An Emotional Security Perspective

E. Mark Cummings
Patrick T. Davies

THE GUILFORD PRESS
New York   London

© 2010 The Guilford Press
A Division of Guilford Publications, Inc.
72 Spring Street, New York, NY 10012
www.guilford.com

Printed in the United States of America

This book is printed on acid-free paper.

Last digit is print number: 9   8   7   6   5   4   3   2   1

Library of Congress Cataloging-in-Publication Data

Cummings, E. Mark.
    Marital conflict and children : an emotional security perspective / by
E. Mark Cummings, Patrick T. Davies.
        p. cm.–(The Guilford series on social and emotional development)
    Includes bibliographical references and index.
    ISBN 978-1-60623-519-5 (hbk.)
    1. Child development.   2. Marital conflict.   3. Problem children.
4. Families—Psychological aspects.   5. Parent and child—Psychological
aspects.   I. Davies, Patrick.   II. Title.
    HQ772.5.C864 2010
    155.9′24—dc22

                                                                2009027108

About the Authors

E. Mark Cummings, PhD, is Professor and Notre Dame Endowed Chair in Psychology at the University of Notre Dame. His research focuses on relations between family processes and child development. Dr. Cummings has served as Associate Editor of *Child Development* and on the editorial boards of numerous other journals.

Patrick T. Davies, PhD, is Professor of Psychology in the Department of Clinical and Social Sciences at the University of Rochester. Like Dr. Cummings, Dr. Davies also studies relations between family processes and child development. He is Associate Editor of *Developmental Psychology* and *Development and Psychopathology*.

Preface

Marital discord is a distressing occurrence in families, with direct consequences for the children. Considerable evidence indicates that children are highly sensitive to parents' discord. Indeed, prolonged exposure to some forms of marital conflict increases the likelihood of children's psychological and physical problems. More broadly, such conflict poses challenges to stable and satisfying interpersonal relations among all members of the family and has the potential for highly negative outcomes. Conflict can readily become uncontrolled and uncontrollable, with even the most well-meaning individuals falling into the escalating social trap posed by intense interpersonal discord, with negative implications for the quality and even continuity of relationships.

Psychological research can play an important role in discovering answers to the complex questions of how best to handle conflict within families. An impressive body of knowledge has accumulated over the years, with many advances since the publication of our first volume on this subject, *Children and Marital Conflict: The Impact of Family Dispute and Resolution* (Cummings & Davies, 1994a). What can be termed a first generation of studies focused on establishing that marital conflict is linked with child maladjustment. By the time our first volume was published, links between marital conflict on the one hand and parenting problems and child adjustment difficulties on the other were well established, but many, many questions remained about the explanatory processes underlying these associations.

Fortunately, there has been an upsurge in the past 15-plus years of studies directed toward identifying the multiple psychological and biological responses activated by marital conflict, with implications for the development of theories for explaining these processes. Advancing ecological validity, home-based studies documenting children's responses to marital conflict have increased. Another concern has been identifying the pathways over time through which marital conflict affects children, based on longitudinal and multimethod measures. The goal is to explain how, why, when, and for which children marital conflict has implications for child adjustment.

This book documents the status of what can be called a second generation of research focusing on processes underlying the effects of marital conflict on children (Cummings & Cummings, 1988; Grych & Fincham, 1990). One finding of this research is that multiple dimensions of children's responding to marital conflict have psychological meaning and significance and are related to their adjustment (Cummings & Davies, 2002). Another finding is that exposure to marital conflict and changes in parenting both contribute to pathways of child development. Process-oriented approaches have advanced an understanding of how children's emotional, social, cognitive, and physiological processes of responding in family and even community contexts are linked prospectively with the children's development over time. The accumulation of knowledge on marital conflict has also precipitated a new research direction: developing evidence-based programs for helping parents handle marital conflict in more constructive ways. Although advice about how to approach conflicts in families abounds in the popular culture, the research findings on marital discord and child adjustment are often not widely known. In this regard, the emergence of translational research aimed at making the findings of empirical research on marital conflict and children more readily available to the public is an exciting development.

A major focus of the present book, *Marital Conflict and Children: An Emotional Security Perspective*, is on explicating "emotional security theory" (EST; Davies & Cummings, 1994) and showing how EST provides a conceptual model for understanding the direct effects of exposure to marital conflict, the indirect effects of marital conflict in the context of parenting, and even the effects of marital conflict in the context of community and political conflict. At this time, a guiding theory is needed to provide a reasonably coherent perspective on the many advances in the study of familywide and extrafamilial pathways and contexts for the effects of marital conflict on children. Theory is also critical for optimal prevention and intervention programs. Given these considerations, EST is employed throughout to provide the guiding perspective and unifying theme for this volume. Although theories in this area are similar in some key respects, and other theories have demonstrated merit, EST (Davies & Cummings, 1994) uniquely incorporates emotional, cognitive, behavioral, and physiological responses to marital conflict into a unifying conceptual model. It is also distinguished from other theories in advocating for much broader views of processes underlying children's development.

AN OVERVIEW OF THIS BOOK

This book provides an up-to-date review of research on marital conflict and children. Although this literature is considered widely, the focus is on research and theory since the publication of our first volume (Cummings & Davies, 1994a). Throughout the present volume, in addition to reviewing and discussing key findings and theory, we endeavor to identify many emerging directions for research, in order to provide a roadmap and stimulus for many advances to come. Toward this end, we also provide methodological tools for new advances in the Appendices, including specific instruments and discussions of advanced topics for multimethod research.

New Directions in the Study of Children and Marital Conflict

Reflecting new directions for conceptualizing the study of children and marital conflict, Chapter 1 reviews evidence that marital discord is a characteristic of "risky families" (broadly defined). Marital conflict is widely and by multiple pathways associated with the development of behavior problems in children. The relation of marital discord and violence to the impact of risky families is considered, including new directions linking marital conflict with the effects of paternal depression and parental alcohol problems on children. We highlight the study of interadult conflict in single-parent families as an important direction for future research.

In Chapter 2, we outline the key elements of a process-oriented approach to the study of marital conflict and children, and introduce EST and the evidence in support of the theory. The building blocks of the process-oriented approach are clearly and carefully described, including notions of the true nature of "mediation" as an explanatory process based on cutting-edge approaches, and the meaning of "moderation" as an explanatory construct. The inherent complexity of the influence of marital conflict on children necessitates a theoretical model to organize, guide, and direct research. Moreover, little sense can be made of the complex pattern of findings without a guiding conceptual model. The exponential increase in knowledge and research directions makes it essential to process and interpret the state of the literature from a coherent, focused theoretical perspective.

EST has some distinct conceptual advantages over some of the other theories in this area. One is its ability to integrate the ways in which children's emotional, physiological, biological, cognitive, and behavioral systems are affected; another is its ability to demonstrate that pathways of development are affected in multiple ways, including direct effects due to exposure or awareness of marital conflict and indirect influences on parenting and other family systems. Moreover, a large body of research has directly and in some cases indirectly tested the assumptions of EST. Given the rapidly accumulating evidence, there is a need to evaluate, within a single volume, the correspondence between the theory and the state of the literature. Chapter 2 provides a seminal, up-to-date explication of EST, including its status in relation to the most recent tests of reciprocal and longitudinal pathways of causal influences on children's development in families.

At the same time, although we highlight the advantages of EST throughout this book, we are not endorsing EST as the only viable theory for explaining the findings from marital conflict research. Other theories, such as the cognitive–contextual framework (Grych & Fincham, 1990), provide important insights into the relationship between marital conflict and children's adjustment. Therefore, we encourage readers to seek out alternative theories to get a complementary picture of the status of research in this area.

Models of Direct Effects

Part II of the book considers the observable effects and implications for child adjustment of exposure to marital conflict and domestic violence. Chapter 3 considers the multiple faces of marital conflict from the children's perspective. We consider how children react to different forms of conflict expression and resolution, including the bases EST provides for differentiating constructive and destructive conflict from the children's perspective. Other advances in recent years are tests of theoretical models for the effects of children's exposure to marital conflict on their adjustment, including theoretically guided tests of mediators and moderators of children's responding. Chapter 4 provides a systematic review of many recent studies that have tested theoretical models for the direct effects of marital conflict on multiple child outcomes; again, it focuses on recent advances from the perspective of EST, including recent tests based on multimethod and longitudinal research designs that support the explanatory value of EST.

Contextualizing Marital Conflict

Part III of the book considers the exciting new directions in this field for understanding marital conflict in multiple contexts: parenting; individual, familial, and extrafamilial processes; and time. Interparental conflict affects children not in isolation, but in the context of multiple family systems and processes. In order to fully understand children's development in discordant families, we must consider the broader pattern of influences on children within the family.

Chapter 5 considers recent advances in the study of what have come to be called "indirect" pathways and processes—that is, the specific and interactive effects within a family of marital conflict, parenting practices, parent–child attachment, and child adjustment. These new directions include tests of models (including longitudinal models) of pathways between and among marital conflict, parenting, and child adjustment. An exciting development described in this chapter is how EST provides a more compelling conceptual explanation for these pathways than past accounts, including advances over the "spillover" hypothesis.

Beyond considering parenting, relatively little research has examined the role of broader family contexts in affecting relations between marital conflict and child adjustment. Therefore, Chapter 6 places marital conflict within these broader familial (e.g., familywide cohesion) and extrafamilial (e.g., peer relationships) contexts to explore the potential value of contextual risk and protective models. Because children exposed to similar histories of marital conflict evidence wide variability in outcomes, identifying characteristics that may amplify or dilute the risk associated with marital conflict can help us understand why some children from higher-conflict homes develop severe psychopathology, while other children evidence resilience and good outcomes. Students and scholars may be especially interested in the comprehensive guide provided for new research directions that will move the field toward a familywide understanding of children's development of adjustment problems, as well as normal development in families.

Chapter 7 considers these issues further by examining development over time in contexts of interparental conflict. Relatively naïve notions abound about the nature of time in research models for child development, and about how time can be incorporated in longitudinal research to advance understanding of causal processes. In fact, there are many pitfalls and challenges for discovering the "truth" of causal processes in the context of the highly complex domain of family functioning. The chapter is devoted to considering cutting-edge issues in this regard, essential for consumers of social science knowledge as well as for the students and scholars.

Future Directions

Part IV of the book is devoted to future directions in research on marital conflict and violence from the children's perspective. There is a need to expand this research to consider the applications of empirical findings to real-world problems, as well as the implications of these findings for understanding the impact of other social systems and processes. In Chapter 8, we consider some research messages that are applicable to real-world problems. The results of studies evaluating the efficacy of programs for communicating the results of empirical research on marital conflict and children to wider audiences are examined. There are increasing questions about whether simply identifying the implications of these results is sufficient to make a difference in the real world for parents, families, and children. At a minimum, there are strong grounds for suggesting that new approaches need to be tried for applications in the real world. Accordingly, we focus in this chapter on the concept of "translational research" and on steps toward advancing translational research in this area.

Chapter 9 is concerned with exporting models and methods derived from research on marital conflict and children beyond the marital dyad—from the study of attachment based on Bowlby's emotional security notions, to the possible relevance of this work for a better understanding of the effects of political violence on children. With regard to the latter, for example, the influence of marital conflict on children can be understood in terms of interrelations among family, community, and culture. Theory in terms of social ecological models may also be applied to understanding pathways of influence, with emotional security posited as a key explanatory mechanism for understanding the effects on children of discord in the family, community, and culture. This chapter considers how the use of EST may serve to guide the interpretation of the influence of multiple levels of social ecological functioning on children's development; we illustrate the discussion with recent work on political violence and children in Northern Ireland.

Appendices

Finally, studying the effects of marital conflict on children poses inherent methodological challenges for investigators. Many scholars or students may not be aware of the latest methodological approaches, including the pros and cons of these approaches. For example, important advances have been made in specific instruments for observationally differentiating dimensions of constructive and destructive conflict behaviors (e.g., see Appendix A) and for assessing children's emotional, behavioral, and cognitive responses to marital conflict (e.g., see Appendices B and C)—all of which are critical for study of processes mediating the effects of marital conflict on children from an EST perspective. These new instruments are not readily accessible, but are critical for optimally studying many of the questions reviewed in this volume. These measures are provided in Appendices A–C. Moreover, creativity and methodological rigor are essential for cutting-edge research in this area. A detailed discussion of the latest methods and approaches for studying children and marital conflict—approaches that may not be widely known to those not reading about them in primary journal sources—is provided in Appendix D to supplement the coverage provided throughout the book. A particularly exciting direction is the study of physiological and biological processes activated by marital conflict, and their role in the impact of marital conflict on children.

In sum, this book updates and treats a variety of themes and issues, including many new topics, pertinent to families, conflict, and conflict resolution from the perspective of children. This is the first comprehensive authored volume devoted to research on family conflict in well over a decade. Many of the studies we cite have been published very recently (i.e., between 2002 and 2009), with additional studies in press. As such, this volume presents a much overdue review, analysis, and update of developments in what continues to be a dynamic and exciting field of study, with coverage provided that is unavailable in any other source.

Contents

PART I

NEW DIRECTIONS
IN THE STUDY OF CHILDREN
AND MARITAL CONFLICT

The effects of marital conflict on children's adjustment were well established by the time *Children and Marital Conflict* (Cummings & Davies, 1994a) appeared. Thus, although further evidence for the risks to children of angry and aggressive family relations has accumulated (e.g., Repetti, Taylor, & Seeman, 2002), our intent even at the outset of this volume is to move beyond acknowledging marital conflict as a risk factor and toward more broadly conceptualizing the role of marital conflict in risky families.

A significant concern is that the impact of conflict and aggression in families on children may be underestimated if one makes the mistake of viewing such conflict as an isolated source of influence. This issue is developed in Chapter 1 with reference to the notion of "risky families" and child adjustment. Repetti and colleagues (2002) have articulately described anger and aggression as central characteristics of risky families that significantly increase the chances of children's maladjustment on multiple levels, including biological and physiological processes.

Extending these notions, we argue that marital conflict is especially pertinent to notions of risky families—not only because of the risk for children associated with exposure to marital conflict, and because of the links between marital conflict and other family processes that affect child adjustment, but also because marital conflict is related both to the occurrence of psychopathology in parents and to the impact of parents' psychopathological symptoms on the children. Thus, unless one recognizes the central role of marital conflict in the creation of risky family environments (broadly conceived) for children, the effects of marital conflict as a child risk factor are likely to be underestimated.

Related to this point, in Chapter 1 we update recent findings further demonstrating interrelations among marital conflict, parental psychopathology, and child adjustment in community families. We extend the notion of risky families and marital conflict to include a wide potential range of community families, as well as families with parents identified as having clinical levels of psychopathology. We argue in that chapter for a very broad appreciation of marital conflict's relevance to a full understanding of the factors and processes that underlie children's risk for adjustment problems, in the context of relations between risky families and children's development.

At the same time, theory is essential to provide guidelines both for clinical work and for making sense of the phenomena found in research. Chapter 2 provides an account of emotional security theory (EST), reflecting the significant theoretical advances that have occurred since the publication of our 1994 volume. Although various conceptual models and theories have been proposed and to some extent tested over the past 15-plus years, we show how EST uniquely meets the needs and requirements for a higher-order conceptualization of children's multiple responses to marital conflict (e.g., emotional, behavioral, cognitive, physiological) and to related family processes (e.g., parental depressive symptoms) as centering around a unifying psychological process (i.e., emotional security). EST has also uniquely provided the inspiration for multiple methodological (statistical and measurement) approaches to studying the multiple processes related to the effects of marital conflict and other risky family processes on children.

Moreover, only EST is firmly grounded in developmental theory (i.e., attachment theory and related developmental theory, with long histories in developmental psychology and psychiatry) and posits bases for integrating emotional security with other psychological processes affecting children in families, including the effects of marital functioning, parenting, and other family factors on child development. Relatedly, relative to other theories of marital conflict, EST has been continually revised and has systematically evolved as a theory since its initial conceptualization. As part of this progress, EST has been subjected to repeated empirical tests of theoretical propositions based on a variety of methods. Advances in the propositions of our theory include numerous demonstrations of the mediating role of emotional security; tests of relations between and among multiple family systems surrounding emotional security and marital conflict; and tests of bidirectional and transactional relations between and among marital conflict, family processes, and children's responses to marital conflict.

Posing a major challenge for investigators is the fact that sensibly grouping or otherwise forming higher-order characterizations of children's multiple response processes around constructs of adjustment or well-being cannot be a simple process of summing or even weighting these reactions according to some statistical or measurement rubric. What is needed in order to accomplish these goals is a theory that is adequately grounded in developmental models and processes, and that also posits higher-order conceptualizations for grouping or otherwise making sense of multiple levels of responding centered around a key developmental construct. As we emphasize throughout the present book, EST uniquely provides a viable conceptual model for research on marital conflict and violence as related to child development—a model that addresses all of these matters and concerns.

CHAPTER 1

Marital Conflict and Risky Families

Marital conflict is not an isolated occurrence in families, but is broadly relevant to notions of risky family environments that may relate to children's adjustment problems. That is, marital conflict and aggression are linked with multiple negative influences on, and multiple negative pathways in, children's development. These influences and pathways extend beyond the effects of exposure to marital conflict per se; they encompass the many family contexts linked with marital conflict. In other words, marital conflict has significant effects on children not only through their direct exposure to it, but also through changes in parenting, family relationships, and multiple family problems (e.g., parental depression and alcohol problems). Thus marital conflict merits consideration whenever one is concerned about how family contexts may relate to children's normal or abnormal development (Davies & Cummings, 2006).

MARITAL CONFLICT AS A CONTRIBUTOR TO RISKY FAMILY ENVIRONMENTS

The following vignette illustrates how many other family stresses may be linked with marital conflict, and how the combination of these factors may have a cumulative effect on a child:

Nicole was the daughter of parents who engaged in relatively frequent displays of interparental hostility and conflict. By adolescence, Nicole had developed significant problems with anxiety and depression. However, numerous family circumstances complicated both Nicole's and her parents' problems. In therapy, it emerged that Nicole's difficulties had multiple sources. Nicole's mother and father both evidenced depressive symptoms. In addition, Nicole's father attempted to self-medicate his symptoms with alcohol, and had thus developed a drinking problem. Moreover, it appeared that in response to these conflicts, the father's alcohol abuse, and other family stresses, the mother's symptoms had developed into major depression. Nicole became highly emotionally distressed when her parents fought—evidencing sensitivity and reactivity to her parents' conflicts, even when these were relatively mild. She felt compelled to mediate the parents' disputes, and to try to alleviate her parents' distress and sadness. Over time, these many family problems took a heavy toll on Nicole's well-being. Her negative reactions and hostility added fuel to her parents' arguments, to their depressive symptoms, and to her father's alcohol abuse. Awareness of Nicole's distress also increased the parents' guilt, anxiety, and distress concerning the course of their conflicts.

This example shows how multiple family factors may have cumulative and interrelated effects on a child. As we will show throughout this book, each of these pathways is supported by research. For example, a clinician who learns that a child has a mother with depression may also want to find out whether there is conflict between the parents, as conflict is another problem often found in homes with maternal depression (Downey & Coyne, 1990). Also illustrated in our vignette is the potential for children's difficulties to affect the parents, and for children to become involved in their parents' disputes, with potentially negative effects. For example, "parentification" may occur; that is, children may come to provide ongoing emotional support for their parents, and this may become linked with the children's own adjustment problems (Peris, Goeke-Morey, Cummings, & Emery, 2008). Thus, in considering marital conflict and child development, one needs to be aware that relations between family and child functioning over time are transactional and bidirectional (Schermerhorn & Cummings, 2008): Children influence their parents' marital relations, as well as vice versa (Jenkins, Simpson, Dunn, Rasbash, & O'Connor, 2005).

Thus marital conflict and aggression frequently contribute to at-risk family environments even when other factors are identified as "the problems." For example, consider the following excerpt from a paper by Repetti and colleagues (2002) on "risky families":

> Risky families are characterized by conflict and aggression and by relationships that are cold, unsupportive and neglectful. These family characteristics create vulnerabilities and/or interact with genetically based vulnerabilities in offspring that produce disruptions in psychosocial functioning (specifically emotion processing and social competence), disruptions in stress-responsive biological regulatory systems . . . and poor health behaviors, especially substance abuse. (p. 330)

As this passage indicates, marital conflict and violence may be linked with insensitivity, neglect, insecure attachment, and lack of parental warmth toward children (Frosch & Mangelsdorf, 2001; Grych, 2002; Kitzmann, 2000; Margolin, Gordis, & Oliver, 2004). Relations have been found between exposure to marital conflict and problems with emotion processing and social competence (Cummings & Davies, 1994a). Marital conflict is also associated with disruptions in stress-responsive biological regulatory systems and risk for physical health problems (Davies, Sturge-Apple, Cicchetti, & Cummings, 2007, 2008; El-Sheikh, Cummings, Kouros, Elmore-Staton, & Buckhalt, 2008; El-Sheikh et al., 2009).

IMPLICATIONS FOR CHILDREN'S SENSE OF EMOTIONAL SECURITY

Throughout this volume, our key emphasis is on the importance of relations between and among marital conflict, emotional security, and child adjustment. The notion that risky family environments have implications for children's emotional security has a long history in developmental psychology, social psychology, and psychiatry (Blatz, 1966; Cassidy & Shaver, 1999, 2008; Waters & Cummings, 2000). For example, applications of attachment theory across multiple disciplines testify to the significance of emotional security to human functioning across the life span (Ainsworth, Blehar, Waters, & Wall, 1978; Bowlby, 1969, 1973, 1980; Cassidy & Shaver, 1999, 2008). Concerning the explanatory processes underlying relations between families and healthy child development, Repetti and colleagues (2002) note:

> In healthy families, children learn that they can count on the environment to provide for their emotional security and their physical safety

and well-being, and they acquire behaviors that will eventually allow
them to maintain their own physical and emotional health independent of caregivers. From this vantage point, a healthy environment for
a child is a safe environment; it provides for a sense of emotional security and social integration and it offers certain critical social experiences that lead to the acquisition of behaviors that will eventually permit the child to engage in effective self-regulation (Basic Behavioral
Science Task Force of the National Advisory Mental Health Council,
1996). (p. 330)

A WORKING DEFINITION OF MARITAL CONFLICT

Marital conflict is not necessarily a predictor of child, marital, or family
problems. Conflict can take many forms, and may include positive as
well as negative elements. It is healthy for marital problems to be discussed in constructive ways. By contrast, avoidance or withdrawal from
marital or family challenges can be more detrimental in the long run
than engaging in openly angry exchanges about these matters can be
(Gottman, 1994; Notarius & Markman, 1993). Discussion of differences
can be highly beneficial if these discussions lead to conflict resolution
or problem solving. In addition to the role of destructive marital conflict and violence as contributors to children's mental health problems,
another theme in this book is the importance of distinguishing constructive from destructive marital conflict behaviors, in order to more
fully appreciate the nature of relations between marital conflict and
child/family functioning.

   In this regard, we propose a definition of "marital conflict," based
on the working definition that we used in diary research about marital
conflict in the home. For these studies, we defined "marital conflict"
as any major or minor interparental interaction that involved a difference of opinion, whether it was mostly negative or even mostly positive
(Cummings, Goeke-Morey, & Papp, 2003a). By using this definition, we
were able to obtain responses about a wide range of marital behaviors,
including verbal aggression, defensiveness, nonverbal hostility, personal
insult, marital withdrawal, and physical aggression on the one hand,
and support, affection, and problem solving on the other. Parents also
recorded their assessments of their own and their partners' emotions
by marking their responses for anger, sadness, fear, and happiness on
10-point scales ranging from 0 ("none") to 9 ("high"). Our findings
indicated that parents' emotional expressions may have just as much

influence as their conflict tactics do on how children view and respond to marital conflict (Cummings, Goeke-Morey, Papp, & Dukewich, 2002). We also found that marital conflict varied widely in the conflict tactics and emotions shown, with many interactions including both positive and negative emotions and tactics.

THE SOCIAL PROBLEM POSED BY MARITAL CONFLICT

The extent of the social problem posed by destructive marital conflict and its contribution to risky family environments merits consideration at this point. Approximately half of all children will experience parental divorce at some period in their lives, and the often significant interparental hostility and discord that can accompany divorce. Many distressed couples who choose to stay together will continue to exhibit marital conflict and turmoil (Emery, 1982). Marriages are most discordant during the early childrearing years (Belsky & Pensky, 1988; Cox, 1985; Glenn, 1990): Marital conflict and discord increase during infancy and early childhood (Belsky & Rovine, 1990; Belsky, Spanier, & Rovine, 1983; Isabella & Belsky, 1985), reaching a peak between early childhood and preadolescence (Anderson, Russell, & Schumm, 1983).

The notion that "problem" marriages increase the likelihood of "problem" children is not new. As long ago as the 1930s, social scientists reported links between marital discord and psychological problems in children (Hubbard & Adams, 1936; Towle, 1931; Wallace, 1935), and support for this association has been consistent over the years (Baruch & Wilcox, 1944; Gassner & Murray, 1969; Jouriles, Bourg, & Farris, 1991; Rutter, 1970). However, until the 1980s, research often simply established correlations between general marital maladjustment and adjustment problems in children. More recent work identifies marital conflict as a key factor in relationships between marital functioning and child outcomes.

First, marital conflict characterizes many distressed marriages. Interactions between members of distressed couples are frequently marked by mutual negativity, escalating anger, and physical aggression (Hotaling & Sugarman, 1990; Margolin, John, & O'Brien, 1989; Markman & Kraft, 1989).

Second, marital conflict is a better predictor of a wide range of children's problems than general marital distress is (Emery & O'Leary, 1984; Johnson & O'Leary, 1987; Porter & O'Leary, 1980). Relationships between marital hostility and child psychopathology are clear even after general marital distress is controlled for (Jenkins & Smith, 1991; Jouriles, Murphy, & O'Leary, 1989).

Finally, marital conflict is more closely associated with children's problems than other individual aspects of distressed marriages are. For example, overt hostility between parents predicts child behavior problems more accurately than marital apathy and covert tension do (Jenkins & Smith, 1991; Rutter et al., 1974). Thus, of all the problems associated with discordant marriages, marital conflict has emerged as the primary predictor of maladjustment in children.

MARITAL CONFLICT AND CHILDREN'S BEHAVIOR PROBLEMS

Although marital conflict is a predictor of child behavior problems, not all, or even most, children exposed to marital conflict develop such problems. Marital conflict is a common occurrence even in harmonious homes. Furthermore, many children do not develop behavior problems even when exposed to very high levels of marital conflict. As we have noted, the effects of marital conflict depend a great deal on how conflict is handled. For example, conflict that is resolved may have relatively benign effects on children (Goeke-Morey, Cummings, & Papp, 2007).

The Extent of the Problem

Associations between marital conflict and children's adjustment problems are typically moderate in magnitude (Grych & Fincham, 1990). On the other hand, few family problems are more closely related to children's poor adjustment than marital conflict, even in "happy" families. Anger between spouses is even more closely associated with negative child outcomes in distressed families. Some evidence suggests that between 40% and 50% of children exposed to marital violence evidence extreme behavioral problems (Jouriles et al., 1989; Wolfe, Jaffe, Wilson, & Zak, 1985). Notably, marital conflict is an even stronger predictor when family stress is high (Emery & O'Leary, 1982; Emery, Weintraub, & Neale, 1982; Grych & Fincham, 1990).

The Importance of Adopting a Process-Oriented Perspective

At the same time, the use of correlations alone to evaluate the effects of marital conflict on child adjustment is misleading in important respects. That is, simple associations are minimally informative with regard to

hildren by influencing
nctioning of family sys-
, 2001; Dunn & Davies,
s do not actually tell us
riented level of analysis,
ldren's problems can be
t significant. As we argue
onflict and child adjust-
ess-oriented perspective
arital conflict and child

INDIVIDUAL PROBLEMS EXPERIENCED BY CHILDREN IN HIGH-CONFLICT HOMES

Externalizing and Internalizing Problems

The vulnerability of children from high-conflict homes to externalizing disorders, including excessive aggression, unacceptable conduct, vandalism, and delinquency, has long been documented (Emery, 1982). For example, Grych and Fincham (1990) reported that between 9% and 25% of the differences between children in externalizing problems were accounted for by marital conflict (see also Buehler, Anthony, Krishnakumar, & Stone, 1997).

At one time, heavy emphasis was placed on externalizing problems in boys as the primary outcome of marital conflict. However, at this point, with the advent of more sophisticated and varied assessments of children's responses, research has clearly documented a wider range of problems as linked with marital conflict. For example, relations between marital conflict and children's internalizing problems, such as depression, anxiety, and social withdrawal, are perhaps even more reliably obtained than relations with externalizing problems. In fact, some studies now even report associations between marital conflict and children's internalizing problems, but only negligible or marginal relations between such conflict and externalizing problems (e.g., Cummings, Schermerhorn, Davies, Goeke-Morey, & Cummings, 2006; Grych, Harold, & Miles, 2003). In earlier research, the opposite trend (i.e., reporting associations between marital conflict and children's externalizing problems, but no relationship between conflict and their internalizing problems) was more often indicated (Fauber, Forehand, Thomas, & Wierson, 1990). One reason for this change is that current research is more sensitive to the relatively subtle behaviors that reflect internalizing problems, or adjustment difficulties in girls; this research places greater reliance on child as well as parent report, including measures of depression, anxiety, and other internalizing outcomes (Davies & Cummings, 1998; Davies, Sturge-Apple, Winter, Cummings, & Farrell, 2006).

Social Skills and Relationships

High levels of marital conflict increase the risk that children will develop dysfunctional social skills and relationships (Grych & Fincham, 1990). Degree of marital conflict predicts more hostile relations with siblings (Dunn & Davies, 2001) and greater problems with peers in school (Parke et al., 2001), including poor interpersonal skills and social competence in school settings. However, by far the most frequently reported link between marital conflict and other social relationships concerns children's relationships with parents, multiple dimensions of which may be undermined (Cowan, Cowan, Pruett, & Pruett, 2007; Krishnakumar & Buehler, 2000; Mikulincer & Goodman, 2006; Schoppe-Sullivan, Schermerhorn, & Cummings, 2007).

Academic Performance

Marital conflict is also linked with diminished academic performance, as manifested by poor school grades and problems in intellectual achievement and abilities. Recent work has begun to shed light on some of the processes and bases for relations between marital conflict and school performance (Harold, Aitken, & Shelton, 2007). For example, attention difficulties have been identified in pathways between children's insecurity about marital conflict and children's school adjustment (Davies, Woitach, Winter, & Cummings, 2008). Pathways have also been identified indicating that sleep problems following from children's emotional insecurity about marital conflict are related to school problems across multiple academic dimensions (El-Sheikh, Buckhalt, Keller, Cummings, & Acebo, 2007; El-Sheikh, Cummings, Buckhalt, & Keller, 2007). On the other hand, constructive marital conflict is linked with children's positive school adjustment (McCoy, Cummings, & Davies, 2009).

　　High-conflict family environments may also contribute to children's interpretations of social situations and interpersonal relations, including family relationships. Thus children in high-conflict homes are more likely to view themselves and their social worlds in overly negative and hostile ways, and to have more negative internal working models of family relationships (Grych et al., 2003; Schermerhorn, Cummings, & Davies, 2008; Shamir, Du Rocher Schudlich, & Cummings, 2001).

Biological Functioning

Risky family environments have been linked with disruptions in sympathetic–adrenomedullary reactivity and limbic–hypothalamic–pituitary–adrenocortical (LHPA) functioning, as well as in other biological response systems (El-Sheikh et al., 2009). Repetti and colleagues (2002) have emphasized the need for further study of biological systems underlying the effects of risky families on children. Ongoing research and future studies hold promise for shedding further light on these effects of marital conflict on child and adolescent outcomes, including the vital questions linked with explanatory and process-oriented models (Davies, Sturge-Apple, Cicchetti, & Cummings, 2008).

FAMILY PROBLEMS EXPERIENCED BY CHILDREN IN HIGH-CONFLICT HOMES

Most studies of the effects of marital conflict on children have sampled relatively normal, intact families. Not surprisingly, some data suggest that links between marital conflict and child difficulties are stronger in families with problems, possibly because children must deal with the "double whammy" of multiple family stressors, including marital conflict (Emery & O'Leary, 1982; Hughes, Parkinson, & Vargo, 1989; Sternberg et al., 1993). For example, Jouriles, Murphy, and colleagues (1991) reported that links between marital conflict and child adjustment were significantly stronger in the face of other risks (i.e., in families with lower socioeconomic status [SES] or with clinic-referred children). The vignette at the start of this chapter provides an illustration of how these multiple family factors may be interrelated.

Relatedly, and consistent with the notion of multiple relations between marital conflict and risky families, marital conflict may figure prominently in the negative impact of various risk environments on children. Marital conflict is often not an isolated family problem, but is associated with other problems within families. Typically, children in a family with a specific dysfunction, such as parental depression or alcoholism, are thought to be at increased risk of adjustment problems.

The marital conflict associated with specific parental dysfunction may be a significant but little-acknowledged factor mediating certain child outcomes.

Studies in recent years have added substantially to the evidence that marital conflict contributes to the impact of multiple family problems on children's risk for both mental and physical health problems. Particular empirical advances have been made in the process-level understanding of the bases for these pathways, and these relations have also been shown in subclinical or community samples (Keller, Cummings, Davies, & Mitchell, 2008; Papp, Cummings, & Schermerhorn, 2004; Papp, Goeke-Morey, & Cummings, 2007), adding to previous evidence based on clinical samples.

Parental Depression

Children of depressed parents are two to five times more likely to develop psychological problems themselves than other children are. They are at greater risk not only for depression and other mood disorders, but also for many other forms of psychological and medical dysfunction (Weissman, Warner, Wickramaratne, Moreau, & Olfson, 1997). One common assumption is that the greater risk for adjustment problems in children of depressed parents is caused either exclusively or primarily by the hereditary transmission of faulty biological structures from the parents to their children. However, biologically based explanations cannot and do not fully account for the association between depression in parents and maladjustment in children (Cadoret, O'Gorman, Heywood, & Troughton, 1985; Reiss, Plomin, & Hetherington, 1991). Moreover, considerable evidence has accumulated that multiple elements of families with depressed parents contribute to the greater likelihood of negative child outcomes in these children (Goodman & Gotlib, 2002). At the same time, many children of depressed parents do not develop psychological problems, highlighting the importance of understanding biological and experiential elements that may contribute to their adjustment.

In particular, marital conflict has been identified as a family factor contributing to adjustment problems in children of depressed parents (Downey & Coyne, 1990). First, interparental anger and aggression are at least moderately associated with parental depression, even in community samples (Whisman, 2001), so that there is a probability that marital conflict will be elevated in such parents. Depressive symptoms are also linked with negative conflict expressions, including increased negative affect, hostility, and withdrawal, as well as with less positive affect (Du Rocher Schudlich, Papp, & Cummings, 2004). Second, the role of marital conflict in the risk for adjustment problems of children of depressed parents has been repeatedly demonstrated, supporting a role in risk for adjustment problems (Cummings, Davies, & Campbell, 2000).

The links between and among parental depression, interparental conflict, and child adjustment problems further support marital conflict as a characteristic of risky family environments (Repetti et al., 2002). Evidence continues to indicate that marital conflict may mediate the relationship between parental depressive symptoms and child adjustment (Davies, Dumenci, & Windle, 1999). Findings on relations among parental dysphoria, child gender, and child adjustment also reveal interesting patterns, including that boys may be more vulnerable in early and middle childhood, whereas girls become more vulnerable during adolescence (Davies & Windle, 1997).

The effects of *paternal* depressive symptoms on children are now being increasingly studied, after being historically neglected (Cummings, Goeke-Morey, & Raymond, 2004; Phares, Fields, Kamboukis, & Lopez, 2005). For example, a study conducted in a community sample (Cummings, Keller, & Davies, 2005) found that marital conflict mediated relations between maternal and paternal depressive symptoms and multiple problems in children. Du Rocher Schudlich and Cummings (2003) reported that depressive marital conflict styles partially mediated links with children's internalizing problems for mothers, whereas these conflict styles fully mediated such links for fathers.

Even subclinical depressive symptoms in parents may affect children. Extending the investigation of family process models of parental dysphoria and child adjustment, Cummings, Schermerhorn, Keller, and Davies (2008) found that children's representations of marital conflict mediated the effects of both paternal and maternal depressive symptoms on child adjustment over time, even with autoregressive controls over earlier levels of adjustment. Moreover, consistent with predictions that risky family environment may engage physiological response mechanisms, Cummings, El-Sheikh, Kouros, and Keller (2007) reported that in the context of interadult arguments, skin conductance reactivity moderated longitudinal predictions of children's internalizing, externalizing, and social adjustment problems, especially for paternal as compared with maternal dysphoria.

Implicating processes of children's emotional security in these pathways, Du Rocher Schudlich and Cummings (2007) reported that this security in the context of particular marital conflict styles mediated the relations between parental dysphoria and child adjustment problems, with similar pathways found for mothers and fathers. Furthermore, in longitudinal analyses, Kouros, Merrilees, and Cummings (2008) found that paternal depression moderated pathways between marital conflict and child adjustment, such that marital conflict was associated with children's greater emotional insecurity 2 years later in the context of paternal depression.

In summary, as elements of risky family environments, both parental depressive symptoms and marital conflict contribute to developmental processes associated with pathways linked with children's adjustment problems. Both wives' and husbands' symptoms are related to interparental conflict in the home (Papp et al., 2007). Although genetic elements surely play a role, substantive evidence supports the inclusion of both environmental and biological processes linked with parental depressive symptoms in any process-oriented explanations for the effects of these family environments on child development.

Parental Alcohol Problems

Parental alcohol problems have well-known deleterious effects on children and families (Chassin, Curran, Hussong, & Colder, 1996; Edwards, Eiden, & Leonard, 2004). However, relatively little is known about the processes involved in the effects of parental alcohol problems on children. Marital problems have long been implicated as a possible mechanism of risk for children exposed to parental drinking (West & Prinz, 1987). At the same time, research has only recently begun to document that parental drinking problems may expose children to higher levels of aggressive and unresolved conflicts (Quigley & Leonard, 2000). El-Sheikh and Flanagan (2001) found that marital aggression mediated the effects of paternal problem drinking on children's internalizing, externalizing, and social adjustment problems. A three-wave longitudinal study, including all appropriate autoregressive controls (Keller et al., 2008), reported evidence for a pathway over time from paternal problem drinking (Time 1) to decreased parental warmth and increased parental control (Time 2) and then to greater child internalizing and externalizing problems (Time 3). This study, in particular, implicated disruptions caused by paternal drinking in both the marital and parent–child relationships, in a complex chain of events involving these processes.

Child Maltreatment

Parental aggression toward children is strongly associated with interspousal aggression (Gelles, 1987; Hughes, 1988; Jouriles, Barling, & O'Leary, 1987). Approximately 40% of the children who are victims of parental physical abuse are also witnesses to spousal violence (Straus, Gelles, & Steinmetz, 1980).

Witnessing spousal abuse alone may contribute to child vulnerability to behavior problems. Children who are *witnesses* of such abuse exhibit problematic behaviors similar to those of children who are *victims* of parental violence. Children who are *both* witnesses and victims of parental violence exhibit higher levels of parent-reported externalizing problems than do children who are *either* witnesses or victims (Sternberg et al., 1993). High levels of marital conflict have been associated with both internalizing and externalizing symptomatology for abused children (Trickett & Susman, 1989). Thus effects attributed solely to child abuse may also reflect the effects of exposure to spousal violence and conflict (Cummings & Davies, 1994a).

Marital Disruption

The impact of interadult conflict on child adjustment is an issue for all family forms and structures; it is not simply confined to intact, two-parent families. Moreover, given the various supports and other sources of financial and other security and stability in two-parent families, conflict between adults may be a more significant problem for child development in other family forms.

For example, the way children function after a parental divorce is affected by the quality of the family environment surrounding the marital separation. The level of parental conflict is an important aspect of the family environment for children whose parents are divorcing. Parental fighting may be a better forecaster of children's functioning after the divorce than either the change in the parents' marital status or the child's separation from one parent may be. In other words, high levels of interadult conflict between the former marital partners may be more closely related to children's behavior problems than the changes in family structure per se (Amato & Keith, 1991; Emery, 1982, 1988).

Marital conflict, moreover, is a significant and influential aspect of family life not only during but before a divorce. A long history of exposure to elevated interparental conflict and anger may well have preceded the divorce, and children's risk for adjustment problems may be a function of this history (Block, Block, & Gjerde, 1988; Block, Block, & Morrison, 1981).

Although some parents are able to reduce conflict after a divorce, divorce as a means of escape from conflict may not be effective. Indeed, parental conflict often increases after a divorce and may continue for many years afterward (Emery, 1988; Johnston, Gonzalez, & Campbell, 1987; Long & Forehand, 1987). Children experiencing elevated interparental conflict after divorce show more adjustment problems than children who experience postdivorce reductions in conflict (Long, Slater, Forehand, & Fauber, 1988).

In fact, stronger relations between interparental conflict and children's adjustment problems are reported for divorced than for intact families. Interparental conflict during the marital dissolution is related to multiple forms of behavior problems in children (Johnston et al., 1987; Slater & Haber, 1984; Wierson, Forehand, & McComb, 1988). Why should these stronger relations be found? One possibility is that marital discord affects children in combination with other stressful circumstances that commonly occur in divorced families. For example, parental dysphoria and other psychological symptoms are frequent responses to divorce. Another possibility is that children are exposed to certain types of fighting that are strongly related to the development of adjustment problems. For example, arguments often center on child-related themes (e.g., custody, child-related expenses or child rearing practices), which are especially disturbing for children (Block et al., 1981; Johnston et al., 1987). Also, parents in divorced families may depend on their children for emotional support (i.e., parentification may occur), or may pressure their children into alliances against the other parent. The stressors related to such role reversals and alliance taking may increase the likelihood of adjustment problems in the children (Buchanan, Maccoby, & Dornbusch, 1991; Wallerstein & Blakeslee, 1989).

A FUTURE DIRECTION: EFFECTS OF PARENTAL CONFLICT IN SINGLE-PARENT FAMILIES ON CHILD DEVELOPMENT

Although a great deal is known about the implications of parental conflict for children in intact, two-parent homes and in divorced families (Emery, 2004; Long & Forehand, 2002), relatively little is known about the role of parental conflict in homes in which parents have never married. The fact that a parent is single does not mean that there is only one adult in a child's life. On the contrary, there may be a stable other adult, and the other adult may be an unmarried parent (e.g., a cohabiting parent); or there may be a series of other adults, including romantic partners, with varying levels of continuity and relationship to the children in the home. There is some evidence that cohabiting relationships are fraught with more conflict than otherwise comparable marital relationships, suggesting that cohabitation is especially important to understand when it comes to predicting emotional security and children. Multiple categories of single-parent families exist, including (1) never married and cohabiting, (2) never married and dating, and (3) never married and not dating. These different family forms may be closely related to the nature and types of parental and family conflict that occur.

However, little is known about relations between parental/family conflict and children's well-being in single-parent families. Given the high and dramatically increasing prevalence of single parents raising children, and the findings that parental conflict contributes to risky family environments in other family forms, the understanding of relations between parental/family conflict and the development of psychopathology in children is a significant question for future research. The percentages of children growing up in single-parent families and/or high-conflict families for at least some portion of their childhoods exceed 50% (Amato, 2007). Conflict processes in these families, including interpartner conflict, may be a significant issue for the children. At the same time, it is a concern that so little research-based evidence about many of these family forms is available, given the significance of the social problem and the great numbers of children affected. It is essential to move forward with the study of factors potentially highly relevant to the well-being of children in single-parent families, including the study of conflict processes and children in these family forms.

With the qualification that there are many gaps in understanding as a function of forms of single-parent families (and that wide individual differences in outcomes among these forms are likely to exist), children in single-parent families are at generally greater risk for behavioral and emotional problems, substance use problems, child abuse and neglect, academic problems in school, and physical health problems (Amato, 2005; McLanahan & Sandefur, 1994; Nock, 2005). Rather than presuming that interpartner and family conflict may be less (or less of an issue) because a marital partner is not present, one can entertain the possibility that conflict may be more frequent and even more severe, with corresponding implications for children's development. One possible hypothesis is that a relative lack of stability and commitment in relation-ships, and the multiple financial and other challenges that often accom-pany single-parent status, may fuel more frequent and more negative forms of conflict in these family environments. The resulting more risky families may foster greater insecurity and greater adjustment problems in the children.

The recognition of the importance of relationship stability and con-flict in single-parent families is evident in the federal support for vari-ous research projects and programs aimed at studying and improving interparental and family relationships in such families. The research includes the Fragile Families and Child Wellbeing Study (McLanahan et al., 2003) and the Building Strong Families project (Dion, Avellar, Zaveri, & Hershey, 2006). Moreover, several of the programs funded in the Healthy Marriage Research Initiative by the Administration for Children and Families are efforts toward remediating and ameliorating parental conflicts in single-parent families. An assumption is that the children of couples who may plan to marry but are not yet married, or don't eventually marry, have a better chance of developing into healthy and well-functioning individuals in stable, low-conflict families.

As suggested above, one challenge is differentiating between effects as a function of the forms of single-parent families. For example, response processes have been investigated in single-parent families fol-lowing divorce (Amato & Keith, 1991; Emery, 1999; Hetherington & Clingempeel, 1992); however, much less is known about single-parent, never-married families, including "fragile families" in which couples are together before the birth of the child and may intend to marry, but remain single (McLanahan et al., 2003).

The models and approaches for studying interparental conflict and children described in this volume provide a starting point for investigat-ing the impact of conflict and aggression on children in single-parent family forms and contexts. These directions also provide bases for advancing our understanding of the role of children's emotional secu-rity in interparental and parent–child relationships in these families. Although research on marital conflict and children provides a strong foundation for process-oriented research on these questions, many similarities and differences may well typify pathways in the various fam-ily environments. Given the many gaps in research on parental conflict and violence in single-parent families, there is substantial impetus for the future process-oriented study of these questions of societal signifi-cance.

SUMMARY AND CONCLUSIONS

Marital conflict and violence are hallmarks of risky families for children. In this chapter, various elements, including parental adjustment problems (e.g., depression, alcohol problems), are described as pertinent aspects of risky family environments associated with marital conflict and violence. Although genetic processes merit consideration in the context of transactional developmental models, overwhelming evidence indicates that environmental processes are highly influential.

The study of parental conflict and violence (including interpartner and dating-related aggression) is essential to an understanding of the constructs of healthy and risky families for children in all family forms, including single-parent families. In this volume, we consider theory, methods, and evidence that have increased and should continue to increase knowledge about processes pertinent to the effects of marital conflict on children. We also examine the possible applications of this knowledge to real-world contexts of prevention, as well as to research on broader social ecologies of conflict, violence, and child development (e.g., political violence and children). These issues pertaining to the process-oriented study of families with marital conflict and violence, EST, and the practical applications of research findings are among the guiding themes for the rest of this book.

CHAPTER 2

The Emergence
of Process-Oriented Approaches

Emotional Security Theory

In Chapter 1, we have made a case that process-oriented study of marital conflict, rather than simple identification of correlations between such conflict and child outcomes, is essential for understanding how marital conflict and the family processes associated with it relate to child outcomes. Moreover, we have alluded to emotional security as a process within children that may hold special significance for conceptualizing how children are affected by marital conflict. In the present chapter, we articulate more fully what we mean by "process-oriented study," and we describe how "emotional security theory" (EST; Davies & Cummings, 1994) may serve as a useful heuristic for guiding important directions in process-oriented research.

To begin with, let us put research on children and marital conflict into historical perspective. A first generation of research established over many years that marital conflict is linked with children's adjustment problems (Emery, 1982). Ongoing research emphasizes the multivariate processes and conditions that elucidate this link. That is, work over the past two decades has been increasingly concerned with advancing understanding of how and why (i.e., "mediators"), and for whom and when (i.e., "moderators"), marital conflict is linked with children's adjustment problems (Grych & Fincham, 1990). These and related directions in research are building blocks of a process-oriented approach to this issue (Cummings & Cummings, 1988) and constitute key elements of what has been described as a second generation of research on children and marital conflict (Grych & Fincham, 2001b).

In further developing key themes of the process-oriented approach to be considered in the present chapter, let us now consider the following example:

> Lois and John came from families with very different relationships between the parents. Lois's parents fought all the time and were typically very angry with each other. John's parents discussed areas of disagreement periodically, but were almost always mutually respectful and resolved most disagreements. One day, Lois's and John's fathers were both late picking them up from a first-grade school play. In both cases, the mothers were very worried. Both yelled at the fathers—even John's mom, because she was so upset. Lois got visibly anxious when her mother behaved that way and tried to make excuses for her father to her mother, becoming involved in the conflict. John, on the other hand, simply went inside to play with his toys, and did not even look up at his arguing and distressed parents.

This vignette highlights the fact that one needs to know more than the contents of the current conflict in order to predict how children will respond to and otherwise be affected by exposure to conflict. That is, an additional element to consider is how each child's conflict history factors into his or her reactions (Davies, Myers, Cummings, & Heindel, 1999; El-Sheikh, Cummings, & Reiter, 1996). In this chapter, we highlight the fact that one needs to account for risk factors and risk mechanisms in order to predict both children's reactions and their adjustment more generally. We further highlight the unfolding processes underlying how and why some children, like Lois, appear to become sensitized to interparental conflict by responding with progressively greater distress over time.

In this chapter, we begin to unravel some of these processes of the influence and impact of marital conflict on children in the context of broader family systems. Our first step, as noted above, is to describe what is meant by a "process-oriented" approach. Such an approach defines key elements and issues for understanding the dynamic mechanisms and conditions that account for relations between marital conflict and child development. At the same time, the complexity of the notions introduced by a process-oriented approach may threaten to overwhelm the investigator or clinician concerned with these questions. Theory is needed to make sense of the potential "chaos" by simplifying and articulating the key issues. That is, to be effective in unraveling causes and effects in this complex pattern of influences, directions in process-oriented research are ideally guided by well-articulated theory.

Addressing this point, another purpose of this chapter is to outline the key concepts and notions of EST (Davies & Cummings, 1994), which has shown increasing promise over the past 15-plus years as a theoretical framework and a source of specific, testable conceptual bases for research and interventions concerned with the influences of conflict processes on children's development (Davies, Harold, Goeke-Morey, & Cummings, 2002). This chapter provides an introduction to many of the research issues from an EST perspective; these issues are also further developed throughout the book (reference is made below, as appropriate, to later chapters that provide further treatment of specific questions).

A PROCESS-ORIENTED APPROACH TO RELATIONS BETWEEN MARITAL CONFLICT AND CHILDREN

As we have argued, in order to understand the complexity of influences associated with relations between children and marital conflict, an approach to conceptualizing and organizing this dynamic family landscape is needed. Figure 2.1 provides a broad framework for a *process-oriented approach* to the study of relations between marital conflict and child adjustment. As indicated in the figure, a process-oriented perspective distinguishes among risk factors, risk mechanisms or processes, and outcomes (Cowan, Cowan, & Schulz, 1996). Although we focus on the many emerging practical, conceptual, and methodological implications of EST in this book, it should be noted that a process-oriented approach is relevant to any theoretical account in this area (e.g., Crockenberg & Langrock, 2001b; Emery, 1989; Grych & Fincham, 1990).

Child Outcomes

"Outcomes" are defined as children's dispositions of behaving, thinking, or feeling that are relatively consistent or stable across time and settings (e.g., family, school, peers). As we demonstrate in this volume, many types of outcomes have been linked with marital conflict, and the number of outcomes related in some way with marital conflict is steadily

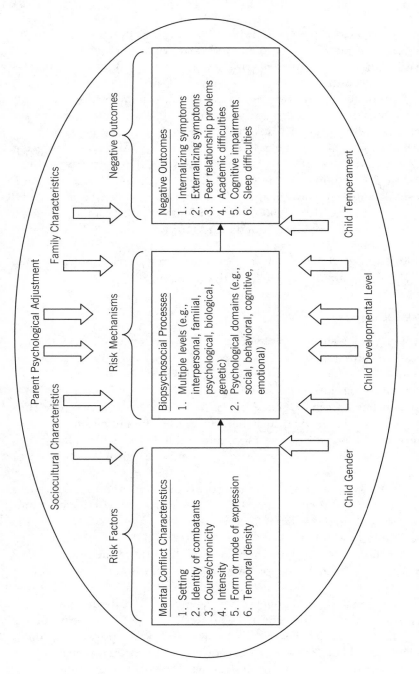

FIGURE 2.1. An overarching process-oriented framework for understanding the role of marital conflict in the lives of children.

expanding (see Chapters 4 and 5). The negative outcomes associated with marital conflict encompass a wide array of psychological problems. In addition, positive outcomes are now also being linked with constructive marital conflict (McCoy, Cummings, & Davies, 2009).

Although internalizing (e.g., anxiety, depression, social withdrawal) and externalizing (e.g., conduct problems, aggression) symptoms have been the primary foci of research, the measurement of outcomes linked with marital conflict has expanded in exciting new directions in recent years, including peer and romantic relationships (Du Rocher Schudlich, Shamir, & Cummings, 2004; Kinsfogel & Grych, 2004; Marcus, Lindahl, & Malik, 2001), physical health (Nicolotti, El-Sheikh, & Whitson, 2003; Wood, Klebba, & Miller, 2000), sleep (El-Sheikh, Buckhalt, Cummings, & Keller, 2007), cognitive functioning (Davies et al., 2008), substance use (Fergusson & Horwood, 1998), pubertal timing (Ellis & Garber, 2000; Papp et al., 2004), and stress hormones (Davies, Sturge-Apple, Cicchetti, & Cummings, 2007; Pendry & Adam, 2007).

Risk Factors

As denoted in Figure 2.1, "risk factors" increase the chances of children's negative outcomes. However, children exposed to risk factors are not doomed to develop psychological or other problems. Indeed, many (if not most) children exposed to any *single* risk factor do not experience any significant form of mental illness or other negative outcomes. Thus the risk is probabilistic rather than certain. At the same time, categorization as a risk factor reflects more than a simple correlation: It requires evidence that a variable precedes the occurrence or intensification of negative outcomes.

In conceptualizing risk, the process-oriented approach advances the multidimensional nature of marital conflict as a risk factor. Characteristics of such conflict related to its potency as a risk factor include the setting in which it takes place; the identity of the combatants (e.g., mother, father, stepparent, unmarried parent, other romantic partner); the chronicity and course of the conflict (e.g., resolution, escalation); the intensity; the form of conflict expression (e.g., physical aggression, verbal aggression, mild anger, disengagement); and the temporal density (e.g., timing between conflict episodes). Moreover, some parameters of conflict do not increase risk, but may well promote positive outcomes in children. Therefore, the process-oriented approach underscores the need to distinguish between destructive and constructive characteristics of conflict.

Risk Mechanisms

The risk associated with marital conflict does not operate in either a static or an instantaneous way. Risk unfolds over time as an influence on children's development. As Cowan, Cowan, and colleagues (1996) have noted, "Risks should be thought of as process. The active ingredients of a risk do not lie in the variable itself, but in the set of processes that flow from the variable, linking specific risk conditions with specific dysfunctional outcomes" (p. 9). Therefore, repeated exposure can be conceptualized as setting in motion dynamic "risk mechanisms," or processes that over time intensify, broaden, and crystallize children's negative outcomes. A risk mechanism is commonly referred to as a "mediator" or "mediating process," which accounts for or explains how and why there is a relationship between a risk factor and an outcome. Consistent with the etiological chain depicted in Figure 2.1, a risk factor is conceptualized as contributing to elevations in one or more risk mechanisms or processes. At this point, we define a couple of terms pertinent to how risk mechanisms are conceptualized in terms of explaining relations between risk factors and child outcomes.

Mediators

"Mediators" are the generative mechanisms by which independent variables such as risk factors (e.g., marital conflict) are linked with child outcomes (e.g., child adjustment). That is, a mediator is the intermediate variable in the link between a potential predictor and an outcome (Baron & Kenny, 1986; Holmbeck, 1997, 2002). As noted above, mediators explain, at least in part, how and why risk factors lead to adaptive or maladaptive outcomes.

In Figure 2.1, the box described as "Biopsychosocial Processes" (e.g., familial, social) includes various possible mediators for relations between interparental conflict and child outcomes. Although testing mediator models would seem on the surface to be a relatively straightforward procedure, researchers sometimes endorse and adopt different criteria for testing mediation. In a traditional form of this notion, Baron and Kenny (1986) argued that several criteria need to be met for mediation, including links (1) between the predictor (i.e., marital conflict) and the outcome (e.g., depression); (2) between the predictor and the proposed mediator (e.g., familial, social); and (3) between the proposed mediator and the outcome. Finally, (4) the inclusion of the mediator in the analyses should result in a substantial reduction in the magnitude of the relations between the predictor and the outcome.

In recent years, investigators have acknowledged the significance of accounting for explanatory processes in any account of mediation as a generative mechanism, and thus have altered the criteria for explaining the link between marital conflict and child outcomes (e.g., Davies et al., 2007; Grych et al., 2003). That is, researchers have realized that the developmental pathway between marital conflict and child adjustment is only understood if the generative mechanism is specified. Specifically, the change has been to drop the first mediational requirement that the risk factor should always be associated with the outcome (MacKinnon, Lockwood, Hoffman, West, & Sheets, 2002; Shrout & Bolger, 2002).

In a sense, the direct link with the risk factor and child outcome, whether present or not, is irrelevant to adequate process-oriented explanation. That is, a developmental pathway is ultimately always a function of some mediating process; when the mediating process is not identified, the pathway is not explained. Now that the necessity of demonstrating direct correlations with child outcomes has been dropped, the focus is on showing how predictors such as marital conflict are related to child outcomes through effects on other variables and mechanisms. This approach to explanatory mechanisms takes into account that even the most robust family risk factors are not directly associated with child adjustment in any absolute or instantaneous way. Rather, risk factors operate over time, frequently slowly and even insidiously, by altering family and child functioning over time.

Moderators

Moderator models are a second class of process models related to the identification of pathways and trajectories between interparental relations and child adjustment. Although moderator models also help us in moving beyond simple documentation of bivariate relations, moderators are fundamentally different from mediators. "Moderators" are conditions or characteristics that alter (rather than explain or link together) the path between marital conflict and children's functioning, such as parental psychological problems or child temperament. In Figure 2.1, arrows run from the moderator to the pathways between marital conflict and child adjustment (mediators), reflecting the fact that the impact of marital conflict on children hinges on the levels of the moderators.

A moderator specifies the strength and/or direction of relations between an independent variable (e.g., marital conflict) and an outcome (e.g., child adjustment)—that is, whether the strength or direction of relations between an independent variable (e.g., interparental conflict) and a dependent variable (e.g., child depression) varies at different levels of another variable (Baron & Kenny, 1986; Holmbeck, 1997, 2002). Moderators reflect the fact that the nature and degree of risk are not necessarily uniform across different conditions and people. For example, risk for adjustment problems in children exposed to marital violence may be disproportionately greater when other family characteristics (e.g., parent–child relationships, family cohesiveness) are dysfunctional. In this case, the link between marital violence and child adjustment disturbances varies, depending on the level of difficulties children experience in the broader family system.

Moderator models specifically address two interrelated questions: (1) Who is, and who is not, at risk? (2) and when is the risk most or least pronounced? Identifying a moderator first involves the delineation of a "synergistic" or "multiplicative" effect between two or more predictors. In other words, a multiplicative model reflects the fact that the co-occurrence of two or more factors, as defined quantitatively by their multiplicative product, has a stronger impact than the sum of those factors considered in isolation. Thus moderators are synonymous with statistical interactions between two or more variables.

As indicated in Figure 2.1, risk mechanisms potentially operate in multiple domains (e.g., social, behavioral, cognitive, emotional) and at multiple levels of analysis (e.g., interpersonal, familial, psychological, biological, genetic). Marital conflict may contribute to negative outcomes by setting in motion negative social (e.g., interpersonal withdrawal), behavioral (e.g., aggression, temper tantrums), emotional (e.g., distress, fear, worries), or cognitive (e.g., negative appraisals of family) processes. These psychological processes are part of an interrelated network of nested factors at different levels of analysis. Other family mechanisms, such as poor parenting or childrearing practices, may help account for associations between marital conflict and children's mental health difficulties (see Chapter 5). Similarly, physiological and genetic mechanisms are also likely to play a role in linking marital conflict and children's negative outcomes.

These pathways and processes associated with marital conflict do not occur in a psychosocial vacuum. As shown in Figure 2.1, marital conflict, risk mechanisms, and outcomes occur in broader family (e.g., unstable relationships, emotional climate) and sociocultural (e.g., poverty, neighborhood quality, social support networks) contexts. Thus another level of analysis in a process-oriented approach involves considering the influence of broader family contexts (see Chapters 5 and 6) and of contexts outside the family (see Chapter 9), all of which may serve as important moderators (or mediators) of outcomes. The characteristics of the individual also matter and may also moderate (or mediate) outcomes; these include developmental (e.g., social perspective-taking ability) and constitutional (e.g., genetic vulnerability, birth complications, difficult temperament) factors (see Chapters 6 and 7).

Although these various factors may also serve as risk mechanisms, they are indicated in Figure 2.1 as moderators, because they are more typically likely to modify the nature or strength of associations (as denoted by the arrows perpendicular to the process model in the figure; see also Chapters 5–7). For example, the impact of marital conflict on negative child outcomes may be weakened for children with positive temperaments or access to supportive adult relationships. Alternatively, prior trauma histories or neuropsychological impairments (e.g., impairments in working memory or inhibitory control) may make children more vulnerable.

Given all these influences and potential pathways, the challenges associated with our process-oriented approach are considerable. As we have noted, the development of theory is also essential—including precise and rigorous hypothesis testing about how children function in the face of marital conflict, especially with regard to the specification of risk mechanisms (Cummings & Davies, 2002). The assumptions and principles of the process-oriented perspective can be regarded as building blocks or tools, whereas theories are needed to guide research toward a more refined and sophisticated understanding of how and why, and for whom and when, interparental conflict is associated with children's difficulties. Although various theories have been proposed (e.g., Grych & Fincham, 1990), in this volume we focus on EST as a guiding conceptualization for understanding process relations between marital conflict and child development.

EMOTIONAL SECURITY THEORY

Overview

EST holds that maintaining a sense of protection, safety, and security is a central goal for children in family settings, including contexts of marital conflict. With regard to risk processes, the organization and regulation of emotional responses are central to understanding how children adapt to marital discord (Davies & Cummings, 1994). Illustrating a "direct pathway" of influence (see Path 2 in Figure 2.2), exposure

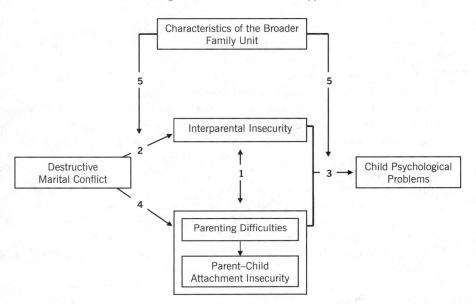

FIGURE 2.2. An EST formulation of the multiple pathways underlying associations between destructive marital conflict and child psychological problems.

to destructive interparental conflict increases children's vulnerability to psychological problems by undermining their emotional security in the interparental relationship—that is, children's confidence in their parents' abilities to manage discord and to preserve family and marital stability, with implications for the children's well-being. A cumulative effect of exposure to destructive marital conflict is that children become sensitized to concerns about preserving emotional security in subsequent contexts of conflict.

A fundamental assumption of EST is that the impact of marital conflict on child adjustment depends on the characteristics of interparental conflict. A critical issue is thus to clarify marital conflict behaviors as destructive or constructive. At the same time, there has been a lack of clarity in the literature with regard to the definition and characteristics of destructive and constructive marital conflict. Addressing this gap, EST provides conceptual and empirical bases for distinguishing between constructive and destructive conflict from the children's perspective. A description of the EST-based empirical research directed toward identifying constructive and destructive conflict is provided in Chapter 3.

Moreover, an observational coding system for coding parents' marital conflict behaviors as constructive or destructive—that is, Conflict in the Interparental System (CIS)—is outlined in Appendix A.

With regard to emotional security as a risk mechanism, EST focuses on identifying whether emotional security about marital conflict reflects processes that explain how and why marital conflict is associated with forms of child maladjustment. Thus the aim is to understand how exposure to marital and family relationships results in changes in children's emotional security over time. In turn, these specific changes in children's patterns of emotional security responding in the context of the family may contribute to broader patterns of psychological adjustment. Accordingly, proponents of EST focus on examining whether signs of insecurity in the interparental relationship (e.g., emotional distress, involvement, negative representations) mediate or account for paths between exposure to marital conflict and children's psychological adjustment.

Consistent with attachment theory, EST accepts the notion that children's emotional security can be enhanced or undermined by the quality of their parent–child relationships. Thus witnessing destructive interparental conflict is thought to increase children's vulnerability to psychological problems by undermining their ability to preserve emotional security within various other family relationships (see Path 4 in Figure 2.2). The erosion of children's confidence in their parents as sources of protection and support within the attachment relationship accounts for many of the deleterious effects of parenting difficulties (e.g., unresponsiveness, intrusiveness, low warmth) on children's psychological adjustment. Although attachment theory and EST share the assumption that differences in children's abilities to utilize their parent–child relationships as sources of safety and security have important implications for their long-term mental health, EST departs from traditional attachment theory in arguing that the maintenance of security is a salient goal in other family relationships as well.

Therefore, growing up with destructive interparental conflict is theorized to undermine a child's emotional security in both the parent–child and interparental relationships. For example, studies have shown that interparental discord uniquely predicts attachment security even after the predictive role of parenting difficulties is taken into account (Frosch, Mangelsdorf, & McHale, 2000; Owen & Cox, 1997). In conjunction with other research indicating that attachment insecurity is a risk factor for child psychopathology (Hilburn-Cobb, 2004), these findings support the hypothesis that children's security in the interparental relationship may account for part of the link between attachment security and child adjustment. Even more central to the conceptualization of EST is the proposal that the sense of security children develop in the context of interparental conflict is distinct from the sense of security they experience in parent–child attachment relationships. For example, the Davies, Harold, and colleagues (2002) research provides support for the hypothesis that children's sense of security in the interparental subsystem is relatively distinct in its composition, family correlates, and developmental implications for the children's adjustment.

Consequently, as shown in Figure 2.2, the two systems are distinct in their substance, correlates, and sequelae, although there may be mutual influence processes between emotional security about the parent–child system and emotional security about the marital system (see Path 1). In further developing this premise, EST specifically proposes two primary pathways by which children's concerns about their security in the context of high levels of interparental conflict may account for their greater vulnerability to adjustment problems: a direct pathway and an indirect pathway (see Path 3 in Figure 2.2). In addition, the effects of marital conflict may be moderated by the operation of other family processes, such as family conflict or cohesion (see Path 5; Chapter 6 provides more development of this question).

Emotional Security as a Goal
Serviced by Regulatory Response Systems

A key element of EST is the specification of component regulatory systems hypothesized to dynamically mediate relations between marital conflict and child development. The articulation of specific, measurable, and conceptually guided response systems in the service of EST advances the testability and therefore the scientific value of the theory. Another assumption of EST is that these response processes can be seen at multiple levels of analysis of response systems, including individual response processes (e.g., emotional reactivity) and higher-order organizations of response processes involving multiple regulatory systems (e.g., variables reflecting multiple reactions to marital conflict, such as emotional reactivity and regulation of exposure to conflict, including behavioral involvement). These elements of EST are consistent with the process-oriented model illustrated in Figure 2.1.

Although preserving emotional security in the interparental relationship is conceptualized as an unobservable, psychological goal, the "set goal" of emotional security regulates and is regulated by at least three domains of regulatory response patterns: emotional reactivity, regulation of exposure to conflict, and internal representations. Threats to the goal of security are posited to activate responding across these domains. Therefore, according to EST, children who demonstrate insecurity in the interparental relationship will evidence greater emotional reactivity; excessive regulation of exposure to subsequent conflict (e.g., parentification responses, mediation, or other behavioral involvements); and negative representations of the interparental relationship. "Emotional reactivity" is characterized by children's negative emotional reactions, including intense, prolonged fear, vigilance, and distress responses to interparental conflict. "Regulation of exposure to conflict" commonly consists of attempts to become behaviorally involved in interparental conflicts as a mediator, confidant, or co-combatant, but it may also take the form of avoidance or other efforts to limit exposure to marital conflict. Finally, "representations" refer to negative (or positive, in the case of constructive conflict; McCoy et al., 2009) expectancies about the implications of interparental conflict for the children themselves and their families (Davies & Cummings, 1994).

Reflecting the adaptive value of these response processes, activation of these regulatory systems may help in achieving some modicum of physical and psychological safety. For example, emotional reactivity may emotionally tag or highlight potential threat in high-conflict homes and energize children to cope with impending adversity. Likewise, expending resources to intervene in conflicts may be an effective way of preserving safety by increasing control over threatening interparental circumstances. Finally, child representations, which are geared toward processing the meaning of interparental conflict for family life, are monitoring systems for identifying interparental events that may undermine the children's own welfare and that of their family members (Cummings & Davies, 1996; Davies, Harold, et al., 2002). Although experiencing elevated emotional insecurity may serve to help safeguard children against the threat posed by high-conflict homes, it may have long-term costs. Thus, in another part of the causal chain (see Path 3 in Figure 2.2), insecurity in the interparental relationship lays the foundation for an array of problems in various domains (e.g., socioemotional, cognitive, physical) of functioning (Cummings & Keller, 2006).

With regard to how emotional security relates to children's various regulatory responses, EST posits that preserving a sense of security in the face of marital conflict is a critical goal that organizes these responses. Protection, safety, and security are among the most salient in the hierarchy of human goals (Waters & Cummings, 2000). EST posits a control systems model in which preserving emotional security in the face of marital conflict is a set goal that influences children's reactions to marital conflict (see Chapter 9 for comparisons with the control systems notions of attachment theory; Bowlby, 1969).

That is, children evaluate marital conflict in terms of the set goal of emotional security, and the emotional security behavioral system is activated if that set goal is threatened. Moreover, if security is threatened, children are motivated to respond in ways aimed at regaining emotional security; in particular, the emotional security response system is serviced by component regulatory systems of emotional reactivity, behavioral action tendencies (e.g., mediation or other intervention), and cognitive appraisals (e.g., internal working models of the marital relationship).

To give a concrete example, if a child observed aggression by one parent toward the other, it would be expected that the child would respond with some combination of negative emotional reactivity, behavioral aggression or intervention, or negative cognitive appraisals. These responses can be thought of as A (affect), B (behavior), and C (cognition)—that is, as the "ABCs" of children's responding to marital conflict (Rhoades, 2008). These responses function as regulatory response systems aimed at regaining the set goal of emotional security about the interparental relationship. At the same time, it follows that children's emotional security about marital conflict can also be assessed by examining the organization of these regulatory response processes.

The emotional security response system thus regulates, organizes, and motivates a child's responses to interparental discord. Notably, some degree of interdependency is expected among these various response systems, as they serve the same goal of preserving security, but each is also assumed to represent distinctive aspects of the emotional security system. Moreover, emotional security can be thought of as a bridge between the child and the world. When the marital relationship is high-functioning, a secure base is provided for the child. Like a structurally sound bridge, a positive marital relationship supports the child's optimal functioning in the context of potentially threatening conditions, fostering exploration and confident relationships with others. When destructive marital conflict damages the bridge, the child may become hesitant to move forward and lack confidence, or may move forward in a dysfunctional way, failing to find the best footing in relations with others or within the self.

How EST Accounts for Sensitization
of Regulatory Response Systems

A much-replicated finding is that repeated or heightened exposure to marital conflict increases children's reactivity, including distress, anger, aggressiveness, and involvement in interadult disputes. This phenomenon is described in terms of a "sensitization hypothesis," and has been widely observed (Cummings, 1994; see also Davies, Myers, et al., 1999; El-Sheikh & Cummings, 1995; Grych, 1998). As a recent example, Schermerhorn, Cummings, and Davies (2008) have reported that changes in children's representations of marital conflict predicted changes in their representations of reactivity to marital conflict over time.

Sensitization is particularly interesting as a challenge for theory, because it is counterintuitive. Thus, in most contexts, one would expect that children would habituate to or get used to stimuli as a function of repeated exposure. The fact that children don't become habituated to marital conflict requires explanation. Accordingly, a test for the cogency of any theoretical approach to understanding relations between marital conflict and children's functioning is to account for sensitization.

A conceptual strength of EST is that it provides a theoretically based explanation for the sensitization phenomenon. That is, according to EST, preserving a sense of security is a salient goal for children in their hierarchy of goals (Waters & Cummings, 2000). The threat accompanying exposure to destructive marital conflict would thus be expected to elevate children's concerns about security—and, in the process, to heighten their reactivity to marital conflict. Moreover, a theoretical proposition of EST is that over time, and with repeated exposure, experiences with destructive marital conflict should progressively amplify the salience of preserving security, and should therefore result in children's successively greater emotional, behavioral, cognitive, and physiological reactivity in these contexts.

The cogency of EST's explanation for how exposure to marital conflict sensitizes regulatory response systems is supported by a growing body of research explicitly testing EST's predictions about the role of these systems. Guided by EST, we (Davies & Cummings, 1998) provided a first empirical test of whether links between marital relations and children's adjustment would be mediated by these specific regulatory systems in the service of children's emotional security—including children's emotional reactivity to marital conflict (i.e., vigilance, distress); their behavioral regulation of exposure to conflict (i.e., involvement, avoidance); and their representations in the context of marital relations.

From a methodological perspective, we (Davies & Cummings, 1998) also illustrated a methodological tenet of EST, which is that constructs must be assessed by means of multiple methods and contexts in order to optimally capture underlying processes. EST is firmly grounded in the developmental psychopathology perspective, which stresses the value of the insights to be gained from using diverse, ecologically sound methods (Davies & Cummings, 2006; Davies & Sturge-Apple, 2007).

Our results (Davies & Cummings, 1998) supported the proposition of EST that child outcomes associated with exposure to marital conflict are mediated by multiple regulatory processes. The results indicated that marital conflict was linked with elevated emotional reactivity and more negative internal representations of marital distress, consistent with the notion of sensitization of regulatory processes in the service of emotional security. Moreover, these regulatory processes were each linked with child adjustment, especially internalizing symptoms, supporting the proposition that processes indicative of emotional insecurity in relation to parental conflict may be factors in child adjustment.

At the same time, despite these encouraging results, questions remained about whether a cumulative impact over time on children's regulatory response systems associated with emotional security could be demonstrated in the context of a longitudinal research design. A recent study (Davies, Sturge-Apple, et al., 2006) tested whether specific regulatory systems could be shown to change over time in response to marital conflict in the context of a longitudinal research design. Consistent with EST's emphasis on differentiating contexts of marital conflict in predicting child outcomes, this study also differentiated interparental withdrawal and hostility as predictors of child adjustment. Moreover, adding to the rigor of tests of sensitization processes purportedly induced by repeated exposure to marital conflict, parental warmth was also included in these model tests, to determine whether sensitization could be demonstrated even when parental warmth was statistically controlled for.

Consistent with the sensitization hypothesis, higher levels of destructive interparental conflict were associated with greater child reactivity over time, including negative affect and cognitions. Notably, both dimensions of marital conflict—that is, interparental hostility and withdrawal—were associated with greater child reactivity to conflict, and these findings remained even with rigorous autoregressive controls over earlier levels of children's regulatory responses and parental warmth. With regard to the impact of these specific dimensions of destructive conflict on specific assessments of reactivity, interparental hostility predicted child overt reactivity over time, whereas interparental with-drawal was uniquely associated with subjective emotional reactivity and negative internal representations of the family. Supporting the inter-pretation of evidence for direct-effects pathways was the finding that when differences were obtained, dimensions of interparental conflict were consistently stronger predictors of child reactivity to conflict than the parenting dimension of parental warmth was. Thus these results provided evidence supporting the idea that the specific regulatory pro-cesses identified by EST change lawfully over time in response to mari-tal conflict; they are also consistent with EST's account of sensitization processes and direct-effects pathways for the effects of marital conflict on children's functioning.

A related question challenging the predictions of EST is whether it can also be shown that sensitization in specific regulatory response sys-tems is longitudinally related to children's adjustment problems. That is, according to EST, experiential histories of marital conflict are postu-lated to increase children's emotional insecurity, as evidenced by high levels of emotional reactivity, hostile representations, and regulation of conflict exposure. Specifically testing these assumptions, Harold, Shel-ton, Goeke-Morey, and Cummings (2004) longitudinally examined rela-tions between and among marital conflict, children's emotional security about marital conflict, parenting, and child adjustment. In this study, distinct pathways of regulatory functioning in response to exposure to marital conflict were differentiated, including children's emotional reg-ulation, children's cognitive representations, and children's behavioral regulation. In addition, an indirect pathway through emotional security about parenting was considered in the same model tests.

Consistent with the hypothesis that each regulatory system contrib-utes to direct-effects pathways, exposure to marital conflict was asso-ciated with children's emotional regulation, cognitive representations, and behavioral regulation. In turn, providing support for the second link in the direct-effects pathway, children's emotional regulation and behavioral regulation were each associated longitudinally with chil-dren's externalizing problems. Moreover, children's behavioral regula-tion was linked with children's internalizing problems. In addition to this support for a direct-effects model (i.e., the links between elevation of children's reactivity and child adjustment over time), evidence was also found for the propositions that these regulatory responses may play a role in other pathways related to child adjustment outcomes. That is, these regulatory systems were each also linked with children's emotional security about parenting, which was in turn also associated with child adjustment. Notably, Owen and Cox (1997) also found support for the notion that exposure to destructive marital conflict may have "spillover" effects that also increase children's attachment insecurity.

In summary, given the centrality of emotional, cognitive, and behavioral response systems to the conceptualization of EST, the cogency of this model is supported by this evidence. That is, these studies demonstrate that specific regulatory responses and multiple pathways act as dynamic processes, each of which individually contributes to the prediction of child adjustment outcomes (see Figures 2.1 and 2.2).

Reciprocal Effects: How Children's Response Systems Influence Marital Conflict

Although children's behavior problems have been shown to influence marital conflict over time (Jenkins et al., 2005), this is not the same as demonstraing children's *agency* in these family contexts—in other words, as showing that children's reactions in the specific context of marital conflict exercise reciprocal and transactional effects on marital conflict over time. A seemingly tacit assumption of much research on marital conflict and children is that the effects only go in one direction: from marital conflict to child adjustment. However, guided by functionalist perspectives on emotion, EST proposes that threats to emotional security organize multiple emotional and behavioral (e.g., mediation, involvement) responses, which in turn are designed to regain acceptable levels of emotional security, including response strategies of mediation and involvement (Cummings & Davies, 1996). Consequently, children's efforts to bring about positive change in destructive marital conflict are anticipated, and are expected from a theoretical perspective to potentially relate to improvements in marital conflict. These issues are thus related to the notion of a reverse or reciprocal direction of effects; that is, children influence marital conflict, as well as vice versa.

This notion of a reverse direction of effects is most cogently supported if the behaviors that children exhibit during marital conflict succeed in affecting this conflict over time. Cummings and Schermerhorn (2003) have defined "agentic behaviors" as actions by children designed to influence family members. In the context of marital conflict, agentic behaviors are active helping behaviors intended to diminish conflict (i.e., involvement or mediation). Given the theoretical bases for expecting children to be motivated to mediate or otherwise try to reduce marital conflict (Grych & Fincham, 1990), and the observed fact that children often do become involved in or attempt to mediate such conflict, it is perhaps surprising that few studies have examined children's agency in the context of the marital relationship as a potential influence on marital conflict over time.

An initial attempt to address this issue (Schermerhorn, Cummings, & Davies, 2005) found that children's perceived agency, which reflected children's impulses to influence family outcomes positively, was associated with reduced marital conflict 1 year later. Although these findings provide some support for the predictions, the focus on children's perceptions rather than their behaviors raises questions about whether children are able to influence marital conflict by their own actions.

To address this issue in particular, Schermerhorn and colleagues (2008) examined these questions in the context of a three-wave longitudinal study. The focus was on children's behavioral responses during marital conflict—specifically, on the impact (if any) of children's regulatory responses during conflict. These categories of regulatory responses posited by EST were examined: children's negative emotional reactivity, behavioral involvement (i.e., agentic behavior), and dysregulated behavior (e.g., "causes trouble").

The results were framed in the context of the three-wave test (i.e., assessments at Times 1, 2, and 3). Consistent with predictions of EST, marital discord at Time 1 predicted children's negative emotional reactivity at Time 2. In turn, negative emotional reactivity was associated with children's agentic behavior and behavioral dysregulation at Time 2. These results thus conform to the prediction of EST that emotional reactivity (emotional insecurity) is associated with children's motivation, organization, and direction toward behaviorally responding to marital conflict (Davies & Cummings, 1994). Moreover, children's agentic behavior at Time 2 was linked with reduced marital conflict at Time 3, whereas children's behavioral dysregulation at Time 2 was associated with increased marital conflict at Time 3, even with autoregressive controls for Time 1 marital conflict in these model tests.

Interestingly, children's behavioral involvement (i.e., agentic behavior) during marital conflict was found to contribute to reducing this conflict over time, although the mechanisms for these effects are unclear. However, children's actions in themselves are unlikely to solve their parents' problems. It is more likely that these children's responses made their parents more aware of the distress being induced in the children, so that the parents chose to have fewer conflicts in the future. By contrast, children's negative, dysregulated behavior did not reduce marital conflict, and therefore did not seem to distract the parents from their conflict, as has sometimes been hypothesized. On the contrary, children's dysregulated behavior during marital conflict appeared to add fuel to their parents' difficulties over time, increasing interparental conflict. Furthermore, children's involvement in marital conflict was not linked with their later development of adjustment problems, whereas children's behavioral dysregulation during parents' disputes was associated with later internalizing and externalizing problems.

Thus the limited available research suggests that reciprocal influences between marital conflict and children's reactions merit consideration as causal pathways in contexts of marital conflict. However, these findings merit further study and some caution in interpretation, especially with regard to characterizing some behavioral reactions to marital conflict as optimal (i.e., agentic behavior) and other reactions as nonoptimal (e.g., dysregulated behavior). Notably, any heightened behavioral response to marital conflict suggests that children's set point for emotional security with regard to marital conflict has been violated, and that children are potentially experiencing emotional insecurity, with possible implications for children's later adjustment problems at some point. For example, children's agentic behavior may have "sleeper effects," relating to somewhat later development of mental health problems.

Another basis for caution about family contexts in which children provide emotional support for their parents is that these responses are linked with parentification, which has been shown to be related to children's adjustment problems and poorer competency in close friendships (Peris et al., 2008). Consequently, a goal for future research is to attempt to identify parameters distinguishing agentic behaviors that are positive and prosocial from involvement in marital conflict that may elicit concern.

Emotional Security as a Higher-Order Organizational Construct: Empirical Support

According to EST, optimal assessment of emotional security focuses on the higher-order organization of multiple response systems, given that each specific regulatory system is posited to provide valuable information about children's emotional security in contexts of marital conflict. EST postulates that concerns about security in the marital relationship reflect an underlying, latent goal system. Although the goal of preserving emotional security motivates each of the regulatory systems, these response systems also each hold distinct information about children's emotional security. Moreover, interplay may occur between and among these response systems in the service of maintaining or regaining emotional security, with response systems having complementary or interchangeable functions at different times, in different contexts, and for different individuals. For example, Billy may show emotional insecurity by overt displays of emotional distress when one parent withdraws from the other during conflicts. Alternatively, Ann may suppress overt forms of emotional responding during a heated argument between her parents, and instead may try to regain security by mediating the parents' conflicts.

Accordingly, assessment of emotional security as a higher-order construct including two or more of these classes of regulatory response processes is likely to be more cogent, complete, and informative than is measurement based on individual regulatory response systems (Rhoades, 2008). In this regard, a strategy has been to form profiles or composites of emotional security based on the measurement of these multiple response systems (Davies & Sturge-Apple, 2007).

Strategies for assessing emotional security about interparental relationships based on multiple dimensions of children's responding, and based on either parent or child report (or both), have been developed to facilitate and stimulate future research on this construct. The latest versions of these measures of emotional security are provided in Appendices B and C of this book; they are brief instruments designed for family researchers (Davies, Forman, Rasi, & Stevens, 2002). These instruments are the Security in the Interparental Subsystem (SIS) scale, completed by children about their own responses to marital conflict, and the Security in the Marital Subsystem—Parent Report (SIMS-PR) scale, which is based on parents' responses about their children's reactions to marital conflict. At the same time, consistent with the commitment of EST to using diverse, ecologically sound methods tailored to specific questions and contexts, assessment of emotional security is not tied to any single approach. Therefore, we encourage the use of multiple other strategies for assessing emotional security. For example, alternative strategies employed in the studies described in this volume have included observational measures based on the revised MacArthur Story Stem Battery, observational measures based on children's reactions to marital conflict, and assessments based on children's responses to analogues of marital conflict (see Chapter 3).

Support for conceptual models is increased when findings are consistent across different research designs, samples, and developmental periods. Pertinent to this point, and also reflecting a higher-order assessment of emotional security in terms of multiple regulatory

systems, Cummings, Schermerhorn, and colleagues (2006) longitudinally tested models of emotional security as explanatory mechanisms
for relations between interparental discord and child maladjustment
in two studies. They examined independent samples of families with
children 9–18 years of age (Study 1) and 5–7 years of age (Study 2). In
these studies, children's sense of emotional security about marital conflict was assessed as an organizational latent variable construct inferred
from multiple classes of response processes (e.g., emotional reactivity,
behavioral involvement).

Despite the differences in samples and age periods, both studies
provided consistent support for the relations posited by the EST model
among interparental discord, emotional security, and child adjustment.
That is, emotional security was identified as an explanatory mechanism
in the adjustment of children ranging in age from kindergarten through
adolescence. Moreover, the pattern of results indicated that emotional
security was related to the explanation of both internalizing and externalizing problems in children. In these studies, emotional security was
an intervening or mediating variable, after controls for earlier levels
of child adjustment. Finally, the cogency of the pattern of results was
supported by the fact that similar findings occurred despite variations
across studies in developmental period; temporal spacing of processes
in relation to other constructs in the model (i.e., concurrent or longitudinal tests, longitudinal tests over varying periods of time); and the
specific strategies for multimethod assessment of marital conflict (e.g.,
observational or questionnaire), and other variables, in the models.

Finally, attachment theory has emphasized the particular importance of emotional security about parent–child relations in infancy
and early childhood; this implies that emotional security in the marital
subsystem may only be important, or may be most significant, for very
young children. In this regard, the findings of Study 2 above supported
emotional security as mediating relations between marital conflict and
child adjustment in early childhood (5–7 years). However, the findings
of Study 1 not only showed that emotional security was also significant
in middle childhood and adolescence, but indicated that the links
between exposure to interparental discord and children's emotional
security about marital conflict were stronger for older than for younger
children in this sample. That is, the links between marital conflict and
emotional security actually *increased* in strength as children moved into
adolescence.

The key demonstration of the Cummings, Schermerhorn, and colleagues (2006) study is that emotional security measured as a higher-

order organizational construct can be shown in the context of a longitudinal research design to serve as an explanatory construct for relations
between marital conflict and child adjustment. Throughout this volume,
we describe other recent studies that support this conclusion; this study
is especially cogent because of the support based on two separate and
independent samples. Another conclusion supported by the Cummings,
Schermerhorn, and colleagues findings is that emotional security about
marital relations is not simply a stage-salient task of early childhood, but
remains an important goal with regard to children's monitoring of the
safety and security of their home environments throughout childhood
and into adolescence.

    A possible explanation for differences between family systems in
the stage salience of emotional security considers differences in these
emotional security systems with regard to children's goals—that is,
differences in the set goal of emotional security between the marital
and parent–child subsystems. In the case of attachment, maintenance
of proximity to parents and use of parents as secure bases for exploration are central goals of this behavioral system; in the case of children's
security in the marital context, Davies and Sturge-Apple (2007) have
proposed that social defense may be a more salient goal than in the
attachment relationship. Although there are scant bases for firm conclusions at this time, these are intriguing notions, reflecting an ethologically based perspective on these two attachment behavioral systems
(Davies & Woitach, 2008). When the social defense notion is considered
in developmental context, concerns about social defense may become
more salient in adolescence with regard to marital conflict, as children
become more aware of (and better understand) the meaning of interparental conflict for their own well-being and that of their families.

FUTURE DIRECTIONS

Future Directions in Process-Oriented Models

From a process-oriented perspective, a goal for the future is the development of more sophisticated process-oriented models that outline a
multiplicity of pathways, conditions, and mechanisms, identifying the
various intra- and extraorganismic characteristics that affect the vulnerability of children. For example, EST postulates that the strength of
mediational pathways between and among interparental conflict, child
emotional insecurity, and child maladjustment may vary, depending on
the operation of processes in the individual or the larger family system

(e.g., cohesion). In other words, examining whether individual-level or family-level processes moderate the unfolding chain of mediating and intervening processes in the link between marital conflict and child maladjustment is a promising direction (e.g., Cummings, Schermer-horn, et al., 2006; Davies, Harold, et al., 2002; Fosco & Grych, 2007; Sturge-Apple, Davies, & Cummings, 2006a, 2006b).

Pattern-based or person-based approaches represent another direction for capturing individual differences in the organization of child functioning in the face of marital conflict (Cicchetti & Rogosch, 1996; Richters, 1997). Various studies have begun to explore ways for identifying organizational patterns at the level of the family (e.g., Belsky & Fearon, 2004; Davies, Sturge-Apple, & Cummings, 2004; Lindahl, 2001; O'Connor, Hetherington, & Reiss, 1998), child coping (Cummings, 1987; Davies & Forman, 2002; El-Sheikh, Cummings, & Goetsch, 1989), and child adjustment (e.g., Grych, Jouriles, Swank, McDonald, & Norwood, 2000).

Longitudinal research designs with three or more measurement occasions have promise for advancing process-oriented understanding, because they permit greater flexibility in charting the nature, correlates, origins, and sequelae of individual differences in developmental pathways (Cummings, Goeke-Morey, & Dukewich, 2001; Willett, Singer, & Martin, 1998; Windle, 2000). New approaches to analysis are helping to identify the interplay among interparental risk factors, risk processes, and multiple trajectories of child functioning (Muthen & Muthen, 2000; Shaw, Gilliom, Ingoldsby, & Nagin, 2003).

EST as a Guide for Future Research

In this chapter and throughout this volume, we provide evidence for the cogency of EST in accounting for relations between family processes, including interparental and parent–child relations and child outcomes. At the same time, EST and various other theories of family processes and child development share some fundamental conceptualizations about processes that underlie the relations between marital conflict and child development (Cummings & Cummings, 2002). For example, EST (Davies, Harold, et al., 2002) and attachment theory (Bowlby, 1969) stress the role of family systems in providing security and protection from harm in times of stress. The cognitive–contextual framework (Grych & Fincham, 1990) and EST (Cummings & Davies, 1996) share the hypothesis that greater sensitization occurs in response to repeated exposure to destructive conflicts, and that this greater sensitization contributes to increases in a child's risk for adjustment problems resulting from exposure to marital conflict. Accordingly, an important future direction is to further refine and articulate EST, including critical tests of theoretical propositions against stringent criteria, and comparisons and contrasts with other theories. These approaches should result in the growth of EST as a conceptual model.

Tests of EST against Stringent Criteria and with Multiple Methods

Critical tests are likely to emerge when theoretical propositions are challenged by rigorous criteria. For example, in addition to longitudinal tests of propositions, EST will be subjected to more stringent testing when causal pathways are modeled with autoregressive controls for prior levels of functioning. Many other questions merit investigation in this context, such as intervals between waves of testing, the role of various possible mediators, and the nature of effects for different outcomes. In addition, knowledge will be further increased when theoretical propositions and constructs are based on multiple research methods, approaches, and designs, including the heightened level of causal inference that can be supported by experiments (Fincham, 1998). Verification of findings based on multiple methods, given that all methods have strengths and weaknesses for interpretation, is essential for cogent demonstration at a process-oriented level of analysis. In Chapter 3, we discuss the merits and possibilities of using multiple methodological and research design approaches in tests of the theoretical propositions posited by EST. Thus, rather than repeatedly relying on only one method or even one instrument to define key concepts, research on EST is more consistent than research on many other theories in advocating and using multiple methods, research designs, and domains of responding to test key predictions (Cicchetti, Cummings, Greenberg, & Marvin, 1990; Cummings & Davies, 1994). Tests in the context of prevention or intervention programs are also potentially informative about the viability of the theory. These directions of study are underway (see Chapters 5–9), but many other critical tests of theory are needed to further explicate EST.

Comparisons with Other Theories

Still another future direction is comparison with other theories. Important differences are evident between EST and these other theories (Davies & Cummings, 2006), and tests of these differences merit further investigation. One question is whether emotional security as defined by EST still contributes to the prediction of children's adjustment, even when constructs from other models are taken into account. For example, attachment theory places greater emphasis on children's behavioral systems for maximizing caregivers' sensitivity and protection, whereas EST emphasizes responses to potentially dangerous or problematic family situations, with one possible goal of social defense systems being to defuse and avoid threat in relation to destructive conflict (Davies & Sturge-Apple, 2007; Davies & Woitach, 2008). Even though EST and attachment theory overlap in important ways (e.g., control systems' functioning centers around issues of emotional security, safety, and protection), these differences in goals provide bases for expecting some differences in prediction.

Rooted in social-cognitive theories of interparental relations, the cognitive–contextual framework places particular emphasis on understanding how the cognitive dimensions of children's appraisals shape the impact of conflict on child adjustment (e.g., Grych & Fincham, 1990, 1993; Grych, Seid, & Fincham, 1992). Children are viewed as active agents who attempt to derive interpersonal meaning from the ways in which their parents manage conflict. Two dimensions of appraisal—that is, perceived threat and self-blame—assume center stage in explaining why interparental conflict increases child vulnerability to psychopathology.

Thus, with repeated exposure to angry, hostile, and unresolved disputes between parents, children are thought to become increasingly likely to perceive parental conflicts as threatening. In turn, these increasing appraisals of threat are thought to predispose children to an increased risk for adjustment problems. When children view themselves as bearing responsibility for reducing interparental and family discord, they may be especially prone to blaming themselves for the maintenance or escalation of interparental difficulties. Increasing feelings of guilt, shame, helplessness, and poor self-worth—outgrowths of these appraisal processes—may develop into broader patterns of adjustment problems. Studies examining perceived threat and self-blame provide support for the proposed pathways (Dadds, Atkinson, Turner, Blums, & Lendich, 1999; Grych, Fincham, Jouriles, & McDonald, 2000; Grych et al., 2003; Kerig, 1998).

In short, then, the cognitive–contextual framework stresses the role of specific response systems of threat and self-blame in affecting child outcomes, whereas EST emphasizes emotional security as a higher-order construct that incorporates emotional, behavioral, and cognitive regulatory systems. Moreover, response systems are conceptualized much more

broadly in EST than in the cognitive–contextual model. In addition to
the emphasis in EST on dimensions of responding beyond appraisals
(e.g., emotional, behavioral), physiological and biological response systems are also seen as pertinent to serving the emotional security control
system (Cummings & Davies, 1996). There is also some recent support
from an EST perspective for relations between biological and behavioral systems in responding to marital conflict. For example, fearful
responses to interparental conflict are linked with the biological stress
response of elevated cortisol reactivity to conflict (Davies, Sturge-Apple,
et al., 2008), and longitudinal pathways between and among interparental conflict, children's cortisol reactivity, and child adjustment have
been identified (Davies et al., 2007).

An important next step in research is to empirically compare and
test the different theories. Conceptually driven tests of the relative usefulness of different theoretical models in explaining relations between
family processes and child outcomes are rare. Moreover, studies designed
to test the validity of theories frequently examine hypotheses that may
be common to multiple theories, and often tests involve comparing a
single conceptual model against the null hypothesis. It is important to
move beyond the all-too-common practice of examining predictions
in relation to the null hypothesis (Fincham, Grych, & Osborne, 1994).
Despite adopting a common goal of distinguishing among risk factors,
risk processes, and outcomes, various theories of interparental discord
offer a diverse array of explanations for why interparental conflict is
deleterious to child functioning. Theories of marital conflict differ most
widely in their accounts of risk mechanisms. For example, whereas some
theories place greater emphasis on children's social-cognitive reactions
to marital conflict as key explanatory processes of risk, other theories
underscore the role of child emotionality. Moreover, still other theories
highlight the value of behavioral or family processes.

Breaking new ground in this regard, the Davies, Harold, and colleagues (2002) research provided direct comparisons among the predictions of various theories about marital conflict and child adjustment.
It assessed emotional security as an explanatory construct in predicting child adjustment, taking into account constructs derived from the
cognitive–contextual framework (Study 2) and attachment theory
(Study 3). The findings of these studies supported the conclusion that
emotional security about interparental relations played an explanatory
role in predicting child adjustment, even when statistical model tests
included constructs from other theories about marital conflict as influences on child adjustment. In a longitudinal analysis involving a British

sample, pathways through emotional security acted as an explanatory mechanism for child internalizing and externalizing symptoms, and remained significant when constructs from the cognitive–contextual framework were also included in the statistical model tests (Study 2). Notably, the cognitive–contextual constructs did not provide complete prediction of pathways when considered in the same statistical model as emotional security, but were significant in predicting pathways to child outcomes when considered in isolation from emotional security. At the same time, emotional security and appraisals of threat and self-blame each played unique, mutually informative roles in understanding pathways between interparental conflict exposure and child adjustment problems. Similarly, in cross-sectional tests based on a U.S. sample of families and children, pathways from interparental conflict to emotional security to child adjustment were significant even when security in the parent–child relationship was included in model testing (Study 3). At the same time, significant but independent pathways were found from parenting to parent–child attachment security to child adjustment.

In summary, correspondence among theories is evident in the common premise that marital conflict directly sets in motion processes within children that lead to stable individual differences in their functioning. Against this backdrop of conceptual similarities, theories do hold distinct assumptions that set them apart from each other. Attesting to the unique role of security in the interparental relationship as an explanatory mechanism in EST versus other major theories, research has shown that pathways between and among interparental conflict, child insecurity, and maladjustment remain robust within larger statistical models that incorporate alternative explanatory processes (e.g., Davies, Harold, et al., 2002) and longitudinal tests of pathways (Cummings, Schermerhorn, et al., 2006; Harold et al., 2004). At the same time, these other models further expand the conceptualization of cognitive (i.e., the cognitive–contextual model) and emotional (i.e., attachment theory) processes, and are complementary in many ways with EST. Each approach merits further study and comparison.

CONCLUSION

In conclusion, considerable progress has been made over the last 15–20 years in developing process-oriented accounts for how and why children exposed to marital conflict are at greater risk for experiencing mental health difficulties. In addition, various theories have been proposed, and many of these theories share a common process-oriented concern with identifying the mechanisms underlying the vulnerability of children exposed to marital conflict; they also share important overlap in their scope of processes. Regrettably, at this stage of the research, simultaneous empirical tests of family process theories are still relatively rare. However, the small number of studies that do examine the relative viability of different theories may provide useful blueprints for such tests (Buehler, Lange, & Franck, 2007; Davies, Harold, et al., 2002).

Although we acknowledge the merits and contributions of other approaches, we adopt the perspective in this volume that EST is especially promising for future advances in process-oriented study of marital conflict from both a familywide (Cummings & Davies, 1996) and a social-ecological (Cummings, Schermerhorn, Merrilees, Goeke-Morey, & Cairns, 2008; see Chapter 9) perspective. Among the various theories, EST is also notably well grounded in developmental theory—firmly based on attachment theory (see Chapter 9) and on evolutionary and ethological perspectives (Davies & Sturge-Apple, 2007; Davies & Woitach, 2008).

Moreover, EST provides an advanced basis for process-oriented perspectives on children and marital conflict. EST offers the most explicit formulation and testable predictions about multiple regulatory processes as distinct pathways. In addition, only EST among the extant theories has proven to be a constantly evolving theory, benefiting from numerous updates since its initial conceptualizations (e.g., Cummings & Davies, 1996; Davies, Harold, et al., 2002; Davies & Sturge-Apple, 2007). Moreover, it has led the way in advancing multimethod approaches to measurement and innovative research designs for the study of family processes and child development (see Chapter 3). EST is also unique among extant theories in providing conceptual bases for higher-order conceptualizations of coping processes related to child adjustment (Davies, Cummings, & Winter, 2004; Davies & Forman, 2002) and tests of how other multiple family systems are interrelated with marital conflict at a process-oriented level of analysis (e.g., Cummings, Schermerhorn, Keller, et al., 2008; Davies, Harold, et al., 2002; Schermerhorn et al., 2008). Finally, up to this point, EST has also led the way in serving as a productive basis for testing and theorizing about of how children's reactions to marital conflict may influence marital conflict over time, and about how family influences may relate to broader social-ecological influences on child development (see Chapter 9).

Thus EST has inspired a virtual explosion of research on marital conflict, family and community processes, and children's adjustment.

At the same time, there is an urgent need for an accessible update of the status of this work. Accordingly, in the remainder of this volume, we endeavor to provide a much-needed advanced review and analysis of the evidence—especially the considerable recent evidence that EST can provide a familywide and social-ecological perspective on family processes and children's functioning and adjustment. In the context of process-oriented analysis of these issues, we also continue to consider other evidence, models, and approaches as they may challenge or improve the predictions of the EST perspective.

PART II

CHILD EFFECTS OF EXPOSURE TO MARITAL CONFLICT

One of the strongest pathways of the effects of marital conflict on children is simply through their exposure to discord between the parents. In spite of the overwhelming evidence for children's sensitivity and responsiveness to exposure to marital conflict, and the findings of links between such exposure and children's long-term well-being and adjustment, some do not recognize that children are affected simply by this exposure. Consider the following example:

> Eddie and Mike, both preschoolers, were playing together in the living room of Eddie's house. Suddenly there was a loud noise from the kitchen as a door slammed, and the children could hear Eddie's parents arguing loudly. The argument went on and on, with both parents storming about, making demonstrative statements. Mike was scared, because he did not know Eddie's parents, and his own parents never fought in such a manner. Looking over at Eddie, however, Mike noticed that Eddie was only mildly concerned. This reflected Eddie's knowledge that his parents might not really be mad at each other, because he knew that both of them cared about cooking, were very demonstrative, and enjoyed the fun and stimulation of a vigorous back-and-forth exchange. Nonetheless, Eddie got up and went into the kitchen to see what was going on. When his parents saw him,

they stopped fighting. His father smiled and jokingly said, "Your mother makes ravioli the wrong way. My mother did it the right way." Eddie's mother said, "Well, it is so sweet that your daddy cares so much about the cooking." The father said happily, "And your mother is such a great cook." The parents then kissed and made up, and both boys went back to playing.

This vignette illustrates that the manner in which parents work out their differences matters a lot, and that the ending of the conflict is relevant to children's final levels of distress. Moreover, children's interpretations of conflict are important. Because Mike interpreted the conflict as hostile, he was scared; Eddie knew from past experience that the conflict might not be serious, and so he was much less concerned. Although Mike showed a lot of visible anxiety, more subtle reactions may actually tell us more about the impact of a conflict. For example, what was Mike's appraisal of the meaning of the conflict? Was his visible anxiety also manifested under the skin in the form of physiological responses? Finally, although the ending seemed constructive, one might wonder whether the ending was a fully constructive process from the children's perspective. For example, was Eddie's mother submitting to the father?

Another example illustrates additional points. Recall the example of Lois, John, and their respective parents from the opening of Chapter 2. Why did Lois exhibit higher levels of distress than John to a comparable conflict? Did her history of exposure to hostile conflicts affect her reactivity? If so, exactly how did it develop? At the same time, John did not grow up in a home devoid of any conflict, so why was he so well regulated in the face of his parents' conflicts? Is it possible that some forms of conflict may actually be benign or even constructive in their effects on how children process and respond to conflict?

The Chapter 2 example demonstrates cumulative effects of exposure, which are evident for Lois but also for John. John's response *to the same conflict* indicates that reactivity is diminished when there is a history of parents' working out differences. Both of these factors— that is, discrimination between types of conflict, and interpretation in the context of the historical meaning of conflict based on children's experiences—are examined further in this part of the book.

These types of evidence are informative about exposure's effects, albeit at different levels of analysis. Children's reactions during exposure to conflicts communicate important information about the relative constructiveness or destructiveness of these types of conflicts from the children's perspective. Chapter 3 provides a systematic review of the latest findings and conclusions regarding the nature of constructive versus destructive conflicts from children's viewpoints.

In Chapter 4, we consider children's reactions as an important element in explaining the processes through which marital conflict influences children's long-term adjustment. Marital conflict does not directly affect children's adjustment. Relations with adjustment are the results of processes set in motion by exposure to or other awareness of marital conflict; over time, these processes come to be related to the development of adjustment problems.

Ideally, models for the impact of exposure to marital conflict on children are tested with relatively complex statistical models that simultaneously include multiple pathways. Creative and advanced testing of process-oriented models for explaining multiple child outcomes has occurred in recent years in the research on EST.

CHAPTER 3

Identifying Constructive
and Destructive Marital Conflict

An important objective in a process-oriented approach is to identify the effects of marital conflict characteristics. In Chapter 2, this point is reflected in Figure 2.1, which indicates that the characteristics of destructive marital conflict are risk factors for children's negative outcomes due to exposure to marital conflict. However, the converse may also be true: If marital conflict is constructive, its characteristics may be initiating factors for children's *positive* outcomes. With regard to model testing, whether marital conflict is constructive or destructive clearly bears on the outcomes of exposure to such conflict.

Although the notion that conflicts can be constructive or destructive is intuitively appealing, there has long actually been very little real basis for making this distinction. Thus the matter has been left to the opinion of experts, or perhaps to general ideas in the popular culture about what may be desirable or undesirable ways to engage in conflict. Unfortunately, these opinions or general ideas can be fundamentally unreliable. For example, at one point a recommendation was made to engage in catharsis when it came to anger toward a partner—that is, to express all the hostility and anger one felt, even to point of hitting the partner violently with a nerf bat or engaging in unbridled expressions of verbal criticism and hostility. These are decidedly bad ideas for any hope of resolving marital disputes amicably!

The goal of this chapter is to advance the concept that marital con-flict can be either constructive or destructive from the children's point of view. First, we consider notions from the developmental psychopathol-ogy perspective that provide a conceptual foundation for the investiga-tion of these issues. Next, the evidence that has accumulated over the past two decades regarding the impact of different forms of conflict on children is examined. We then present criteria derived from EST that support distinctions between constructive and destructive conflict, and consider recent studies that have employed conceptual and empirical criteria from EST to identify constructive and destructive marital con-flict behaviors. Finally, future directions and questions are examined.

THE IMPORTANCE OF DIFFERENTIATING MARITAL CONFLICT BEHAVIORS

At the outset, the topic of marital conflict and children's functioning should be put in some perspective. Conflict is normal and unavoid-able in marriages, especially if one defines "conflict" broadly to include any disputes, disagreements, or expression of untoward emotions over everyday matters between the parents (e.g., chores, childrearing, visit-ing relatives; see Chapter 1). Despite the seeming assumption in pre-1980s research that marital conflict is a homogeneous stimulus, marital conflict in everyday life varies on multiple dimensions (Cummings & Cummings, 1988). Thus different forms of marital conflict may have different effects on children (Cummings & Davies, 2002): Given the centrality of such conflict to family circumstances, children's repeated experiences with some forms of marital conflict may have lasting, highly negative effects, but other types may have relatively benign effects.

Questions thus remain about the nature and definitions of con-structive and destructive marital conflict from the children's perspec-tive. Making reliable and well-defined distinctions between these types of conflict behaviors may be critical for the practical application of find-ings from research in this area—that is, the development of programs or approaches to teach parents how to handle conflict better for the sake of their own and their children's welfare. For example, teaching such distinctions may form a solid foundation for psychoeducational programs for parents about how to handle everyday disputes.

A particularly intriguing issue is whether there are actually conflict behaviors that can be called "constructive" from children's perspective. Past work has been limited to showing that some behaviors (1) have non-negative effects on observing children (i.e., the children are not distressed), or (2) reduce negative reactions (as in the case of children observing a compromise between the parents after a lengthy conflict). It is questionable whether simply failure to induce distress, or even to reduce distress, is an adequate criterion for the existence of truly constructive conflict behaviors. The classification of conflict behaviors as constructive also requires a demonstration that these behaviors actually *improve* children's well-being or functioning.

A DEVELOPMENTAL PSYCHOPATHOLOGY PERSPECTIVE

The principles of developmental psychopathology provide bases for exploring notions of constructive as well as destructive conflicts (Davies & Cummings, 2006). The developmental psychopathology perspective emphasizes the significance of context. Applied to the study of marital conflict and children, this perspective demands a contextual analysis of the dynamic implications for child development of multiple and specific forms of marital conflict (Cummings, Davies, et al., 2000).

Pertinent to the present topic, another emphasis that follows from a developmental psychopathology perspective is appreciation for the possibility that a given class of family processes can be either positive or negative, depending on expression and other contextual factors. The principle of the mutually informative value of studying normal and abnormal development and processes (Sroufe, 1990) calls for a complementary consideration of both positive (e.g., protective) factors and outcomes (e.g., competence in the face of risk) and negative (e.g., risk and potentiating) factors and outcomes (e.g., psychopathology) associated with marital conflict behaviors.

In the sense of expressing disagreement and having differences of opinion, conflict is an everyday characteristic of marital relationships. Disputes, disagreements, or expressions of negative emotions over everyday matters are common occurrences in marital and family life. Not only may children adapt to marital discord, but some forms of conflict expressions and resolution may *theoretically* advance children's well-being. At the same time, specific forms of marital discord are related to risk for psychopathology both in parents (Du Rocher Schudlich, Papp, & Cummings, 2004) and in children (El-Sheikh et al., 2008). Thus, in principle, given the contextual richness of family conflict, some forms of marital conflict may have negative effects and others may have benign or constructive effects.

Another pertinent contextual concept that emerges from the developmental psychopathology perspective is an emphasis on the dynamic interactions between an active organism and the environment (Cummings, Davies, et al., 2000). This perspective on children as active agents also calls attention to the importance of understanding children's particular perspectives on marital conflict, rather than simply the external characteristics of marital conflict behaviors (e.g., volume, intensity) (Cummings, Davies, & Simpson, 1994). Children are inherently better sources of information about the constructiveness or destructiveness of marital conflict from their own perspectives than outside observers or even their parents can be. It follows from the emphasis on understanding children's processes of responding as a multidimensional construct that multiple aspects of children's responding may indicate the meaning of marital conflict from their perspective. That is, their emotional, behavioral, cognitive, or physiological responses, or their higher-order patterns of responding to conflict (Maughan & Cicchetti, 2002), may each and all provide insights into the impact of conflict on them. The emphasis on the importance of the psychological as well as expressive meaning of context further necessitates differentiating the topography of marital conflict, rather than treating such conflict as a global stimulus.

At the same time, from an organizational perspective, multiple and alternative forms of expression of marital conflict can have similar implications from the children's perspective (Davies, Myers, et al., 1999). For example, multiple behaviors may have similar meanings from the children's perspective as representations of either constructive or destructive conflict. Thus goals at this level of analysis should include differentiating the effects of specific expressions of conflict from the children's perspective, as well as identifying higher-order categories or organizational meanings of conflict behaviors—in other words, categories of constructive or destructive conflict (Davies & Cummings, 2006). Conflict behaviors that pose risk are significant to studying the impact of abnormal marital processes on children's adjustment and may merit classification as destructive, whereas behaviors valuable to understanding the role of marital conflict as compensatory or protective processes may qualify for categorization as constructive. These influences must also be understood in the context of time; over time, specific marital conflict behaviors may contribute to normal and/or abnormal developmental trajectories in children. Broader patterns of functioning in families may also be related to the effects of specific forms of marital conflict on children (Davies, Cummings, & Winter, 2004). Notably, risk associated with marital conflict is probabilistic rather than certain (Sroufe, 1997), and the impact of exposure to marital conflict expressions must be weighed in terms of the broader family context (Davies, Harold, et al., 2002).

Although some forms of marital conflict tactics, strategies, and communications have emerged as risk factors—that is, they probabilistically increase children's risk for adjustment problems and negative reactivity (see below)—much less is known about possibly protective or compensatory marital conflict behaviors. Although considerable reference is made to constructive conflict as a hypothetical concept in the literature, until recently there was little actual evidence to support the existence of constructive conflict behaviors, or even the criteria for evaluating their existence. Even now, relatively little is known in the context of process-oriented and longitudinal research designs about marital conflict as a protective factor or contributor to resiliency processes (Egeland, Carlson, & Sroufe, 1993; Luthar, Doernberger, & Zigler, 1993; Masten, Best, & Garmezy, 1990).

However, it is one thing to posit hypothetically or even to test probabilistically that marital conflict can be either harmful or beneficial. It is another to be guided by theory in testing which conflict tactics fit these specifications, including tests based upon well-defined conceptual and/ or operational criteria for constructive and destructive conflicts from the children's perspective. Although theory and evidence have accumulated to *suggest* categories of marital conflict as risk (destructive) or compensatory (constructive) factors (Cummings, 1998), a gap has existed between these suggestions and the articulation and exploration of explicit, conceptually based criteria for classifying and ordering marital conflict behaviors.

CRITERIA FOR CONSTRUCTIVE AND DESTRUCTIVE CONFLICT BEHAVIORS DERIVED FROM EST

The framework in Figure 2.1 highlights the significance of adequately defining marital conflict as a risk (or, alternatively, a protective) factor, since all that follows in this process-oriented account of children's development in the face of exposure to marital conflict is based on this starting point. Consistent with the principles of the developmental psychopathology perspective, current theory and research on children and marital conflict indicate the following: (1) The effects of parental conflicts on children are more a function of children's perceptions of the meaning of such conflicts for themselves and their families than simply a function of the conflicts' frequency or even their physical character- istics; and (2) the meaning of conflicts is most informatively discerned from multiple dimensions of children's responding, including cogni- tions, emotional reactions, coping behaviors, and even physiological responses (Crockenberg & Forgays, 1996; Cummings, 1987; Davies & Cummings, 1994; El-Sheikh et al., 1989; Harold et al., 2004; Wilson & Gottman, 1995). Accordingly, it follows that examining children's evalu- ations of meaning is the most appropriate approach to understanding the behaviors and categories of constructive versus destructive con- flicts.

However, although the "meaning of conflict" is intuitively appealing as a basis for distinguishing forms of conflict from the children's per- spective, it is also inherently a vague and ill-defined notion. For example, what are the goals that guide children's appraisals (Crockenberg & Lan- grock, 2001a)? With regard to these issues, EST provides operational and conceptual foundations for defining meaning and distinguishing goals guiding children's responses to conflicts; it thereby yields both operational and conceptual bases for distinguishing constructive and destructive conflicts from the children's perspective (Davies, Harold, et al., 2002; Goeke-Morey, Cummings, Harold, & Shelton, 2003).

According to EST, the meaning of marital conflicts is related to children's assessment of emotional security implications, which can be discerned operationally from the children's emotional, behavioral, and cognitive reactions. These responses in the service of emotional security are related to children's histories of exposure to marital conflict, and are also identified theoretically as mediators of children's adjustment over time (Davies, Harold, et al., 2002; Harold et al., 2004). Moreover, following from developmental psychopathology's emphasis on identify- ing continua of functioning as well as discrete categories (Cicchetti et al., 1990; Cummings, 1990), the goals for research on discriminately marital conflict as constructive or destructive are twofold: (1) *categoriza- tion* (differentiating more precisely the effects of specific expressions of conflict as constructive or destructive), and (2) *ranking* (ordering the relative effects of conflict behaviors within higher-order groupings or categories of constructive and destructive conflict, from the children's perspective).

With regard to the categorization of marital conflict, a function- alist perspective on emotions (Campos, Mumme, Kermoian, & Cam- pos, 1994) and pertinent theory (Fabes, Leonard, Kupanoff, & Mar- tin, 2001) suggest that children's *emotional reactions* should provide an especially revealing window into the impact of marital conflict on their functioning. Accordingly, the emotional security hypothesis is that marital conflict tactics eliciting more negative than positive emotional reactions should be considered "destructive," since such responding suggests that children's security is reduced. By contrast, marital conflict tactics resulting in more positive than negative emotional reactions should be classified as "constructive," given that such responding implies enhanced security. Thus children's emotional reactions to specific conflict behaviors provide bases for classifying these behaviors as constructive or destructive.

In addition to providing bases for classifying conflicts as constructive or destructive, these criteria based on EST provide bases for ranking conflict tactics according to their relative effects, adding to the specificity of assessment. That is, conflict tactics can be rated on continua derived from the response criteria proposed by EST. Rating on continua reduces potential errors in measurement associated with categorical classification as destructive or constructive, because it provides additional information about conflict tactics that may be on the borderline between destructive and constructive (e.g., "calm discussion"), and it provides representations of the distinction between extreme and mild expressions within particular categories (e.g., "physical aggression toward the spouse" vs. "nonverbal hostility").

Further criteria for emotional security derived from EST also provide bases for ordering marital conflict behaviors along continua from highly destructive to highly constructive. These criteria are based on regulatory systems in the service of the emotional security system, including behavioral involvement, cognitive representations, or internal working models (Davies & Cummings, 1994). Thus children's efforts at regulating exposure to interparental conflict (e.g., becoming involved in conflict or taking sides through triangulation), or the nature of their expectations about resolution (e.g., positive or negative cognitions), also provide criteria for assessing the relative impact of conflict behaviors from the children's point of view, and therefore bases for evaluating behaviors as relatively constructive or destructive.

EVIDENCE FOR THE IMPACT OF DIFFERENT FORMS OF CONFLICT

The notion that some behaviors may be constructive and others destructive *from the children's perspective* has received support from two decades of research suggesting that different forms of conflict may have very different implications for children's functioning.

Physical Aggression

In laboratory analogue studies, children reported that they perceived conflicts involving aggression as more negative, described more negative emotional reactions to these conflicts, and/or reacted more negatively to them than to conflicts that did not involve aggression (E. M. Cummings, Vogel, Cummings, & El-Sheikh, 1989; see also J. S. Cummings, Pellegrini, Notarius, & Cummings, 1989; Laumakis, Margolin, & John, 1998; O'Brien, Margolin, John, & Krueger, 1991). This finding has received support from paternal reports of children's reactions in the home (Cummings, Zahn-Waxler, & Radke-Yarrow, 1981). Exposure to physical violence has also been related to children's adjustment problems (Doumas, Margolin, & John, 1994; Fantuzzo et al., 1991; Holden, 1998; Jouriles et al., 1989; Kempton, Thomas, & Forehand, 1989; McDonald & Jouriles, 1991).

Ballard and Cummings (1990) reported that children reacted as negatively to analogue presentations of parental aggression toward objects as to interpartner aggression. In addition, Jouriles, Norwood, McDonald, Vincent, and Mahoney (1996) found that other forms of marital aggression (e.g., insulting or swearing at the partner; throwing, smashing, or kicking something; threatening to hit or throw something at the partner) and marital violence were each correlated with children's adjustment problems in a marital therapy sample and a women's shelter sample, respectively. Furthermore, the other forms of marital aggression assessed were related to children's adjustment problems even after the frequency of marital violence was controlled for.

Verbal Hostility

Exposure to verbal aggression (yelling, verbal threats, anger expressions) elicits distress in children (E. M. Cummings et al., 1989; Cummings, Ballard, & El-Sheikh, 1991) and is also linked with child adjustment problems (Davies, Harold, et al., 2002; Johnston et al., 1987). Some types of verbally hostile conflicts contain messages that children find especially disturbing—as much so as exposure to marital violence. Laumakis and colleagues (1998) reported that conflicts involving threats to leave and physical aggression elicited similar high levels of negative reactions from children. Moreover, such conflicts elicited more negative emotional reactions and predictions of negative outcomes than did conflicts with name calling, negative voice, or positive affect.

The notion that verbally hostile conflicts about child-related themes are more distressing than conflicts about other topics of conflict has received support (Grych, 1998; Grych & Fincham, 1993; see also Davies, Myers, & Cummings, 1996), including associations with adjustment problems (Jouriles, Murphy, et al., 1991; Snyder, Klein, Gdowski, Faulstich, & LaCombe, 1988). Recently, Shelton, Harold, Goeke-Morey, and Cummings (2006) reported that hostile child-related conflicts resulted in more mediation efforts by children than other forms of conflict did.

In one of the few studies to examine children's reactions to actual marital discussions of disagreements in the laboratory, Easterbrooks, Cummings, and Emde (1994) reported that toddlers with parents who almost always expressed conflict in mutually respectful and emotionally well-modulated tones evidenced little distress in reaction to a conflictual discussion between parents. On the other hand, parental anger expression, which was relatively uncommon, was associated with negative emotional reactions by these children.

Nonverbal Hostility

In addition to overt conflict behavior, the withdrawal of parents from conflict may signal marital distress to children. Katz and Gottman (1997a) reported that husband withdrawal, indexed by observationally based codes of husband anger and stonewalling, predicted children's increased risk for adjustment problems. Cox, Paley, and Payne (1997) found that marital withdrawal was more predictive of child outcomes than was marital conflict per se. Another study reported that both mothers' and fathers' avoidance and capitulation were related to children's behavior problems (Mahoney, Lape, Query, & Wieber, 1997).

Children's reactions to laboratory analogue presentations of nonverbal conflict or the "silent treatment" indicate that they are significantly distressed by these behaviors (Ballard & Cummings, 1990; E. M. Cummings et al., 1989). In some studies, children's reactions to nonverbal conflicts between adults are indistinguishable from reactions to verbal conflicts (e.g., Cummings, Ballard, & El-Sheikh, 1991). DeArth-Pendley and Cummings (2002) evaluated children's reactions to different forms of nonverbal marital conflict, showing that few youngsters made discriminations between different forms of marital conflict behaviors, and that their reactions to nonverbal conflict were similar to their reactions to verbal conflict. Adults' nonverbal expressions of fear elicited the most negative reactions from children. Links with adjustment problems have also been reported for stonewalling, the silent treatment, sulking, or withdrawal (Jenkins & Smith, 1991; Katz & Gottman, 1997a, 1997b; Katz & Woodin, 2002; Kerig, 1996).

However, few studies have compared responses to specific behaviors linked with risk, so the relative risk associated with different negative behaviors is difficult to ascertain. Moreover, the pattern of findings has been inconsistent across studies for some behaviors; these findings thus provide little theoretical foundation for evaluating the meaning and process-related impact of conflict behaviors from the children's perspective.

Conflict Resolution

Laboratory analogue research has suggested that complete resolution of conflict may largely ameliorate the negative effects of exposure to conflict (E. M. Cummings et al., 1989). One study found not only that children's distress diminished when conflicts were resolved, but that it diminished as a function of the degree of resolution; that is, the specific forms of conflict resolution mattered (Cummings, Ballard, El-Sheikh, & Lake, 1991). Compromise elicited the least negative reactions, and continued verbal hostility or the "silent treatment" received the most negative reactions. Submission, topic change, and apology resulted in responses suggesting that children viewed these endings as reflecting partial resolutions. Thus children may benefit from any progress toward resolution; in other words, distress reactions may be reduced even when parents do not fully resolve conflicts, and children may also benefit from learning about later resolution of conflict. Finally, if both the emotional and informational contents of conflict resolution suggest that matters have been worked out, this may serve to diminish children's negative reactivity (Shifflett-Simpson & Cummings, 1996). Interestingly, Kerig (1996) reported that marital conflict resolution was consistently associated with reduced child adjustment problems, whereas negative elements of conflict (e.g., frequency) were associated with increased adjustment problems.

Furthermore, conflict resolution may sometimes ameliorate the negative impact on children of exposure to marital violence. Cummings, Ballard, El-Sheikh, and Lake (1991) found ameliorative effects of messages about conflict resolution on children's emotional responses to conflicts that included physical aggression, as well as conflicts that were nonverbal or verbal in nature. Similarly, El-Sheikh, Cummings, and Reiter (1996) found that conflict resolution ameliorated children's negative emotional reactions to each of these types of conflicts, including physically aggressive conflicts. Moreover, in this instance children were asked to respond as though the actors were their parents.

However, it should be noted that children were responding to analogue presentations of interparental aggression and subsequent resolution in many of these studies. Although the actors' resolutions appeared genuine, there was no history of prior conflict in these analogue contexts to compromise the apparent sincerity of the resolutions. As we argue throughout this book, children react to the meaning of conflicts for marital and family relations on the basis of their past histories of exposure to conflict, as well as the nature and form of current conflict stimuli. Although the questions await empirical study, children's responses to resolution may not be positive if marital violence or other forms of extreme marital discord have occurred chronically in the past within the family, even if these conflicts have been followed by supposed resolutions. On the other hand, conflict resolution may be relatively uncommon in high-conflict homes, so that such endings to conflicts might well carry more (rather than less) weight for such children. Consistent with this notion, Hennessy, Rabideau, Cicchetti, and Cummings (1994) found that physically abused children from high-conflict homes benefited more, rather than less, from conflict resolution than a comparison group did.

Parental Postconflict Behaviors and Verbalizations

Research has also indicated the importance of parental postconflict behaviors and verbalizations. Somewhat surprisingly, children's distress reactions are reduced greatly even when adults have resolved conflicts behind closed doors, only indicating resolution by a change to positive affect after the adults emerge from the room they entered in the midst of conflict. Children also benefit from hearing brief explanations that conflicts are resolved, or even that conflicts are not resolved but that parents expect that they will be. Moreover, children benefit from information about resolution, including explanations of conflict resolution by parents, parents' expressions of optimism about the ultimate outcomes of conflict, and information suggesting the resolution of conflicts behind closed doors (Cummings, Simpson, & Wilson, 1993; Cummings & Wilson, 1999). On the other hand, postconflict explanations that conflicts were in fact not resolved, or even that conflicts were not resolved but that this was okay for one reason or another (e.g., "It's okay to disagree"), were much less beneficial or not beneficial at all (Cummings & Wilson, 1999).

Recently, we (Gomulak-Cavicchio, Davies, & Cummings, 2006) reported that mothers indicated that they would communicate with children after marital conflicts about 80% of the time, and that most of these communications would reflect relatively constructive depictions of the conflicts. Specifically, these communications most often emphasized the warmth, harmony, and stability of family relationships or downplayed the negative implications of family disputes. However, these postconflict communications did *not* change links with child adjustment beyond the relations associated with exposure to interparental conflicts, and sometimes had unintended consequences. For example, positive messages appeared to amplify the risk posed by marital conflict when families were in fact experiencing significant discord, consistent with the "relational fit" hypothesis (Winter, Davies, Hightower, & Meyer, 2006).

These results thus support the notion of conflict resolution as a "wonder drug" for marital conflict from the children's perspective, although they also indicate that many conflict endings do not constitute a complete resolution from this perspective—including some endings that many parents may regard as an adequate form of resolution (i.e., one partner's giving in to the other). Moreover, although there is some support for the idea that postconflict communications about resolution may be beneficial, the nature of these communications is critical, as is the family context with regard to the level of discord. Interestingly, given the widespread acceptance that conflict resolution is ameliorative for children's exposure to marital conflicts, some important questions remained until recently about the role of resolution in affecting children's reactions. Limited support was evident until very recently for relations between conflict resolution and actual positive responses and outcomes in the children (Kerig, 1996); that is, resolution had only been shown to reduce negative reactivity (Cummings, Ballard, El-Sheikh, & Lake, 1991, 1993; Davies, Myers, et al., 1999).

SPECIFYING CONFLICT BEHAVIORS AS DESTRUCTIVE OR CONSTRUCTIVE, BASED ON EST

Recent work has begun to classify and order marital conflict behaviors as destructive or constructive, based on the conceptual and empirical criteria of EST. For example, Goeke-Morey and colleagues (2003) examined the responses of 11- and 12-year-old U.S. and Welsh children to laboratory presentations of marital conflict behaviors. In this study, behaviors eliciting significantly more negative than positive emotions in response to analogue presentations of conflict behaviors were classified as "destructive," based on the principle that the induced negative reactivity reduced children's sense of emotional security. In contrast, behaviors resulting in more positive than negative behaviors were categorized as "constructive," based on the principle that the induced positivity indicated increased well-being.

These criteria thus provided bases for identifying higher-order categories or organizational meanings of constructive and destructive conflict behaviors. When these criteria were applied, support, problem solving, and affection were identified as constructive behaviors. That is, children's reports of positive emotional responding were significantly greater than their reports of negative emotional responding to these behaviors. Moreover, supporting the decisiveness of these classifications, effect sizes were relatively high (ranging from 0.36 to 0.76 across all comparisons for the two cultures). Notably, these constructive conflict behaviors were represented as occurring in the context of negative conflict situations—in fact, the same contexts as for behaviors classified as destructive conflict behaviors. Thus, even when behaviors were presented in the context of otherwise negative and conflictual interactions between the parents, children nominated primarily those to which they had positive emotional responses. These results thus provided initial support for the existence of behaviors occurring during the course of marital conflicts that are constructive, with evidence that children's emotional security is increased by exposure to these behaviors.

When the criteria derived from EST for classifying behaviors as destructive from the children's perspective were applied, threat to the intactness of the marriage, direct physical aggression toward the spouse or aggression with objects, marital pursuit and withdrawal, nonverbal anger, and verbal hostility met criteria for classification as destructive behaviors. In these instances, negative responding was much greater than positive responding; again, effect sizes were all high, ranging from 0.44 to 0.89 (12 comparisons).

Comparisons among emotional responding to these behaviors also provided bases for differentiating among specific expressions of conflict within the categories of constructive and destructive conflict. A continuum from most destructive to most constructive conflict behaviors was identified, with direct physical aggression toward the spouse, physical aggression toward objects, and threats to marital intactness at one extreme, and affection and support at the other. Moreover, also consistent with criteria based on EST, children's cognitive representations of marital conflicts and behavioral coping responses (i.e., mediation, avoidance) supported these distinctions along a continuum from destructive to constructive conflict behaviors. The same classifications of marital conflict behaviors as constructive or destructive were generally found for both the U.S. and Welsh samples, with the relative orderings of behaviors along a continuum from destructive to constructive remarkably similar for these behaviors. The degree of correspondences across the cultures adds to confidence in the classification and continuum-based scoring.

The developmental psychopathology perspective advocates the demonstration of convergences among findings based on multiple methodologies (Cummings, Davies, et al., 2000). Consistent with this perspective, children's reactions to various forms of parental conflict behaviors in the home were examined in a related series of studies based on parental diaries about marital conflict (Cummings et al., 2001). These studies also addressed issues of the external validity of findings, by testing whether the constructive and destructive conflict behaviors identified were the same or similar in the home as in the laboratory.

The results from the diary studies were consistent with the distinctions between constructive and destructive marital conflicts reported in the laboratory analogue studies (e.g., Goeke-Morey et al., 2003). Cummings, Goeke-Morey, and Papp (2003b) examined whether the occurrence of specific behaviors during marital conflicts in the home significantly changed children's emotional responding, with the criteria for constructive conflict being an increase in positive emotionality, and the criteria for destructive conflict an increase in negative emotionality. Based on children's reactions, affection, support, and calm discussion in contexts of otherwise destructive conflict emerged as constructive behaviors during everyday marital conflicts in the home, whereas threat, personal insult, verbal hostility, defensiveness, nonverbal hostility, withdrawal, and personal distress qualified as destructive behaviors during such conflicts. Moreover, parents' reports of destructive conflict tactics in the diaries were related to global assessments of aggressive marital conflict tactics, children's exposure to marital hostility, and marital dissatisfaction, whereas reports of constructive conflict tactics had the opposite relations with marital relationship characteristics. These results supported the diary reports as representative of everyday marital functioning in the home. In addition, children's responses during marital conflicts in the home were linked with their adjustment: Children's positive emotionality in response to conflicts was related to less risk for adjustment problems, and all dimensions of children's negative emotional reactivity (negative emotionality, sadness, anger, fear) were associated with increased risk for adjustment problems. These findings thus indicate that children's immediate emotional responding during everyday marital conflicts, presumed to be indicative of their emotional security, is linked with their adjustment.

Research on constructive and destructive conflict behaviors and children's reactions in laboratory-based studies has tended to focus on the issue of parents' strategies and tactics during conflicts, rather than on parents' emotionality during marital conflicts (for an exception, see Shifflett-Simpson & Cummings, 1996). However, the importance of emotional communication during interparental conflicts has long been stressed in marital conflict research focusing on adults' functioning and adjustment (Gottman & Gottman, 1999; Markman, Floyd, Stanley, & Storaasli, 1988). A study addressing this issue via the home diary method (Cummings et al., 2002) found that parents' positive emotionality during conflict in the home emerged as another constructive conflict behavior, based on children's highly positive emotional responding to it. By contrast, parents' negative emotionality during marital conflict merited classification as a destructive conflict behavior, based on the negative emotional reactions shown by children in the home. Further supporting the notion that parental emotions as well as behaviors per se may be related to children's emotional security about conflicts, Cummings and colleagues (2003a) reported that both mothers' and fathers' diary reports about interparental conflicts indicated that emotions and behaviors in the marital subsystem were linked to children's emotional and behavioral reactions in a manner consistent with a familywide model of emotional security (Cummings & Davies, 1996).

Matters of long-standing concern in the literature on abnormal child development have been the links between marital discord and children's aggressivity/conduct problems (Emery, 1982). An intriguing research direction in this regard has involved testing these links (Cummings, Iannotti, & Zahn-Waxler, 1985). Children's behavioral dysregulation (e.g., aggression) in the face of marital conflict can be conceptualized as an index of emotional security, related to notions of emotional reactivity, and therefore as providing a further test of the cogency of these classifications of behaviors as constructive or destructive. Demonstrating links between exposure to destructive marital conflict and increases in children's aggression in the home, and links between these responses and children's adjustment, also advances the notion of destructive conflict as a risk factor for children's behavior problems from a process-oriented, developmental psychopathology perspective.

Laboratory studies have reported that exposure to conflicts between adults (Cummings, 1987; Cummings, Iannotti, & Zahn-Waxler, 1985), including parents (Davis, Hops, Alpert, & Sheeber, 1998), increased verbal and physical aggression in children ranging from 2 to 18 years of age. Higher aggression has also been reported in 5-year-old physically abused boys following exposure to interadult conflicts involving their mothers in laboratory play sessions (Cummings, Hennessy, Rabideau, and Cicchetti, 1994). Furthering our understanding of possible underlying processes, Davis and colleagues (1998) conducted sequential analyses of children's reactions in a laboratory marital conflict resolution task. Aggressive responding by children (both girls and boys) was sequentially related to interparental conflict. In findings indicating a type of differential reactivity to the parents, both boys and girls were more likely to aggress against their mothers than their fathers when evidencing aggression following marital conflict. However, boys more significantly showed these responses to attacks by the mothers on the fathers, whereas girls more prominently evidenced these behaviors to attacks by the fathers on the mothers.

However, these studies still did not resolve questions about the validity of the argument that exposure to marital conflict is a situational influence on child aggression—that is, questions about ecological validity. Tests of these notions based on home diary approaches can address these concerns on multiple fronts, because relations are indexed (1) between the parents, rather than between parents and strangers, or simply between strangers; (2) in the home as opposed to in the laboratory; and (3) during everyday contexts of marital discord, rather than in response to marital conflict resolution paradigms or other structured contexts for marital interactions. The pertinent issues are whether only destructive conflicts are linked with children's risk for aggression, and whether constructive conflict may actually *reduce* the occurrence of aggression (consistent with the notion of compensatory or protective processes).

In response to these questions, Cummings, Goeke-Morey, and Papp (2004) examined 8- to 16-year-olds' immediate responses to exposure to everyday interparental conflicts in the home, as reported in separate diaries kept by mothers and fathers. Consistent with the developmental psychopathology emphasis on multimethod research, with its attendant strengths for increasing confidence in the validity of the results (Cummings, Davies, et al, 2000), children's reported aggressive responses to exposure to analogue presentations of marital conflict in the laboratory were assessed in addition to the diary records. Conflict tactics were grouped into destructive and constructive categories, based on the findings of prior research, as well as on the conceptual and theoretical criteria derived from the emotional security hypothesis. In addition, parents' positive emotionality and negative emotionality were distinguished in the diary reports.

The results supported the generalizability of findings based on laboratory methodologies (e.g., Cummings et al., 1985) by showing that children's aggression increased in the home during everyday conflicts between the parents. Extending this literature on marital conflict and aggression to include distinctions between destructive and constructive conflict, this study showed that aggression only increased in response to destructive conflict tactics and parents' negative emotionality during conflicts. Moreover, conflict topics during conflicts presumed to be threatening to children (e.g., child-related themes) also heightened the likelihood of aggression.

At the same time, further supporting the notion that some conflict behaviors may have beneficial effects on children's functioning, both constructive conflict tactics and positive emotionality were found to decrease the probability of children's aggression during everyday conflicts. Adding to confidence in this pattern of findings, the fathers' and mothers' separate diary reports, and the children's responses to analogue presentations of constructive and destructive conflict tactics, *all* showed support for these relations. For example, of all aggressive responses reported by children in reaction to analogue marital conflicts, 96% occurred in response to destructive conflict tactics and only 4% occurred in response to constructive conflict tactics.

Consistent with the relevance of children's aggressive responding during exposure to marital conflict to notions of the constructive or destructive effects of certain categories of marital conflict behavior, aggressive responding to interadult conflicts in both the home and laboratory predicted children's externalizing behavior problems, including scores in the clinical range on externalizing behavior problems (e.g., aggression).

A gap in this literature has been the lack of home-based observational evidence that resolution actually affects children's reactions to marital conflict. As a result, questions might be raised about the external validity of the results—that is, the extent to which findings hold for actual everyday marital conflict resolution in the home and children's reactions. Moreover, although work has shown that conflict resolution reduces children's negative emotional reactions to marital conflict, there have been no tests of whether conflict resolution actually *increases* children's emotional security about marital conflict. Thus there has been no evidence that conflict resolution is necessarily *constructive* from the children's point of view.

Addressing these gaps, Goeke-Morey and colleagues (2007) recently provided an especially comprehensive test of relations between conflict resolution and children's responses. Specifically, they assessed mothers' home diary reports of marital conflict resolution (i.e., compromise, apology, submission, agreement to disagree, withdrawal) and of children's responses, along with the reactions of children to analogue presentations of these same conflict endings in the laboratory. Children's responses strongly supported the highly ameliorative effects of conflict resolution and positive emotionality on children's responses to interparental conflicts in the home. Moreover, children's happy or positive emotional responses were substantially elevated in response to conflict resolution, supporting the idea that children's emotional security is increased by observing the resolution of marital conflicts. By contrast, lack of resolution was linked with children's elevated negative emotional reactions, as well as with other responses reflective of emotional insecurity about these interactions (e.g., children's triangulation or involvement in the parents' conflicts; children's dysregulated behaviors of aggression in response to conflict).

Children's responses to conflict resolution were related to their broader adjustment, with negative emotionality in response to conflict related to both their internalizing and externalizing problems—findings further supporting the significance of conflict endings to the impact of marital conflict on children. The significance of specific conflict endings, including the emotionality of these endings, was also supported by the results demonstrating these relations for the first time in the home; the laboratory results based on analogue tests were generally consistent with the findings based on diary reports.

Compromise emerged as being the most constructive conflict ending from the children's perspective, according to multiple dimensions of regulatory responses indicative of emotional security (emotional reactivity, mediation or intervention, and behavioral dysregulation) observed in the home and laboratory. Positive emotionality by parents in the home during conflict endings was also a constructive conflict ending from the children's perspective. Parents' negative emotionality and withdrawal both qualified for classification as destructive marital conflict endings, and the perceived destructiveness increased further when parents withdrew in fear. Children's responses to parental apologies elicited a more nuanced reaction; that is, apology was seen as constructive when accompanied by positive emotionality, and as destructive when linked with negative emotionality.

Moreover, some conflict endings demonstratively *altered* for children the negative impact of witnessing destructive conflict in the home. In particular, parents' positive emotional expressions at the end of conflict lessened the impact of destructive conflict tactics. Interestingly, compromise between the parents predicted that children would perceive the conflict as constructive, regardless of the level of negative emotion and destructive conflict tactics during the conflict episode.

Although parents and children similarly evaluated many aspects of how conflicts ended, some behaviors, such as submission and apology, were less likely to be seen as constructive by the children than by the parents. A particularly pronounced difference between parents and children in evaluating conflict endings was seen in the home-reported data: Parents viewed submission as positively linked with conflict resolution, whereas children reacted to submission as at best a partial resolution, and at worst a destructive conflict ending. This finding is consistent with past work on children's reactions to submission (e.g., Cummings, Ballard, et al., 1991); even when parents may view submission as constituting an adequate way of working things out, children are much less sanguine about one parent's "winning" at the expense of the other. In this instance, children may actually be more sensitive than the parents to the broader implications of these behaviors for the longer-term relationship between the parents, although this question merits further empirical study.

Thus, consistent with EST, children can be seen as primarily concerned with whether interparental conflicts pose real and continuing threats to the family. Conflict resolution effectively ameliorates these concerns, although effects vary as a function of the specific conflict endings; some behaviors seen by parents as "resolution" (i.e., submission, apology) are less likely to be viewed this way by the children.

FUTURE DIRECTIONS

Although inroads have been made into identifying constructive and destructive conflict on the basis of theoretically guided criteria, many questions remain. As indicated in Figure 2.1, the relative constructiveness or destructiveness of marital conflict is only a starting point for testing process models about the effects of marital conflict on children's development. Departing from the traditional emphasis on marital conflict as a homogeneous risk factor, research is needed that differentiates the impact of multiple forms of marital conflict tactics or emotions on children over time. Many studies of marital conflict and children continue to rely on relatively global measures of destructive marital conflict. Coding systems have recently been developed for classifying marital conflict behaviors as destructive or constructive according to EST. These coding systems can support more fine-grained assessments of marital conflict based on theoretically guided criteria in future research (see Appendix A), as well as more rigorous assessments of emotional security processes (see Appendices B and C); both types of assessments are critical to exploring process-oriented models for the effects of marital conflict on children (see Figure 2.1).

An important future direction will be investigation of the long-term implications of constructive conflict. There is limited support for the conclusion that children actually benefit in terms of their adjustment and well-being from exposure to constructive conflict; only a handful of studies have examined relations between exposure to constructive conflict and children's adjustment (e.g., Du Rocher Schudlich & Cummings, 2007), with very few demonstrations in longitudinal contexts (e.g., see McCoy et al., 2009; Chapter 4). Many other questions remain, including whether children learn to be more constructive in their own relationships in conflict situations—for example, during conflicts with parents, siblings, or peers—as a result of observing constructive conflicts between the parents. Another important future direction will be to further investigate the impact of positive and constructive dimensions of marital conflict on dimensions of children's positive social functioning.

CONCLUSION

In this chapter, addressing a critical gap in the study of relations between marital conflict and child adjustment, we have reviewed research on distinctions between constructive and destructive marital conflict from the children's perspective. The emotional security hypothesis has been advanced as providing theoretical and operational bases for more cogent criteria for distinguishing these forms of conflict from the children's perspective. In the next chapter, we consider findings from longitudinal research designs for evaluating direct effects of exposure to marital conflict—including further evidence supporting emotional security as a mediating process, and the patterns of multiple child outcomes that have been linked with exposure to marital conflict.

CHAPTER 4

Testing Process-Oriented Models of the Direct Effects of Exposure to Marital Conflict

One of the strongest pathways of the effects of marital conflict on children is perhaps the simplest one: through their exposure to discord between the parents. In earlier chapters, we have reviewed conceptual propositions and selected empirical evidence that EST provides an explanatory model for child outcomes of exposure to marital conflict. Chapter 2 has provided not only a conceptual account of how children's concerns about emotional security may explain the risk posed by destructive marital conflict for children's long-term adjustment, but an initial review of key studies supporting direct effects on children of exposure to such conflict. We have also shown that children are sensitive to many variations in qualitative aspects of interparental disputes, including whether the disagreements are resolved. Chapter 3 thus encourages readers to think of marital conflict more broadly as having potentially constructive as well as destructive properties across multiple domains of child functioning. However, though the focus on constructive and destructive properties in Chapter 3 is valuable, it does not elucidate how properties of marital conflict engender response and coping patterns in children that ultimately explain individual differences in the children's patterns of mental and physical health. Taken together, these chapters leave questions unanswered about how and why different dimensions and properties of marital conflict may actually be associated with different child outcomes. In this chapter, we further address these questions, expanding discussion of pathways and processes affected by children's exposure to marital conflict—that is, "direct-effects models"—to consider process-oriented model tests including multiple child outcomes linked with exposure to marital conflict. We also provide further evidence for effects of multiple forms of marital conflict and emotional security as explanatory processes (see Figure 2.1).

Study has traditionally focused on internalizing and externalizing adjustment problems (Emery, 1982). However, multiple child outcomes may follow from marital conflict. Moreover, the transactional nature of developmental pathways further increases the possibility of diverse patterns of outcomes. At a conceptual level, these notions are reflected in the construct of multifinality derived from the developmental psychopathology perspective (Cummings, Davies, et al., 2000). Moreover, as indicated throughout this volume, conceptual and empirical bases in EST support the idea that multiple domains of child outcomes may be affected by marital conflict (Davies & Cummings, 2006).

The significant impact of exposure to marital conflict on children's emotional, social, cognitive, and physiological responses supports a premise of direct-effects models: That is, exposure to multiple forms and expressions of marital conflict may affect multiple domains of children's functioning. Demonstrations of direct effects on children's regulatory responses are readily accomplished—for example, by observing children's responses during exposure to marital conflict; questioning children about their reactions to particular interparental disputes; or in other ways measuring reactions, including physiological reactions (e.g., Cummings et al., 2007; Davies, Sturge-Apple, et al., 2008; El-Sheikh et al., 2009; see Appendix D). For example, consider the following report by a mother about her 20-month-old child's reactions:

> "I was very upset about, well, I still had the flu virus and I wasn't feeling very well. And the house was a shambles, where the children had been running and pulling out toys, and the dishes had not been done, and there were clothes on the floor (they played mommies). So the house was in bad shape. So I put Clara to bed and I made Tommy go to his room to rest. And then I ran down to the kitchen to put away some of the things that were out of the refrigerator in there, and the

things that would spoil. And Dick was in the kitchen and I yelled at him, 'I don't care if this house stays a mess forever, I am not picking up another damn thing.' And I screamed at the top of my lungs, I was mad and I was furious. . . . And in a squeaky voice . . . I heard Clara say, 'Mommy, shut up.' She said this about three times." (Cummings et al., 1981, p. 1276)

The sensitivity of children as bystanders to others' emotions and behaviors is sometimes underestimated. As a case in point, Chapter 5 describes attempts to conceptualize marital conflict as being spuriously associated with children's adjustment through its co-occurrence with other family processes (e.g., parenting styles). In contrast to such assumptions, careful observational studies have demonstrated that children are highly attuned and responsive to angry emotions between adults. The goal of this chapter is thus to review the empirical support for direct-effects models of pathways between multiple forms of marital conflict and multiple child outcomes (Figure 2.1).

MODELS TESTING DIRECT EFFECTS

Misconceptions about Direct Effects

There are misconceptions about process-oriented models for direct effects of exposure to marital conflict. For example, showing associations between marital conflict and child adjustment, or even showing that these pathways remain after other pathways are accounted for (e.g., Baron & Kenny, 1986), does *not* constitute cogent evidence for direct effects from a process-oriented perspective. That is, these types of data are insufficient to support process-oriented models of direct effects because such findings do not identify the within-child processes that are engaged by exposure to marital conflict, and that therefore contribute to pathways for the effects on child outcomes. Support for these pathways requires showing links between marital conflict and children's response processes (e.g., children's emotional, cognitive, behavioral, or physiological reactions), and in turn between these response processes and child outcomes (Rhoades, 2008).

Increasing the Cogency of Evidence for Direct Effects

Thus relations with child outcomes are the results of processes that are set in motion by exposure to or other awareness of marital conflict, and that over time come to be related to the development of adjustment problems. The strongest evidence is provided in the context of longitudinal model tests. Further criteria have recently been added for the most cogent demonstrations of pathways between and among marital conflict, mediating mechanisms, and child outcomes. For example, controls for earlier levels of mediating or outcome variables—sometimes termed "autoregressive controls"—increase confidence that any effects on child adjustment can be attributed to change over time in the identified processes, rather than to concurrent relations between variables (Cole & Maxwell, 2003). Confidence in tests of mediating processes is also increased when they are supported by additional tests of the operation of mediating processes, such as "bootstrapping" (MacKinnon et al., 2002). Longitudinal multimethod tests and the construction of latent variables for constructs based on multiple assessments are additional examples of sophisticated statistical modeling that improve our ability to explain how, why, when, and for whom marital conflict has implications for multiple child outcomes. These elements are represented in recent studies of marital conflict aimed at explaining multiple child outcomes, which are reviewed in this chapter.

Historical Trends in the Study of Direct Effects

"Direct effects" of marital conflict are mechanisms of influence on children resulting from repeated exposure to marital conflict itself. We introduced this terminology (Cummings & Davies, 1994a) to distinguish the impact of exposure from that of "indirect effects" through other relationships (e.g., parenting) in the family (see Chapter 5). At the same time, longitudinal or advanced statistical tests of models of the processes contributing to child outcomes had not yet been conducted. Thus the notion of a "developmental psychopathology of angry homes" (discussed in Cummings & Davies, 1994a) was mostly a promissory note for future research at that time. Tests of direct-effects pathways awaited further articulation of conceptual models of exposure to marital conflict on children, the fortuitous development of advanced methods and statistical modeling techniques for assessing mediating processes, and the use of longitudinal studies to address these issues.

Notably, all of these things have now happily come to pass. In particular, a substantial body of research pertinent to multiple child outcomes has accumulated, especially in the past few years. Accordingly, this chapter addresses the earlier gaps in its review of the growing evidence from process-oriented studies of direct paths and processes for predicting multiple child outcomes, including additional tests of EST's explanations for mediating processes (see also Chapters 2 and 5). Among the directions reviewed are pathways associated with constructive marital conflict, fathers' marital conflict behavior, and pathways to the prediction of school functioning. Finally, we consider future directions for identifying mechanisms and processes accounting for relations between marital conflict and child outcomes—including new directions for the study of transactional relations and physiological processes, both of which are conceptualized in EST as mediators of the effects of marital conflict.

STUDIES EXPLORING MULTIPLE CHILD OUTCOMES DUE TO DIRECT-EFFECTS PATHWAYS

Constructive Conflict, Emotional Security, and Positive Outcomes

In terms of model testing, we have focused to this point on how destructive marital conflict undermines children's emotional security about marital relations, leading to links with child adjustment problems. Conversely, observing constructive conflict between parents may serve to increase children's confidence in the safety and security of marital functioning, by showing that even such difficult, challenging, and potentially threatening matters as interparental disputes can be effectively handled by the parents. Clinicians and family researchers have long speculated about the possibly beneficial effects of constructive conflict. Armed with a growing corpus of conceptual and empirical knowledge, we are now better positioned to provide more authoritative conclusions about how constructive conflict may promote children's adjustment by increasing children's emotional security about marital relations (Cummings & Davies, 2002).

Furthermore, the notion that exposure to constructive conflict may foster children's emotional security is supported by the recent diary, analogue, and laboratory observational studies reviewed in Chapter 3, which show that exposure to various forms of constructive conflict expression (e.g., problem solving, positive affect, compromise, or other forms of conflict resolution) may actually lead to increases in children's positive affect and decreases in behavioral and cognitive indicators of insecurity. These findings indicate that exposure to constructive conflict may have positive effects on the regulatory systems associated with responding to marital conflict, including increasing children's emotional security about such conflict. At the same time, there has been little investigation of the long-term implications of constructive conflict, to demonstrate that children actually do benefit in terms of their adjustment and well-being from exposure to this type of conflict.

On the other hand, an element of common wisdom is that children may benefit from observing constructive conflict, in terms of learning lessons for better handling their own conflicts with peers and in other relationships. This notion enjoys relatively wide currency in the mass media, and it appears in frequent observations by clinical experts and others concerned with family relations. Social learning theory conceptualizations (Bandura, 1973) are often referenced to support this and similar points. However, there is actually virtually no empirical evidence over many years of study that social learning theory principles account for the effects of marital conflict on children (e.g., Cummings et al., 1981). In direct comparisons, we have recently shown that EST provides a cogent explanation above and beyond social learning conceptualizations for children's reactions to forms of marital conflict (Davies, Harold, et al., 2002). Moreover, for these points to be established empirically, longitudinal research that identifies the ordering of processes in links between specific properties of marital conflict, emotional security, and child adjustment is needed, to show that constructive conflict improves children's functioning over time in a manner consistent with EST. That is, in order to substantiate the bases for these relations, it is important to determine the sequence of processes accounting for why and how marital conflict is related to positive outcomes.

To address this gap, a three-wave longitudinal study (McCoy et al., 2009) examined relations between and among constructive and destructive conflict, children's emotional security, positive parenting (i.e., couples' warm parenting), and children's prosocial behavior. Even after controls for prior levels of children's prosocial behavior, children's elevated emotional security mediated between constructive marital conflict and children's increased prosocial behavior over time. Moreover, the relations found between constructive conflict, emotional security, and increased prosocial behavior over time remained even with controls for parenting (i.e., with parenting included in the statistical model testing). By contrast, destructive conflict was associated with reduced emotional security and decreased prosocial behavior over time. These results thus highlight the need to further investigate the impact of positive and constructive dimensions of marital conflict on dimensions of children's positive social functioning.

Fathers and Mothers, Emotional Security, and Multiple Child Outcomes

Marital conflict involves the conflict behaviors of both fathers and mothers. At one level, this is surely an obvious point. At the same time, it makes the relative lack of investigation of fathers in marital context all the more remarkable. Nonetheless, even in the absence of systematic study, there are various truisms about the role of fathers versus mothers in marital conflict—some of which, unfortunately, have received little support from research. Among these truisms are that children are affected more by the behavior of the same-sex parent, or that fathers' conflict behaviors are more distressing for children than mothers' conflict behaviors are (Cummings & O'Reilly, 1997). In fact, relatively little is known about the impact of the specific behaviors of fathers and mothers during marital conflict. In addition to further advancing our understanding of marital conflict as a stimulus by differentiating the effects of the conflict behaviors of mothers and fathers, research on the impact of each parent's behavior can also further define mothering and fathering in family and marital contexts (Goeke-Morey & Cummings, 2007).

Long-Term Effects of Fathers' versus Mothers' Marital Aggression

Although recent work has begun to disaggregate the impact of the specific behaviors of mothers and fathers on children's exposure to marital conflict (see Chapter 3), relatively little was previously known about the implications for children's adjustment of the aggressive behavior of each parent during marital conflict. Addressing this gap, El-Sheikh and colleagues (2008) examined relations between marital aggression (psychological and physical) and children's mental and physical health, with children's emotional insecurity assessed as an explanatory variable for these relations. Distinctions were made between marital aggression against fathers and mothers as predictors of child adjustment, with family socioeconomic status (SES), parental ethnicity (African American or European American), and child gender examined as moderators. Notably, aggression directed against *either* parent was associated with similar pathways to children's adjustment problems, even when aggression against the other parent was included in the statistical model. Aggression directed against either the mother or the father was linked with children's increased emotional insecurity, and emotional insecurity was in turn associated with children's adjustment problems, including internalizing problems, externalizing problems, and posttraumatic stress disorder (PTSD) symptoms. With regard to tests for possible moderators, no differences were found as a function of whether parents were African American or European American, and pathways also did not differ according to family SES or child gender.

The results underscore that aggressive behavior toward either fathers or mothers in the context of marital conflict poses threats to children's emotional insecurity about marital relations, with implications for children's adjustment. The pattern of findings is consistent with the results of laboratory and analogue studies indicating highly similar reactions by children to conflict behaviors exhibited by parents of either gender toward parents of the other gender (see Chapter 3).

Moreover, with regard to tests of previously developed hypotheses about parent gender, no evidence was found that behaviors of same-sex parents elicited greater insecurity in the children (see also Davies, Harold, et al., 2002, Study 1), or that fathers' conflict behaviors were more disturbing or damaging than mothers' conflict behaviors were. Both these points held across the ethnic groups studied. Marital aggression by *either* mothers or fathers was linked with both boys' and girls' emotional security and risk for adjustment problems, including PTSD.

Fathers in the Broader Family Context

At the same time, parents' marital conflict behaviors do not affect children in isolation, but should also be considered in the broader family context. An extensive review of the relevant literatures has called attention to the importance of considering fathers' behavior within the broader family context (Cummings & O'Reilly, 1997). In this regard, Cummings, Goeke-Morey, and Raymond (2004) presented a framework for the study of fathers' influences on children in the context of marital conflict and family functioning. This framework considered multiple pathways of fathers' influences on children over time in marital and family contexts, in order to clarify the familywide implications of marital conflict. The following pathways were included: (1) fathers' actual marital conflict behaviors, (2) spillover of these behaviors into fathering and father–child relationships, and (3) exposure to fathers' psychological functioning. Moreover, in the context of all these influences, children's patterns of coping and response processes, including emotional insecurity, were seen as contributing to explanations for children's adjustment outcomes.

Testing this model specifically in terms of emotional security processes as explanatory variables, Schacht, Cummings, and Davies (in press) examined longitudinal relations between fathers' behaviors and children's adjustment in marital and family context through inclusion of autoregressive controls over earlier levels of each construct in the model. Notably, children's emotional security was found to be a mediating variable in relations between paternal processes and children's internalizing and externalizing problems, with specific pathways to child adjustment through children's emotional insecurity for paternal depressive symptoms, paternal marital conflict behavior, and paternal parenting.

In summary, these results suggest that children evaluate the marital conflict behaviors of fathers and mothers similarly from an emotional security perspective. Thus, for fathers as well as mothers, emotional security processes are related to pathways between and among marital conflict, other family stresses, and child adjustment.

Emotional Security and Children's School Functioning

The effects of exposure to marital conflict on children may also extend outside the family context to include school functioning. Another thread of common wisdom, apparent among teachers and other school personnel, is that children with significant adjustment or academic problems are frequently troubled by discord and turmoil in the home. That is, anecdotal reports by teachers and conversations with school and counseling psychologists often convey the strong opinion that home problems play a major role in the school difficulties of many students.

Further supporting this point, correlational evidence has accumulated to indicate relations between marital conflict on the one hand and school and peer problems on the other (Grych & Fincham, 2001b). However, it remains true that little is known about the processes underlying these relations. For example, there have been relatively few tests of formal models for relations between marital conflict and school functioning, and little progress has been made in identifying the mechanisms or processes that may account for these relations. The possibility that third variables may account for these relations is heightened by the relative lack of longitudinal studies, especially investigations that include autoregressive controls over prior levels of functioning (e.g., Time 1 functioning) in predicting long-term outcomes (e.g., Time 2 or Time 3 outcomes).

Researchers working from an EST perspective have recently begun to address these questions, testing conceptually driven models aimed at advancing a process-oriented understanding of relations between marital conflict and social/academic problems in school. One realization that has emerged in the conceptualization of these models is that a fuller understanding of these relations is likely to require extending explanatory models based on EST to include additional processes. That is, even when emotional security may play a role in child outcomes, additional processes should be considered in developing fully articulated models of children's school problems.

Insecure Representations of Family Relationships and School Performance

Children's emotional insecurity about family processes may hypothetically affect school performance for a variety of reasons. One hypothesis is that exposure to marital conflict diminishes children's school performance by undermining their capacity to sustain attention. That is, children's heightened concerns about their own safety and security in the family may increase the likelihood of attention difficulties, with negative effects on school performance. To address this hypothesis, Davies, Woitach, and colleagues (2008) examined relations between and among children's insecure representations of interparental relations, attention difficulties, and school adjustment in the early elementary school years, in the context of a three-wave longitudinal design. Multiple methods were employed in addition to questionnaires, including observer ratings of children's insecure representations of interparental relationships in a story completion task, as well as computerized task assessments of attention difficulties. The results of analyses indicated that children's attention difficulties were associated with increases in school problems over a 1-year period (even with autoregressive controls over earlier attention difficulties and school performance), accounting for 34% of the association between insecure representations of marital relations and children's school problems.

Marital conflict may also affect children's functioning in school through its effects on children's representations of family relationships, including interparental and parent–child relationships (Grych, Wachsmuth-Schlaefer, & Klockow, 2002; Shamir et al., 2001). According to EST, children's internal representations of family relationships act as potential mechanisms of risk for pathways to child adjustment problems, by serving as schemas for interpreting the consequences and meaning of interpersonal processes. Therefore, another hypothesis about the impact of emotional security processes for school functioning is that insecure representational models of relationships due to marital conflict foster insecure internal representational models for other social relationships, which then act to undermine children's social functioning in school settings.

A study addressing this possible pathway to school adjustment problems (Sturge-Apple et al., 2008) longitudinally examined multiple pathways from marital problems (interparental conflict) and parenting problems (parental emotional unavailability) to children's insecure representations of multiple family relationships (interparental, parent–child) to children's school adjustment. The findings supported the predictions of EST about possible relations between children's concerns with insecurity in the home and their socioemotional functioning in school. Specifically, interparental conflict was related to children's insecure representations of interparental and parent–child relationships, which contributed as explanatory variables to children's emotional and classroom engagement difficulties. Moreover, pathways from interparental conflict to parental emotional unavailability contributed to familywide models of emotional insecurity, which in turn were linked with children's socioemotional problems in schools (see Chapter 5 for more on indirect-effects pathways).

A study extending this line of research further (Bascoe, Davies, Sturge-Apple, & Cummings, in press) examined children's information processing about peers as an explanatory mechanism for relations between insecure representations of interparental relationships and school adjustment. Consistent with EST, children's insecure representations of the interparental relationship were specifically linked with negative peer information-processing patterns, which in turn predicted increases in school maladjustment over a 1-year period. Reflecting strong support for EST as an explanatory account for these relations, these pathways were robust even after tests against alternative hypotheses. That is, pathways supporting an EST model remained significant even after the roles of representations of parent–child relationships, trait measures of child negative affect, and SES were taken into account as predictors in the analyses. These results suggest that children's negative representations of peers constitute another class of processes that help to explain how children's insecurity in interparental contexts may undermine their adjustment in school. Furthermore, the findings support the premise that children's representations of interparental relationships serve as templates for processing and responding to stressful peer events.

Sleep Problems and School Performance

There is intuitive appeal to the notion that insecurity about the family due to parents' fighting may foster sleep problems, and thereby may serve to diminish school achievement. Although the study of the relations between sleep and functioning in adults is an increasingly active area of research, surprisingly little work has been directed toward understanding children's sleep problems, including family contexts for sleep problems and their impact on children's functioning in schools. Mona El-Sheikh, Joseph Buckhalt, and their research teams are leading the way in exploring relations between marital conflict and sleep, including relations among marital conflict, child sleep problems, and child adjustment (El-Sheikh, Buckhalt, Mize, & Acebo, 2006). For example, El-Sheikh, Buckhalt, Cummings, and colleagues (2007) showed that when marital conflict increased children's emotional insecurity about interparental relations, children's sleep was disrupted. In this study, sleep was assessed via the objective recording method of actigraphy. In turn, disruptions in the duration and quality of sleep were associated with children's emotional and behavioral problems at home and with their emotional and academic problems in school.

El-Sheikh, Buckhalt, Keller, and colleagues (2007) subsequently extended this investigation to include relations among emotional insecurity, children's difficulty sleeping, and children's specific academic performance problems. In this instance, emotional security was assessed in terms of both children's emotional security about parent–child relations (i.e., attachment) and their emotional security about the interparental relationship. Interestingly, insecurity about marital conflict, but not attachment insecurity, predicted sleep problems. Sleep problems constituted an intervening variable between children's insecurity about marital relations and multiple effects on children's academic performance, including lower scores on math, language, and verbal and nonverbal school ability scales. However, sleep problems were not a factor in the impact of attachment insecurity on child adjustment, although children's emotional security in the parent–child relationship was directly linked with reading and language scores. The sleep problems were more closely related to academic achievement for both African American children and children of lower SES.

The El-Sheikh, Buckhalt, Keller, and colleagues (2007) findings not only further underscore the significance of children's emotional security in the family for school performance; they also suggest that qualitatively different pathways for child outcomes may be associated with the marital and parent–child systems. One interpretation is that emotional security about marital relations has more pervasive effects on children's regulatory processes (including sleep) than security about parent–child attachment does, because emotional security about interparental conflict is more closely aligned with social defense as a set goal than the attachment behavior system is (see Davies & Sturge-Apple, 2007; Davies & Woitach, 2008). At the same time, the results also further support the significance of both attachment and the quality of marital relationships for children's school functioning.

Although these results emphasize that children's emotional security about marital relations is relevant to children's functioning in schools, they also suggest that research examining pathways from marital conflict to emotional security to children's school performance may not cover all possible meditational and causal chains. That is, in order to account more fully for children's school functioning, additional processes and factors may need to be included in tests of causal models.

In summary, the studies described in this chapter provide powerful additional support for the explanatory value of emotional security as a construct, as well as for the value of assessment based on higher-order latent variables reflecting multiple pertinent regulatory systems. Notably, findings emerged even in analyses that subjected the data to rigorous tests, such as controlling for prior levels of adjustment and taking into account the contributions of constructs from other major (and related) theories. However, emotional security was at times one of several mechanisms mediating relations between marital conflict and child adjustment, suggesting the need for more complex models of explanatory processes to account for child outcomes.

FUTURE DIRECTIONS

Emotional Security and Transactional Relations among Family Systems

An advanced understanding of causal processes requires consideration of children's effects on marital conflict, as well as the impact of marital conflict on children's functioning. Moreover, the developmental process is ultimately transactional—involving pathways of influence that go back and forth between families and children, and between different subsystems of the family, over time. Researchers working from an EST perspective have been grappling with these issues.

The notion of "transactional relations among family systems" refers to the mutual interplay among family and child influences, such that each element of the family is theoretically in a state of constant change in relation to other elements over time. Cicchetti, Sroufe, and colleagues have especially pioneered the view of child development as a product of mutual influences among different developmental subsystems over time (Carlson, Sroufe, & Egeland, 2004; Cicchetti, Toth, & Bush, 1988). However, empirical tests that truly reflect this level of analysis are rare—reflecting (1) the considerable demands from an empirical and data-analytic perspective, and (2) the relative lack of specificity in the conceptualization of transactional relations among developmental systems. With regard to the second difficulty, Schermerhorn and Cummings (2008) have proposed a new framework for "transactional family dynamics." This framework is concerned with myriad ways family members influence one another as transactional processes—that is, as influence processes continuously moving in both directions over time.

These themes are relevant to conceptualizing direct effects as well as other influence processes in families (see Chapters 5–7). Many gaps remain in our knowledge about child effects of exposure to marital conflict from a transactional perspective, including questions about relations among emotional security processes in marital and other family systems. For example, an issue of particular interest in EST concerns mutual influence processes at the level of children's representations of multiple family relationships (Bretherton, 1985).

Addressing this issue, we (Schermerhorn et al., 2008) longitudinally examined links among children's representations of the security of multiple family relationships over time. Beginning in kindergarten, children engaged in a story stem task each year, tapping children's representations of multiple family relationships. Representations of different family relationships were found to be interrelated over time. Most pertinent to an understanding of direct effects was the finding that representations of marital conflict were related to representations of reactivity to conflict. In addition, mutual influence processes were identified between representations of security about marital conflict and security of parent–child relationships, and between security in father–child and security in mother–child relationships. These results thus add to support for a familywide model of emotional security: Security in multiple family systems, and security between mother–child and father–child attachments, have been demonstrated as predictors of each other over time.

In summary, progress is being made within the context of EST toward testing child effects on marital conflict and examining transactional relations among multiple family systems, including marital conflict and children's responses to exposure to marital conflict. At the same time, although these efforts at clarifying developmental processes are off to a promising start, the exploration of these issues is in an early phase, both empirically and conceptually (Schermerhorn & Cummings, 2008). Thus a more important objective for the future is to continue to advance from multiple perspectives toward further understanding of mediating and moderating processes and developmental trajectories, including the direct effects of conflict on children. Chapters 5–7 review additional important directions for advancing these important themes in the future.

Greater Incorporation of Physiological Assessments into Direct-Effects Models

Finally, a vitally important area for future research is the fuller incorporation of physiological and biological processes into models of marital conflict's direct effects on children. A fundamental assumption of EST is that temperament and biological processes are very important for understanding not only the effects of exposure to marital conflict on children, but effects related to attachment security (Cummings & Davies, 1996). Moreover, research inspired at least in part by EST has made important recent advances in the study of the roles played by biological processes (Cummings, El-Sheikh, Kouros, & Buckhalt, 2009). Among the pertinent findings, Davies and colleagues (2007) recently demonstrated the role of child adrenocortical functioning in pathways between interparental conflict and child maladjustment. Cummings and colleagues (2007) showed that children's skin conductance reactivity, partly in response to marital conflict, moderated longitudinal relations between parental dysphoria and children's internalizing, externalizing, and social adjustment problems (see also Erath, El-Sheikh, & Cummings, 2009). Finally, in a series of studies yielding complementary findings, El-Sheikh and colleagues (2009) demonstrated interactions among marital conflict and the parasympathetic and sympathetic branches of the autonomic nervous system (the PNS and SNS, respectively) in the prediction of child externalizing problems.

Elsewhere in this volume (see especially Appendix D), we consider further the conceptual and methodological bases for these future directions. Because research in this area is in such early stages, identifying the multivariate interplay between physiological functioning and marital conflict in predicting child functioning is a central task for future studies.

A common misunderstanding is that examining physiological processes in isolation from psychological processes is adequate. In one of the repeated calls for research to integrate children's physiological and psychological responses to family stress (Cummings, Davies, et al., 2000; Fox, Hane, & Perez-Edgar, 2006; Katz, 2001), Katz (2001) aptly stated: "It is only through integrating our understanding of both biological and behavioral processes that we can get a complete picture of the effects of marital conflict on the whole child" (p. 207). Therefore, it is critical for future research to develop integrative measurement strategies that capture the "meaning" of physiological responses within the context of psychological processes.

Second, linking psychological and physiological domains of responding requires careful synchronization of measurement, particularly if the focus is on capturing psychophysiological indices of reactivity to stress. Different physiological systems have distinct temporal windows of reactivity (see Fox et al., 2006). For example, brain electrical activity occurs over a span of milliseconds following exposure to specific types of stimuli (e.g., adult angry faces) (e.g., Curtis & Cicchetti, 2007; Pollak, 2005; Pollak & Tolley-Schell, 2003), whereas the time course for measures of cardiovascular reactivity involves a span of seconds. Other indices, such as the release of neuroendocrine hormones (e.g., cortisol), are reactive to stressors for several minutes (e.g., 20–40 minutes) following exposure (Dickerson & Kemeny, 2004; Gottman & Katz, 1989; Matthews, Gump, & Owens, 2001). Accordingly, optimal analysis hinges on successfully coordinating the temporal courses of the physiological and psychological domains of responding.

Third, because physiological domains of reactivity do not necessarily "behave" in the same way, decisions about the inclusion of physiological measures must be grounded in a thorough understanding of the architecture, organization, and function of each response system. For example, studies of children's psychophysiological reactivity to interadult conflict have focused on specific indices of cardiovascular reactivity, including heart rate, blood pressure, and finger pulse volume (e.g., Ballard, Cummings, & Larkin, 1993; El-Sheikh, 1994; El-Sheikh et al., 1989). Although these studies have highlighted the importance of integrating the study of physiological responding with that of children's psychological adaptation to marital conflict, a limitation of this research is that such measures are products of multiple organismic products (see

Katz, 2001). For example, heart rate is multiply determined by different regions of the brain, bodily functions (e.g., respiration), metabolic activities, and motoric functions, as well as by basal heart rate level (Fox et al., 2006). Thus, although heart rate reactivity to stress has often been interpreted as an index of arousal, distress, or fear, it is also a marker for a multitude of other processes.

Conceptual and methodological innovations over the last decade offer new opportunities to achieve a multilevel understanding of how children cope with marital conflict. For example, it is now possible to capture more precise indices of cardiovascular stress reactivity (vagal tone, pre-ejection period), stress hormones (e.g., α-amylase, cortisol, catecholamine), and physiological markers of the cognitive–affective processing of negative stimuli (e.g., event-related potentials, startle reflex measures) (Fox et al., 2006; Granger et al., 2006; Quigley & Stifter, 2006). Conceptual efforts to distinguish different physiological systems and their functions are likely to provide useful heuristics in deciding on specific physiological assessments.

New conceptualizations underscore the importance of capturing how distinct but interrelated physiological systems may help elucidate the link between family discord and child functioning (e.g., Repetti et al., 2002; Repetti, Taylor, & Saxbe, 2007). The SNS, the PNS, and the limbic–hypothalamic–pituitary–adrenocortical (LHPA) axis are basic components of psychobiological reactivity to stress that hold great potential for increasing our understanding of how children cope with marital conflict at multiple levels. For example, "allostatic load" models conceptualize children's biological reactivity to family stress as mediating mechanisms in pathways between family adversity and children's mental and physical health (Evans, 2003; Lupien, King, Meaney, & McEwen, 2001; Susman, 2006). In these models, some components of children's biological systems are governed by the goal of preserving their physical and psychological integrity in the threatening context of high-conflict homes. Although alterations to physiological systems may initially serve the adaptive functions of monitoring and coping with potential danger stemming from family conflict, changes in physiological reactivity to stress are theorized to result in wear and tear on the body and to culminate in physical and mental health problems (Cicchetti, 2002; Katz, 2001; Repetti et al., 2002; Susman, 2006).

Some evidence on associations between marital conflict and physiological functioning support the allostatic load models. For example, exposure to marital conflict and discord has been associated with higher baseline levels of cortisol (Pendry & Adam, 2007; Saltzman, Holden,

& Holahan, 2005). Providing an intriguing pattern of complementary findings, another study has identified children's dampened cortisol reactivity to interparental conflict as a mediating mechanism linking exposure to interparental conflict with subsequent externalizing symptoms (Davies et al., 2007).

However, not all physiological indices are likely to serve as mediators. Some physiological systems act as moderators of marital conflict (Cummings et al., 2007; Steinberg & Avenevoli, 2000; see Chapter 7). For example, a high level of vagal tone, which is stable and relatively resistant to family stress, may serve as a protective factor for children in high-conflict homes (Katz, 2001; Porges, Doussard-Roosevelt, Portales, & Suess, 1994). Supporting this prediction, the relationship between marital conflict and children's psychological and health problems is significantly weaker for children who evidence high basal vagal tone and vagal tone suppression to stressful events (El-Sheikh, Harger, & Whitson, 2001; El-Sheikh & Whitson, 2006; Katz & Gottman, 1995, 1997a, 1997b).

CONCLUSIONS

In conclusion, since our first volume (Cummings & Davies, 1994a) appeared, considerable advances have been made in testing process-oriented models of direct effects. These tests have included assessments of the processes that mediate and/or moderate relations between exposure to marital conflict and child adjustment in the context of EST. Other important directions have included delineating developmental pathways longitudinally and beginning to articulate transactional developmental processes.

In relation to Chapter 2, in this chapter we further contextualize the study of direct effects by broadening the applicability of these models to multiple dimensions (i.e., constructive, destructive) of marital conflict and multiple domains of child functioning (e.g., sleep, cognitive processes, school adjustment, physiology). In relation to Chapter 3, we provide a more thorough account of the conceptual ordering of children's concerns about security in the face of multiple forms of marital conflict, including indices of child adjustment and adaptation along a pathway model of unfolding risk and compensatory processes.

These tests of emotional security as explanatory variables for child development have added to a process-oriented understanding of relations between marital conflict and child adjustment. The recent work is also highly impressive methodologically, especially when studies are conducted longitudinally and meet demanding statistical criteria to support causal interpretation (autoregressive controls, bootstrapping, additional indirect-effects tests). Notably, many of the studies reviewed in this chapter satisfy most or all of these statistical and methodological criteria.

An important direction for the future is to continue to advance from multiple perspectives toward a further understanding of mediating and moderating processes and developmental trajectories. This chapter and Part II in general have focused on delineating direct effects of exposure to marital conflict, as shown in Figure 2.1.

However, a more complete account of child outcomes must also consider the effects of the broader family system, including family processes as mechanisms of effects and also as moderating influences. In Part III, we consider these so-called "indirect effects" of marital conflict on children, as reflected in Figure 2.2.

CONTEXTUALIZING
MARITAL CONFLICT

Marital conflict does not occur in an interpersonal vacuum. Rather, it is an inextricable part of a broader network of familial, extrafamilial, and developmental processes that also hold a key to understanding how children adjust in the face of conflict between parents. The following clinical cases drawn from Johnston, Roseby, and Kuehnle (2009) provide poignant illustrations of why conflict between separated parents must ultimately be examined in the broader interpersonal and developmental context.

> *Family A*: "When 5-year-old Sally expressed a wish to call her father on the phone and tell him how she learned to jump rope that day, her mother withdrew into sullen anger. Inexplicably, to Sally, her mother was 'too tired' to read her the usual bedtime story that evening." (p. 33)

> *Family B*: "For weeks after his wife left the marriage, Mr. L. kept Lisa home from school to keep him company, to comfort him. Later, when the mother recovered custody of the child, this man lavished bribes and promises of exciting outings on the little girl, but then failed to turn up for the scheduled visits. When his wife refused to talk with him, he would tearfully tell the distraught child good-bye, that he would never see her again—and then he

would return the next day to renew his pleadings. Whenever his wife left the child in the care of the grandmother, he would take the little girl away with him, claiming she had been deserted; then he would drop her off with sundry acquaintances for her care. The child was constantly asked to plead the father's case with the mother: 'Ask her, "Where do you belong?" Tell her I love her and want her back!' When first seen in counseling, Lisa was a dazed, flaccid child. She lacked spontaneity and seemed vacant, joyless, and withdrawn. She made no demands and waited uncomplainingly for someone to attend to her needs, as if she had entirely given up any sense of herself as a viable person." (p. 37)

Beyond the risk posed by exposure to the discord between the parents, several processes operating in these families can potentially be unhealthy for the children. However, drawing this rather common-sense conclusion is simply not enough to place anyone in a position to understand and better the lives of these children and their families. From the perspective of psychologists, the pressing challenge is determining how the joint interplay between parental discord and these other family characteristics may alter the course of the children's adjustment. In both families, parents are exhibiting notable difficulties in their ability to rear their children—particularly in the ability to be sensitive and responsive to their children's needs. At the same time, important differences are evident in the form of their parenting problems. In Family A, the childrearing problems appear to occur mainly in the form of the conditional disengagement and rejection shown by Sally's mother; in Family B, the father–child interactions reflect a high degree of enmeshment and role reversal, in which Lisa carries the responsibilities and burdens of being the father's confidante, therapist, and caretaker. One fundamental question is whether these impairments in parenting partially or even fully account for the children's vulnerability when they witness interparental conflict. Still another challenge is to determine whether the different forms of parenting in the two families may carry different developmental implications for the children's adjustment.

In both families, the parents also appear to be suffering from considerable psychological pain in the form of depression, anxiety, and possibly other difficulties. Could witnessing their parents struggle with mental health issues be having an impact on the children's adjustment, even if this struggle is not directly manifested in direct interactions with the children or the estranged partners? If it is affecting their adjustment, does it carry as much punch as the stressfulness of experiencing parents fight or interact with the children in potentially detrimental ways? Might it also serve as a mediating mechanism that accounts for at least part of the association between the marital conflict and the children's adjustment problems? Alternatively, might it exacerbate or compound the risk created by the children's witnessing marital conflict?

The challenge becomes even more formidable with a broader look at some of these families' characteristics that may also come into play in affecting how the children cope and adjust. In both families, understanding the relationship between the children and their parents, siblings, and close extended relatives would help to provide a more comprehensive picture of the resources and adversities faced by the children. For example, it is possible that the presence of supportive kin may reduce or offset any risk posed by parent–child or interparental difficulties. Nested within this possibility are also myriad unanswered questions: Does it matter for each of these possibilities who is involved in the relationship with the children (i.e., sibling, mother, father, extended family member)? What specific psychological characteristics (e.g., responsiveness, disclosure, instrumental support) provide the most benefits for the children? Are some types of relationships likely to make matters worse for the children? If so, why do some types of relationships with family members help children from high-conflict homes, whereas others only amplify their vulnerability to problems?

Family systems theory further reminds us that each family may also have very different sets of implicit rules or guidelines for transmitting and sharing information and resources. For example, in Family A, the maternal love withdrawal may signify a broader pattern of cold, distant, and disengaged family relationships. In contrast, the father's behavior in Family B may signify a broader pattern of overly close or enmeshed family relationships that do not permit adequate personal space for the development of children's autonomy. Alternatively, the relationship between the father and Lisa may reflect an unhealthy alliance against the mother. Each of these patterns of broader family functioning may have very different developmental implications for the children. For example, in Family B, certain developmental competencies (e.g., capacity for empathy, social perspective taking) are likely to underlie Lisa's ability to assume the responsibilities of caretaker and therapist.

Moreover, other individual and family factors may relate to child outcomes. For example, over time the burden of attempting to solve complicated adult problems may have "sleeper effects" that slowly wear and tear at Lisa's psychological adjustment. At the same time, Lisa's preexisting temperamental, personality, and developmental characteristics may help to allay some of the damaging effects of experiencing high levels of family discord. Thus part of the process of unraveling the folds in the family tapestries would require identifying broader patterns of family functioning and understanding how they affect the children's developmental pathways over time. In addition, both families' functioning takes place in the broader context of socioeconomic conditions, neighborhoods, schools, communities, and cultures. Each of these ecological characteristics may in itself alter the magnitude or form of the association between the marital conflict and children's adjustment.

To address these important issues, the next three chapters provide coverage of the progress made in contextualizing the study of marital conflict within the broader family, ecological, and developmental milieu. We begin this coverage in Chapter 5 by exploring how parenting may explain why children exposed to discord between parents are at greater risk for developing psychological problems; our particular focus is on EST as a theoretical model for how marital conflict relates to parenting and child adjustment. Next, in Chapter 6, we describe advances in understanding how other familial and extrafamilial processes may elucidate pathways between marital conflict and children's adjustment; again, we consider these matters primarily from the perspective of EST. Finally, we explore in Chapter 7 how embedding the study of marital conflict in the broader developmental context over time further informs an understanding of children's adjustment and mental health, with particular analysis of the dynamic role of the emotional security system within this context.

CHAPTER 5

The Role of Parenting
in the Context of Marital Conflict

Indirect Pathways and Processes

Another pathway for the effects of marital conflict on children is through parenting and other family processes. The cases of Families A and B described in the introduction to this part of the book underscore an important point: The burdens experienced by children from discordant homes result not just from witnessing marital conflict, but also from an increased likelihood of parenting problems. In this chapter, we focus on discussing pathways and processes for relations between and among marital conflict, parenting, and child outcomes, including the EST account of what we describe as "indirect-effects models." As illustrated in Figure 2.2, this terminology is rooted in the basic presumption that marital conflict can increase risk for maladjustment *indirectly*, through its association with disruptions in parent–child and family relationships.

MODELS OF INDIRECT EFFECTS

Historical Trends in the Study of Indirect Effects

The proposition that parenting contributes to the link between marital conflict and child adjustment is not new. For example, in an early and classic review of the literature on interparental conflict and children, Emery (1982) highlighted the possibility that several co-occurring forms of family adversity, including parenting problems, may explain part of the association between interparental conflict and child adjustment.

From a process-oriented perspective, numerous family processes are potential mechanisms in the link between marital conflict and child functioning. Parenting or childrearing styles have received the most attention. For example, from a social learning perspective, the stress and strain of marital problems may undermine parents' abilities to manage children through adequate supervision, open communication, and enforcement of rules for appropriate child conduct. Lax monitoring or discipline may have two major consequences. On the one hand, it limits the opportunities for maritally distressed parents to "catch" children being good. Thus, in the terminology of social learning theory, distressed parents may not positively reinforce children's prosocial behavior by providing positive consequences for appropriate child conduct. On the other hand, the lax supervision means that negative consequences often do not follow bouts of child misbehavior.

Since these early formulations, other notions have been considered in process-oriented models of marital conflict. For example, marital and parenting disruptions may exact a damaging toll on the quality of parent–child relationships. Attachment theory formulations posit that children's difficulties in using parents as a secure base of support and protection may explain the vulnerability of children exposed to high levels of marital conflict. Family systems theory notions highlight the co-occurrence of marital problems with parents' problems in serving as a cohesive team in rearing their children (Cowan & McHale, 1996; McHale, 1997; Sturge-Apple, Davies, & Cummings, 2006a). Thus, rather than supporting each other in their roles as socialization agents, parents who are experiencing marital difficulties may undermine and disparage one another in their parenting roles. In turn, parents' difficulties in working together as a team in rearing children may increase children's psychological problems (e.g., Belsky, Putnam, & Crnic, 1996; Belsky, Woodworth, & Crnic, 1996; McHale & Rasmussen, 1998; Schoppe-Sullivan, Mangelsdorf, & Frosch, 2001).

Misconceptions about Indirect Effects

Variations are evident in the strength attributed to mediating family mechanisms. Historically, some rather extreme assumptions about parenting disturbances as explanatory mechanisms have been made.

These approaches have postulated that parent–child relationship disturbances account completely for how and why interparental discord is related to child adjustment (e.g., Erel, Margolin, & John, 1998; Fauber et al., 1990; Fauber & Long, 1991; Patterson, DeBaryshe, & Ramsey, 1989).

Some investigators point to a handful of studies finding that associations between marital conflict and child adjustment are reduced to a negligible magnitude after inclusion of co-occurring parenting difficulties as mediators (Buehler, Benson, & Gerard, 2006; Erel et al., 1998; Fauber et al., 1990; Fauber & Long, 1991; Mann & MacKenzie, 1996; Patterson et al., 1989). Problems with such approaches include (1) the use of models that are inappropriately reductionistic, in the face of overwhelming evidence for more influences and more complex pathways (Emery, Fincham, & Cummings, 1992); and (2) inadequately conceptualized research designs, in which parenting variables are much more rigorously measured and outnumber marital conflict or violence variables as predictors by a ratio of 5:1 or higher (e.g., Gerard, Krishnakumar, & Buehler, 2006; Krishnakumar, Buehler, & Barber, 2003; Levendosky, Huth-Bocks, Shapiro, & Semel, 2003). Even in these contexts, marital conflict is still often directly associated with children's outcomes (e.g., Buehler & Gerard, 2002; Krishnakumar et al., 2003; Levendosky et al., 2003; Levendosky, Leahy, Bogat, Davidson, & von Eye, 2006; Webster-Stratton & Hammond, 1999).

These approaches thus reflect misconceptions of pathways concerning relations between interparental conflict and child outcomes. From our analysis of the literature, there is little or no evidence to support the notion that parenting practices are the only or even the primary mechanisms of effect (e.g., Davies, Harold, et al., 2002; Frosch & Mangelsdorf, 2001; Webster-Stratton & Hammond, 1999). Carefully controlled experimental manipulations of interadult conflict have repeatedly shown that the destructive forms of such conflict cause elevated levels of distress and aggression in children (see Cowan & Cowan, 2002; Cummings & Davies, 2002). In contrast to the extensive evidence for direct effects based on experimental and observational studies, there is little support at this level of analysis for indirect effects. Finally, what direct-effects models propose is not simply a pathway from marital conflict to child adjustment, but a pathway from marital conflict to some mediating process (e.g., emotional security) to child adjustment (Davies, Harold, et al., 2002; Grych et al., 2003; see Chapter 4). Competing tests of direct- and indirect-effects pathways have often not fully conceptualized or specified the direct-effects pathways.

On the other hand, models that recognize indirect pathways as aspects of the plurality and diversity of developmental pathways are valuable representations of research findings. An appropriate conceptualization is that marital conflict is associated with greater child problems via (1) a direct pathway, in which the stress of witnessing disputes between parents alters children's psychological functioning; and (2) one or more indirect pathways, whereby marital conflict also incurs part of the risk through its association with parenting and family disturbances (see Figure 2.2).

DIRECTIONS IN EXPLORING PATHWAYS OF INDIRECT EFFECTS

The Need for Theory

Although researchers have been exploring indirect-path propositions for many years, relatively little progress has been achieved in formulating integrative *theories* of the processes linking marital conflict, parenting, and child adjustment. Thus, in spite of the publication of influential studies further documenting the existence of indirect paths in recent years, we are nearing the point of diminishing returns in terms of making this point at a strictly empirical level of analysis. At this juncture, virtually every parenting dimension has been explored as a factor that may elucidate the link between marital conflict and child adjustment. Innovative theory development is needed for this line of work to progress beyond showing correlations and toward explaining the processes accounting for pathways between marital conflict and child development. In accord with our overarching aim in this volume of outlining an EST perspective, we review and critique the study of indirect paths through the lens of EST. In particular, we address how EST can direct us toward a conceptual understanding of the role parenting plays in models of marital conflict.

The Importance of Indirect Pathways

There is little room for doubt about answers to this question: Do parenting difficulties play a role in accounting for the association between marital conflict and child adjustment problems? At this stage of research, there is strong empirical support for the notion that parenting disturbances constitute a key class of explanatory mechanisms. For example, Sturge-Apple and colleagues (2006b) found that parents' emotional unavailability to children was a key explanatory mechanism linking histories of destructive marital conflict with subsequent child adjustment problems (see also Schoppe-Sullivan et al., 2007). Moreover, intervention studies have provided support for the hypothesis that parenting is a mediator of marital conflict. For example, programmatic work by the Cowans and their colleagues showed that parents' participation in interventions designed to improve their marriages also promoted effective parenting practices and subsequent child adjustment. Interestingly, although participation in another program designed to improve parenting practices also improved subsequent child adjustment, it did not yield any enhancement in marital quality (Cowan & Cowan, 2002; Cowan, Cowan, & Heming, 2005; see also Cowan et al., 2007).

Moreover, recent studies that simultaneously assess child experiences with parenting practices (i.e., an indirect path) and child reactions to interparental conflict (i.e., a direct path) within models of child psychological adjustment find evidence for the operation of both pathways. For example, the Davies, Harold, and colleagues (2002) study found that multi-informant constructs of emotional insecurity in the interparental relationship and parent–child relationship disturbances each mediated the link between marital conflict and adolescent internalizing and externalizing symptoms. A study using a multimethod, longitudinal design (Sturge-Apple, Davies, Winter, Cummings, & Schermerhorn, 2008) showed that parent–child relationship processes and children's insecure internal representations of the interparental relationship were each intervening mechanisms in the link between marital conflict and teacher reports of children's emotional and classroom difficulties.

The Need to Study New Sets of Process-Oriented Questions

At the same time, at this advanced stage of research, the preponderance of evidence indicates that parenting difficulties are one part of a broader set of multiple, diverse pathways linking marital conflict to children's adjustment. Thus, if we are to sustain the vitality of indirect-path research, we need to begin to ask a new series of process-oriented questions: Why and how do parenting dimensions serve as explanatory mechanisms? Addressing such questions can provide useful guides for addressing other central questions in indirect-path models, including these: What specific dimensions of parenting appear to be the most destructive for children exposed to marital conflict? How can parenting be conceptualized as part of a broader constellation of family processes, which in themselves might serve as explanatory mechanisms? In the remainder of this chapter, we examine each of these questions from the perspective of EST.

THE SPILLOVER HYPOTHESIS

The "spillover" hypothesis posits that parental negative affect stemming from unresolved spousal disputes carries over into parental interactions with children, including unresponsiveness, rejection, and inconsistent child management (e.g., poor monitoring, inconsistent or hostile discipline) (e.g., Engfer, 1988; Erel & Burman, 1995; Floyd, Gilliom, & Costigan, 1998). Socialization models of parenting are enlisted to explain children's subsequent vulnerability to negative child outcomes (Barber, 1996; Gray & Steinberg, 1999; Steinberg, Lamborn, Dornbusch, & Darling, 1992; Stolz, Barber, & Olsen, 2005).

However, a limitation of this perspective is that the notion of spillover does not articulate what processes are carried over from marital to parenting relationships. That is, the interrelations between the marital conflict and parenting are not specified in terms of either specific testable hypotheses about mediating processes, or a unifying conceptual model linking the spillover and socialization components of the explanation. From a process-oriented perspective, an adequate foundation is not provided for further specifying how and why parenting acts as a mediator in the context of marital conflict. A model that systematically integrates theories of parenting and marital conflict is necessary for advancing this next generation of research questions and hypotheses.

Although relationship perturbations, coping processes, negative affect, and personality attributes have been discussed as possible mechanisms, little attention has been devoted to developing precise conceptual and operational definitions and hypotheses, including testing the relative merits of different mediating mechanisms (see Davies, Sturge-Apple, & Cummings, 2004; Grych, 2002). For example, the spillover notion that "affect and behavior generated in one relational setting transfer to other relationships" (Buehler et al., 2006, p. 267) appears at first glance to be straightforward and testable. In fact, the spillover hypothesis does little to sort out the multiplicity of emotional processes that may underlie links between marital conflict and parenting, or to indicate how such processes may be transferred from one relationship context to another over time. Testing these predictions requires well-articulated perspectives on the multiple possible affective processes by which interparental problems affect parenting. For example, the marital subsystem may undermine parenting through (1) amplification of negative appraisals and attributions of children; (2) constriction of resources devoted to childrearing activities; and/or (3) disruption of parental problem solving and facilitation of reflexive, dysregulated parental response patterns (Dix, 1991). The processes that account for why parenting problems in high-conflict homes increase child vulnerability to psychological difficulties also need further specification. For example, exposure to parenting sets in motion multiple processes within children (e.g., affective, motivational, social information processing), which ultimately need to be identified.

EST AS AN EXPLANATORY MODEL FOR INDIRECT PATHWAYS

EST provides another model of indirect pathways. A strong point is its balance between parsimony and scope in accounting for how and why parenting mediates between marital conflict and child outcomes. Rather than introducing an array of theories (e.g., social learning theory, information-processing theory) to explain the mediating role of parenting, EST provides a coherent conceptualization of how parenting problems following marital conflict may undermine children's goal of protection from physical or psychological harm. Given the assumption that protection from harm is significant in the hierarchy of human goals, when difficulties in achieving security are pronounced and prolonged, the eventual results are diminished resources for other developmental tasks.

EST thus postulates multiple ways in which parenting problems associated with marital conflict disrupt children's security in family relationships. Figure 5.1 provides a synopsis of the pathways through which marital conflict is proposed to influence children's adjustment by indirectly affecting parenting processes. Path 1 is derived from attachment theory; the proposition is that parenting difficulties interfere with children's long-term adjustment by compromising the attachment relationship between parents and children, including the function of providing protection. Impairments in parental responsiveness to children undermine children's confidence in parents as sources of protection (Bowlby, 1969, 1973, 1980; Goldberg, Grusec, & Jenkins, 1999; McElwain & Booth-LaForce, 2006). This indirect path thus reflects a negative impact on the children's ability to form secure relationships with their parents.

EST also posits that parenting problems may also increase children's worries about security in the interparental relationship (see Path 2). Expressions of parental disengagement, unresponsiveness, and rejection toward children undercut security in the interparental relationship, affecting emotion regulation, self-confidence, and self-efficacy. That is, parenting difficulties, as correlates and sequelae of marital conflict, exact a toll on children's psychological adjustment by compromising their parent–child attachment security and also further undercutting their sense of security in the interparental relationship, over and above the effects due to direct exposure to marital conflict.

Tests of these predictions provide promising support for these pathways. Supporting Path 1 in Figure 5.1, Davies, Harold, and colleagues (2002) study found that parenting difficulties characterized by low levels of warmth, emotional rejection, and poor monitoring of children's activities mediated the link between marital conflict and parent–child attachment security. In turn, parent–child attachment insecurity mediated the link between parenting difficulties and adolescent internalizing and externalizing symptoms. Notably, these findings were consistent with those of studies identifying (1) parenting difficulties as mediators of links between marital conflict and parent–child attachment insecurity (Frosch et al., 2000; Owen & Cox, 1997) and (2) parent–child attachment insecurity as mediators in the link between parenting difficulties and child adjustment problems (Carlson, 1998; Madigan, Moran, Schuengel, Pederson, & Otten, 2007; Shields, Ryan, & Cicchetti, 2001).

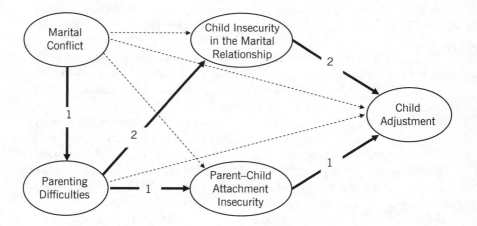

FIGURE 5.1. A model depicting the two pathways through which marital conflict is proposed to influence children's adjustment by indirectly affecting parenting processes. The destructive bold arrows denote key processes outlined in the indirect-path component of EST. Dashed arrows designate other important pathways in models of marital conflict.

At the same time, the 2002 study extended past work by simultaneously examining the entire chain of intervening processes proposed in the indirect-effects hypothesis. However, the results did not support Path 2 in Figure 5.1: After exposure to interparental conflict was taken into account, parenting was not associated with children's insecure responses to interparental conflict.

Recent studies utilizing more rigorous designs (e.g., longitudinal data, multiple methods) provide support for *both* of the indirect-pathway predictions derived from EST. In accord with Path 1, Sturge-Apple and colleagues (2008) found that observed displays of low parental warmth and responsiveness with children served as an intervening mechanism in the link between observational measures of destructive marital conflict and children's insecure representations of their parents' abilities to serve as a source of support and protection for them under times of stress. In turn, these insecure representations of the parent–child relationship served as a key intervening mechanism in the link between low parental warmth and teacher reports of children's problems with engaging with classroom activities in school.

This same study (Sturge-Apple et al., 2008) identified a multivariate pattern of results corresponding with the second conceptual pathway. More specifically, low levels of parental warmth, which co-occurred with high levels of marital conflict, were uniquely associated with children's insecure representations of the interparental relationship even after the role of marital conflict as a predictor of insecure representations was specified. In turn, these insecure representations of interparental relationships predicted concurrent levels of poor classroom engagement and emotional maladjustment to school, as well as increases in emotional problems over a 2-year period. Further increasing confidence in the stability of this pathway, a multimethod structural equation modeling analysis indicated that low parental warmth was an intervening mechanism in the link between marital disengagement and children's subjective reports of their negative emotional reactivity to a simulated interparental conflict (Davies, Sturge-Apple, Winter, Cummings, & Farrell, 2006).

MORE PRECISE EST CONCEPTUALIZATIONS OF INDIRECT PATHS

These findings provide a promising theoretical foundation for elucidating why parenting may mediate pathways between marital conflict and child maladjustment. However, because EST is a developmental theory, advances in EST have been largely geared toward characterizing how children process, respond, and adjust to the interplay among marital conflict and accompanying parenting difficulties. Thus, despite some notable headway in accounting for why parenting processes in high-conflict homes may ultimately have a negative impact on children's development, greater theoretical precision about several of the indirect pathways is needed. In the following discussion, we describe how EST conceptualizations may help meet this need.

Directionality in Paths

Most contemporary conceptualizations of family process acknowledge the reciprocal transactions between and among different family subsystems (Cox & Paley, 1997). Consequently, it is not usual to propose that marital conflict and parenting difficulties influence each other in a bidirectional manner. Moreover, there is growing recognition that other family factors may act as third variables contributing to the association between marital conflict and parenting problems.

However, although identification of the multiple pathways involved in the association between marital conflict and parenting has led to a fuller appreciation of the complexity of family processes, it occurs at some cost. Gains in scope can result in significant reductions in parsimony and precision. Without a balance between scope and precision, there is risk of falling into the trap of accepting increasingly weak, vague, and timid statements about how all family factors mutually influence each other.

We are not proposing a return to models that reduce the complexity of children's development to a small set of elementary, unidirectional processes. At the same time, sharper and bolder theoretical statements are needed to explain the indirect pathways parsimoniously. Future progress will require developing and testing theoretically guided hypotheses about which specific indirect pathways are likely to be the strongest in the broad constellation of processes.

EST acknowledges that the association between marital conflict and parenting is likely to be the product of bidirectional influences plus the impact of other family variables. In addition, the tenets of EST provide a promising foundation for more precise predictions regarding the causal structure underlying the link between marital conflict and parenting. Like family systems theory, EST accepts the assumption that the marital relationship is the cornerstone or hub of the broader system of relationships in the family. In this regard, marital conflict should be more powerful as a causal agent in altering parenting than parenting should be as an etiological factor in subsequent marital relations.

Empirical results from a wide array of studies provide considerable support for this hypothesis. For example, novel experimental designs have shown that mothers who were randomly assigned to participate in a conflictual interaction with their partners were less attentive to their sons in an ensuing parent–child interaction task than mothers who participated in a nonconflictual interaction were (Jouriles & Farris, 1992). Likewise, hierarchical linear analyses with daily diary measurements of family stress indicated that marital tensions were followed by a disproportionately higher likelihood (in the range of 41–60%) of stress in both mother–child and father–child interactions the following day (Almeida, Wethington, & Chandler, 1999). Longitudinal research has further shown that observations of destructive marital conflict (i.e., withdrawal, hostility) predicted subsequent decreases in parental emotional availability in both mother–child and father–child interactions 1 year later (Sturge-Apple et al., 2006a, 2006b). A study exploring reciprocal associations between marital and parenting difficulties over a 1-year period yielded some support for the role of marital discord as a predictor of greater parenting difficulties. At the same time, parenting difficulties did not predict subsequent changes in marital problems (Davies, Sturge-Apple, & Cummings, 2004). Although findings are not always consistent (e.g., Belsky & Hsieh, 1998; Schoppe-Sullivan, Mangelsdorf, Frosch, & McHale, 2004), findings from the few existing studies exploring the interplay between marital discord and parenting difficulties suggest that marital discord is more consistently an antecedent of parenting than it is a consequence of parenting.

Marital Conflict and Attachment in the Marital Relationship

Although the spillover hypothesis is a prevailing model guiding research on the interplay between marital conflict and parenting, it says little about how and why anger, distress, and preoccupation are carried from the marital to the parent–child subsystem. Simply relying on the maxim that negative affect in the marital relationship spills over into the parent–child relationship does not account for why marital difficulties predict cumulative decrements in parenting over periods of months or years (Sturge-Apple et al., 2006a, 2006b).

Marital Conflict Behaviors as Manifestations of Attachment Quality

An EST perspective provides theoretical bases for why distress may proliferate across family subsystems over long periods. If attachment theory is extended to adulthood, marital conflict behaviors (e.g., escalating hostility, disengagement, warmth) can be seen as manifestations of the quality of the attachment bond. That is, marital conflict behaviors signify individual differences in the partners' ability to use each other as sources of support in the family, particularly during stressful or conflictual times (Cowan, Cohn, Cowan, & Pearson, 1996; Crowell, Treboux, & Waters, 2002; Mikulincer, Florian, Cowan, & Cowan, 2002). In support of this premise, research has shown that adult attachment insecurity is lawfully associated with tense, unstable, fickle romantic relationships (Crowell et al., 2002; Mikulincer et al., 2002). Moreover, romantic relationships are characterized by elevated levels of aggression, threats, and discord when the adults exhibit difficulties in utilizing their partners as a secure base (see below). These problems may be expressed through indistinct, indirect, and inconsistent signals for support; ineffective use of partners for facilitating emotion regulation; and insecure working models of the relationships (Crowell et al., 2002; Treboux, Crowell, & Waters, 2004). As both a cause and an outcome of destructive marital conflict (Mikulincer et al., 2002; Treboux et al., 2004), insecurity in the adult relationship may erode childrearing abilities.

Priming Negative Responses to Childrearing

Insecure attachment in the marital relationship deprives spouses of the opportunity to use each other as sources of support to alleviate distress (Mikulincer et al., 2002). Thus negative affect and attributions resulting from interparental conflicts are more likely to continue or escalate for prolonged periods of time after a conflict has ended. These responses may prime parents to respond negatively to challenging childrearing tasks.

Undermining Representations of the Self and Marital Partner

Because the attachment relationship between partners is a primary source of caregiver support in many cultural settings, problems in this attachment relationship may undermine the parental role by having a deleterious effect on the partners' general representations of themselves and each other. Over periods of months or years, these progressively negative global attachment representations may insidiously alter how adults approach their roles as caregivers (Rholes, Simpson, & Friedman, 2006; Sibley & Overall, 2007).

Difficulties in Using the Partner as a Secure Base

Attachment insecurity in the marital relationship may also compromise the ability to meet basic needs in other psychological systems. Caregiving, including the function of providing support for dependents, is central for understanding how spillover operates. In fact, the caregiving system is so closely intertwined with the attachment system that it is commonly viewed as a component of the adult attachment relationship (e.g., Ainsworth, 1985; Crowell et al., 2002). For example, an influential system for coding secure-base behavior in adult attachment relationships is based on the partners' ability to effectively provide support to and receive support from each other (Crowell et al., 2002; Treboux et al., 2004). Thus it is possible that difficulties in utilizing partners as a base of support not only may be linked with subsequent difficulties in offering support to caregivers, but may also undermine the adults' ability to be sensitive and responsive to the needs of their children.

From an EST perspective, Davies, Sturge-Apple, Woitach, and Cummings (in press) recently examined the conditions and mechanisms underlying the transmission of distress from the interparental relationship to parenting difficulties for parents of kindergarten children. Even with autoregressive controls, pathways were found between interparental conflict and parenting difficulties—including parental psychological control and insensitivity to child negative affect—over a 2-year period for fathers. Moreover, fathers' attachment insecurity in the marital relationship significantly mediated the pathways between interparental conflict and parenting difficulties. The mediational role of adult relationship insecurity in pathways between interparental discord and fathering difficulties remained even when adult depressive symptoms were included as a possible mediator and rival predictor in the analytic models. Thus the results lend support to the notion that more global forms of negative affect are not necessarily the operative processes underlying the transmission of disturbances from the interparental to the parent–child relationship. Support was found for the notion that attachment insecurity fostered by doubts about the availability of one's partner as a source of support may undermine the caregiving system, impeding adults' ability to be sensitive and responsive to the needs of their children.

EST Conceptualizations of the Effects of Different Marital Conflict Behaviors on Parenting

Inconsistencies in extant findings indicate considerable variability in the role parenting plays in pathways between marital conflict and child adjustment. Although perturbations in parenting are robust mediators of marital conflict in many studies (e.g., Erath, Bierman, & the Conduct Problems Prevention Research Group, 2006; Lindsey, MacKinnon-Lewis, Campbell, Frabutt, & Lamb, 2002; Low & Stocker, 2005; Sturge-Apple et al., 2006a, 2006b), null findings on the role of parenting as an explanatory process are not uncommon (e.g., Frosch & Mangelsdorf, 2001; Katz & Windecker-Nelson, 2006; Skopp, McDonald, Jouriles, & Rosenfield, 2007; Stocker & Richmond, 2007). Process-oriented models such as EST can be useful for identifying sources of heterogeneity in these indirect pathways.

Conflict in Secure Marital Relationships May Be Healthy

One central source of variability may lie in how marital conflict is expressed. In other words, it is plausible that associations between marital conflict and parenting practices are stronger for some forms of conflict than for others. From an EST perspective, simply airing adult grievances in mildly or moderately angry ways is not necessarily detrimental to the parenting role. In fact, we theorize that adults who are able to use their partners effectively as bases of security are more likely to be open to identifying, discussing, and repairing emerging sources of problems in marital relations than are adults with insecure attachments.

For example, secure representations of marital relationships may provide individuals with more latitude to explore their current relationship circumstances at deeper and more incisive levels that are generally free of defensive processes (Curran, Hazen, Jacobvitz, & Sasaki, 2006). As a result, expressions of anger do not necessarily reflect destructive relational or intrapersonal processes. Rather, for the subset of marriages characterized as secure, angry displays may signify a deeper commitment to repairing, maintaining, and improving the marital relationship. If this is the case, however, we would expect that the anger would be constructive in helping to organize and focus attention on the resolution of issues. Therefore, from our theoretical perspective, anger expressed in mild to moderate forms as an aspect of broader progress in resolving significant relationship issues is unlikely to undermine parenting processes.

Verbal and Physical Hostility Are Expected to Predict Heightened Parenting Problems

Conversely forms of conflict characterized by physical violence, verbal aggression, and/or threats of abandonment may be manifestations of deeper adult attachment difficulties and may pose significant problems for the ability to assume the full responsibilities and demands of parenthood. From our perspective, interpersonal antagonism in the form of verbal aggression and threats may disrupt parents' abilities to serve as socialization agents by undermining their ability to use the marital relationship as a forum for both successfully accessing social resources and honing aptitude in serving as a source of support (Wampler, Riggs, & Kimball, 2004).

Moreover, if hostility reflects a broader pattern of oppression, intimidation, or violence in the relationship, it may be an even stronger predictor of parenting problems as a proxy for the operation of multiple adult attachment relationship dysfunctions. Under these dire conditions, the intimate relationship not only fails to serve as a base of support and a prototype for refining caregiving practices in times of family challenge; it also serves as a source of significant threat to the psychological and physical welfare of the adult victims of the violence. If these propositions are valid, we might expect that marital violence would be uniquely associated with parenting impairments *even after* other forms of destructive marital conflict that may occur are taken into account. Although no study has explored this specific research question, to our knowledge, some findings indirectly support this contention. For example, qualitative reviews of the literature have noted that associations between marital and parenting difficulties appear to be higher in domestic violence samples (Appel & Holden, 1998; Margolin & Gordis, 2003).

Withdrawal Is Also Problematic for Parenting

Emotional disengagement or indifference may also play a distinct role as an antecedent of parenting. Conceptualizations of the long-term stability of marriage suggest that withdrawal may even reflect a more destructive process than hostility, because withdrawal may result in the accumulation of unresolved issues and in progressively greater emotional abandonment and detachment between spouses (Christensen & Heavey, 1990; Gottman, 1994). Consistent with this assumption, Cox, Paley, Burchinal, and Payne (1999) found that spousal withdrawal, rather than spousal hostility, predicted diminished parental responsiveness in parent–infant interactions at both 3 and 12 months. A study of an older sample of early elementary children (Sturge-Apple et al., 2006b) further reported that marital withdrawal was a unique predictor of subsequent decreases in both mothers' and fathers' emotional availability to their children over a year. In fact, marital withdrawal was a significantly stronger predictor of diminished paternal emotional availability than marital hostility was.

Within an EST conceptualization, one possible explanation is that spousal apathy or indifference may take a toll on parenting because it is a marker for one of the last stages in the deterioration of the adult attachment relationship. For example, behavioral signs of withdrawal and indifference (e.g., tuning out the partner's feelings, downplaying painful relationship events, reluctance to rely on the partner for caring) during conflict events are thought to reflect a broader pattern of avoidant or dismissing attachment in adult relationships (Wampler et al., 2004). In turn, adult endorsement of more avoidant attachments in romantic relationships during pregnancy was found to be associated with less desire to have children and greater parenting stress when the children were 6 months of age. Moreover, these associations were robust even after potential third variables were taken into account, including the participants' and their partners' depressive symptoms, attachment anxiety, and marital satisfaction (Rholes et al., 2006).

DIFFERENTIAL PREDICTION OF PARENTING PATHWAYS FROM AN EST PERSPECTIVE

Pathways from Marital Conflict to Parenting

The power of parenting as a mediator in pathways involving security may further depend on the form of parenting practices under consideration. Without the use of theory as a guide, determining which specific types of parenting are central mediators is next to impossible. Parenting is a complex construct in itself, with multiple layers and dimensions.

For example, in "parenting styles," which are defined as broad characterizations of the climate of parenting, there are multiple ways parents can serve as socialization agents. Parenting styles that are posited to correlate with destructive marital conflict and help to explain its risk for children include (1) poor behavioral management, or difficulties in managing and controlling children; (2) greater psychological control, characterized by manipulation and exploitation of the parent–child bond (e.g., love withdrawal, guilt induction); and (3) lack of support, as defined by low levels of warmth and acceptance. Within classes of parenting styles, there are distinct ways of expressing childrearing difficulties. For example, poor behavioral management may be reflected in lax monitoring of child activities, lenient or inconsistent discipline, or harsh punishment techniques.

EST conceptualizations may help to refine the focus on the identification of affected parenting behaviors in indirect-effects pathways. If both interparental and parent–child attachment processes are central mechanisms in the associations between/among marital conflict, parenting, and child adjustment, then mediational paths should be shaped by emotional relationship processes in the family. That is, marital conflict should be most likely to influence emotion-laden domains of parenting; for instance, difficulties in using the partner as a secure base for regulating distress should be linked with diminished empathy and sensitivity in caregiving. Our review in our initial exposition of EST indicated that all 13 studies that assessed emotion-oriented dimensions of parenting (i.e., emotional rejection, hostility, or unresponsiveness) reported significant relations between marital conflict and parenting (Davies & Cummings, 1994). Relatedly, a meta-analysis indicated that the associations between marital conflict and parenting were significantly stronger for the childrearing domains of acceptance and harsh punishment, which are also emotion-laden behaviors, than for lax control (Krishnakumar & Buehler, 2000).

Pathways from Parenting to Child Outcomes

According to EST, emotional dimensions of parenting may affect children's long-term psychological adjustment through parent–child attachment relationship processes. Parental warmth or coldness, support or lack of support, and availability or rejection in the context of managing child behavior (e.g., harsh discipline) are theorized to affect children's long-term adjustment in relation to their ability to utilize their parents as bases of support and protection. Studies support child–parent attachment security as a mediator between emotional availability or rejection and child adjustment (DeWolff & van IJzendoorn, 1997; Waters & Cummings, 2000).

Other domains of parenting may also serve as explanatory processes in links between marital conflict and child adjustment. For example, there is overwhelming support for inconsistent discipline and lax monitoring as critical to understanding children's adjustment (Crouter & Head, 2000; Patterson & Yoerger, 1997). Yet our contention is that the socialization processes set in motion by these forms of parenting are more likely to be forged by other mechanisms that are not as closely related to the propositions of EST—for example, behavioral contingencies that reinforce misbehavior, as articulated in social learning theory.

By the same token, the premise that security processes may assume greater significance in explaining the mediating role of emotional dimensions of parenting does not rule out the possibility that security may still help to account for indirect pathways that are traditionally emphasized in other theories (Cummings & Davies, 1995). For example, in the literature, information-processing and social learning theories have been predominantly invoked to explain how lax monitoring and broader indices of behavioral control serve as intervening mechanisms in associations between marital and child functioning (Davidov & Grusec, 2006; Grusec & Goodnow, 1994; Snyder, Cramer, Afrank, & Patterson, 2005). Children's sense of security may still carry explanatory weight for understanding these particular indirect-effects pathways. For example, slipshod or inconsistent discipline strategies may signify a lack of structure, predictability, and organization, and thus may create doubts about parents' ability to protect and support children in times of need (Greenberg, Speltz, & DeKlyen, 1993). Thus, from an EST perspective, it is plausible that children may resort to angry, disruptive attempts to exert some control in parent–child relations or to draw the attention of a lax parent (Crittenden, 1992; Cummings & Davies, 1995). In a similar vein, children's confidence in their parents as supportive figures may be undercut by their experiences with volatile bouts of parental hostility or inexplicable love withdrawal, which commonly occur in the context of harsh or intrusive discipline strategies (Bowlby, 1980; Cummings & Davies, 1995; Hoffman, 1994; Kobak, Cole, Ferenz-Gillies, Fleming, & Gamble, 1993).

Other aspects of parenting may help to elucidate indirect-effects pathways even further. For example, in contrast to the relatively broad construct of "parenting styles," "parenting practices" are defined as caregivers' use of effort and other specific resources to achieve specific socialization goals. Thus, whereas parental involvement as a "parenting style" has been characterized as the extent to which a parent is "committed to his or her role as a parent and to fostering optimal child development" (Maccoby & Martin, 1983, p. 48), parental involvement as a "parenting practice" is defined as "the dedication of resources by a parent to the child within a given domain" (Grolnick & Slowiaczek, 1994, p. 238). Much of the work of exploring links between and among marital conflict, parent–child processes, and child adjustment have operationalized emotional availability and loosely related constructs (e.g., support, acceptance, sensitivity, responsiveness) as global parenting styles. Thus warmth, support, or responsiveness is defined as a broad parental characteristic or trait that is consistent across tasks and socialization contexts.

Yet there are strong theoretical bases for examining parental emotional availability in terms of specific parenting processes, in order to delineate more precisely the security processes underlying these indirect pathways. The attachment bond is not conceptualized as cumulative functioning related to all aspects of the parent–child relationship. Rather, it is concerned specifically with the formation of a close emotional relationship related to secure-base behavior and the provision of support (Waters & Cummings, 2000). Thus it follows that some aspects of emotional availability or responsiveness are about matters other than emotional security.

Such assumptions, though implicit in the literature, have not undergone systematic empirical testing. For example, Stolz and colleagues (2005) suggested that parental warmth and support should predict children's social initiative through multiple processes, some of which may index attachment processes, whereas others reflect the promotion of affiliation and relatedness. From an EST perspective, the critical question is what specific elements of parenting are central mediators in pathways between marital conflict and children's attachment security. Given that the attachment system is particularly salient during times of distress, many researchers have called for a new level of specificity by proposing that parental responsiveness in contexts of child distress and support seeking is a more central antecedent to attachment than general "climate" characterizations of availability and warmth are (Goldberg, Grusec, & Jenkins, 1999; Thompson, 1997, 1998). Thus some elements of broad "style" characterizations of support may be particularly relevant to attachment (e.g., ability to use a caregiver effectively to allay distress), whereas other dimensions of support (e.g., mutual enjoyment in recreational activities) may be relevant to other domains or systems of functioning (e.g., affiliation). Consistent with this assumption, maternal sensitivity to infant distress at 6 months was a significant predictor of infant attachment security at 15 months even after the nonsignificant role of maternal sensitivity to children in nondistressing situations was taken into account as a predictor of attachment (McElwain & Booth-LaForce, 2006).

In placing this work within theorizing about the indirect-pathway component of EST, a critical next step in the literature will be further identifying how "emotional" parenting practices, characterized by the dedication of resources to helping children regulate their distress, operate in broader models of marital conflict, attachment, and child adjustment. As a first step in elaborating on this conceptualization, it will be important to capture the multidimensional nature of such parenting practices. Literatures on emotion coaching and parental coping with child negative affect indicate that parental reactions to child distress can be expressed in multiple ways. For example, in contexts of child distress, parents may become distressed themselves, minimize or downplay their children's emotional experience, reject or punish their children, offer emotional or instrumental support, or assist children in overcoming the problem that originally evoked the distress. As yet, it is unclear which specific dimensions of parenting practices may be particularly likely to accompany marital conflict, and in turn to increase children's attachment difficulties and psychological symptoms. As research by Katz and Windecker-Nelson (2006) suggests, destructive marital conflict may be associated with some forms of emotional parenting practices but not with others. Accordingly, advances in the indirect-path component of EST will hinge in part on understanding how mediational pathways involving the joint role of marital conflict and parenting practices, child attachment security, and child adjustment may vary as a function of the ways parents respond to child distress.

FUTURE DIRECTIONS

Parenting as a Mediator in the Broader Constellation of Family Processes

As we conclude this chapter, it is also important to take stock of how security pathways involving marital conflict, parenting, and child adjustment may operate within the broader system of processes in the family. Infusing principles of family systems theory into EST is a particularly promising direction for future work.

The Compensatory Hypothesis

First, in recognition that all families do not have the same experiences of indirect-effects pathways, family systems theory provides a useful set of conceptual tools for identifying patterns of individual differences in the pathways between marital and parent–child subsystem processes and their implications for child adjustment. For example, according to the "compensatory" hypothesis, some parents who are facing high levels of discord may defy the odds of experiencing parenting difficulties (Belsky, Youngblade, Rovine, & Volling, 1991; Cox et al., 2001; Engfer, 1988). In fact, some caregivers may respond to some of the most adverse marital circumstances (e.g., recurring and severe violence) by consciously attempting to offset children's vulnerability to this adversity through increasing their effectiveness as parents (e.g., Levendosky & Graham-Bermann, 2000; Levendosky et al., 2003).

When "Warmth" Is Not What It Seems

By the same token, family systems theory cautions against interpreting increases in positive parenting in high-conflict homes at face value. Further reflecting diversity in possible indirect-effects pathways, interparental discord may engender parental attempts to fulfill lingering intimacy needs in the parent–child relationship. These attempts may be manifested overtly in parental warmth, but such expressions of parental warmth may be part of a broader pattern of parent–child relations characterized by high levels of parent–child triangulation, enmeshment, and intrusiveness (Kretchmar & Jacobvitz, 2002; Marvin & Stewart, 1990; Stevenson-Hinde, 1990). Thus, in these parenting contexts, these expressions of "warmth" may reflect a type of emotional unavailability. Accordingly, it may play a mediating role similar to that played by other forms of emotional unavailability in our indirect-path conceptualization. More specifically, an enmeshed, intrusive pattern, which may misleadingly seem to contain elements of "warmth," may be more prevalent in high-conflict homes and may serve as a potent risk factor for the development of insecure attachment (Davies, Cummings, & Winter, 2004; Kretchmar & Jacobvitz, 2002). Thus greater attention to the underlying meanings of different patterns of relations between marital conflict and parenting will further advance our understanding of the many indirect pathways involving marital conflict, parenting, and children's attachment security.

Spillover in the Context of Broader Family Processes

Family systems theory also provides a rich foundation for developing hypotheses about the sources of variability in interdependencies among the marital and parent–child subsystems and their implications for children. Family perturbations and stressors may provoke subsequent reorganizations in family functioning. Accordingly, the strength and nature of pathways between/among the marital subsystem, the parent–child relationship, and children's adjustment are theorized to vary as a function of properties of the larger family unit (Grych, 2002; Minuchin, 1985; O'Connor, Hetherington, & Clingempeel, 1997). Interpreted in terms of EST conceptualizations, adult and child attachment insecurity processes may be particularly related to spillover across marital, parent–child, and child subsystems when adults are experiencing psychological and social vulnerabilities. As one illustration, Margolin and colleagues (2004) found that parental violence in the marital relationship potentiated the concurrent link between marital hostility and both paternal and maternal parenting difficulties (see also Floyd et al., 1998). Likewise, in our own research, we have found that the strength of associations between marital discord and subsequent changes in both mothers' and fathers' acceptance of their children varied depending on maternal depressive symptoms, maternal relationship insecurity, and child-rearing disagreements (Davies, Cummings, & Winter, 2004).

Family systems processes may also help to account for heterogeneity in associations between parenting difficulties and child attachment processes. For example, pathways between parenting difficulties and child adjustment may be stronger when adults are unable to fulfill their intimacy needs within the interparental relationship or exhibit overt displays of vulnerabilities in the presence of the children. In support of this hypothesis, clinical observations suggest that the dependency and distress underlying resistant attachment patterns serve a stabilizing function in some families by diverting attention away from serious interparental problems or fulfilling the intimacy needs of parents in disengaged marriages (Byng-Hall, 1999; Marvin & Stewart, 1990; Stevenson-Hinde, 1990).

However, not all family perturbations necessarily play a uniform role as moderators of these indirect paths. In still other cases, some family perturbations may dilute the role of parenting in predicting attachment by overriding or superseding its risk. For example, Raikes and Thompson (2005) reported that low parental sensitivity was only associated with greater attachment insecurity when toddlers were in homes characterized by high levels of emotional risk (e.g., anger, violence, instability). However, further inspection of the interaction revealed that high levels of family adversity did not buffer children from the risk associated with experiencing maternal insensitivity. Rather, the potent risk associated with negative family climate appeared to supplant the risk of maternal insensitivity in predicting attachment insecurity. Given that domestic violence and excessive family anger were the two most prevalent indices of the measure of negative family climate, the role of negative family climate as a powerful and unique predictor of attachment insecurity further underscores the viability of direct paths between broader interparental and family processes and children's security processes in the parent–child relationship (see Chapter 4 for more details).

Missing Ingredients?

The focus of family systems theory on capturing broader patterns of family functioning than traditional dyadic relationship constructs also highlights the possibility that indirect-path models may be missing key aspects of the parenting and socialization environment. For example, the interplay between marital discord and parenting difficulties may be further advanced by the study of coparenting relationship processes, or, more specifically, the ability of parents to serve as a cohesive team in rearing their children (Cowan & McHale, 1996; McHale, 1997; Sturge-Apple et al., 2006a, 2006b). The principle of interdependency in family systems theory postulates that spousal discord reflects a larger constellation of transactional influences with coparenting disturbances, as perturbations in any one subsystem reverberate through other family relationships in a negative reciprocal cycle (e.g., Cox et al, 2001; Minuchin, 1985; Westerman, 1987). For example, emotional difficulties with a spouse may be especially likely to be manifested in coparenting disruptions, as attempts to undermine the spouse's authority in the family may be a powerful way to seek retribution for perceived emotional injustices stemming from the interparental relationship.

In accord with these hypotheses, marital conflict has been associated with various disruptions in the ability of parents to coordinate childrearing activities, including disengagement, triangulation, hostility, and disparagement (e.g., Davies, Sturge-Apple, & Cummings, 2004; Floyd & Zmich, 1991; Katz & Gottman, 1996; McHale, 1995; McHale et al., 2004; Schoppe-Sullivan et al., 2004). Likewise, recent evidence suggests that competitive coparenting relations were uniquely associated with both mothers' and fathers' perceptions of infant attachment insecurity, even after statistical controls for several parent–child interaction properties and caregiver demographic characteristics (Caldera & Lindsey, 2006). In short, coparenting and broader family-level processes (e.g., disengagement, enmeshment) may be usefully conceptualized as distinct classes of socialization constructs that may play similar roles as mediators in the indirect paths between marital conflict and children's attachment insecurity and maladaptation.

CONCLUSION

The study of parenting as an explanatory mechanism in pathways between marital conflict and child adjustment is an important direction for research. However, identifying inherent characteristics of "bad parenting" as mediators of links between marital conflict and child adjustment is no longer ground-breaking. Research is needed to determine how and why parenting practices are mediators of the link between marital and child outcomes, and to identify the sources of variability in the strength of the pathways. Contemporary models of the interplay between marital conflict and parenting are largely based on relatively undeveloped post hoc theories that leave gaps regarding the question of why parenting problems may contribute to the link between marital conflict and child adjustment. Guided by EST, this chapter introduces conceptual bases for developing and testing a more satisfactory theory of indirect-effects pathways. We encourage other investigators to develop complementary models that will help to bridge the gap between theory and research in this area.

CHAPTER 6

Contextual Vulnerability and Protective Models

In broadening the scope of marital conflict models to include parenting and family-level processes, Chapter 5 provides some additional insight into the multiple ways difficulties between parents may be associated with child adjustment. Yet our treatment of associations between marital conflict and children's adjustment also highlights the significant variability among children exposed to very similar levels and forms of discord between their parents. Even with conceptual and methodological advances in precisely assessing multiple forms of marital conflict and their proposed explanatory mechanisms, the processes underlying marital conflict typically account for only a modest to moderate proportion of children's individual differences in their coping and psychological adjustment. For example, witnessing physical violence between parents is a particularly potent risk factor. In fact, children who are exposed to severe domestic violence are as much as seven times more likely to exhibit clinically significant behavior problems than are children in the general population (Cummings & Davies, 1994; McDonald & Jouriles, 1991). Yet it is also that case that most children from violent homes do not experience clinically significant levels of psychopathology at any one time (Hughes, 1997; Hughes, Graham-Bermann, & Gruber, 2001).

These observations raise a central question: Why do children exposed to similar conditions in the marital subsystem often develop so differently? To return to the two families introduced at the beginning of Part III, it is apparent that many other contextual factors beyond marital conflict and child reactivity to family stress may help to account for why children may experience distinct developmental outcomes, despite their exposure to similar patterns of conflict between parents (see also Jouriles, McDonald, Norwood, & Ezell, 2001; Jouriles, Spiller, Stephens, McDonald, & Swank, 2000). For example, the impact of marital conflict on children may ultimately depend on the types of relationships children form both inside and outside the family—and, at an even broader level, on neighborhood, community, and cultural factors. Conversely, moving toward more micro-level analysis—that is, identifying specific attributes of children (e.g., temperament, physiological characteristics)—can also assist in understanding the conditions under which the risk of exposure to marital conflict is most and least pronounced.

In this chapter, we explore the latest work on how contextual conditions and characteristics may help to inform individual differences in the nature and magnitude of associations between marital conflict and child functioning. These influences are described as "Characteristics of the Broader Family Unit" in Figure 2.2. The first part of the chapter addresses the multiple ways in which context may help to alter pathways between marital discord and child functioning. We specifically introduce a vulnerability and protection model from the developmental psychopathology literature, to provide a backdrop for understanding the different ways contextual factors may modify how marital conflict affects children. Using this model as an organizing framework, we focus in the remainder of the chapter on coverage of recent trends and future directions in research on three substantive domains related to the characteristics of the broader family as context: (1) children's intrapersonal attributes, (2) familial characteristics, and (3) ecological contexts. Consistent with our overarching emphasis on EST, we stress the utility of EST propositions in advancing an understanding of contextual factors.

A DEVELOPMENTAL PSYCHOPATHOLOGY MODEL OF RISK AND PROTECTION

From a developmental psychopathology perspective, individual development is regarded as operating within an open system characterized by an ongoing transactional interplay between an actively changing organism and a dynamic context (Cicchetti, 1993; Davies & Cicchetti, 2004; Granic & Hollenstein, 2003). As such, a derivative conceptualization is that the developmental pathways set in motion by marital conflict will lawfully vary as a function of the broader multilevel matrix of contextual characteristics. Accordingly, diversity of outcomes in the face of comparable patterns of risk is accepted as a basic component of any developmental psychopathology model. In fact, developmental psychopathologists use the term "multifinality" to reflect the expectation that exposure to a single risk factor, such as marital conflict, will result in a diverse set of developmental outcomes. Thus the developmental course of each child is unique because of the specific transactions between and among the child's prior and current experiences in family and ecological contexts, as well as his or her own attributes, resources, and histories of adaptation.

As moderators are particularly powerful and direct sources of heterogeneity in outcomes of children exposed to adversity, the identification of moderators is currently a thriving enterprise in the study of marital conflict. Distinctions between two specific classes of moderators are particularly useful in more precisely specifying the nature of moderating effects. On the one hand, "vulnerability factors" (also called "potentiating factors") are specific types of moderators that amplify the association between interparental conflict and child maladjustment. Thus the search for vulnerability factors can effectively answer two questions: Who is *most* at risk? And when is the risk *most* pronounced?

For example, it is possible that the relationship between marital conflict and poor child adjustment may be stronger for children with difficult temperaments. For illustrative purposes, Figure 6.1 provides a hypothetical graph of the role of difficult temperament as a vulnerability factor. The x- and y-axes reflect different levels of the proposed predictor (i.e., marital conflict) and outcome (i.e., child adjustment), respectively. Plotted within the graph are two lines representing the association between marital conflict and child adjustment for children with different temperaments. Both lines indicate that exposure to greater marital conflict is associated with poorer adjustment. However, there is a difference in the slope of the line for children with different temperamental characteristics. Specifically, the steeper slope of the solid line indicates that the magnitude of the relationship between marital conflict and poorer child adjustment is stronger for children with difficult temperamental characteristics. Thus the pattern of findings suggests that difficult child temperament is a potentiating factor: It amplifies the risk of exposure to marital conflict for children.

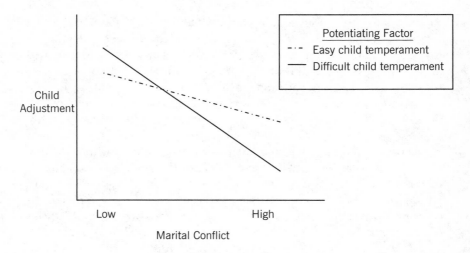

FIGURE 6.1. A hypothetical graph of difficult child temperament as a vulnerability factor moderating the association between marital conflict and child functioning.

On the other hand, "protective factors" or "buffers" are specific types of moderators that reduce or offset the risk associated with exposure to interparental discord. Consequently, the objective of identifying protective factors answers a pair of questions complementing the questions answered by the search for potentiating factors: Who is *least* at risk? And when is risk *least* pronounced? Figure 6.2 offers a hypothetical diagram of the protective effects of peer support. The two lines plotted within the diagram represent the association between marital conflict on the *x*-axis and child adjustment on the *y*-axis when children have high versus low levels of peer support. When we compare the slopes of the two lines, the slope of the solid line indicates that increasing exposure to marital conflict is associated with progressively lower adjustment when children experience low levels of peer support. Conversely, the high, flat slope of the broken line indicates that children who benefit from high levels of peer support also enjoy a high level of psychological adjustment, regardless of their level of exposure to marital conflict.

The protective factor in Figure 6.2 is so strong that it completely offsets the risk normally posed by marital conflict. The portion of the broken line circled in the figure represents a subgroup of children with high levels of exposure to interparental conflict. So they are experienc-

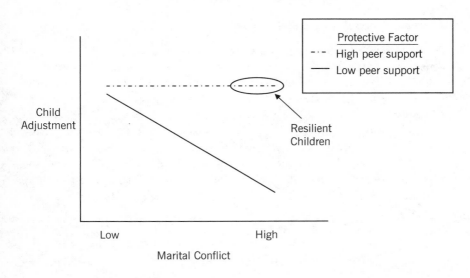

FIGURE 6.2. A hypothetical graph of peer support as a protective factor moderating the association between marital conflict and child functioning.

ing high levels of adversity or risk. But the key here is that they look no different in their rates of psychopathology from the children evidencing low risk. Rather, they are exhibiting a level of functioning similar to that of children who exhibit no problems at all. Thus this illustrates the operation of "resilience," or the ability of children to adapt fairly well despite exposure to considerable adversity. Although understanding resilience is a central task in understanding how marital conflict affects children, simply identifying a group of children who are relatively well adjusted despite their exposure to risk is not particularly valuable or satisfying in itself. The ultimate question that begs to be answered is this: Why are these children so resilient? Or, more specifically, what are the sources of their positive adjustment in the face of risk? The search for protective factors helps to identify these specific sources of resilience. For example, in the case of Figure 6.2, the children who are doing well in the context of high levels of marital conflict share a common benefit of high levels of peer support. Although tests of moderation are useful starting points for determining how contextual factors may inform models of marital conflict, further conceptual scope and precision are needed for a full understanding of how these factors operate.

Alternative Models of Contextual Factors

At the level of broadening the conceptual scope, tests of moderation must be balanced by the consideration of alternative models for the role of contextual characteristics in models of marital conflict. Figure 6.3 provides a visual depiction of three complementary ways in which contextual factors may inform multivariate frameworks of interparental conflict. Models 1 and 2 in Figure 6.3 illustrate that mediational pathways may best capture the interplay between interparental conflict and a given contextual characteristic in the prediction of child maladaptation. Because it is often plausible to interchange interparental conflict and many contextual characteristics in conceptual roles as mediators of

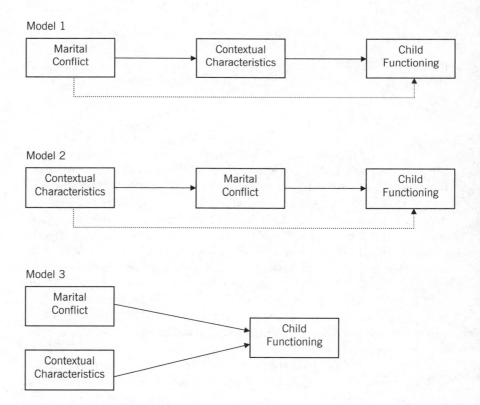

FIGURE 6.3. Conceptual models depicting alternative forms of interplay between marital conflict and contextual characteristics in the prediction of child functioning.

one another, precisely mapping the etiological pathways remains a critical challenge in the literature. Consistent with the indirect-path models
of parenting described in Chapter 5, the first model proposes that contextual attributes may reduce the strength of direct and indirect pathways by partially mediating or accounting for the effects of interparental conflict. Thus alternative contextual characteristics may also serve as
mechanisms that help to explain why children exposed to destructive
interparental conflict are at greater risk for developing psychopathology. In contrast, the second model postulates that contextual characteristics may influence child coping and adjustment indirectly, through
their associations with interparental conflict. Thus mediational pathways may be reversed; that is, interparental problems may be more proximal mediators of the more distal effects of contextual characteristics
on children's adjustment. For example, in Chapter 9 we discuss findings
from research on political violence and children in Northern Ireland, in
which interparental conflict is a more proximal mediator than community violence. The final model illustrates the possibility that mediational
or causal chains may not adequately reflect the nature of the relationship between interparental conflict and a particular contextual characteristic in predicting child maladaptation. Even though the two factors
may fail to explain one another's effects, the third model in Figure 6.3
indicates that interparental conflict and any given contextual risk can
still operate as unique predictors of children's functioning. Although
the ability of an additive contextual factor to explain the potency of
marital conflict as a risk factor is likely to be noticeably weaker than it
would be in a role as a mediator, it may still modestly weaken the magnitude of the link between marital conflict and child functioning in its
role as a rival predictor.

Multiple Dimensions of Vulnerability and Protection

At the level of conceptual precision, additional taxonomies have been
offered to increase specificity in distinguishing between protective and
vulnerability effects. In one of the more prominent taxonomies, Luthar
and colleagues draw important distinctions among types of protective
factors. Whereas the general term "protective factor" is reserved for
unique predictors of adjustment that have a beneficial effect on children
regardless of the level of risk, these researchers also specifically identify
three forms of protective effects that reflect moderation (Luthar, 1993;
Luthar & Cicchetti, 2000; Luthar, Cicchetti, & Becker, 2000). An "ameliorative protective effect" diminishes, but does not completely offset,

the potency of the vulnerability associated with interparental conflict. A "neutralizing protective effect" is even more pronounced, in the sense that marital conflict becomes benign at high levels of the protective factor. That is, associations between interparental conflict and child psychological problems, which are robust at low levels of the protective factor, actually evidence a negligible relationship at high levels of the protective factor. Finally, "enhancing protective effects" occur when higher levels of interparental conflict are actually associated with less symptomatology (or better adjustment), despite having harmful effects at low levels of the protective factor.

Classification schemes may also be useful in more richly and precisely characterizing the effects of vulnerability factors. For example, Luthar and colleagues (2000) distinguish between *vulnerable-stable* and *vulnerable-reactive* effects. The former reflects when a general disadvantage occurs when an attribute is present, despite changing levels of stress, whereas the latter occurs when the overall maladjustment with the attribute is greater at increasing levels of stress. Discriminating between what we term "active catalysts" and "inert catalysts" may further illustrate this point. Both types of factors catalyze risk, in the sense that they are moderators amplifying the link between processes in high-conflict homes and child maladjustment. However, the difference lies in their direct effects on the outcome. Whereas active catalytic agents have direct negative effects on children's outcomes, inert catalytic factors pose no direct risk for child adjustment on their own (e.g., Brown & Harris, 1978; Goodyer, 1990; Rutter, 1983). Why may this distinction be important? Well, in the case of an inert catalyst, a specific variable may look like a benign factor that has little or no power as a direct predictor of risk. Thus, on the surface, it may be overlooked as having little relevance to understanding how children develop psychological problems. Yet it does carry a more insidious peril for children who are exposed to high levels of marital conflict. That is, although it is harmless alone, its effects lurk deviously below the surface by compounding the risk of children from high-conflict homes. In contrast, an active catalytic agent is a more obvious and dangerous "double whammy" for children, because it serves as both a predictor of children's psychopathology and a moderator that excerbates the deleterious effects of marital discord. Despite the conceptual significance of such taxonomies and their successful application to several areas in developmental psychopathology, these fine-grained distinctions have yet to be integrated systematically into the study of marital conflict.

Summary

In summary, tests of moderation are among the most powerful ways to identify sources of variability in the outcomes of children from high-conflict homes. The value of a developmental psychopathology approach is that it helps to explicate the specific ways in which contextual factors may alter marital conflict processes as moderators, and at the same time offers alternative models for how such factors may alter children's security and adjustment as distal predictors, additive predictors, or mediators. In the rest of this chapter, we apply this framework to organizing findings on some of the central contextual characteristics in the study of marital conflict. In attempting to provide a parsimonious account of risk and protection that spans multiple topics in developmental psychopathology, Garmezy (1985) has offered a tripartite framework consisting of (1) child dispositional attributes, including temperament, personality, and gender; (2) family characteristics, including family climate, parenting practices, and parent psychopathology; and (3) extrafamilial characteristics, including friendships, community, and ethnicity/culture. For example, we show in Chapter 9 how factors at each of these levels relate to the influence of political violence on children in Northern Ireland. We selectively discuss below how these three classes of contextual factors may help to increase our knowledge about models of marital conflict. In keeping with the broader theme of this book, we specifically explore how EST can serve as a guide to identifying and interpreting organism–environment models of marital conflict.

CHILDREN'S INTRAPERSONAL ATTRIBUTES

As a fundamental class of moderator models, organism–environment or diathesis–stress models have been particularly valuable heuristics in exploring the role played by child characteristics in the wide range of outcomes among children exposed to marital conflict (e.g., Wachs, 1991; Windle & Tubman, 1999). The environmental or stress component of these models consists of exposure to dimensions of marital discord. The organism or diathesis component of these models includes such personological characteristics as temperament, behavioral dispositions, personality traits, and appraisal and attribution styles. Grounded in this broader framework, the original process-oriented model and more recent theoretical frameworks have stressed the importance of identifying children's intrapersonal attributes that may serve to potentiate or protect children from the effects of marital conflict (Cummings & Cummings, 1988; Davies & Cummings, 1994; Grych & Fincham, 1990). For illustrative purposes, we briefly address three types of personological characteristics: gender, temperament/personality, and physiological functioning (see Chapter 8 for information on the role of age).

Child Gender

It is difficult to draw any clear-cut, simple conclusions regarding the role of child gender in models of marital conflict. Large-sample studies and meta-analyses have largely failed to find support for the role of child gender as a moderator (e.g., Buehler et al., 1997; Jouriles, Bourg, et al., 1991; Kitzmann, Gaylord, Holt, & Kenny, 2003). Likewise, when studies do report that gender is a significant moderator of marital conflict, the findings do not uniformly indicate that either gender is necessarily more vulnerable to marital conflict (Davies & Linsday, 2001). Adding to the complexity, even studies from the same laboratory often yield very different findings. For example, in one study supporting a female vulnerability hypothesis, marital conflict was associated with lower levels of peer interactions only for girls (David & Murphy, 2007). Yet the results of another study by the same investigators could be interpreted as supporting a male vulnerability model, because marital conflict in this study was associated with greater distress reactions to adult conflict only for boys (David & Murphy, 2004).

So this raises a critical question: What role, if any, does child gender play as a moderator of marital discord? The most parsimonious interpretation is that it does little to explain variability in the outcomes of children exposed to marital conflict. It is plausible that the sparse, complex, and sometimes contradictory findings are simply happenstance artifacts of the large number of gender analyses that have been reported in the literature. The null findings on gender as a moderator in the meta-analytic studies adds credence to this interpretation.

However, prior meta-analyses have been limited in their predominant focus on bivariate relationships between marital conflict and global child adjustment measures (e.g., internalizing and externalizing symptoms). Therefore, an alternative interpretation is that a more fine-grained process analysis of the intervening mechanisms linking marital conflict with global child adjustment measures might reveal previously undiscovered gender differences in the risk posed by marital conflict. That is, gender might operate more consistently as a moderator in links between (1) marital conflict and children's reactivity to conflict, and/or

(2) children's reactivity to conflict and their psychological adjustment (Davies & Lindsay, 2001). Still, although it is premature to discard child gender from models of marital conflict, work on EST does not point to gender as being a primary source of variability in children's vulnerability to marital conflict. For example, EST does not completely ignore child gender. Yet gender is not conceptually regarded as a central moderator of individual differences in the mediational role played by emotional security in the links between marital conflict and child outcomes. In other words, although expressions of insecurity may end up differing as a function of child gender, there is no theoretical reason at this point to expect that one gender should be more inherently vulnerable than the other to difficulties in preserving security. In support of this assumption, mediational pathways involving emotional security have not varied significantly as a function of child gender in the major empirical tests reported in the literature (e.g., Cummings, Schermerhorn, et al., 2006; Davies & Forman, 2002; Davies, Harold, et al., 2002; Davies, Sturge-Apple, et al., 2006; DuRocher Schudlich & Cummings, 2007; El-Sheikh et al., 2008; Harold et al., 2004). Thus, even though some studies do find that boys and girls differ in their tendency to experience some signs of insecurity's (Davies & Lindsay, 2001), these main effects do not appear to translate into insecurity playing a stronger mediating role in marital conflict models for one gender than for the other.

In spite of the paucity of evidence for the role of gender as a moderator of emotional security pathways, the predominance of null or weak findings may result from several problems in the literature. In reviewing the literature on gender and marital conflict, Snyder (1998) noted that "recent gender findings are often packaged within studies not designed to examine them specifically and seem to have been accumulating in the 'background' of research on marital conflict and child adjustment" (p. 392). Unfortunately, this observation is nearly as applicable today as it was over a decade ago, because repeated calls to integrate gender more fully into models of marital conflict have largely been ignored in favor of explicating the role of family processes as contextual factors (Davies & Lindsay, 2001; Snyder, 1998). An all-too-common result is a research design that does not have sufficient statistical power to test authoritatively the role of gender in the very quantitatively demanding multivariate blends of mediator and moderator models.

In fact, even larger samples and more sensitive measurement batteries and research designs may be necessary to uncover potential gender differences in child vulnerability to marital conflict. For example, it is possible that gender moderates links between exposure to specific parameters of marital conflict (e.g., gender of parent, mode of conflict expression) and children's responses to such conflict (e.g., Crockenberg & Forgays, 1996; Shelton et al., 2006). Likewise, the moderating role of gender may vary as a function of developmental period. According to the "gender intensification" hypothesis, the increasing physical differentiation between boys and girls is paralleled by increasing differentiation and development of gender roles (Hill & Lynch, 1983). As a consequence, girls are socialized into valuing close interpersonal relations and emotional connectedness, especially in family relationships. In turn, this greater concern and preoccupation with maintaining harmonious family relations may increase girls' sensitivity to interparental conflict and cause them to react more negatively to it than boys do (Davies & Lindsay, 2004; Davies & Windle, 1997). In support of this premise, Davies and Lindsay (2004) found that stronger pathways between marital conflict and internalizing symptoms in early adolescence for girls than for boys was largely explained by the girls' tendency to experience high levels of interpersonal connectedness.

However, numerous unresolved questions remain. If adolescent girls' heightened vulnerability to marital conflict is mediated by their greater communal tendencies, why are pathways between marital conflict and emotional security not stronger for girls? One possibility is that boys and girls may experience different circumstances and exhibit different responses, which cumulatively make neither gender more or less susceptible to the antecedents or consequences of insecurity. For example, the heightened interpersonal connectedness experienced by girls may be interpreted as increasing their sensitivity and reactivity to marital conflict, and ultimately their concerns about their emotional security (Davies & Lindsay, 2004). Yet this may be offset by boys' tendencies to exhibit heightened agency or interest in the self (Helgeson, 1994). In the context of repeated exposure to marital conflict, boys may exhibit comparable levels of emotional insecurity, due to their greater focus on self-protection. Consistent with this interpretation, David and Murphy (2004) reported that perceptions of marital conflict in late adolescence differentially predicted specific dimensions of insecurity in subsequent interadult conflicts as a function of gender: Whereas boys experienced greater self-reported distress, girls were more likely to develop pessimistic representations of the relationship implications of the adult conflict.

Another possibility is that the same gender-differentiated characteristic may have both protective and vulnerability functions that counteract each other. For example, high levels of interpersonal connectedness may potentiate the mediational role of emotional security for girls by amplifying their reactivity to discord. Yet, by the same token, the greater interpersonal sensitivity and social skills that underlie greater connectedness may permit girls to identify the source of adversity more readily and to enlist more effective strategies for processing and coping with conflict. In sum, future progress in identifying the role of gender as a contextual factor will hinge on the development and testing of more fine-grained and complex models.

Child Temperament and Personality

EST hypothesizes that dimensions of temperament and personality function as both potentiating and protective factors in associations between interparental conflict and children's coping and adjustment (Davies & Cummings, 1994). Dimensions of temperament specifically reflect individual differences in characteristic ways of behaving that are largely constitutional in origin, emerge early in life, and evidence relatively high stability across time and context. Because individual differences in temperament are by definition relatively resistant (though not immune) to the effects of environmental factors, temperament is regarded as a better candidate for serving as a moderator or unique predictor than as a mediator in pathways between marital conflict and child functioning.

Consistent with this premise, initial empirical tests of this hypothesis have revealed that some dimensions of temperament serve as moderators in associations between marital discord and child adjustment. At this early stage of research, temperamental indices reflecting the abilities to flexibly shift and focus attention (i.e., "attentional control") and to forestall dominant responses in favor of more adaptive subdominant responses (i.e., "effortful control") have been most consistently identified as protective factors in models of marital conflict. For example, Davies and Windle (2001) found that task orientation, which is an index of attentional control, may have a neutralizing protective effect by serving to offset the heightened risk of adolescents exposed to marital discord (Luthar et al., 2000). Whereas marital discord was a significant predictor of subsequent delinquency and depressive symptoms for adolescents who exhibited poor task orientation, associations between marital discord and these outcomes were negligible for teens with good task orientation.

In fact, there is even some evidence to suggest that effortful control may, in the terminology of Luthar and colleagues (2000), have "enhancing" protective effects. David and Murphy (2007) specifically found that marital conflict was only associated with problematic peer relationships for preschoolers who exhibited low levels of effortful control. In contrast, an opposite relationship between marital conflict and poor peer relationships was found for children who were high in effortful control. That is, exposure to marital conflict actually predicted lower levels of problems in peer interactions when children were high in effortful control. If this finding is replicated in future research, it would suggest that children with high levels of effortful control may actually thrive in the face of higher levels of adversity. Thus, consistent with challenge models, even elevated levels of marital conflict may be relatively mild or manageable challenges that may precipitate the development of a wider repertoire of coping strategies (Davies & Cummings, 2006). The key qualification, however, is that this type of steeling or toughening is only applicable for children who already demonstrate a capacity to regulate behavior through high levels of effortful control.

However, findings on the moderating role of child temperament and personality attributes are far from resolved. A primary unresolved issue is whether major dimensions of difficult temperament actually serve as potentiating or vulnerability factors in models of marital conflict. For example, whereas some studies find support for the role of infant negative emotionality as a vulnerability factor that exacerbates the negative effects of marital conflict (e.g., Pauli-Pott & Beckmann, 2007), other studies do not support the role of distress as a moderator of marital discord (e.g., Crockenberg, Leerkes, & Lekka, 2007). Likewise, examining a multidimensional composite of "difficult temperament" (i.e., negative mood, rigidity, withdrawal) as a moderator in associations between marital discord and adolescent adjustment did not yield any significant findings (Davies & Windle, 2001). Thus cataloguing the occurrence and nature of moderating effects across the full range of temperament and personality characteristics in models of marital conflict remains a central task (David & Murphy, 2004).

As knowledge of these moderating effects accumulates, understanding why children with certain dispositions are more vulnerable to marital discord will also be a critical research objective. An overarching assumption of EST is that difficulties in temperament and personality may potentiate the risk of marital conflict by progressively amplifying difficulties in children's ability to preserve a sense of security in high-conflict homes (Davies & Windle, 2001). First, children with difficult temperament and personality attributes may exhibit progressively greater sensitivity and emotional reactivity with repeated exposure to marital conflict. Thus difficult temperament may serve as a vulnerability factor that magnifies links between marital conflict and signs of emotional insecurity (e.g., negative emotional reactivity). Second, various psychological attributes may also prompt children to rely on narrow, rigid, and maladaptive ways of coping with interparental conflict (Grych & Fincham, 1990). These attributes—such as inflexibility in the face of changing environmental events, proclivity to experience negative moods, and poor attentional focus—may directly compromise their ability to regulate their emotional reactivity, and ultimately their ability to achieve a sense of security in the marital relationship. In research supporting the potential operation of these mechanisms, David and Murphy (2004) showed that the association between exposure to marital conflict in late adolescence and greater distress in response to simulated adult conflicts was particularly pronounced for individuals who experienced difficulties in regulating their emotions. Third, it is possible that transactional processes are operating: Difficult child temperaments may tax already fragile family relationships, and the resulting exposure to greater family conflict may further fuel children's insecurity (Davies & Cummings, 1994; Davies & Windle, 2001). Precisely pinpointing the mechanisms that explain or mediate the moderating effects of temperamental and psychological attributes will be critical in future research.

Child Physiological Attributes

Multiple-levels-of-analysis models in developmental psychopathology underscore that children's individual differences may be manifested not only in behavioral or psychological processes, but also in physiological functioning. Because there are so many dimensions and domains of physiological responding, a central ongoing task in research is to identify the specific roles and functions of each physiological component in links between marital conflict and child adjustment. On the one hand, there is a consensus that many distinct systems of physiological functioning (e.g., the SNS, PNS, and LHPA; see Chapter 4) share the characteristic of environmental sensitivity. As such, these systems all exhibit reactivity in some form to at least some types of environmental stressors. Yet they may differ substantially in the plasticity of their responses to cumulative environmental events over more prolonged periods.

At one extreme on the continuum of system plasticity, some physiological substrates may be constitutional processes that develop early in life, are highly stable over time, and are relatively resistant to the impact of family stress (Katz, 2001). Thus biological differences may serve as predictors of child adjustment in and of themselves in models of marital conflict. Moreover, consistent with organism–environment models, these types of physiological indices may best be regarded as moderators that alter the risk posed by marital conflict. At the other extreme of the plasticity continuum, coherent patterns of individual differences in other physiological attributes may emerge over time as functions of exposure to different histories of marital conflict. Thus these physiological systems may be more dynamic, flexible, and open to change. In accordance with allostatic load models, such assumptions lead to the notion that repeated exposure to marital conflict may undermine children's psychological functioning by creating wear and tear on physiological systems. Notably, because biological plasticity is viewed as occurring along a continuum, moderating and mediating functions of biological systems in models of marital conflict need not be mutually exclusive.

At this early stage of research, the best illustration of a biological system with low biological plasticity to family adversity is the vagal system. In support of organism–environment frameworks, vagal tone and vagal regulation are two indices of physiological functioning that have been most consistently identified as moderators of marital conflict. As reflections of the hardiness of the PNS (see Appendix D for details), higher vagal tone and greater vagal regulation (i.e., suppression of vagal tone during stress or challenge) are conceptualized as components of emotion regulation. Consistent with this assumption, high vagal tone and vagal regulation in response to interpersonal stressors (e.g., interadult conflict) are consistently associated with more optimal physical, emotional, and social functioning in children (e.g., Eisenberg et al., 1996; El-Sheikh et al., 2001; Gottman & Katz, 1989; Porges, Doussard-Roosevelt, Portales, & Greenspan, 1996). Moreover, the protective function of high vagal tone and vagal regulation for children from high-conflict homes is now well documented (i.e., El-Sheikh et al., 2001; El-Sheikh & Whitson, 2006; Katz & Gottman, 1995, 1997a, 1997b). In the terminology of Luthar and colleagues (2000), this form of protective effect is most commonly characterized as either (1) "ameliorative," reflecting a partial, but not full, diminution, in the risk associated with marital conflict; or (2) "neutralizing," as evidenced by negligible risk for children who have high levels of vagal tone. However, at this stage of the research, the conditions that might account for variations in the power of vagal tone as a protective factor (i.e., neutralizing vs. ameliorative) have yet to be systematically identified.

In the middle portion of the biological plasticity continuum, other physiological indices appear to function as both mediators and moderators. For example, skin conductance reactivity (SCR) is emerging as a robust, albeit complex, moderator of links between family adversity and child adjustment (e.g., Cummings et al., 2007; El-Sheikh, 2005; El-Sheikh, Keller, & Erath, 2007). Research by El-Sheikh and colleagues specifically showed that a high level of SCR to interadult conflict appeared to serve as a vulnerability factor in associations between marital conflict and both concurrent and subsequent adjustment problems for girls. In the terminology of Luthar and colleagues (2000), the form of the moderation most closely resembled a "reactive" vulnerability effect: SCR magnified the associations between marital conflict and a host of physical and mental health difficulties (El-Sheikh, 2005; El-Sheikh, Keller, et al., 2007). However, for boys, SCR largely failed to serve as a moderator in either study. In fact, the single significant interaction involving boys' SCR reflected a different form of moderation, characterized by Luthar and colleagues as a "stable" vulnerability pattern: Boys with *lower* levels of SCR exhibited high levels of externalizing symptoms, regardless of their level of exposure to marital conflict. Moreover, consistent with the allostatic load model and the potential plasticity of the SNS (Cicchetti, 2002; Katz, 2001; Repetti et al., 2002; Susman, 2006), SCR to interadult anger mediated the link between marital conflict and internalizing symptoms for boys.

Still other physiological systems may be characterized as further along the continuum of biological plasticity. LHPA functioning may be one system in which individual differences are forged over time through differential exposure to psychosocial adversity. For example, such forms of family discord as parental withdrawal, dysphoria, stress, and severe types of maltreatment (e.g., co-occurrence of physical and sexual abuse) have demonstrated associations with individual differences in cortisol activity (Cicchetti & Rogosch, 2001; Essex, Klein, Cho, & Kalin, 2002; Field et al., 2001; Gunnar & Vazquez, 2001; Heim, Ehlert, & Hellhammer, 2000; Pine & Charney, 2002). Similarly, the little research conducted on the interplay between marital conflict and children's cortisol functioning has indicated that marital difficulties are associated, albeit complexly, with individual differences in children's cortisol levels. For example, greater marital difficulties have been associated with *higher* daily levels (i.e., "baseline" levels) of cortisol (Pendry & Adam, 2007; Saltzman et al., 2005). However, the role of cortisol functioning in models of marital conflict may be different when cortisol reactivity to stressors is considered. For example, emerging evidence suggests that children's *diminished* cortisol reactivity to conflict between parents is an intervening mechanism in the link between such conflict and subsequent increases in externalizing symptoms (Davies et al., 2007). Similarly, at least one study suggests that dampened cortisol functioning may also serve as a vulnerability factor that amplifies associations between family conflict and child maladjustment/health problems (El-Sheikh et al., 2008).

Although empirical identification of physiological dimensions in studies of marital conflict over the last decade attests to the promise of a multiple-levels-of-analysis approach to understanding the effects of marital conflict, it is still unclear how these processes map onto psychological processes of security. Therefore, we believe that it is no longer enough simply to continue cataloguing the moderating and mediating roles of physiological processes in models of marital conflict, without simultaneous consideration of the broader pattern of children's psychological functioning. For example, it is possible that higher levels of vagal functioning and vagal suppression may reflect constitutional differences in children's abilities to preserve their emotional security in the interparental relationship. Thus, in efforts to map "psychological" meaning onto *psycho*physiological activity, EST may explain or account for the moderating effects of vagal functioning in associations between marital conflict and child adjustment. EST may also help to contextualize the study of more plastic physiological systems. For example, cortisol activity and reactivity may serve as intermediary processes in pathways between marital conflict and child adjustment because they are part of a large system of responses reflecting individual differences in the experience of insecurity in the interparental relationship. Invoking psychological theory as a guide in further interpreting and contextualizing models of physiological functioning is likely to facilitate a new, exciting direction of work on marital conflict.

FAMILY ATTRIBUTES

Individual differences in children's experiences within the larger family system may also help to explain the heterogeneity of children's outcomes in high-conflict homes. However, unlike many of the dimensions of intrapersonal attributes (e.g., gender, age), family characteristics may play key roles as both moderators and mediators of child adjustment. For the sake of brevity, we illustrate the utility of adopting a family systems approach by limiting our scope to illustrative examples of parenting practices and broader family-level processes. However, as the description of the parental psychopathology and community processes identified in the Northern Ireland research (see Chapter 9) highlights, it is important to bear in mind that many other familial and extrafamil-ial characteristics are likely to play key roles in developmental psychopa-thology models of marital conflict.

Parenting Practices and Parent–Child Relations

Considerable evidence for the role of parenting variables as mediators of marital conflict (e.g., Cowan, Cohn, et al., 1996; Fauber et al., 1990; Gonzales, Pitts, Hill, & Roosa, 2000; Harold, Fincham, Osborne, & Conger, 1997) does not rule out the possibility that a substantial subset of parenting variables may serve as protective or vulnerability factors. From an EST perspective, such a prediction is certainly viable. The sup-port and safety afforded by good parent–child relationships have been hypothesized to buffer children from the effects of interparental con-flict. Likewise, children who must grapple with both marital discord and parenting difficulties may face a "double whammy" that exponentially increases their psychological burdens and distress. Yet the predominant focus on exclusively testing parenting practices as mediators, without balanced consideration of their possible roles as protective or vulner-ability factors, leaves the issue open to considerable theoretical specula-tion.

Important questions remain about whether specific dimensions of parenting or parent–child relationships may be best conceptualized as possessing (1) broad power as unique predictors of outcomes across a wide range of marital conflict conditions, (2) effects as moderators that magnify or attenuate associations between marital conflict and child functioning, or (3) some blend of the two functions. Some dimensions of parenting do not appear to vary as a function of experiences with even very severe marital difficulties, in the form of violence and bat-tering (e.g., Katz & Windecker-Nelson, 2006; Rossman & Rea, 2005). However, when results do not support the role of parenting dimensions as mediators, many such dimensions do continue to predict child out-comes even after the role of marital conflict as a predictor is taken into account (Frosch & Mangelsdorf, 2001; Rossman & Rea, 2005). Thus these findings suggest that some parenting variables may confer broad protective or vulnerability effects that forecast children's functioning, regardless of the children's level of exposure to marital problems.

Evidence is also emerging to support the role of various parenting dimensions as moderators of marital conflict. However, given the early stage of this research, the forms of these moderating effects require further specification and are likely to vary in complex ways, depending on the dimension of parenting under consideration. For example, parental "emotion coaching" (characterized by attempts to help children identify, process, and cope with negative affect) was identified as a neutralizing protective factor. In contrast to the significant associations between domestic violence and child psychological problems in families low in emotion coaching, domestic violence was unrelated to child psychological problems when parents engaged in high levels of emotion coaching (Katz & Windecker-Nelson, 2006). Findings by Frosch and Mangelsdorf (2001) further highlight the possibility that more global forms of parenting (i.e., warm vs. hostile, instrusive parenting) may alter associations between marital conflict and child adjustment in different ways. In reflecting an enhancing protective effect, higher levels of marital conflict were actually associated with lower levels of symptomatology for children whose parents were high in warmth. Children who experienced low levels of parental warmth exhibited relatively high levels of behavior problems, regardless of their level of exposure to marital conflict. Within the taxonomy of Luthar and colleagues (2000), maternal hostile parenting most closely resembles a reactive vulnerability factor. In particular, associations between marital conflict and children's psychological problems were particularly pronounced for children who also faced high levels of maternal hostility and intrusiveness.

In future research cataloguing parenting and parent–child relations as moderators in the outcomes of children, an important task will involve integrating theory as a guide to addressing the question of why the risk of exposure to marital conflict varies across childrearing conditions. EST specifically posits that parenting difficulties may alter the risk of marital conflict by heightening children's sensitivity and reactivity to conflict. The moderator component of this general assumption is that children are particularly likely to regard marital conflict as a threat to their security when they have no opportunity to gain support from attachment figures in times of stress (Davies, Harold, et al., 2002). However, in considering the additive component of the assumption, it is important to understand whether parenting may also serve as a direct predictor (not just a moderator) of children's security concerns about the marital relationship. Parenting difficulties in themselves undermine the necessary building blocks for efficiently preserving a sense of security in the face of interparental problems; they take a serious toll on the development of emotion regulation skills, self-confidence, and self-efficacy in children (Davies & Cummings, 2006).

If these two assumptions are correct, then they may highlight the significance of at least some forms of parenting difficulties as "active catalysts" (e.g., Brown & Harris, 1978; Goodyer, 1990; Rutter, 1983). As we have noted earlier in this chapter, this designation should not be regarded lightly, as it indicates that these specific parenting practices have a particularly damaging double effect—directly increasing the vulnerability of children, and also catalyzing the risk of marital conflict. In empirical tests of parenting difficulties, such difficulties (including extreme forms of problems) have been shown to uniquely predict signs of children's insecurity in the face of adult conflict. For example, comparisons of abused and nonabused children have revealed that abused children may be particularly sensitive to interadult conflict, as evidenced by greater fear, aggression, and intervention (Cummings et al., 1994; Hennessy et al., 1994). Likewise, more subtle forms of parenting difficulties (reflected in low levels of parental warmth) are also associated with higher levels of child-reported negative emotional reactivity to interparental conflict, even after prior histories of exposure to marital conflict are taken into account (Davies, Sturge-Apple, et al., 2006). Direct tests of moderator models have also indicated that signs of insecurity (i.e., greater perceptions of threat, diminished coping efficacy, higher anxiety, and greater involvement in parental conflicts) are especially pronounced when children experience high levels of interparental and parent–child aggression (Gordis, Margolin, & John, 1997; Grych, 1998).

However, EST does not rule out the possibility that parenting difficulties may moderate marital conflict in other ways. For example, extreme parenting perturbations in the form of maltreatment may overwhelm children's coping capacities in some family contexts and thus override any deleterious effects posed by interparental conflict (Sternberg et al., 1993). Moderating effects under these conditions would be more than likely to assume the stable vulnerability pattern described by Luthar and colleagues (2000). The overriding toll of forms of maltreatment would specifically be evident in stable levels of elevated insecurity across both high and low levels of exposure to marital conflict. Reflecting the other component of the interaction, marital conflict would only exhibit a dose–response relationship with insecurity in the absence of maltreatment.

If insecurity in family relationships coalesces over time into symptomatology, as EST suggests, then a next important step for research is to trace the moderating effects of parent–child relationship properties across the intersection of processes and outcomes (e.g., symptomatology) in greater detail (Appel & Holden, 1998; Hotaling, Straus, & Lincoln, 1990). EST provides a rich set of predictions about how the implications of children's emotional security for their subsequent psychological problems may vary, depending on their experiences with childrearing (Davies, Harold, et al., 2002; Davies, Winter, & Cicchetti, 2006). Children's worries about marital problems are specifically likely to take a toll on their psychological adjustment when they must contend with disengaged or rejecting parents and significant doubts about the availability of their parents in times of distress. The only study to test this hypothesis (Davies, Harold, et al., 2002) found that associations between insecurity in the interparental relationship and early adolescent maladjustment were significantly more pronounced when a child experienced high, rather than low, levels of parenting difficulties and parent–child relationship insecurity.

Family-Level Characteristics

Building a familywide model of emotional security also necessitates moving beyond the study of parenting processes and toward understanding marital conflict within the broader constellation of family processes. Accordingly, family systems theory, with its focus on processes in the broader family unit, may serve as a useful heuristic for integrating the study of marital conflict in the broader family context. According to the principle of "holism" in family systems theory, the meaning of any perturbation in a specific family relationship or subsystem cannot be fully deciphered without an understanding of the relationship structures, boundaries, power distributions, and communication patterns of the other family subsystems and the whole family unit (Cox & Paley, 1997; Davies & Cicchetti, 2004). Thus, within our familywide model, the impact of marital conflict on children's emotional security and adjustment is assumed to depend in part on the quality of the larger family system. For example, marital conflict may assume a more benign meaning for children in the context of cohesive, autonomy-supportive relationships in the family. Conversely, the deleterious effects of marital conflict on children may be amplified by family processes that reflect high levels of discord, chaos, and disengagement.

Consistent with this notion, Davies and colleagues (2004) reported that high levels of interparental discord served as the common denominator in two higher-order profiles of relationship functioning across interparental, coparental, and parent–child subsystems. Specifically, disengaged families experienced overly rigid, inflexible, and distant relationship boundaries that were manifested in high levels of family discord, hostility, and detachment across family subsystems; enmeshed families exhibited weak boundaries across family subsystems, and as a result displayed high levels of conflict, hostility, and psychological control. In comparison to children from cohesive families, who experienced warmth, affection, and flexible but well-defined boundaries in family relationships, children from enmeshed families showed elevated signs of insecurity in the interparental relationship across all five assessment domains (i.e., behavioral distress, behavioral avoidance, threat appraisals, involvement impulses, and subjective distress). Children from disengaged families also exhibited higher levels of insecurity in the interparental relationship, but the signs of insecurity were largely confined to subjective rather than behavioral indices (e.g., threat appraisals, involvement impulses) of responding to marital difficulties. Further embedding the study of family boundaries in mediational models of children's symptomatology was the finding that emotional security was a consistent mediator in the links between family enmeshment or disengagement and children's internalizing and externalizing symptoms.

Identification of more specific dimensions of family characteristics has also proven fruitful in informing an understanding of children's adaptation to marital conflict, particularly within an EST perspective. From the children's perspective, signs of broader family vulnerabilities may indicate that marital conflict is more likely to disrupt family functioning and threaten the children's well-being. For example, the confluence of marital conflict with other family-level risk factors may increase the likelihood that marital hostility will spill over into parent–child relationships. In research supporting this assumption, "family instability," which is defined as the degree to which families fail to provide continuity, cohesiveness, and stability for children, has been shown to potentiate associations between marital conflict and children's insecurity (Davies, Harold, et al., 2002). Another, though rarely tested, possibility is that family-level risk factors may create a "double whammy" for children by not only sensitizing their security concerns when they are faced with high levels of marital conflict, but also magnifying the toll insecurity takes on for their long-term adjustment outcomes.

However, it is also important to refrain from overpathologizing marital conflict. Under some family conditions, high levels of marital conflict may not necessarily translate into greater insecurity or adjustment problems for children. Thus an ongoing challenge is to identify the family conditions that may help to counteract the risk posed by marital conflict and children's concerns about insecurity. For example, high rates of positive affect or support in the context of anger and conflict may reduce children's emotional insecurity, thereby "freeing" them to reach a better understanding of how people manage and resolve disputes. Prior evidence suggests that perceptions of family support protected children who were exposed to marital discord from developing psychopathology (Davies & Windle, 2001). From the standpoint of EST, a key question is whether support or cohesion in the broader family unit helps to attenuate the pathways between (1) marital conflict and children's insecurity, (2) children's insecurity and their maladjustment, or (3) both. Although few studies have explored these questions, one study (Davies, Harold, et al., 2002) suggested that family cohesion may safeguard children against risk by reducing the probability that children's concerns about security in the interparental relationship will crystallize into broader forms of psychological maladjustment. Whereas family cohesion did not moderate associations between marital conflict and children's insecurity, associations between insecurity and their maladjustment were significantly lower in magnitude for children who experienced high levels of family cohesion.

In the overall analysis, we still know relatively little about the joint influence of marital conflict and family-level processes on children's security and adaptation. Future advances will depend on expanding the scope of inquiry in two ways. First, casting a broader net in testing the role of family processes will help extend the knowledge base on family system processes. For example, EST has proposed that marital conflict may be less threatening to children if it is simply part of a larger tendency for parents to express both positive and negative affect in the family (Davies & Cummings, 1994). Yet this proposition remains largely untested. The only study that has examined it, to our knowledge, did find some indirect support for it in demonstrating that associations between marital conflict and children's insecurity were significantly weaker when parents exhibited high levels of expressiveness in the marital relationship (Davies, Harold, et al., 2002). Moreover, advances in the conceptualization and assessment of family-level, triadic, and sibling processes will provide fruitful opportunities to embed the study of the effects of marital conflict within the family system (e.g., Cummings & Davies, 2002; Grych, Raynor, & Fosco, 2004; Leary & Katz, 2004; McHale, 2007).

Second, it will be useful to provide a broader account of children's security in the family unit. Simultaneous consideration of children's security across multiple family relationships may offer one fruitful step in this direction (e.g., Davies, Harold, et al., 2002; Sturge-Apple et al., 2008). For example, in extending the notion of holism in family systems theory, familywide conceptualizations of children's security also assume that children's security in the whole family unit cannot be fully captured by the aggregate of assessments of security within each of the family relationships. Thus new models and assessment tools are now available for exploring children's overall evaluation of their whole family units as sources of threat and security (Forman & Davies, 2003, 2005). Reflecting the potential significance of this research direction, appraisals of security in the family unit as a whole uniquely predict children's psychological symptoms, even after controls for children's insecurity in specific family relationships (Forman & Davies, 2005).

ECOLOGICAL CONTEXTS

In an editorial statement for the *Journal of Family Psychology* over a decade ago, Parke (1998) noted that "one of the major challenges over the next decade is to better understand the interplay between family and other social systems" (p. 4). However, despite additional calls for contextualizing the study of family and developmental processes within broader ecological settings (e.g., Garcia Coll, 2005; Kazak, 2004), progress in integrating ecological factors into the study of marital conflict has been slow.

Race, Ethnicity, and Culture

Although families in different cultures and subcultures may exhibit both similar and distinct family dynamics (Parke, 2000), we still know very little about interrelations between marital conflict and children's coping and adjustment in cultural groups other than middle-class European Americans (Lindahl, Malik, Kaczynski, & Simons, 2004). Race or ethnicity, which may be considered a rough proxy for various cultural differences, may provide a useful way of understanding the specificity and universality of process relations between marital conflict and child adjustment. For example, McLoyd, Harper, and Copeland (2001) have hypothesized that Hispanic and African American children may be less susceptible to interparental conflict, because extended family networks increase children's access to sources of support, and cultural norms serve to limit the proliferation of anger into the broader family system. From this perspective, the mediational role of parenting processes and children's emotional security may be regarded as more (or only) applicable to European American families. In support of this possibility, ethnic specificity in spillover of family stress has been documented by stronger associations between family stress and family conflict in European American families than in Hispanic families (Barrera, Li, & Chassin, 1995). Moreover, authoritarian styles of parenting, characterized by low warmth and high levels of control, are stronger and more consistent predictors of psychological adjustment problems in European American families than in Hispanic and African American families (Lindahl & Malik, 1999).

At the same time, it is premature to conclude that the direct- and indirect-path components of EST are necessarily stronger or more applicable to families of specific races or ethnicities, for three primary reasons. First, studies that more closely capture the specific pathways outlined in EST do not readily support the role of ethnicity or race as a moderator. The only direct test of the role of race as a moderator of emotional security indicated that pathways among marital conflict, children's emotional insecurity, and their psychological symptoms did not vary for African American and European American families (El-Sheikh et al., 2008). Likewise, associations between dimensions of marital conflict and children's reactivity and adjustment evidence more similarities than differences in comparisons of (1) Mexican American and European American families (Tschann, Flores, Pasch, & Marin, 1999; however, see Buehler et al., 1998, for evidence of differences), and (2) Chilean and European American families (Cummings, Wilson, & Shamir, 2003). Finally, parenting-as-mediator models of marital conflict are remarkably similar across studies that have independently utilized samples of predominantly middle-class European American families and samples of multiethnic low-income families (Fauber et al., 1990; Gonzales et al., 2000; Lindahl et al., 2004); such studies thereby fail to support the hypothesis that the effects of marital conflict may vary across ethnicity or race.

Second, although studies of race and ethnicity provide convenient starting points for the study of culture, they are unrefined markers of more central psychocultural processes. Thoroughly examining the applicability of EST across cultural or subcultural conditions will require a new generation of research that is designed to directly capture relevant cultural and subcultural processes. Expectations that family processes have different developmental implications across races or ethnicities are commonly predicated on the assumption that there are differences in cultural beliefs. For example, greater emphasis on the importance of the family over individual interests (i.e., *familismo*) and on respect for self and others (i.e., *respeto*) in Hispanic families than in non-Hispanic families may change the meaning of marital processes for families and children (Halgunseth, Ispa, & Rudy, 2006; Lindahl et al., 2004; McLoyd et al., 2001). Yet research on marital conflict has rarely, if ever, directly assessed such culturally rooted beliefs. Moreover, wide variability in the adoption of specific cultural beliefs within any given racial or ethnic group should serve as a reminder that race and ethnicity are not synonymous with culture and resulting beliefs (e.g., Cabrera, Shannon, West, & Brooks-Gunn, 2006; Halgunseth et al., 2006).

Third, as complex, socially constructed designations, race, ethnicity, and culture often co-occur with other ecological characteristics, including economic and community factors, family structure, and racial and ethnic discrimination (McLoyd et al., 2001). Therefore, analyses of these characteristics may further increase our understanding of cultural factors in models of marital conflict. If research does demonstrate that such factors as impoverishment or community violence alter the effects of marital conflict and children's emotional security, it will be important to explicate the precise form of moderation. For example, it is possible that exposure to these factors increases children's vulnerability to marital conflict processes. Specifically, in a reactive pattern of vulnerability (Luthar et al., 2000), mediational pathways between/among marital conflict, child concerns about security, and child adjustment may be magnified for children exposed to other forms of sociodemographic adversity (Cummings, Davies, et al., 2000; Margolin & Gordis, 2003). Alternatively, some child maltreatment studies suggest that stable vulnerability patterns may be operating, whereby the potent risk posed by forms of economic and community adversity may override or supersede the impact of marital conflict and insecurity in the interparental relationship on children's adjustment (e.g., Okun, Parker, & Levendosky, 1994; Trickett, Aber, Carlson, & Cicchetti, 1991).

Peer Relations

Research on the interplay between marital relationships and children's peer relationships has focused on documenting links between marital conflict processes and difficulties with peers. Exposure to marital discord has been shown to be a consistent predictor of fewer friendships and poor relations with peers (e.g., Gottman & Katz, 1989; Lindsey, Colwell, Frabutt, & MacKinnon-Lewis, 2006; Stocker & Youngblade, 1999). EST further posits that children's insecurity in the marital relationship is a central mechanism through which marital conflict increases the likelihood of peer difficulties. Consistent with this view, a recent study (Bascoe et al., in press) identified children's hostile information processing of peer events as an intermediary mechanism in the associations between children's insecure representations of marital relationships and their increases in aggression over time.

However, research to date has predominantly examined poor peer relations as *consequences* of experiences with destructive marital conflict; few studies have explored the potential role of friendship and peer relationships as *moderators* of marital conflict. Notably, there are compelling bases for expecting that peer processes may function better as moderators than as outcomes of marital conflict processes, at least under some conditions. For example, some studies find negligible associations between peer relationship quality and experiences of marital conflict (e.g., Lindsey et al., 2002). Moreover, a complementary, but largely untested, conceptualization has stressed that peer and friendship quality may actually buffer children from the deleterious effects of interparental conflict (Wasserstein & La Greca, 1996). Some studies do support the hypothesis that peer support and availability protect children from the deleterious effects of marital conflict (Rogers & Holmbeck, 1997; Wasserstein & La Greca, 1996), whereas other studies have failed to find any moderating effects (Jenkins & Smith, 1990).

Additional research is needed to resolve the complexity of these initial results. Progress in this area will require specification of moderator models that are sensitive to the multidimensional nature of peer relations and the underlying mechanisms accounting for the beneficial effects. Assumptions derived from EST may facilitate such specification. For example, warmth and emotional support in peer relationships may be key peer dimensions that safeguard children with insecurity about the marital relationship from developing broader psychological problems.

CONCLUSIONS

It is evident that vulnerability and protective models have become increasingly important tools for understanding the wide variability in the outcomes of children who are exposed to similar levels of marital conflict. Although the task of identifying moderators in models of marital conflict is far from complete, the extant findings indicate that associations between marital conflict and children's coping and adjustment may be altered by factors at multiple layers, including child, familial, and extrafamilial characteristics. In order to increase our knowledge in this area, it will be important to cast a broader net in identifying characteristics that might serve as vulnerability and protective factors.

At one end of the continuum, a common assumption is that protective factors are synonymous with inherently positive characteristics. However, this assumption is not always correct. The identification of inert catalytic agents is a perfect case in point, as they appear benign in isolation, but synergistically increase vulnerability in the presence of a risk factor such as marital conflict. Moreover, some factors may actually be interpreted as salubrious but still may potentiate the deleterious effects of marital conflict. For example, a high level of "communion" or interpersonal connectedness is commonly documented as a healthy attribute. Yet communion is also a potentiating factor when coupled with marital conflict, as it has been shown to amplify the association between marital conflict and greater child symptomatology (Davies & Lindsay, 2004).

At the other end of the continuum, it is also the case that inherently negative characteristics do not have a singularly uniform effect of amplifying the risk associated with marital conflict. Rather, some of the more inherently negative attributes may best be designated as stable vulnerability moderators, because their potency as risk factors overrides any impact marital conflict may have on children's adjustment. Furthermore, as Chapter 9 details, other pathogenic factors (e.g., community violence and parent psychopathology) may elucidate pathways between and among marital conflict, emotional security, and child adjustment.

Finally, integration of EST with models of vulnerability and protection in developmental psychopathology can provide a firm foundation for advancing future moderator tests. On the one hand, EST can provide valuable guidance in addressing *why* contextual factors alter the magnitude of associations between/among marital conflict and child adjustment. On the other hand, risk and protective models of developmental psychopathology can provide valuable guidance in understanding the conditions that are likely to magnify or attenuate the mediational pathways between/among marital conflict, emotional security, and child adjustment. To address the goal of further integrating our model of marital conflict within a developmental psychopathology perspective, the next chapter discusses the interplay between marital processes and child adaptation across development.

CHAPTER 7

Development over Time in Contexts of Marital Conflict

A comprehensive process-oriented view of the dynamic interplay between family and child processes also requires consideration of *time* and *developmental process*. Taking a process-oriented perspective means moving beyond single "snapshots" to capturing children's changing response processes in the context of shifting risk and protective factors over time and developmental periods. The goal is not simply to show that marital conflict predicts later adjustment, but to identify the dynamic patterns of causal processes that underlie pathways of development in context over time. For a fully articulated process-oriented explanation, timelines should be included in Figures 2.1 and 2.2. In this chapter, we explore how considering time and developmental process in the study of marital conflict takes the field in exciting new directions.

THE EMOTIONAL SECURITY SYSTEM SEEN THROUGH A DEVELOPMENTAL LENS

Examining the emotional security system through a developmental lens generates additional questions. For example, do the signs of security change over time? Put differently, is there systematic variation across age or developmental periods in the "look" of security? Even after considering normative changes, we must address the question of consistency in individual differences in insecurity across time and development.

The Structure and Operation of the Emotional Security System during Development

Developmental continuity or change in the emotional security system has long been a concern (Cicchetti et al., 1990). However, the focus has been on attachment, with little consideration of the organization of children's emotional security about the marital relationship over time. Because a premise of EST is that multiple regulatory response processes serve the same goal system, some correspondence among indicators of children's emotional reactivity is expected. A major question for future research is this: How do the meaning and pattern of relations among these indicators change over time?

If the functioning of these response patterns in the service of emotional security holds evolutionary significance (e.g., Davies & Sturge-Apple, 2007), structural stability and temporal consistency among security responses would be expected. Children's fearful distress, avoidance, involvement, and triangulation, and their negative appraisals in the face of marital conflict, should interrelate in ways that evidence similarities across developmental periods (particularly when the time lag is relatively short). Plasticity should also be evident: Developmental processes are likely to transform the structure of the system by triggering alterations in the functioning of its specific elements. For example, as children progress into adolescence, they become increasingly adept at inhibiting overt expressions of distress. Thus, although overt distress is likely to reflect difficulties in preserving security across childhood and adolescence, its salience as an indicator of insecurity in the broader organization of responding to conflict may decrease over time.

From a variable-based perspective, change across different developmental periods from infancy through adolescence may be manifested in transformations in the factor structure of the security system. For example, consistent with the orthogenetic principle in developmental psychopathology (Cummings, Davies, et al., 2000; Werner, 1957), structural changes in the emotional security system may signify differentiation processes as dimensions and levels expand and diversify (e.g., increases in the number or levels of factors, or increasing complexity of their interrelations).

The further exploration of person-based approaches to understanding stability and change in the structure of the emotional security system over time is another important goal for future research. For example, Davies and Forman (2002) distinguished among children on the basis of differences in their higher-order organization of responding across multiple response domains, including subjective and overt indices of emotional reactivity, regulation of exposure to conflict, and the quality of their internal representations. The higher-order patterns included the following: (1) "Secure" children exhibited well-regulated, mild forms of concern and distress, and confidence in their parents' ability to manage disputes so as to maintain family harmony; (2) "preoccupied" children showed high levels of vigilance, anxiety, and involvement across behavioral and subjective indices of responding; and (3) "dismissing" children downplayed conscious experiences of threat in the interparental relationship (i.e., low subjective distress and negative representations).

However, at this early stage of person-based research, little is known about the nature of stability and change in these patterns of emotional security. Davies and Sturge-Apple (2007) have recently proposed a social defense conceptualization of the organization of the emotional security system, based on ethology and evolutionary psychology. In this system, an "insecure–camouflaging" strategy is characterized by dissembling or inhibiting overt signs of distress in a way that reduces children's salience as targets of hostility by angry adults during bouts of marital problems. As children become increasingly adept at regulating and masking their overt emotions through middle childhood and into adolescence, the camouflaging strategy may emerge as an increasingly prevalent pattern. Thus undifferentiated forms of insecurity in early childhood may evolve into more differentiated and complex styles of responding, such as the camouflaging pattern, as children get older.

Developmental Stability and Change in Emotional Security

Another developmental thesis in EST is that individual differences in children's security responses to marital conflict have long-term implications for the children's adaptation and adjustment (Cummings & Davies, 1996; Davies & Cummings, 1994). Notably, EST studies have focused on the psychological and physical health sequelae of security. Children who exhibit elevated signs of insecurity in the interparental relationship show a wide array of problems, including internalizing symptoms, externalizing symptoms, school difficulties, disturbances in peer relationships, physical ailments, attention problems, and sleep troubles (Cummings, Schermerhorn, et al., 2006; Davies, Cummings, & Winter, 2004; Davies, Woitach, Winter, & Cummings, 2008; Du Rocher Schudlich & Cummings, 2007; El-Sheikh, Buckhalt, Keller, et al., 2007; El-Sheikh et al., 2008). However, the risk processes linking security and children's mental and physical health outcomes do not occur instantaneously. Rather, differences between children in responding to conflict are theorized to evidence consistency over time as they progressively (and often gradually) intensify, broaden, and coalesce into broader patterns of child psychopathology.

The premise that individual differences in emotional security must evidence some consistency over time in order to evolve and develop into broader difficulties has been neglected in earlier research. EST conceptualizes the emotional security system as a relational construct with some degree of temporal stability. Consistency over time reflects tendencies to utilize previously developed patterns as guides for interpreting and reacting to subsequent threatening events in the marital subsystem (Carlson et al., 2004; Davies, Harold, et al., 2002). Thus, as components of the emotional security system, differences between children in emotional reactivity, regulation of conflict exposure, and internal representations should evidence continuity over time. However, against this backdrop of stability, adaptation to family stress is a product of the ongoing interplay between an actively changing organism and a dynamic environment (Cummings, Davies, et al., 2000). Thus, consistent with the documented plasticity of the parent–child attachment system (e.g., Belsky, Campbell, Cohn, & Moore, 1996; Oppenheim, Emde, & Warren, 1997), the magnitude of developmental stability in individual differences in child reactivity to conflict is hypothesized to be moderate. Consistent with this hypothesis, longitudinal studies have documented moderate stability in individual differences in children's reactions to conflict over periods of a year or two in childhood (Cummings, Schermerhorn, et al., 2006; Davies, Sturge-Apple, et al., 2006).

Models of children's emotional development further highlight the possibility of normative changes in children's reactions to interparental conflict over longer developmental spans of childhood and adolescence (Caspi & Bem, 1990). Cross-sectional studies have shown that younger children report greater subjective distress and fear in response to conflict than preadolescents and adolescents do (Brown, Covell, & Abramovitch, 1991; Cummings, Ballard, et al., 1991; Davies, Myers, et al., 1999). Responses by younger children may reflect underlying tendencies to blame themselves for adult anger (Covell & Abramovitch, 1987), to appraise interpersonal disputes as direct threats to their well-being (Cummings, Ballard, & El-Sheikh, 1991), and to exhibit low perceived competence and emotion dysregulation in stressful contexts (El-Sheikh & Cummings, 1995). With increasing age, children develop more negative representations and expectations of future adult relationship quality after witnessing adult disputes, and report greater impulses to mediate adult disputes (Cummings et al., 1991; Davies et al., 1996; Davies, Myers, et al., 1999). Although these studies provide firm bases for expecting normative changes in multiple domains of child responding to interparental conflict, little is yet known about the presence and nature of change in distress, involvement, and avoidance in response to interparental conflicts across childhood and adolescence. Future theoretical and empirical work addressing this gap is imperative.

DEVELOPMENTAL APPLICABILITY OF PROCESS PATHWAYS IN EST

Although EST proposes that emotional security processes remain important mediators of mental health problems across childhood and adolescence (Cicchetti et al., 1990; Davies & Cummings, 2006), developmental transformations during the course of childhood and preadolescence may alter the magnitude of both direct and indirect pathways between and among interparental conflict, family processes, child emotional security, and child maladjustment. Proposed mediational pathways may vary as a function of two developmental processes: age or developmental period, and experiential history.

Age or Developmental Period

In initial forays into addressing issues of development as a moderator of marital conflict and security processes, age is commonly used as an expedient, albeit imprecise, proxy for developmental periods (Cummings & Davies, 1994; Grych & Fincham, 1990; Mahoney, Jouriles, & Scavone, 1997). At this early juncture, it is difficult to decipher whether children in any specific age group or developmental period are, in any broad sense, more vulnerable to interparental conflict or insecurity than other age groups. For example, in addressing bivariate links between marital conflict and child adjustment, some research indicates that associations between marital discord and child adjustment may be stronger for preschool children than for older children (Kitzmann et al., 2003; Mahoney, Jouriles, et al., 1997). However, other research suggests that adolescence may be a period of greater vulnerability to marital difficulties (Sim & Vuchinich, 1996). Still other studies have failed to find evidence for any moderating effects of age (Buehler et al., 1997; Gerard & Buehler, 1999; Johnston et al., 1987).

Because age is a general marker for numerous changes in biological and experiential processes, there is no easy answer to the question regarding which age is most vulnerable to the effects of marital conflict. The most precise answer to this question is that it depends on the area of functioning under consideration. For preschool children, regulatory mechanisms underlying children's security in the marital relationship may be more easily overwhelmed by exposure to marital conflict. In comparison to older children, preschool children are predisposed to experience fear, self-blame, and threat in response to such conflict (e.g., Covell & Abramovitch, 1987; E. M. Cummings et al., 1989; Davies, Myers, et al., 1999; Jouriles et al., 2000; Kitzmann et al., 2003), as well as low levels of perceived competence in coping (Cummings, Ballard, & El-Sheikh, 1991; Grych, 1998) and limited ability to enlist coping strategies to regulate affect (El-Sheikh & Cummings, 1995). This evidence suggests that insecurity in the marital relationship may be a more powerful mediator of pathways between marital conflict and child adjustment during the preschool years.

However, this hypothesis can be challenged on several bases. First, age is largely explored as a predictor of adaptation to conflict only within main-effects models. Main-effects analyses do not permit authoritative conclusions about whether age is a moderating factor that amplifies or weakens the effects of marital conflict on children's difficulties. Figure 7.1 provides a hypothetical illustration of this issue. If we only look at the effects of age without considering the effects of marital conflict, the findings indicate that preschool children respond with greater distress to such conflict than older children do. Yet this does not mean that marital conflict is a stronger predictor of maladjustment for preschoolers than for older children. It's quite the opposite! Analysis of the more complex interaction reveals that marital conflict is related to child adjustment during the early school years, but *not* during the preschool period.

Second, developmental changes suggest that children exposed to marital conflict may exhibit a different constellation of vulnerabilities as they grow older. As a result, it is possible that older children experience as much insecurity in the face of marital conflict as preschool children do, or perhaps even more. For example, as children grow older, greater

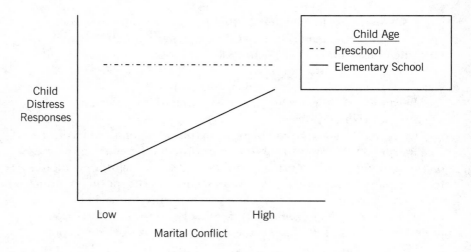

FIGURE 7.1. Graphic depiction of the danger of interpreting age differences in psychological liabilities as necessarily meaning that age is a moderator amplifying the risk posed by marital conflict to children's adjustment.

use of symbolism and the emergence of new ways of modulating emotion may precipitate changes in the ways the children respond to family conflict (Denham, 1998; Greenberg & Speltz, 1988). Gains in social perspective-taking ability may also raise children's concerns about the safety of their parents and of the family unit as a whole. Therefore, adversity in family contexts outside the parent–child relationship, such as interparental discord, may assume greater salience as children begin to grapple with worries about stressful family events and the implications of these events for their own welfare and that of the family system (Cicchetti et al., 1990).

Third, adolescence ushers in a unique profile of responses that may, in some respects, heighten children's vulnerability to marital conflict. For example, in a sample of 8- to 17-year-old children, Cummings, Schermerhorn, and colleagues (2006) found that the relationship between marital conflict and children's emotional insecurity was stronger for older children. One possible interpretation is that the challenge of successfully resolving numerous stage-salient tasks and marked increases in normative stressors (e.g., puberty, school transitions) during adolescence may accentuate the risk associated with living in high-conflict homes (Gest, Reed, & Masten, 1999; Windle & Davies, 1999). In addition, relative to those of younger children, adolescents concerns about security in high-conflict homes and their negative developmental implications may be amplified by their increased sensitivity to adult problems, longer histories of exposure to interparental conflict, and stronger dispositions to mediate in conflicts (Davies & Cummings, 2006).

Experiential Histories of Marital Adversity and Insecurity

A developmental psychopathology model of security posits that experiential histories of interparental difficulties during earlier developmental periods uniquely predict children's outcomes during subsequent times, even after consideration of contemporaneous psychosocial experiences. Highlighting the significance of early experience is the concept of "hierarchical motility," or the idea that prior psychological organizations and experiences emerge in new, dynamic forms of functioning during development (Cicchetti & Cohen, 1995; Cummings, Davies, et al., 2000). Applied to emotional security, this concept suggests that earlier developmental experiences may leave an indelible imprint on subsequent patterns of insecurity, and ultimately on children's trajectories of adjustment over time (Davies, Winter, & Cicchetti, 2006). Children's security and adjustment are products not only of contemporaneous marital adversity, but also of their prior histories of experiences with such adversity. For example, with emergent social role-taking capacities and the assumption of multiple social roles, emotional security conceptualizations indicate that children must increasingly grapple with concerns about the safety of their caregivers and its implications for their own well-being (Cicchetti et al., 1990). Thus early experiences with interparental conflict may precipitate novel, protracted patterns of functioning, even in the face of subsequent changes in interparental and family dynamics (Cummings & Davies, 1995).

Supporting the predictions about the unique significance of prior experiential histories, Sroufe, Egeland, and Kreutzer (1990) found that early family experiences and child adaptation continued to account for child functioning in elementary school, even after statistical controls for contemporaneous experiences. The active rejection of this hypothesis by some researchers only amplifies the importance of addressing these questions. For example, some developmental theorists have argued that contemporary environmental circumstances, in evidencing stability from earlier experiences, fully mediate or account for associations between early experience and subsequent adjustment (Kagan, 1980; Lamb, 1984). Thus documenting whether prior exposure to marital conflict and concerns about security uniquely predict child functioning, above and beyond current experiences with these risk processes, is another important direction for future research.

CHARTING UNFOLDING DEVELOPMENTAL PROCESSES

Prospective longitudinal research is an urgent requirement for greater understanding of time-related effects. Identifying the temporal ordering of variables in the context of longitudinal research designs gives a much better indication of the causal relations between and among variables than simply showing that the variables may covary, as in cross-sectional research. EST offers direction in testing how classes of stress and coping processes, and child characteristics and family background factors, dynamically mediate and/or moderate the relations of particular contexts with stimulus characteristics of marital relationships and children's developmental outcomes. In this section, we describe the important theoretical and methodological parameters for building and testing a developmental model of EST.

Stability and Change in Marital Adversity

Since the publication of our original book over 15 years ago (Cummings & Davies, 1994a), there has been substantial progress in prospectively documenting associations between marital conflict and children's adjustment problems (e.g., Cummings, Schermerhorn, et al., 2006; Davies, Sturge-Apple, et al., 2006; El-Sheikh, Keller, & Erath, 2007; Harold & Conger, 1997; Ingoldsby, Shaw, Owens, & Winslow, 1999; Sturge-Apple et al., 2006b). These studies thus constitute an important first step in the study of risk processes over time. However, even these state-of-the-art longitudinal studies assess marital conflict as a static trait at a single point in time. Such assessments do not fully correspond with the developmental assumption that both marital conflict and child functioning are dynamic processes changing over time (Cummings et al., 2001; Fincham et al., 1994).

Testing whether marital conflict at a single time point is associated with subsequent changes in child functioning only captures one temporal window of directionality. Some developmental models suggest other, more dynamic forms of influence. For example, at least under some conditions, increases in marital problems may be associated with corresponding increases in children's adjustment. Consistent with this alternative conceptualization, Cui, Conger, and Lorenz (2005) reported that changes in marital conflict were better predictors of adolescent trajectories of psychological problems than initial, static levels of marital conflict were.

Static conceptualizations of marital conflict run counter to notions of the importance of temporal dimensions of marital conflict. Distinctions between transient and enduring risk and protective factors provide an excellent case in point (Cicchetti, 1989; Cicchetti & Toth, 1995). Whereas transient factors reflect relatively short-term, temporary "states," enduring factors may last over periods of years. Because different couples face unique arrays of dispositions, challenges, and stressors, it is likely that there is considerable interfamilial variability in the enduring versus transient nature of marital conflict. Guided by this assumption, EST proposes that children are likely to be sensitive to both stability and change in marital problems. For example, the degree of risk posed by marital conflict may be a function of the chronicity of the parents' problems.

The Dynamic Role of Emotional Security Processes over Time

Delineating the temporal windows within which developmental processes operate is a formidable challenge for contemporary theories, and EST is certainly no exception. For example, in one of the pathways of risk posited by EST, repeated exposure to destructive marital conflict is thought to sensitize children gradually and cumulatively to concerns about their security in the marital relationship. However, as the vague qualifying terminology of "gradually and cumulatively" attests, the time lags required for this unfolding process to occur have yet to be specified. Questions about the timing of security processes also pertain to other pathways in the EST model. For example, there is lack of clarity about the timing of spillover processes from the marital to the parent–child subsystem, as lag times for the operation of spillover range from seconds or minutes (e.g., Jouriles & Farris, 1992) to hours or days (e.g., Almeida et al., 1999) to months or years (e.g., Cowan et al., 2007; Sturge-Apple et al., 2006b). Although the affirmative documentation of spillover processes across diverse time frames testifies to the robustness of these processes, a question for future research is whether different dynamic processes underlie the transmission of disturbance over different temporal windows (Davies & Sturge-Apple, 2006).

Recent theoretical and empirical advances in charting the sequelae of emotional security have begun to articulate some of the processes that may underlie emerging patterns of adaptation and maladaptation.

For example, concerns about emotional security may require an expenditure of biopsychological resources that ultimately increases children's risky behavior and mental health problems through multiple pathways. That is, difficulty in garnering security may create deviations in homeostatic balance and efficient psychobiological resource allocation that reverberate across multiple levels of functioning. In one proposed pathway, insecurity in family relationships may result in neurobiological dysregulation and accompanying problems with maintaining homeostasis and mounting effective physiological responses to stress. The LHPA axis and one of its hormonal products (i.e., cortisol) are components of the neuroendocrine system, which may play a key role in shaping the developmental sequelae of insecurity in the family (see Appendix D for further details on the LHPA axis). When children are concerned about their security in the face of destructive interparental conflict, the resulting emotional distress and vigilance are theorized to be accompanied by disruptions in the efficiency of the LHPA axis in marshaling resources to cope with threatening events. In turn, these disruptions are hypothesized to undermine children's physical and mental health insidiously over time (Davies, Winter, & Cicchetti, 2006).

Supporting the first link in this unfolding process model, a recent study found that children's distress behaviors were consistent, unique predictors of their elevated cortisol reactivity to marital conflict (Davies, Sturge-Apple, et al., 2008). Although this study did not explore links between cortisol reactivity and children's adjustment over time, empirical documentation of associations between elevated cortisol reactivity to stressors and greater psychological problems provides some support for the second link in this mediational chain (e.g., Ashman, Dawson, Panagiotides, Yamada, & Wilkinson, 2002; Granger, Weisz, & Kauneckis, 1994; Klimes-Dougan, Hastings, Granger, Usher, & Zahn-Waxler, 2001).

In another proposed pathway in EST, insecurity in family relationships is theorized to increase children's vulnerability to psychopathology by undermining neuropsychological functioning, including focused attention, working memory, and response inhibition. If concerns about security deplete children's biopsychological resources, as EST suggests (Davies, Winter, & Cicchetti, 2006), this depletion may disrupt attention and neuropsychological systems (e.g., working memory, inhibition) that require large reservoirs of resources to operate. Recent empirical support for the mediational role of attention problems lends some credence to this hypothesis (Davies, Woitach, et al., 2008). Structural equation models specifically revealed that observer ratings of children's insecure representations of the marital relationship predicted computerized task assessments and parent reports of children's attention difficulties 1 year later. In turn, children's attention difficulties were associated with increases in teacher reports of school problems over a 1-year period.

Developmental Trajectories

A developmental psychopathology framework assumes that there are multiple developmental trajectories of child adjustment (Bowlby, 1973; Sroufe, 1997), with disorder defined by successive and changing patterns of deviation from normality resulting from the interplay between intra- and extraorganismic processes. Prospective longitudinal research is therefore one of the most urgent requirements for exploring these trajectories. In recognition of this need, studies are increasingly employing longitudinal tests of marital conflict, with a common objective being the assessment of continuity and change in child functioning over two time points. However, the form, direction, and shape of developmental pathways can only be identified with cogency by collecting more than two measurements over time. That is, the pattern of continuity or change in development can only be more reliably demonstrated by assessing individuals' functioning on multiple occasions over a period of time, and tracking how the individuals change or remain the same over that period.

In providing direction to the objective of tracing children's trajectories of adjustment over time, developmental psychopathology conceptualizes development as a series of stage-salient challenges that emerge as prominent at a given period and remain important throughout an individual's lifetime (Cicchetti, 1993). Because these developmental challenges constitute a period of normative transition for most (if not all) individuals and require significant reorganization in functioning, some level of change and discontinuity is expected by definition (Graber & Brooks-Gunn, 1996). At each developmental stage, individuals are faced with resolving a number of significant tasks across multiple domains of functioning. Table 7.1 lists the major developmental challenges from birth through adolescence (see also Chase-Lansdale, Wakschlag, & Brooks-Gunn, 1995; Cicchetti, 1991; Sroufe & Rutter, 1984).

Given that these tasks are already challenging in themselves, their successful resolution may be particularly sensitive to the risks associated with marital conflict and children's insecurity (Cummings, Davies, et al., 2000). In accordance with this premise, EST postulates that interparental conflict may ultimately increase long-term patterns of maladaptation by disrupting children's abilities to resolve developmental

TABLE 7.1. Developmental Challenges Faced by Children from Infancy through Adolescence

Developmental period	Stage-salient challenges
Infancy	Modulation of arousal Physiological regulation Harmonious, synchronous interactions with caregivers Secure attachments with primary caregivers Interpersonal trust
Toddler	Awareness of self as distinct Exploration of social and object worlds Emotion regulation and management Awareness and responsivity to standards Mastery, persistence, and problem solving Autonomy Sociability Understanding of internal emotion states of others
Preschool	Flexible self-control Self-reliance Initiative Awareness of social roles Gender role development Establishing effective peer relations Empathy and prosocial behavior
Middle childhood	Social understanding (equity, fairness) Gender constancy Same-sex friendships Peer relations and reputation Sense of "industry" (competence) Social agency School adjustment Internalization of standards of conduct
Adolescence	Flexible perspective taking Abstract thinking Moral reasoning Reconciling "ideal" world with "real" world Loyal same-sex friendships Establishing romantic relationships Balancing emotional autonomy with relatedness to parents Identity development Interpersonal intimacy Sexuality Risk management (e.g., substance use, sexual relations)

challenges (Davies, Winter, & Cicchetti, 2006). Through the process of hierarchical motility, old psychological characteristics and structures, while not evidencing a one-to-one correspondence with new forms of functioning, are specifically carried over and incorporated into evolving new structures over time (Cicchetti & Cohen, 1995). For example, in toddlerhood, difficulties with security evidenced in emotion dysregulation and negative working models of family relationships may prevent children from successfully resolving the task of developing peer relationships in childhood (Amato & Booth, 2001). Moreover, successful negotiation of each newly emerging developmental task is thought to depend in part on adequate differentiation and integration of earlier stage-salient tasks (Cicchetti, 1993). For example, difficulties in establishing close same-sex peer relationships during childhood are thought to increase the likelihood of problems with involvement in romantic relationships during adolescence, by depriving children of opportunities to address such relevant stage-salient tasks as flexible social perspective taking and interpersonal intimacy (Brendgen, Vitaro, Doyle, Markiewicz, & Bukowski, 2002; Connolly, Furman, & Konaski, 2000; Feiring, 1996; Furman & Wehner, 1994). Failure to resolve these tasks may increase the probability of developing along maladaptive trajectories of adjustment (Graber & Brooks-Gunn, 1996). Thus, in these cascading models, individual differences in resolving developmental tasks may help to explain how and why marital conflict and children's concerns about emotional security increase children's mental health problems (Davies & Cummings, 2006).

Transactional Models

Transactional approaches assume that child adaptation to adversity is an evolving product of the interactions between a dynamic child and an ever-changing, multilayered ecological context. According to the principle of interdependency in family systems theory, the functioning of any one individual or relationship is regulated by the characteristics of other individuals or relationships in the family (Davies & Cicchetti, 2004). Consequently, the interplay between/among family relationships and child development is assumed to be reciprocal in nature. In research supporting this hypothesis, not only was marital conflict found to be a predictor of increases in children's psychological problems over time, but children's externalizing symptoms also predicted greater marital conflict over a 2-year period (Jenkins et al., 2005). Testifying to the potential robustness of bidirectional processes in high-risk families, the power of child behavior problems in the prediction of marital difficulties was particularly strong in more complex, problematic family contexts containing stepparents (Jenkins et al., 2005; see also O'Connor & Insabella, 1999). Furthermore, in one of the strongest tests of bidirectionality between marital and child functioning to date, Cui, Donnellan, and Conger (2007) examined the reciprocal interplay among marital conflict and adolescent symptomatology in a series of cross-lagged autoregressive analyses at three time points, spaced 1 year apart. Consistent with transactional models, adolescent depressive and delinquency symptoms served as both outcomes and predictors of marital conflict. Moreover, marital conflict served as a critical intermediary process linking the reciprocal relations between adolescent maladjustment and marital dissatisfaction.

Signifying another type of bidirectional process, children's patterns of responding to interparental problems may also affect the nature and course of interparental problems. In his behavioral conceptualization of family violence, Emery (1989) proposed a transactional cycle of effects between children and the marital subsystem. In the initial series of unfolding processes, children respond to witnessing violence with higher levels of distress, which in turn precipitate specific attempts on the part of the children to alleviate their distress through disruptive behaviors (e.g., aggression, yelling). In the subsequent phases of this reciprocal cycle, children's misbehavior is posited to broaden and intensify in subsequent conflicts, because it serves a function of distracting parents from engagement in the aversive ongoing conflict. In elaborating on this theme, EST has further postulated that children's intervention strategies (e.g., mediation) in marital conflicts may help them to attain a sense of security by interrupting the course of escalating conflicts before they substantially threaten the family system (Davies & Cummings, 1994).

Although misbehavior, distress, triangulation, and intervention strategies may temporarily distract parents from ongoing conflict, there is considerable disagreement about the long-term impact of children's patterns of responding on the interparental relationship. Some conceptualizations underscore that children's reactivity to adult problems may increase their salience as targets of family hostility and amplify the proliferation of discord across family subsystems (Emery, 1989); other models suggest that children's reactivity to conflict may alert parents to their offspring's distress and motivate them to resolve their differences (Schermerhorn et al., 2005; Schermerhorn, Cummings, DeCarlo, & Davies, 2007).

CONCLUSIONS, CAVEATS, AND FUTURE DIRECTIONS

It is important to note that steady progress in understanding marital conflict processes over time has led to some very fruitful research directions. Exciting insights are reflected in the theoretical acknowledgment and empirical documentation of the complex developmental processes involved in understanding the dynamic interplay between the changing child in the context of a changing marriage. Yet future progress in this area will require a broader appreciation of the complexity of advancing models of dynamic processes.

Although temporal lags between assessments of a risk factor and an outcome are ultimately necessary to test the assumption that a variable can only be caused by values of a preceding variable, even the most robust risk factors and processes may lose predictive power in models of child development as the time between the assessment of the risk factor and the outcome increases. Long spans between the risk factor and outcome (e.g., years) increase the probability that the risk associated with marital conflict may be diluted by the emergence of multiple causal pathways, competing etiological factors, and random factors that add methodological noise to the empirical tests (see Shrout & Bolger, 2002). Notably, if there are resulting null findings, these do *not* necessarily disconfirm the potential role of either marital conflict or emotional security in models of child psychopathology. Instead, effects may be seen through more sophisticated process-oriented models of change over time and developmental process.

Introducing smaller temporal lags (e.g., months) may seem like an obvious solution, but these designs may reduce statistical power for different reasons. For example, in one of the most rigorous longitudinal models, the risk factor or process at Time 1 is specified as a predictor of a Time 2 outcome after the Time 1 assessment of the outcome is controlled for. Allowing the Time 1 outcome to predict the Time 2 outcome provides an estimate of the stability of the outcome, thereby leaving the proposed predictor in the position of predicting the leftover variance or change in the Time 2 outcome. However, the high stability of many psychological outcomes (e.g., aggression) over periods of months limits the power of the risk factor or process to predict the outcome by limiting the leftover variance in the Time 2 outcome. The final result is often an overly conservative analytic model that may yield inaccurate estimates of the association between variables—and, in some cases, findings that are the opposites of the predictions (Bradbury, Cohan, & Karney, 1998; Bradbury & Karney, 1993; Karney & Bradbury, 1995). In fact, the tendency for researchers to select outcomes with high test–retest reliability may actually dilute the power and accuracy of some longitudinal models by increasing the stability of the outcomes across time.

In conclusion, we cannot emphasize strongly enough that EST does *not* propose that marital conflict and emotional security are such overpowering predictors that they will necessarily predict children's functioning across all conditions and time frames in terms of simple bivariate relationships. Our proposal is that marital conflict and security processes, like most risk factors and processes in developmental psychopathology, play important roles in understanding the development of individual differences in children's functioning across settings and time periods in terms of multivariate-pathways models. Accordingly, understanding the boundaries of the developmental applicability of EST propositions will be an important step in our future work. The ultimate objective for future research is to identify the temporal windows and contextual conditions that underlie the process relations between and among marital conflict, emotional security, and child adjustment.

PART IV

FUTURE DIRECTIONS

Child development research, including work on children and marital conflict, has wide potential applicability and value beyond its disciplinary confines. Moreover, the high quality of the social science practiced provides a strong basis for our belief that the messages of our discipline *should* have wider currency, for the benefit of society. Unfortunately, this potential contribution is often not realized, and it is increasingly apparent that proactive steps need to be taken to extend the purview of the scholarship.

This part of the book is concerned primarily with future efforts to increase the applications and uses of child development research in general and the body of scholarship on relations between/among marital conflict, emotional security, and child adjustment in particular. First, in Chapter 8, we outline bases for translating the research on marital conflict and children into prevention programs to help ameliorate conflict and adjustment problems in families. We hope that this chapter will increase interest in such translational research; it both highlights the need for and value of such programs, and provides suggestions for further work in this area.

As its title suggests, Chapter 9 is concerned with stimulating consideration of the applicability and value of the literature described in this book in multiple ways and at multiple levels of analysis. For example, we encourage social scientists working at different levels of analysis of social problems (e.g., political scientists) to consider the potential value of child development findings, models, and theories for shedding light on such problems. The point is illustrated specifically with regard to the study of political violence and peace processes. As a Fellow of Notre Dame's Joan B. Kroc Institute for International Peace Studies, one of us (E. Mark Cummings) has been struck over the years not only by the great important of peace studies, but also by how peace studies—and negotiators of peace accords, for that matter—often only deal with the "top layers" of the peace process in seeking conflict resolution. At the same time, we wonder how long peace accords will last if the effects on communities, families, and children are not factored into the negotiations. The utility of also considering the effects on children is illustrated by a theoretical model and ongoing line of research being conducted in Northern Ireland on political violence and child development.

In closing, we are hopeful that these new directions, and the many others described throughout this volume, will stimulate future advances in this vibrant and rapidly growing area of research, advancing knowledge in this area and its applicability to many other issues in the years to come.

CHAPTER 8

Applications of Findings and Translational Research

Knowledge about marital/family conflict and children is potentially applicable to real-world situations and settings. That is, the impact of this conflict on children is of more than academic concern. To the extent that such conflict creates distress for children and is linked with the development of mental health problems, it constitutes a significant social problem. The well-being and stability of all couples are potentially compromised by interpersonal conflicts (Cowan, Cowan, & Schulz, 1996), and problems stemming from marital conflict appear across a broad range of community families (Amato & Booth, 2001; Emery, 1999), including families without clinically significant difficulties (Cowan, Cowan, & Schulz, 1996; Liberman, Van Horn, & Ippen, 2005). As we have reviewed in Chapter 1, marital conflict is associated with a host of adjustment problems across family members—including depression, alcohol problems, and divorce in adults, and behavioral, emotional, and academic problems in children. Thus it is desirable for these findings to be made available and accessible to the public.

Moreover, popular advice about how to handle conflicts within families often has little foundation and is even sometimes potentially destructive. For example, at one point some "experts" commonly advocated the practice of fully ventilating anger as desirable and good for all parties. For example, if one partner didn't like something about the other partner, this feeling was to be expressed fully. Nerf bats were recommended so that partners could ventilate their hostilities by (safely) hitting each other. Unfortunately, hostility begets hostility. The notion that expression of aggression is releasing—the "catharsis" hypothesis—has not fared well in the research literature. The following two case examples illustrate the importance of parents' receiving research-based information.

Family A: Cindy and Michael Smith were the parents of an adolescent named Bobby. Cindy and Michael were having interparental conflict over issues related to Bobby's autonomy. It felt as if they could never "get on the same page" for parenting. One day Cindy began watching a TV talk show on popular approaches to parenting and marital conflict. After watching the show, Cindy decided that she would employ some of the techniques she learned. She went to the local toy store and purchased three super-soaker water guns. Cindy informed Michael and Bobby that they were to use the water guns to express their aggression. They would then have a family conversation once everyone had had a chance to "get it all out." This technique did not work out: Cindy ended up soaking wet in her work clothes, Michael got angry, and Bobby stormed up to his room. One year later, the Smith family was still often unable to have a conversation without conflict. Cindy and Michael could not agree on many parenting issues, especially with regard to Bobby's autonomy, and their relationship with Bobby remained strained.

Family B: Jackie and Matthew Jones were the parents of an adolescent named Billy. Jackie and Matthew began to have interparental conflict over issues related to Billy's autonomy. It felt as if they could never "get on the same page" for parenting. One day while reading her daily newspaper, Jackie came across an ad for an educational program based on research and aimed at teaching families better ways to handle marital and family conflict. She encouraged Matthew and Billy to get involved by informing them of the compensation they would receive for participating. While attending the workshops, Jackie, Matthew, and Billy learned constructive and valuable communication techniques, and were reassured about the normality of conflict. Jackie and Matthew also got valuable information on the importance of security in their relationship. After 4 weeks of classes, the parents felt that they were on a better path and were able to communicate more effectively, both with each other and in negotiating autonomy issues with Billy. One year later, Jackie and Matthew felt that their relationship remained improved. Their parenting and relationship with Billy also remained improved, who felt closer to his parents and also experienced an adequate sense of autonomy.

The different experiences of Families A and B highlight the importance of the quality of the information. In the case of Family A, the TV presentation, which was based on antiquated assumptions with no basis in research findings, provides a sobering reminder that such assumptions may not only fail to help a family, but also run the risk of further undermining family relationships. In recognition of the contrasting success experienced by Family B, practitioners and public policy makers are increasingly calling for the development of evidence-based programs.

Responding to these concerns, in our previous volume (Cummings & Davies, 1994a) we provided a brief summary of conclusions, implications, and guidelines supported by the body of research that had accumulated to that point on children and marital conflict. Our hope was that this review would both inform clinical practice and inspire translational research aimed at more fully informing the public about evidence-based findings. One aim of this chapter is to revisit, update, and review these findings and conclusions with practical implications that are supported by recent research.

However, our major aim is to describe and advocate for the extension of translational research into the development of actual prevention programs. Concerns are increasing about the apparent assumption that just publishing or publicizing research results is sufficient to result in the implementation of such findings by parents or even practitioners. There are relatively many steps between making the public aware of findings and actually enabling individuals to take appropriate advantage of the results. For example, simple exposure to key findings in scientific journals or the popular media is unlikely to give practitioners sufficient bases or foundation to implement these findings fully in their practices. Moreover, parents and other laypersons may have limited understanding of research results that they may read about in the popular media.

TRANSLATIONAL RESEARCH AS AN EMERGING DIRECTION IN DEVELOPING PREVENTION PROGRAMS

Translational research is an emerging direction for more effectively presenting research-based conclusions in the form of practically valuable programs for the public. A key concern is that the outcomes of these programs must be evaluated according to high scientific standards.

Support for Prevention Approaches in Developmental Psychopathology Concepts

The developmental psychopathology tradition provides conceptual support for prevention approaches as efficient and effective ways to reduce mental health problems in children. Specifically, the identification of processes underlying children's risk for developing adjustment problems is assumed to provide bases for earlier and more effective preventive interventions, before such problems become full-blown and therefore resistant to amelioration (Cummings, Davies, et al., 2000). Given the well-established links between negative marital conflict strategies and children's adjustment problems, prevention efforts aimed at changing parents' conflict tactics hold particular promise for altering family dynamics and family risk and protective processes. Research identifying the characteristics of constructive and destructive conflict supports the development of programs for teaching parents how to handle interparental conflicts more effectively for the sake of their children (Shifflett & Cummings, 1999; Webster-Stratton, 1994). Moreover, EST provides a theoretical foundation for guiding such programs. Additional findings regarding the processes mediating and/or moderating relations between marital conflict and children reviewed in this volume provide further possible content for prevention programs.

The New Emphasis on Translational Research in Both Science and Public Policy

The growing emphasis on translational research in both scientific and applied arenas has challenged researchers and practitioners alike to apply science to intervention and prevention programs. For example, new editorial guidelines at journals such as the *Journal of Family Psychology* now uniformly challenge contributors to outline how empirical findings may inform clinical practice and public policy (Kazak, 2004; Parke, 1998). Likewise, modifications in the organization and priorities of funding agencies like the National Institute of Mental Health signify an overarching commitment to translating research in the behavioral and social sciences into practical efforts at understanding and reducing mental illness (Dingfelder, 2004; National Advisory Mental Health

Council Behavioral Science Workgroup, 2000; see also Institute of Medicine, 1994). Accompanying these changes in the "infrastructure" of the behavioral sciences is progress in addressing many other significant gaps between behavioral theory/science and treatment/policy initiatives (Cicchetti & Toth, 2006; Toth & Cicchetti, 2006).

In addition, greater demands are being made on practitioners by funding agencies to demonstrate how science informs the development of prevention and intervention programs. Notably, EST and the process-oriented approach provide a strong scientific basis for prevention programs on children and marital conflict. Knowledge of methodology is also required to test the effectiveness of these programs. Many intervention and prevention programs (e.g., those conducted at schools or clinical treatment centers) are increasingly demanding some scientific verification of the success of these clinical and community services for children. Thus it is becoming more and more necessary for practitioners to be well versed in methodology (Heatherington, Friedlander, & Greenberg, 2005).

Translational Research Programs on Children and Marital Conflict

Although there are various meritorious programs exemplifying translational research, including programs for couples based on research concerning couples (e.g., Blanchard, Hawkins, Baldwin, & Fawcett, 2009; Laurenceau, Stanley, Olmos-Gallo, Baucom, & Markman, 2004; Markman et al., 1988), the development of programs based on empirical research into the relationships between marital conflict and child outcomes, and based on an explicit theory of these relationships (i.e., EST), is a unique direction. Thus we devote much of the rest of this chapter to discussing the development and implementation of such programs. However, because translational research is still an emerging area, how to go about conducting it may not be widely known or understood. Thus it is useful to consider how this approach may be used to disseminate evidence-based information about children and marital conflict more effectively and appropriately.

Accordingly, our goals in what follows are twofold. First, we plan to continue the summary of conclusions in the area of children and marital conflict that we began in our 1994 book. Our goal is again to provide an accessible overview of the practical implications of the scientific evidence on interadult conflict and child outcomes. We briefly and selectively update the points made in the 1994 volume, and add new findings and conclusions supported by subsequent studies.

Second, we go beyond this aim of summarizing selected bottom-line messages to provide a guide to the development of translational research programs. Following a consideration of the definitional and methodological characteristics of translational research, and a review of requirements for such research, we consider some recent examples of translational research programs on marital conflict and children.

SELECTED EMPIRICAL FOUNDATIONS FOR TRANSLATIONAL RESEARCH

Children's Responses to Marital Conflict

Anger Expression and Conflict Are Normal

The angry behavior and conflicts of parents, when extreme, increase the risk for less-than-optimal socialization of children—including depression and anxiety, as well as risk for aggression and behavior problems. Moreover, high levels of aggressive responding to conflict in the home have been directly linked with adjustment problems (see Chapters 1, 2, and 4). However, an overly strong focus on pathological outcomes runs the very real risk of promoting a distorted view of the role anger expression can play in family life.

Anger is a natural part of life; everyone, including parents, sometimes becomes angry. Conflict may sometimes be necessary to work out important marital and family issues that could cause further and more serious problems if left unattended. Also, the attempts of parents to suppress angry emotional expression may have a negative effect on children; it is questionable whether parents can truly hide anger from children simply by not verbalizing it. Recent work indicates children's sensitivity to nonverbal conflict in the home (Cummings, Goeke-Morey, et al., 2003a), and also suggests that withdrawal may have more negative effects than hostility on parenting and child adjustment (Sturge-Apple et al., 2006b).

The overall message of research is that within certain ill-defined bounds, exposure to anger between adults is unlikely to create difficulties for children. There is every reason to believe that children can handle normal levels of anger in the home, even though it may be stressful for them while it is going on.

A general stereotype is that the more parents argue and the more demonstratively they argue, the greater the likelihood of negative outcomes for children. This is too simple a view of conflict expression and is ultimately misleading. It appears quite possible that parents may argue a lot but still be close and have happy marriages, with no ill effects on the children. Some parents clearly enjoy continual, stimulating back-and-forth exchanges and do not interpret disagreements as necessarily significant or negative. For others, even a minor expression of disagreement carries with it relatively dramatic meaning and interpretation.

The past 15-plus years of research have underscored that the underlying messages of communication, and children's interpretations and responses to those messages, are more important to the impact on children than the mode of communication is. For example, as shown elsewhere in this volume, children's responses to marital conflict have been shown to critically mediate the effects of this conflict on the children. In fact, in some studies, no relations are found between children's exposure to marital conflict and their risk for adjustment problems until their processes of responding are taken into account. At the same time, we would argue that even when relations between marital conflict and children adjustment are found, they can only be explained by taking into account children's processes of responding (e.g., emotional insecurity, self-blame, threat).

In our 1994 volume (Cummings & Davies, 1994a), we noted that relatively little was then known about what constitutes constructive versus destructive conflict. Thus we speculated that children's observations of parents' anger and conflict may be necessary experiences in their development of adequate coping skills and skills for relating with others, and that these experiences may teach them valuable lessons about human relations. However, the existing evidence about what dimensions of conflict behavior might be constructive was limited to demonstrations in analogue studies that some conflict behaviors had non-negative effects; as yet, there was no evidence that any conflict behaviors might have positive effects.

As indicated in Chapter 3, great strides have since been made in identifying behaviors occurring in the contexts of actual conflicts, including conflicts in the home, that have *positive* effects on children's functioning (e.g., McCoy et al., 2009). Thus, beyond simply not showing elevated distress in response to some marital conflict behaviors, children actually report and express elevated positive affect in response to some forms of marital conflict. Thus affirmative evidence for constructive ways of handling conflicts, rather than simply evidence for non-toxic effects, now exists in abundant supply—including evidence based on parental report in the context of actual conflict episodes.

In sum, it would be unfortunate indeed if this book and the literature reviewed in it were misinterpreted to indicate that parents should
never express conflict or hold their angry feelings in. The evidence
against such recommendations has become even more substantial since
1994. The basis of concern for children is essentially how anger is handled during and after arguments, not whether it is expressed.

Children Are Sensitive to Interadult Anger

Although children can cope with most anger expression effectively,
they are also exquisitely sensitive, discriminating, and reactive to anger
expressions by others, especially parents. They seem almost like emotional Geiger counters. While children may not obviously signal their
awareness, research suggests that they often accurately understand the
emotional content of their parents' communications. Children show
discriminated and distressed responses to parental anger at an early
age—by 6 months of age, according to some research (Cummings &
Davies, 1994a).

The distress and disruption induced in children by exposure to
interadult and interparental conflict are documented in many different
types of responses. Although these reactions are sometimes relatively
subtle behaviors, parents are able to report reliably on these behaviors even when they are involved in marital disputes (Cummings et al.,
2002, 2003a), and they are readily detected when children's responses
are videotaped (Davies, Sturge-Apple, et al., 2006). Another exciting
direction in identifying children's sensitivity to conflict has been demonstrating the impact of exposure to marital conflict on biological
regulatory processes (Cummings et al., 2007; Davies et al., 2007; El-
Sheikh, 2005; El-Sheikh et al., 2001, 2009; El-Sheikh & Whitson, 2006).
For example, Davies, Sturge-Apple, and colleagues (2008) showed that
children's distress responses (especially fear) to interparental conflict
were consistent, unique predictors of their elevated cortisol reactivity
to conflict, especially for children exhibiting high levels of involvement
in conflicts.

Commonly reported responses by children to interadult anger
include facial expressions of distress; gestures and actions indicative of
fear and anxiety; and behaviors or self-reports indicative of angry, sad
or fearful reactions. Children may also become aggressive or otherwise
behaviorally dysregulated, or may be drawn into parents' disputes, making attempts to mediate interparental disagreements by negotiating

between the parents. Studies have repeatedly demonstrated children's efforts at making the parents feel better emotionally by comforting the parents or helping the parents work out their differences.

Recent work has added sleep disruptions to the domains of functioning affected by marital conflict. For example, El-Sheikh, Buckhalt, Cummings, and Keller (2007) found that marital conflict was linked with children's sleep disruptions, and that children's emotional insecurity about their parents' marital relationship was an intervening variable in this link. In turn, the sleep problems were associated with children's behavioral, emotional, and academic problems (see also El-Sheikh et al., 2006). These finding suggest that a fundamental aspect of biological functioning, sleep, is affected by insecurity in children induced by marital conflict, with consequences for multiple dimensions of children's functioning.

Bases for concern about the implications for marital conflict for school performance have increased substantially in recent years, including new evidence about the processes underlying links between marital conflict and school problems. Extending the study of relations between/ among marital conflict, emotional security about marital conflict, and sleep problems further, El-Sheikh, Buckhalt, Keller, and colleagues (2007) showed that this pathway was related to several aspects of school performance, including math, language, and both verbal and nonverbal achievement scores (see Chapter 4).

Other processes reflecting relations between children's emotional insecurity about marital conflict and school performance are also under investigation. For instance, Davies, Woitach, and colleagues (2008) identified a pathway from marital conflict to children's insecure representations about marital conflict, and from emotional insecurity to children's attentional difficulties 1 year later. In turn, the attentional difficulties were associated both concurrently and longitudinally with school problems. These findings add to the evidence for the impact of children's emotional insecurity about marital conflict on their functioning outside the home, particularly in school.

Supporting a "sensitization hypothesis," evidence has continued to mount over the past 15-plus years that the more often fights occur in the home, the more likely children are to react with aggression, anger, distress, and mediation. Children from angry home environments are more sensitive than other children to adults' conflicts. For example, children are much more likely to intervene in parental conflicts when they are from angry homes. Similarly, children from angry home environments are more distressed by adults' fights than others and are more likely to become aggressive toward others.

Thus children do not get used to marital conflict or accustomed to it; rather, they become sensitized to it, and as a result become more vulnerable to emotional, behavioral, cognitive, and physiological reactions that may lead to adjustment problems. A long history of research supports the sensitization effect (e.g., Cummings et al., 1981), which is thought to hold a key to understanding the increased risk for adjustment problems associated with repeated exposure to marital conflict and discord (Cummings, 1994). More recently, sensitization effects have been demonstrated in the laboratory under controlled conditions (Davies, Myers, et al., 1999) and also longitudinally (Davies, Sturge-Apple, et al., 2006) (see Chapter 2).

Notably, EST takes an integrated view of emotional, behavioral, and cognitive responding as indicative of sensitization to conflict. Thus this theory moves beyond a focus on any single dimension of responding (e.g., cognitive or emotional), and provides conceptual and empirical bases for regarding multiple dimensions of children's reactions as revealing vulnerability to adjustment problems. Again, much research conducted since the publication of our 1994 volume supports EST in accounting for the effects of marital conflict on children. To facilitate future research, two standardized instruments for assessing emotional security are provided in Appendices B and C.

Children Respond Differently to Different Forms of Anger

Although interparental conflict and disagreement are normal, everyday occurrences, high levels of such conflict do increase children's risk for mental health problems. This has been documented repeatedly in research conducted over many years. Differences in how parents handle conflict account for many of the differences in the effects on children. Notably, many conflicts include both constructive and destructive conflict expressions; thus the critical matters are the relative constructiveness of conflict and the extent to which conflicts are resolved (Cummings et al., 2003b; Goeke-Morey et al, 2007). A review of findings pertinent to making recommendations for parents about handling conflict destructively versus constructively is provided in Chapter 3. These results are also central to the psychoeducational program for parents described later in this chapter (Cummings, Faircloth, Mitchell, Cummings, & Schermerhorn, 2008).

The findings of field, experimental, and analogue studies thus provide a consistent picture: The impact of marital conflict varies as a function of how parents fight. Although sensitivity and reactivity to parental anger in children are normal and are found at an early age, heightened sensitivity is linked with destructive forms of anger expressions between parents. High levels of reactivity can in fact be regarded as dysfunctional, since they are associated with long-term negative child developmental outcomes.

Another key message of research over the past 15-plus years is that both fathers' and mothers' anger and hostility during marital conflict affect children's adjustment. Moreover, the theoretical processes accounting for the effects of both parents' marital conflict behaviors on children may be similar. For example, El-Sheikh and colleagues (2008) showed that emotional security was a viable explanatory mechanism for the influence of marital aggression on child adjustment, including internalizing, externalizing, and PTSD symptoms. Moreover, the findings extended EST by showing in both African American and European American families that marital aggression against the father as well as the mother had negative implications for children's emotional security and adjustment outcomes.

Marital Conflict Affects Children by Affecting Parenting

Great progress has been made in the past 15-plus years in clarifying relations between/among marital conflict, parenting, and child adjustment. Relatively little was known about this pathway at the publication of the 1994 volume. As indicated in Chapter 5, there are now numerous demonstrations that parenting is one of the pathways mediating the effects of marital conflict on children, including longitudinal demonstrations of these relations. More precisely, however, marital conflict affects children both directly though exposure and indirectly by changing family processes, including parenting and other family processes (e.g., sibling relations).

A particularly intriguing direction for more complete understanding of relations between marital conflict and parenting is research examining the effects of specific forms of conflict on parenting as a pathway for influencing child outcomes. Thus, Sturge-Apple and colleagues (2006b) recently showed that hostility and withdrawal from interparental conflict affected parental emotional unavailability, leading to increased adjustment difficulties among children. Interestingly, consistent with other work suggesting the impact of relatively less overt forms of conflict, withdrawal during marital conflict was a stronger predictor in this pathway than hostility was.

Bidirectional Effects

A traditional view is that marital conflict affects children. However, there was scant consideration until recently of how children may influence marital conflict. Recent studies make clear that these bidirectional pathways exist. For example, children's behavior problems are longitudinally related to marital conflict (Jenkins et al., 2005).

As another example, children's reactions during marital conflict have been related to marital functioning. Thus, consistent with the sensitization hypothesis, Schermerhorn and colleagues (2007) found that interparental conflict was related to children's negative emotional reactivity, which in turn was related to children's mediation in parental conflict and dysregulated behavior. Children's mediation was found to be longitudinally predictive of decreased interparental discord, whereas dysregulated behavior was associated with increased marital conflict and children's adjustment problems. This research suggests that children's tendencies to react to marital conflict may affect the course of marital conflict over time, but questions remain as to why these relations are obtained.

Relatedly, for many years it has been posited that family processes are mutually influential and related in transactional ways over time. Although this notion is central to a familywide perspective on interrelations between/among marital conflict, family processes, and child adjustment, these assumptions have recently been subjected to tests. One study (Schermerhorn et al., 2008) showed that children's representations of emotional security about the marriage, the mother–child relationship, and the father–child relationship were mutually influential over time.

Principles for Parents' Anger and Conflict Expression

Guidelines and principles for how parents can fight constructively for the sake of the children have been much further developed since 1994. First, there is support for the existence of constructive conflict from the children's perspective, as opposed to certain behaviors' simply inducing less negative emotionality than others in the children. Moreover, a continuum of behaviors in terms of relative destructiveness–constructiveness has been identified and supported by careful laboratory and home-based studies, providing bases for much clearer guidelines for parents on how to handle conflicts.

Second, the processes accounting for the effects of marital conflict on children have been much more clearly identified; the result is a greater understanding of how, when, and why children are vulnerable or resilient in the face of marital conflict. With the publication of several major theories, and increasing publication of valuable tests of these theories' propositions, there is a rich conceptual foundation for understanding these relations. In particular, EST provides an organizational and theoretical model (1) for integrating the multiple emotional, behavioral, cognitive, and physiological responses known to be influenced by exposure to marital conflict; and (2) for conceptualizing common processes by which marital conflict and affected family systems may lead to children's adjustment problems. These directions are particularly useful for practitioners dealing with distressed marriages and families, as well as for parents.

Don't Hold Anger In

We sometimes refer to the "silent treatment" as "middle-class anger." We middle-class types tend to think that if we don't say anything, children won't notice that anything is wrong. But they most definitely do notice, and it makes them anxious.

There is now evidence that chronic nonverbal anger expression can pose even more problems than verbal anger over time. Verbally unarticulated and unexpressed hostility between parents is a potential ongoing source of stress for children. No resolution of the parents' conflict is possible, because the issues are never put on the table.

Don't Go Overboard When Fighting

Going overboard in marital conflict is destructive not only for marriages, but also for children. The message from research is even clearer than in 1994: Partners should at least control their anger expression sufficiently that they do not engage in any physical aggression. Physical anger expression is not only the most distressing form of anger expression from a child's immediate perspective; it is the form that has most clearly and consistently been linked with the later development of mental health problems in children.

Principles for Conflict Resolution

One of the most exciting findings in this area is evidence that resolution greatly reduces children's negative emotional reactions to interadult conflict. This point was already well established by the publication of the 1994 book, including that the degree of resolution matters. The main advance in recent years has been to document the ameliorative effect of conflict resolution in actual incidents of marital conflict in the home, including differences in responding as a function of the degree of resolution (Goeke-Morey et al., 2007).

DEFINITION AND AIMS OF TRANSLATIONAL RESEARCH: BUILDING PROGRAMS BASED ON EMPIRICAL FOUNDATIONS

A next step for work in this area is effectively making these findings available to parents and practitioners. In the 1994 volume, we referred to the need to disseminate research findings on marital conflict and child development to practitioners and parents. In the intervening years, efforts to accomplish this goal have received various labels, among them "translational research." Although it remains true that limited progress has been made toward meeting this goal, progress has at least been made on outlining some of the key issues for accomplishing this work, and some initial studies have been published.

Translational research aims to bridge gaps between scholarly wisdom and the application of this knowledge in practice. Optimal programs cull key findings, principles, and concepts from scholarly and academic directions, and translate these elements into applied programs that are both applicable and effective in the "real world." Just how this can be accomplished is rarely explicitly considered, however. Steps in the development of optimal translational research include (1) identifying messages or conclusions in research that may have practical implications, (2) creating evidence-based prevention or intervention programs, and (3) rigorously evaluating the efficacy of these programs.

The gaps addressed by translational research merit further discussion. Just as it is not enough to generate research and theory in the hope that parents or practitioners will eventually benefit from the availability of this information in the scientific literature, it is not enough simply to develop programs that have good intentions for helping children and families. In addition to being presented in formats that are accessible and appealing to the public, programs need to be informed by the available research on the one hand, and evaluated for their efficacy on the other. Although many well-meaning policies and programs are designed to ameliorate children's and families' problems, there are frequently disconnects between the messages and characteristics of applied programs and the relevant scholarly research base. That is, the elements of applied programs may be no more than loosely based on actual evidence, even when the term "evidence-based" is used to describe these programs. Moreover, many applied programs are rarely if ever subjected to rigorous evaluation; this limits both confidence in the effectiveness of these programs and opportunities to improve the programs over time (Grych & Fincham, 1992).

Specifically, we discuss the necessary steps in developing a program on marital conflict and children—a program that achieves the aim of making research-based information helpful for children and families. One direction is preventing marital discord for the sake of children in community samples, but there are others (see Turner & Dadds, 2001). Focusing on this direction, we selectively provide examples from trials aimed at translating evidence about marital conflict's effects on children into prevention programs for community families (Cummings, Faircloth, et al., 2008; Faircloth & Cummings, 2008).

STEPS IN DEVELOPING TRANSLATIONAL RESEARCH

The development of translational research at the level of procedures and materials is unfamiliar for many investigators trained in scholarly research traditions. At the same time, individuals comfortable in applied contexts may have limited understanding of scholarly traditions for gathering and evaluating evidence, including research design issues essential to advancing the scientific bases for applied programs, and sophisticated approaches to evaluation. These facts present significant and fundamental challenges to achieving the goal of developing programs that effectively make the best empirical research available in the context of adequately evaluated applied programs.

Culling Key Findings, Principles, and Concepts from the Scholarly Literature

A critical aspect of translational research is that programs must be closely based on "empirical foundations." This term is sometimes used rather loosely. Attention to this aspect of program development is critical; one cannot "give away" research if one does attend first to whether the program adequately reflects the relevant research.

What Are the Key Findings?

An initial step is to discern the key messages from research that might serve as bases for a prevention program. In our own work (e.g., Cummings, Faircloth, et al., 2008), we decided to focus on information about specific ways parents can handle conflicts for the sake of the children. This element of the program was relatively straightforward to decide upon, as a core goal for us over the past two decades has been to conduct research with implications for parents on the distinctions between constructive and destructive conflict from the children's perspective. This research is especially reviewed in Chapter 3 of this volume, although pertinent evidence is cited throughout the volume. Moreover, prevention research has been little informed by empirical research on marital conflict and children, reflecting the problem described throughout this chapter of spanning the gap between research findings and the effective application of these findings in the real world.

What Is the Theory?

There is a general agreement that optimal intervention programs are informed and guided by a theoretical framework (Borkowski, Smith, & Akai, 2007; Nation et al., 2003). Theory both serves to integrate program elements into a cohesive whole and provides participants with a "big-picture" view of the program's message. Tests of theory can also contribute to an understanding of the conceptual bases for any success of the program.

EST has provided the theoretical basis for our translational research program. This theory has been described in detail in Chapter 2 of the present volume. The principles of EST were included as program elements. That is, to foster parents' understanding of the principles and concepts underlying the program's educational components, the significance of maintaining emotional security among family members even during conflicts was stressed, including the importance of secure interparental attachment, secure parent–child attachment, and children's emotional security about the interparental relationship. Parents were encouraged to keep the value of these relationships foremost in their minds, even when they were faced with threatening or intense conflict situations.

Is There Other Work That Merits Consideration?

Although translational research requires a focus on the topic at hand (in our case, children and marital conflict) to do justice to the relevant empirical literature, other directions in practice and theory may also merit consideration. Thus, although our work was intended to address a unique gap by translating research findings on marital conflict and children into prevention materials, we also sought to be aware of and benefit from successful aspects of adult marital conflict interventions. Elements employed in couple therapy and research were incorporated into our program, especially marital communication training approaches (Gottman & Gottman, 1999; Markman & Floyd, 1980; Rogers, 1965). That is, building upon intervention techniques receiving empirical support in the literature on interventions for marital conflict, we provided parents with opportunities for active training in handling such conflict. These elements added to the diversity of the program materials, which is another characteristic of successful prevention programs (Borkowski et al., 2007).

Translating Basic Research into an Applied Program

The development of effective program materials is as much art as science. Although a consensus is emerging on the characteristics of the best programs (Borkowski et al., 2007; Nation et al., 2003), the development of materials that translate research knowledge into an effective program remains a significant challenge. Moreover, demands may vary, depending on the goals of the program. For example, the common wisdom is that prevention efforts should be comprehensive, but at the same time it is important to determine the "right amount" of treatment (Borkowski et al., 2007). Moreover, in some instances—especially for the goals and samples addressed by prevention programs—briefer programs may be more effective (van IJzendoorn, Bakermans-Kranenburg, & Sagi-Schwartz, 2003).

Thus it is not necessarily the case that "more is better" in a program for community families. Investigators must be careful not to provide either too little or too much treatment, so that participants are either left with inadequate information, or are overwhelmed by the number of visits and amount of material in the program. When too much is asked of participants (e.g., too many visits, too much time required for the treatment), a program may experience high attrition levels, which ultimately influences researchers' ability to evaluate the program's effectiveness. Cummings, Faircloth, and colleagues (2008) endeavored to strike a balance between "too little" and "too much" by asking families to participate in four visits that lasted on average 2½ hours; this represented a compromise between a single visit (Faircloth & Cummings, 2008) and an extensive series of visits. This level of participation proved manageable for many community families, as indicated by low attrition levels during the course of the 4-week program.

Deciding on Program Format and Emphases: The Psychoeducational Approach as an Example

Clinical intervention and prevention trials are typically intended for different audiences and may be better served by different formats for communicating information. A program's target population and goals must be considered in decisions about the best mode for presenting work. One possible way of presenting translational research for community families in prevention trials is the psychoeducational approach. This approach may be especially comfortable for academics and is highly amenable to the purpose of translating research findings into "user-friendly" presentations for laypersons. Of course, this method ideally will not consist of simply lectures on the topic, at the risk of losing the interest of participants; lectures are best supplemented with active, engaging approaches and activities.

The psychoeducational approach may be less appropriate for clinical samples or therapeutic interventions, although some benefits for divorced couples have been indicated (Shifflett & Cummings, 1999). It may be most appropriate in a prevention program for community samples (Blanchard et al., 2009). Any decision about program format should also weigh the type of information that the program developers wish to convey. For example, the goal of conveying research-based knowledge about marital conflict and children is a good fit for this approach.

There are bases for holding that community families can benefit from the presentation of information about family functioning in this way (Blanchard et al., 2009; Webster-Stratton, 1994). Teaching parents "to understand and identify which aspects of their behavior are detrimental to child adjustment can be a powerful intervention in itself" (Turner & Dadds, 2001, p. 403). Educational programs may increase knowledge, leading to improvements in behavior and increased capabilities to handle future problems (Morgan, Nu'Man-Sheppard, & Allin, 1990). Particularly important for prevention efforts are findings that such programs may be less daunting and more appealing to more individuals than intensive interventions (Pehrson & Robinson, 1990). Group methods of dissemination are also more cost-effective than individual methods (Johnston, 1994), which is another consideration if relatively large groups of community families are the intended audience. Of course, if the focus of the program is on transfer of knowledge, it is essential that the information be sound and likely to benefit parents and families. Carefully ensuring that information is firmly based on the latest research will ensure that this goal is achieved.

Varied Teaching Methods

In addition to the art of attempting to present the appropriate amount of treatment, preventive approaches are more effective if they employ multiple teaching methods, so that the information being conveyed is interesting and engaging (Borkowski et al., 2007). Presenting the material by utilizing several different modes of instruction helps to keep the participants' attention, as well as to make the material memorable. For example, information for adults may be presented by means of Power-Point, games, one-on-one training, and small-group discussions. For programs designed for children, puppets, stories, and games are among the possible vehicles for conveying information.

Participant Satisfaction

Related to these points, another important goal is to assess how much families enjoy the program, which ultimately relates to the program's potential to reach as many families as possible. Administration of a consumer satisfaction questionnaire at the end of the program is valuable for ensuring that the information has been conveyed in appealing ways to participants.

Well-Trained Staff and Positive Relationships with Participants

Well-trained and enthusiastic staff members are essential to delivering and presenting the program materials (Borkowski et al., 2007). The staff must receive extensive training, to ensure that the program is being administered appropriately and consistently. It is also vital that staff members create a warm relationship with participants, to make the environment one in which everyone is comfortable. A warm environment invites participants to ask questions whenever they please and helps them to feel at ease, both of which are fundamental to an optimal learning environment for a parent education program. Quality checks on staff members' interactions with participants, as well as formal assessment of participant satisfaction, help to ensure that a warm, comfortable environment is created for each family. These elements are vital to reducing attrition and successfully recruiting all family members when this is required (including mothers, fathers, and children).

Manualized Programs

Manualized program materials contribute to the uniform and consistent presentation of the program, and also foster the replicability of the program by other investigators. That is, having manualized protocols minimizes discrepancies among different individuals' ways of administering the program. It is important to ensure that all members of the research team follow a manualized protocol that outlines all elements and features of the program. A separate manual unit for each visit is ideal.

Fidelity Checks

Quality checks should be performed randomly throughout the project to ensure that the protocol is being followed. That is, observers should be trained to watch the visits to score treatment fidelity and ensure that standards for adequate treatment fidelity are met.

Evaluating the Efficacy of the Translational Program

Another critical element for optimal translational research is appropriate research design and evaluation to demonstrate the efficacy of the program. This element may be either missing from or inadequate in many applied research projects (Grych & Fincham, 1992). We next provide discussion of some of the requirements and opportunities for adequately conducting this phase of translational research, as well as some of the obstacles to doing so.

Randomized Controlled Trials

Critical to the interpretability of findings is that participants are randomly assigned to conditions, including treatment and control conditions. Otherwise, it is not possible to determine whether any results are attributable to the treatment condition or to preexisting differences between the groups. Randomized controlled trials are increasingly required for publication in top referred journals and are the standard for prevention trials. Decisions about control conditions are critical, including whether to use a no-treatment control (e.g., a wait-listed control group; Faircloth & Cummings, 2008) or a control group that carries more demanding tests for treatment efficacy. In the Cummings, Faircloth, and colleagues (2008) study, the comparison group was a self-study control group; this group was given text-based resources that presented findings on marital conflict, parenting, and children comparable to those presented in the treatment condition. Thus similar information was made available to both groups, but the control group was based on a self-help model (see Wolchik et al., 2000). This approach reduced the likelihood of treatment outcomes due to placebo effects, but also raised the possibility that both the treatment and control groups would evidence gains, thereby reducing the likelihood of treatment effects.

Pretesting, Short-Term Follow-Up, and Long-Term Follow-Up

Pretesting is essential, to control further for the possibility that preexisting differences are contributing to treatment effects. Another major concern is to show that treatment effects are relatively enduring (i.e., not evident only at end-of-treatment testing). Thus follow-up testing (e.g., 6-month and 1-year follow-ups) is needed to establish the value of prevention programs more fully. Long-term follow-up tests may be especially important for prevention trials, as benefits may only emerge over time for participants who are at risk but do not yet demonstrate problems. In the case of programs for preventing marital conflict, benefits for children may be expected to be found from improved marital conflict behavior, but these effects are not necessarily immediately apparent. That is, changes in marital conflict may need to be in place for some time before researchers can reasonably expect that child adjustment will be beneficially affected. Thus Cummings, Faircloth, and colleagues (2008) found that child adjustment improved in parental treatment conditions, but only over time and as a function of improvements in marital conflict behavior.

Multimethod Assessments

Given the focus of prevention trials on administering programs, there is a temptation (and, to some extent, a need) to minimize the demands of assessment. Assessment packages are also necessarily limited in research that focuses on developmental process. However, the goal of providing cogent evidence for the value of a prevention trial means that appropriate assessment must not be neglected. In particular, using only questionnaire measures of intended outcomes may limit the interpretability of outcomes in some cases, since such measures are susceptible to social desirability effects. Questionnaires may also be relatively imprecise in documenting program effects and may produce smaller effects than observational assessments (Blanchard et al., 2009). For example, extant marital conflict instruments make relatively few distinctions among types of marital conflict behaviors.

For this reason, assessment measures should be developed to document whether the most specific outcomes targeted by the program are affected. For example, an important measure for a psychoeducational program may be a questionnaire to test parents' knowledge of program materials—for example, the best ways to handle marital conflicts (Cummings, Faircloth, et al., 2008; Faircloth & Cummings, 2008).

In addition, observational records of marital conflict behaviors in the laboratory permit investigators to obtain much more detail about any changes in these behaviors, as well as more objective data on any such changes. In the Cummings, Faircloth, and colleagues (2008) study, observational records provided valuable indices of positive changes in marital conflict behaviors associated with participation in the program.

Finally, researchers may want to document that any changes that occur are seen in the home as well as the laboratory. Thus it may also be worth obtaining records of changes in marital conflict behaviors in the home. For example, use of diary recording procedures can increase the ecological validity of program effects (Cummings et al., 2003a, 2003b). The coding of marital conflict in the home on the basis of parents' diary records is being pursued in an ongoing prevention project for parents and adolescents.

INITIAL STUDIES TO ACCOMPLISH A TRANSLATIONAL RESEARCH OBJECTIVE: PARENT EDUCATION ABOUT MARITAL CONFLICT AND CHILDREN

In this section, we review some recently completed translational studies of marital conflict–focused psychoeducational prevention programs. These studies provide additional examples of how such research can be conducted.

A One-Visit Program

Faircloth and Cummings (2008) used questionnaire-based evaluations to test the effectiveness of a one-session prevention program for improving marital conflict resolution skills, as well as parents' knowledge about marital conflict. Fifty-five couples with an oldest child no more than 6 years of age were randomly assigned to either an immediate-treatment group ($n = 41$) or a 6-month wait-listed control group ($n = 14$), with assessments at pretest, posttest, and 6-month and 1-year follow-ups.

A unique feature of the intervention was that *the implications of marital conflict for the children* were central in the presentation of all program materials, which were based on the extensive empirical and theoretical work on children and marital conflict (Cummings & Davies, 1994a, 2002). Another portion of the program taught couples specific principles, skills, and techniques they could use to identify destructive behaviors, understand them, and replace them with constructive behaviors. Finally, a 19-item questionnaire was developed to assess couples' knowledge of the effects of marital conflict on children and the family, providing a targeted assessment of the psychoeducational program's effectiveness.

Results indicated that the program was effective in improving parents' knowledge about marital conflict across all assessment periods (but without comparisons to the control group), and in increasing parents' knowledge (relative to that of the wait-list control group at the posttest). Couples in the treatment group also displayed less hostility in front of their children 6 months after the program, and showed improvements in conflict tactics at both follow-ups, relative to their levels in preprogram assessments.

Thus parents participating in this evidence-based parent education program about marital conflict showed greater knowledge about constructive versus destructive conflict tactics and resolution strategies. Other findings suggested that parents' increased knowledge about optimal marital conflict strategies might be related to improved behavior during marital conflicts. However, although the findings supported the value of this one-visit program, limited posttest comparisons between treatment and control conditions, and the reliance on self-report about marital conflict, limited the potential interpretations of this program. Moreover, the presentation of the evidence-based information about marital conflict was constrained in a single session. Thus greater gains seemed possible with the presentation of a more extensive prevention program.

A Four-Visit Program

Cummings, Faircloth, and colleagues (2008) tested a more elaborate program, including much more extensive parent education about marital conflict; they also tested a psychoeducational component for children. Specifically, a four-session psychoeducational program about marital conflict for community families was developed. Couples with children between 4 and 8 years of age were randomly assigned to one of three groups: (1) a parent-only group ($n = 24$), (2) a parent–child group ($n = 33$), or (3) a self-study control group ($n = 33$). Both fathers and mothers participated in parent programs. Assessments were conducted at pretest, posttest, and 6-month and 1-year follow-ups. As noted earlier, the four-session approach represented a balance between very short (Faircloth & Cummings, 2008) and lengthy (i.e., clinical treatment) programs. The program was also more explicitly guided by EST, emphasizing the significance of maintaining the quality of emotional bonds among all family members during marital conflict.

More constructive and less destructive marital conflict was observed at all assessments for treatment groups. Most evident were changes in conflict behaviors indicating that parents changed their basic orientation with their partners in conflict situations; their new approach included being more respectful of their emotional relationship with each other, as well as fostering the security of family relationships. Specifically, after participation in the psychoeducational program, parents were more supportive of their partners, more emotionally positive during interactions, more likely to advance toward the resolution of arguments, and more constructive during conflict discussions. All these findings were consistent with the program's message that preserving and advancing the quality of emotional relationships in the family is more important than dominating the outcomes of arguments.

These changes were also linked with improvements in other family processes. That is, changes in marital conflict in the treatment group were linked with positive changes over time in marital satisfaction, parenting, and child adjustment. Changes in knowledge over time were linked with changes in conflict behaviors as well, suggesting that knowledge might be an active agent in improvements found in the treatment group. In addition, it is encouraging that over time, positive changes in marital conflict were linked with positive changes in marital satis-faction, parenting, and child adjustment. The program did not target these broader family processes, so such changes were expected to be contingent on improvements in marital conflict (Cowan & Cowan, 2002; Cowan et al., 2005, 2007).

The possibilities for implementation of these findings in commu-nity samples were further increased by the high consumer satisfaction with the program. The results supported the hypothesis that improve-ments in marital conflict in community samples can be accomplished in the context of a relatively brief program, and that these changes may be sustained in relation to a control group for at least 1 year. The find-ings thus further supported the promise of brief psychoeducational pro-grams for marital conflict in community samples.

A 2-Year Follow-Up

Faircloth, Schermerhorn, Mitchell, Cummings, and Cummings (2009) recently tested the long-term efficacy of this four-session prevention program. Couples with children between 4 and 8 years of age who had previously participated in either treatment condition or the control con-dition of the earlier study were contacted again and asked to complete a 2-year follow-up assessment. Compared to the control group, both treatment groups demonstrated greater knowledge about the effects of marital conflict on families, as well as behavioral improvements in constructive conflict (specifically, problem-solving behaviors), at the 2-year follow-up. Moreover, these changes in marital conflict knowledge and behavior were linked with improvements in other family processes, including marital satisfaction, parenting, and child adjustment. The findings thus supported the long-term efficacy of this program. These findings suggest that even brief psychoeducational programs for educat-ing community samples about family processes (marital conflict, in this instance) can serve to prevent problems, with positive implications for marriages, parenting, and child development.

CONCLUSIONS AND FUTURE DIRECTIONS

Given the implications of marital conflict for children's adjustment prob-lems, the findings from research on marital conflict and children are of interest to parents and practitioners concerned with the well-being of children. Increasing the potential value of this work, research conducted since our 1994 volume was published has made great progress in clarifying the distinctions between constructive and destructive conflict from the perspective of the children, as well as the processes underlying children's vulnerability and resilience in the face of marital conflict. At the same time, this literature has become so extensive (conceptually as well as empirically) that our review of research-based conclusions, implications, and guidelines has necessarily been selective and illustrative. The work in this area has progressed to the point where an entire volume could easily be devoted to its practical implications (Jouriles, McDonald, Stephens, Norwood, Spiller, & Ware, 1998; Turner & Dadds, 2001).

A next step for future research will be further exploration of program elements for children as well as parents. With regard to marital conflict, the focus should remain on parent programs, since parents are by definition the persons best able to ameliorate marital conflict as a stressor. Although efforts have been explored to teach children to cope more effectively with marital conflict (e.g., the parent–child program in Cummings, Faircloth, et al., 2008), the evidence for the efficacy of this approach for the children is very modest (Mitchell, McCoy, Cummings, Faircloth, & Cummings, in press; see also Wolchik et al., 2000). Given that it is realistic for children to be concerned about marital conflict, the benefits that can be obtained by teaching children to cope with it better are probably limited. At the same time, reciprocal and bidirectional relations are found between child and parental conflict behavior (Jenkins et al., 2005), so a program component that teaches children to handle their own conflicts with parents and others more constructively may hold more promise for the children's own adjustment, as well as for family relationships and marital conflict. This direction may be most valuable in adolescence—a period in which parent–child conflict is high and when children are cognitively most likely to benefit from a psychoeducational approach.

However, as we have indicated, simply identifying and communicating these findings may have only have limited benefits. Another next step will be translational research that develops programs for delivering this information more effectively to parents and practitioners. Given the widespread risk posed by marital conflict for marriages, children, and families, and the fact that the optimal point for remediation is the period before discord becomes severe, programs for community families may be a particularly promising direction. Accordingly, another goal for this chapter has been to lay foundations for this application of research findings. Again, there are various other possible directions, issues, and possibilities, so this review has also inevitably been limited to illustrative points and examples.

In closing, the rapid growth of research and theory on marital conflict and children is exciting and encouraging. At the same time, given the implications of this research for real-world problems, an ongoing concern is how to make its results applicable in the real world. We hope that this chapter will serve to stimulate further advances in this area of work.

CHAPTER 9

Beyond the Marital Dyad

From Bowlby to Political Violence

Research on marital conflict and children has implications for a better understanding of other contexts influencing children's development, beyond the marital dyad. The many methodological directions described throughout this volume for investigating the effects of marital conflict on children are potentially useful for exploring these other contexts. The complexity of influences operating in the family, and the challenges involved in studying these relations, have necessitated the development of sophisticated and unique research approaches. The solutions and theory advanced in the marital conflict area can serve as models for solving other problems in research on complex socioemotional contexts affecting child development (e.g., school contexts, peer relations, sibling relations).

Marital conflict is also a factor in phenomena traditionally thought to create risk for children for other reasons. For example, marital conflict is intimately related to the impact of risky families on children (Repetti, Taylor, & Seeman, 2002), and is closely tied to the impact of parental depression (Cummings & Davies, 1994b; Downey & Coyne, 1990) (see Chapter 1). Marital conflict is not an isolated influence, but should be considered in developmental pathways in multiple other social-ecological contexts. Unfortunately, interparental conflict and violence are often ignored or neglected. For example, despite over two decades' worth of evidence for relations between/among parental depression, marital conflict, and child adjustment, many studies and even reviews of parental depression and children that are otherwise quite outstanding continue to neglect marital conflict as an environmental influence on children's socioemotional development (e.g., Goodman & Gotlib, 1999).

In this chapter, the implications of marital conflict research and EST are extended to topics perhaps not traditionally considered pertinent to relations between marital conflict and children. Themes vary from connections between EST and attachment theory in the Bowlby tradition, to the contributions made by marital conflict and emotional security to the impact of political and community violence on children. Notably, these are only illustrative examples. Conflict in families plays a role in multiple other ecological contexts pertinent to the development and well-being of children—for example, parental alcohol problems (see Chapter 1).

A FAMILYWIDE MODEL OF EMOTIONAL SECURITY

Although we have considered *empirical* relations between marital conflict and other family systems, these demonstrations have focused primarily on the statistical links between marital conflict and other family processes. This section focuses on the further development of theoretical foundations for conceptualizing these relations. Although these relations may be based upon numerous different contexts of risk and resilience for children, the premise is that *similar underlying processes of emotional security* may account for the impact of multiple family systems on children's development. This discussion thus advances the notion of a familywide model of emotional security (Cummings & Davies, 1996).

Attachment Theory

In our experience, there is considerable interest in the relations between attachment theory and children's emotional security about marital conflict as articulated in EST. Given the extent to which this issue has arisen in our professional communications with colleagues, and given the significance of both attachment and EST to models of risk and resilience, this topic merits further discussion.

First, secure-base conceptions are fundamental to both attachment theory and EST (Cummings & Davies, 1996; Waters & Cummings, 2000).

According to attachment theory, the emotional bonds between parents and children are sources of security for children in times of stress (Cicchetti et al., 1990). These notions are extended by EST to include other family processes, including marital conflict and its effects on children; EST thus emphasizes the role of multiple family relationships in contributing to children's security (Cummings & Davies, 1996).

Although attachment theorists have focused on emotional security in the parent–child relationship (primarily the mother–child relationship), the concept of extending secure-base notions beyond mother–child attachment has a long history. Notably, Ainsworth (1989) acknowledged the lifelong significance of attachment, and Bowlby (1949) recognized the need to take the family into account in considering children's security and distress (see also Byng-Hall, 1995; Marvin & Stewart, 1990). However, at least until recently, attachment theory has been largely confined to identifying parenting attributes (e.g., maternal responsiveness) as predictors of attachment in isolation from other family systems (Thompson, 1997).

EST was developed in part to address this gap. That is, although it seemed evident both logically and from observations of children's reactions that exposure to marital conflict would affect their emotional security (Cummings et al., 1981), no theoretical model existed to account for this possibility. Thus, instead of being an alternative theory, EST was intended from the outset to be a logical extension of attachment theory (Davies & Cummings, 1994). EST postulates that although a child evaluates interpersonal contexts in relation to multiple goals, safety and security are among the most salient in the hierarchy of human goals (Waters & Cummings, 2000). Rather than positing that security is only relevant to the mother–child attachment relationship, EST hypothesizes that children develop a sense of security in the context of the interparental relationship that is distinct (but not orthogonal) in its substance, origins, and sequelae from attachment security (Davies, Harold, et al., 2002). EST also emphasizes understanding the role of fathers in the context of marital relationships, including the significance of father–child attachment (Cummings, Goeke-Morey, & Raymond, 2004).

In both EST and attachment theory, children are posited to have a set goal of maintaining emotional security, consistent with Bowlby's (1969) propositions. When this set goal is violated—for example, due to stress in the context of the parent–child or interparental relationship—children are motivated to take action to regain the goal (Cummings & Davies, 1996). In the case of exposure to the threat of separation from the mother, an infant may respond by seeking proximity or contact with the mother on her return in order to regain emotional security, or by engaging in avoidance or behavioral dysregulation in the case of an insecure attachment. EST proposes parallels between threats to emotional security in parent–child relationships and threats for security posed by marital conflict: When exposed to marital conflict, children may respond by mediating in parents' conflicts, or by engaging in avoidance or behavioral dysregulation in the case of an insecure response pattern (Davies & Forman, 2002). At the same time, compared to attachment behavioral systems (Ainsworth, 1969), social defense systems are uniquely activated by exposure to marital conflict and violence (Davies & Sturge-Apple, 2007; Davies & Woitach, 2008).

Thus the secure-base system, with emotional security as its set goal, is conceptualized as central not only to the functioning of the parent–child attachment relationship (Bowlby, 1969), but to children's functioning in the context of marital conflict (Davies, Harold, et al., 2002). Moreover, both the attachment and marital conflict behavioral systems, like other fundamental psychological processes, have biological bases (Cummings & Davies, 1996) and are hypothesized to be reflected in biologically based response processes (Davies et al., 2007; Davies & Woitach, 2008). Both control systems as expressions of personal relationships in families are constructed through experience, and are theorized to play a role in the organization of behavior and emotion in family relationships. Thus the child's attachment to the parents, and the child's response to the relationship between the parents—including the interparental attachment relationship (Cummings et al., 2005) and experiences with constructive as well as destructive marital conflict (McCoy et al., 2009)—are revealed in the operating characteristics of an underlying control system that takes into account information about the child's state, the state of the environment, and the child's past and current experiences with the caregivers (Bowlby, 1973; Davies, Harold, et al., 2002; Davies, Sturge-Apple, et al., 2006).

Both attachment theory and EST refer to the role of self-regulatory processes in the service of emotional security, including children's emotional and cognitive appraisals of situational and contextual challenges and threats, and the influence of these appraisals on emotional and behavioral responding. In both conceptualizations, emotional reactions reflect children's evaluations of events and are conceptualized as playing a role in organizing and motivating children's responses to threats (Bowlby, 1969; Davies & Cummings, 1994). Over time, these emotionally based self-regulatory patterns, which reflect the relative security or insecurity afforded by children's experiential histories with parents in multiple situations, are seen as characterizing children's functioning in response to current experiences (Davies, Sturge-Apple, et al., 2006). Such responses constitute one class of processes derived from day-to-day experiences with the parents, reflecting their success in providing security for children in stressful situations. That is, these responses index self-regulatory structures derived from experience that serve to guide current responding (e.g., Bowlby, 1973; Schermerhorn et al., 2008).

Another process emphasized by both attachment theory and EST involves the cognitive processes or "internal working models" that mediate relations between children's experiential histories and their outcomes. The issue is how children represent and organize their cognitions about themselves and their relationships with others as a function of experiences with their parents, particularly in times of stress (e.g., separation, marital conflict), and how their expectancies about the parents' behavior and affect relate to their ongoing functioning in regard to the set goal of emotional security. Both approaches also call attention to the fact that relationship experiences with the parents over time (e.g., emotional responsiveness, exposure to marital conflict) lead to generalized expectancies regarding the self, the world, and others. These internal working models emerge in some form early in development, and continue to evolve as a function of experiences in the family throughout development.

Accumulating evidence suggests that these cognitions resulting from children's experiences with parents in both parent–child attachment (Bretherton, Ridgeway, & Cassidy, 1990) and marital conflict (Schermerhorn et al., 2008) are keys to understanding the processes that underlie the effects of attachment and marital conflict, respectively, on children's development (Shamir, Du Rocher Schudlich, & Cummings, 2001). These internal representations may underlie the impact of stable family circumstances on the continuity of developmental trajectories; alternatively, changing internal representations due to altered family circumstances (e.g., newly emotionally unavailable parents, heightened marital conflict) may relate to discontinuities in developmental pathways. Thus relations between attachment theory according to Bowlby and EST are evident on multiple levels of analysis, including the organizational construct (Cicchetti et al., 1990) that behavioral, emotional, and cognitive responses may serve the goal of maintaining emotional security in children's responses to parent–child and marital systems (Davies & Cummings, 1994; Davies, Harold, et al., 2002).

Moreover, EST extends Bowlby's account by positing that interparental conflict is associated with child adjustment through multiple pathways involving both the parent–child and interparental systems associated with emotional security processes. Parenting difficulties accompanying interparental conflict are proposed to be related to child adjustment problems, in part through their association with attachment security between the parents (Davies, Harold, et al., 2002). In addition, EST postulates that interparental conflict may be associated with child psychological problems by directly undermining child security in the parent–child relationship (Frosch et al., 2000; Owen & Cox, 1997). Unanswered questions remain about the role of parenting processes in children's security in the interparental relationship. For example, sensitive parenting may facilitate children's emotion regulation across multiple family contexts, and thereby assist children in their goal of preserving security in the interparental context.

Empirical support is accumulating to support a familywide model of emotional security. For example, one study (Davies, Harold, et al., 2002) reported distinct pathways to child adjustment from emotional security about both the parent–child and marital relationships (see also Sturge-Apple et al., 2008). Moreover, Harold and colleagues (2004) found longitudinal support for cognitive, emotional, and behavioral responses to marital conflict as pathways to child adjustment, as well as for attachment as a pathway relevant to the effects of marital conflict on child adjustment. More recently, Schermerhorn and colleagues (2008) found interrelations longitudinally among cognitive indicators of emotional security about marital conflict, father–child relationships, and mother–child relationships, with evidence for transactional interrelations among these response processes over time. Finally, evidence indicates support for a familywide model of emotional security across multiple family systems, including relations between insecurity in the interparental system and familywide profiles of cohesive, disengaged, enmeshed, or adequate families (Davies, Cummings, & Winter, 2004).

Parental Psychopathology

Many conceptualizations of family adversity share the assumption that children's difficulties in preserving a sense of security and safety in the family are among the primary sources for several serious psychological disorders emerging from parental psychopathology, such as depression, anxiety disorders (including PTSD), and conduct disorder (Davies & Cummings, 2006; Greenberg, 1999; Johnston & Roseby, 1997). Familywide perspectives on risk and resilience in children (Cummings & Davies, 1994b) implicate marital and family conflict, including conflict in single-parent homes (Amato, 2005), in multiple family processes affecting children's risk for adjustment problems.

At the same time, although progress has been made in identifying multiple family processes that may be related to the impact of parental psychopathology on children, relatively little is known about the specifics of these processes. Emotional security emerges as one factor among several (e.g., genetic factors, social learning) that may be involved in the operation of multiple family systems associated with parental psychopathology in elevating children's risk for adjustment problems. For example, with regard to parental depression and child development, disturbances in attachment have long been implicated both theoretically and empirically in the development, maintenance, and intergenerational transmission of depressive problems (Cummings & Cicchetti, 1990). Higher rates of marital conflict are found in homes with parental depression, as well as higher rates of insecure attachments (Cummings, DeArth-Pendley, Du Rocher Schudlich, & Smith, 2000). In addition, familial patterns of dysfunctional emotional communication and psychological unavailability characterize these homes (Goodman & Gotlib, 1999). Thus it seems logical that emotional security concerns should be elevated in children of depressed parents, and that these concerns may play a role in such children's elevated risk for adjustment problems (Cummings, DeArth-Pendley, et al., 2000). A future direction is the move to process-level study—that is, understanding how and why the interplay between parental psychopathology and marital conflict increases children's vulnerability to problems through security processes.

EST as a specific articulation of a relational systems approach has similarities to other models for the development of children of depressed parents. For example, Lee and Gotlib (1991) speculated as to why different forms of family disturbance predict common child outcomes. They proposed that there may be common pathways (e.g., emotional processes in family systems) through which multiple forms of family disturbances (e.g., marital conflict, parental depression) exert their effects, including children's sense of security or confidence in their parents. Lyons-Ruth (1995) argued for process-oriented models centering on relations among systems within depressive family contexts; she noted that two particularly promising relational contexts were attachment relationships and hostile marital relations (see also Goodman & Gotlib, 2002).

Emotional security thus emerges from multiple perspectives as a promising construct for understanding child development in families with parental depression. Relations between parental depression and insecure attachment in children have been reported (Cummings & Cicchetti, 1990). As another example, Cummings and colleagues (2005) found that increased parental depressive symptomatology (either mother's or father's dysphoria) was related to increased marital conflict, insecure marital attachment, less parental warmth, more psychological control in parenting, and multiple negative child outcomes. This study highlighted the particular roles of marital conflict and of parents' emotional security in the interparental relationship in mediating child outcomes due to *both* paternal and maternal dysphoria; that is, it called attention to the attachment relationship between the parents, as well as other conceptualizations of emotional security (e.g., parent–child attachment), in accounting for risk or resilience associated with child development outcomes in these families.

Recent research also indicates that children's emotional security regarding the interparental relationship plays a role in child outcomes in association with parental depressive symptomatology. In a study of a community sample, Du Rocher Schudlich and Cummings (2007) reported that parental depressive symptoms (either mother's or father's dysphoria) were linked with child adjustment through distinct mediating family processes, including marital conflict and parenting. Notably, children's emotional security in the context of particular marital conflict styles mediated relations between parental dysphoria and child adjustment problems, with similar pathways found for mothers and fathers. At the same time, although the results implicated both marital conflict and children's emotional security about marital conflict in pathways leading to child outcomes, the findings clearly left room for other possible pathways and processes.

Future researchers are urged to consider additional possible explanatory processes, and also to extend these emotional security models to other forms of psychopathology. For example, links between/among parental alcohol problems, marital conflict, and child adjustment argue for the inclusion of marital conflict and emotional security in explanatory models for the impact of parental alcohol problems on children (El-Sheikh & Flanagan, 2001). Recent work has longitudinally identified marital conflict as a process mediating the effects of paternal alcohol problems on child adjustment (Keller et al., 2008). Another recent study has implicated emotional security as a process mediating the effects of paternal problems (alcohol problems, dysphoria) on child adjustment over time (Schacht, Cummings, & Davies, in press).

The Relevance of Marital Conflict and Emotional Security to Extrafamilial Conflict Processes

Mutual Influences among Multiple Levels of the Social Ecology

Marital conflict and emotional security may also be relevant to understanding the impact of extrafamilial conflict processes on children, such as community and political conflict and violence. For example, political conflict processes (e.g., ethnic conflict) may have effects on communities, families, and children that are significant both to understanding the full impact of these processes, and to achieving long-term success at the societal level in resolving political conflicts (Lovell & Cummings, 2001). Moreover, although community and political conflict and violence have been little examined with regard to family processes, they may affect family relationships and children's emotional security about both community and family.

Thus both family and community conflict are highly pertinent to peace studies. Although peace studies have traditionally focused on political conflict resolution, conflict resolution is needed at multiple levels of the social ecology, including community and family. Empirical, conceptual, and methodological lessons from the study of conflict in families may be potentially valuable for understanding conflict processes at multiple other levels of analysis, including sectarian, ethnic, and other forms of political conflict.

However, these questions have rarely been posed, and little is known about conflict processes from the perspective of a social-ecological analysis that takes into account multiple levels of societal functioning. Such a perspective calls for theory-driven research, innovative study designs, new methodological approaches, consideration of multiple influences and complex ecological processes, and sophisticated analytic methods (Feerick & Prinz, 2003; Prinz & Feerick, 2003).

In the remainder of this chapter, we begin to explore these issues. We start with a consideration of marital conflict and associated processes as pathways for understanding the effects of community conflict and violence.

Community Conflict and Violence

Exposure to community violence may exert a negative influence on children's psychological adjustment (Garbarino, Dubrow, Koselny, & Pardo, 1992; Mabanglo, 2002; Stein, Jaycox, Kataoka, Rhodes, & Vestal, 2003). Such exposure is particularly linked with children's development of externalizing disorders, especially violence and aggressiveness in males (Attar & Guerra, 1994; Cooley-Quille, Turner, & Beidel, 1995; Jenkins & Bell, 1994; O'Keefe, 1997). However, other emotional, cognitive, and behavioral problems have also been identified (Kuther, 1999; Singer, Anglin, Song, & Lunghofer, 1995), including depression and stress symptoms (Berton & Stabb, 1996; Gorman-Smith & Tolan, 1998). Although some studies find no differences in exposure to community violence as a function of child age or gender (Cooley-Quille et al., 1995; Richters & Martinez, 1993b), other studies report that males and older children are more likely to be victims or witnesses of such violence (Jaycox et al., 2002; Richters & Martinez, 1993b).

Community violence exposure has also been linked to poor academic performance in urban elementary school children, with evidence for mediation through symptoms of depression and behavior problems (Schwartz & Gorman, 2003). Negative effects may include disruptions in children's capacities for self-regulation and control (Maughan & Cicchetti, 2002; Schwartz & Proctor, 2000), as well as the development of social-cognitive biases toward attributing more hostile intentions to others (Earls, 2003), which may foster children's aggressive responding toward others (e.g., Crick & Dodge, 1994, 1996).

Some studies indicate that marital conflict and domestic violence may be affected by community or cultural contexts of violence (Martinez & Richters, 1993; Richters & Martinez, 1993b). That is, both families and children may be affected by exposure to community contexts of conflict and violence, with effects seen even in very young children (Cooley-Quille et al., 1995; Farver, Natera, & Frosch, 1999). Moreover, violence in the community and violence in the home are interrelated in affecting children (Lynch & Cicchetti, 2002; Margolin & Gordis, 2000). Families with high levels of exposure to community violence are characterized by high conflict and a lack of cohesion (Cooley-Quille et al., 1995).

On the other hand, community violence and family violence may be distinct influences on children's maladaptive psychological functioning: Exposure to family violence has been found to be associated with child adjustment even when relations between community violence and child psychopathology are nonsignificant (Muller, Goebel-Fabbri, Diamond, & Dinklage, 2000). Maternal distress (i.e., maternal symptomatology) has also been implicated as mediating links between community violence and early child behavior problems (Linares et al., 2001). Other studies indicate that poor parental monitoring, as well as exposure to community violence, contributes to children's self-reported violent behavior in elementary and middle school (Singer et al., 1999).

Studies have also examined the effects of exposure to violence in different ethnic and cultural groups. Exposure to violence has been related to psychological adjustment in African American children (Flowers, Lanclos, & Kelley, 2002). Exposure to violence in communities and schools may be dramatically higher for high-risk urban youth (Berman, Kurtines, Silverman, & Serafini, 1996; O'Keefe, 1997; Selner-O'Hagan, Kindlon, Buka, Raudenbush, & Earls, 1998; Singer et al., 1995). Violence exposure before, during, and after immigration has been linked with mental health problems in immigrant (Spanish, Korean, Russian, Armenian) children (Jaycox et al., 2002). Children in foster care are also at risk for exposure to violence, and such exposure has been linked with distress symptoms (Stein et al., 2003). Notably, among African American adolescents living in communities with a high level of violent crime, carrying a weapon was associated with previous exposure to violence, victimization, and family conflict (DuRant, Getts, Cadenhead, & Woods, 1995).

In summary, although exploratory investigations of community and family conflict/violence support interrelations between community and family functioning, many gaps remain in the study of these questions. In particular, the quality of evidence may be regarded as more exploratory and suggestive than authoritative, and these relations have not yet been demonstrated in the context of advanced hypotheses testing, including testing of the specific relations between social-ecological contexts and child outcomes. Moreover, little progress has been made in the specification of process-oriented models, including processes that may mediate the effects of community and/or family conflict on children (e.g., emotional security processes), or the elements that may serve as moderators (e.g., age, gender, or ethnicity). Later in this chapter, we consider new studies that begin to address these next steps.

Political Conflict and Violence

Another, even higher-order level of analysis of societal conflict processes concerns political conflict and violence. There are major gaps in the study of how civil strife, terrorism, ethnic conflict, and other forms of political violence are related to child development (Barber, 2004; Feerick & Prinz, 2003). Process-oriented studies of the effects on children are rare, particularly investigation of the psychological factors involved in the etiology and mechanisms of these effects.

Children in ecological contexts of political violence (e.g., ethnic conflict) may be exposed to multiple levels of violence simultaneously.

For example, children may be exposed to political expressions of hostility in multiple media; conflict and violence in the community; and conflict and violence in the family. Few satisfactory definitions of political violence pertinent to children's development have been formulated. Such violence generally occurs in the context of clashes between groups (e.g., different religious sects or ethnic groups), but conflict within one's own group may also become elevated due to political violence—for example, as a result of the breakdown of controls within the community over lawlessness. Multiple forms of conflict within the family may be affected as well, including interparental conflict and adolescent–parent conflict. Few studies have examined the many issues pertaining to political violence exposure, including interrelationships between different types of such exposure (Mabanglo, 2002). Definitions of, and boundaries between, political and community violence are also little examined (Trickett, Duran, & Horn, 2003). Moreover, scant research has taken into account the broader contexts of children's exposure to conflict and violence, including broader cultural or political influences related to the impact of such exposure on children and families.

The limited research supports the importance of family, community, and other social contexts for understanding child outcomes in contexts of political conflict and violence (Joshi & O'Donnell, 2003; Shaw, 2003). Gibson (1989) emphasized the importance of considering contextual (e.g., immediate experiences with political violence), interpersonal, and intrapersonal (e.g., variations across individuals in coping abilities) factors in accounting for the impact of stress on children in situations of political violence. Among interpersonal factors, Gibson identified the family as the most important and consistent mediator of stress; significant family factors included a supportive and harmonious family environment, parents' display of concern for children, and parents' serving as sources of self-direction for children in everyday tasks. In a review of the available research at that time, Elbedour, ten-Bensel, and Bastien (1993) reported evidence that children suffered from chronic and acute stress in war. Moreover, the impact of war on children was found to be a dynamic interaction among multiple processes, including the breakdown of community, the disruption of families, and the children's own psychological characteristics. Finally, Punamaki (2001) reported that multiple factors were related to children's positive developmental outcomes during a period of intense political violence in Chile. Positive mental health and social competencies in children were predicted by (1) a family atmosphere of low conflict and high cohesion, and (2) effective coping strategies (e.g., a positive and optimistic view of the future).

A SOCIAL-ECOLOGICAL MODEL OF CONFLICT'S EFFECTS ON CHILD DEVELOPMENT

A Framework for Conceptualizing Multiple Influences

Children's exposure to conflict and violence may affect them at multiple levels of individual and societal functioning, with each level capturing a unique grouping of these effects (Prinz & Feerick, 2003). Marital conflict may be involved in multiple pathways of the effects of conflict processes on children. Moreover, in areas affected by political violence, including multiple elements of the social ecology of political violence contributes to a more complete understanding than would be achieved by focusing on only one level of analysis. A challenge is to conceptualize the most relevant and pertinent ways in which social ecologies of political or community violence influence children's adjustment. Various possible levels of analysis (e.g., economic, political, institutional, educational, individual) of the effects on children in multiple regions of the world with ethnic conflict have been described (Initiative on Conflict Resolution and Ethnicity [INCORE], 1995).

An organizational framework is needed for conceptualizing the effects of conflict at these multiple levels of societal influence as processes related to child development. In a highly influential model, Bronfenbrenner (1979, 1986) and others (e.g., Cicchetti & Lynch, 1993) proposed an ecological–transactional framework for a more complete understanding of the effects of social environments on children. This framework consists of several nested levels in differing degrees of proximity to children's functioning. First, the "macrosystem" involves cultural beliefs and values that reflect societal and governmental functioning, and may affect community, family, and child functioning. This level of functioning includes processes that characterize political discord and conflict at the level of interrelations between conflicting groups.

Next, the "exosystem" consists of the influences of neighborhood and community violence on children and families. Better relations between groups achieved at the level of political processes (the macrosystem), however, may or may not translate into relations between groups at the community (exosystem) level. Moreover, relations between political processes and community behaviors may vary widely from one community to the next. Measuring neighborhood and community contexts for child development is more complex than is sometimes understood, since differences in perceptions of and experiences with violence may vary substantially across different elements of a community (Guterman, Cameron, & Staller, 2000). Accordingly, a framework recognizing possible variability within neighborhoods may be a more promising approach (Coulton, Korbin, & Su, 1996, 1999).

Third, the "microsystem" reflects, in large part, the effects of family environment. Variations in marital and parent–child relations are among the most prominent and variable influences of family contexts on children (Cummings, Davies, & Campbell, 2000). Highlighting the significance of this level of analysis for contexts of conflict and violence, Richters and Martinez (1993b) reported that adversities and pressures in the exosystem (community-level violence) were not directly related to children's adaptational failure. Instead, risk for adaptational failure only increased when such adversities reduced the quality of children's microsystem—that is, the stability and safety of their homes (Berkowitz, 2003; Gorman-Smith & Tolan, 1998; Lynch & Cicchetti, 2002). Relations between conflict in the community and conflict in the family are increasingly reported (Halpern, 2001; Kaslow, 2001).

In longitudinal research based on this social-ecological perspective, Lynch and Cicchetti (1998) reported that child maltreatment and exposure to community violence were each related to children's psychological functioning, with evidence that these contexts mutually influenced each other over time. Linares and colleagues (2001) found that community violence and family aggression each predicted early behavior problems in children; the effects of these experiences in this high-risk sample were mediated by mothers' increased psychological symptomatology. Exposure to family violence may moderate relations between exposure to community violence and adolescents' adjustment, with adolescents exposed to high levels of both types of violence evidencing the greatest risk for psychological distress (LeBlanc, Self-Brown, & Kelley, 2003). Moreover, one of the strongest predictors of lowered propensities toward violent crime among children in high-crime neighborhoods is a marital context factor—that is, a stable two-parent family (Raudenbush, 2003).

Finally, "ontogeny" is the most proximal level of analysis and is the level of the child's own development, including processes of psychological functioning. Multiple processes are candidates at this level of analysis, including genetic or biological vulnerabilities to stress or reactivity to conflict processes (Cummings et al., 2007; Davies et al., 2007; Davies, Sturge-Apple, et al., 2006; Harden et al., 2007). Children's emotional security (Davies, Harold, et al., 2002) and social attitudes (Cairns, 1987; Cairns & Mercer, 1984; Crick & Dodge, 1994) are also among the factors that may be affected by political, community, and family contexts of conflict and violence (Lovell & Cummings, 2001). The multiple levels of the social-ecological context may be interrelated in affecting children's dispositions toward adaptive (e.g., social competence) or maladaptive (e.g., behavior problems) development (Cicchetti & Lynch, 1993). In addition, individual differences in children's characteristics may mediate the impact of exposure to violence (Grych, Jouriles, et al., 2000; Maughan & Cicchetti, 2002).

The Significance of Adopting a Process-Oriented Approach

As we have discussed in Chapter 2, a key goal for a second generation of research on children exposed to conflict and violence is moving beyond simply demonstrating correlations between exposure to violence and child adjustment problems to identifying the psychological processes that contribute to children's adjustment outcomes (see also Holden, Stein, Ritchie, Harris, & Jouriles, 1998). The family and psychological processes (e.g., emotional security) proposed to mediate the effects on children of conflict and violence in broader ecological contexts merit particular consideration. Throughout this volume, we have reviewed the growing evidence for relations between/among multiple family processes, emotional security, and child adjustment. Lovell and Cummings (2001) have extended this notion to include community and political discord, hypothesizing that conflict and violence in these ecological contexts also influence children's sense of emotional security—both directly as a result of exposure, and indirectly as a result of influences on family functioning (e.g., marital conflict and violence).

Extending the notion of emotional security to include emotional security in community and political contexts is consistent with the notion that extrafamilial factors may also influence children's sense of emotional security. One might expect that emotional security in this extended sense would be especially important in areas of political violence, because of the threat to community well-being and safety posed by such violence. At the same time, the functioning of the community may also be a source of threat for children in other areas not touched by politically motivated violence per se, such as inner-city or high-crime neighborhoods in the United States.

The effects of community conflict and violence on family and adolescent functioning may also vary as a function of the apparent bases for the behavior. Sectarian community violence can be seen at the local level, as an expression of conflict between opposing ethnic groups. Or violence at the community level may reflect "ordinary crime" that may be found in any culture, regardless of the broader political context.

Given the facts that politically motivated community violence or other sectarian conflict may be more unpredictable (e.g., terrorism) and may pose a greater threat to the integrity of the political system and therefore the social order, this form of community conflict may be especially closely related to family and child adjustment. At the same time, there have been no direct tests of these notions—partly due to the difficulty of distinguishing politically and nonpolitically motivated community conflict, and partly due to the fact that these issues have rarely been systematically studied in areas of political discord.

Parental characteristics are also posited to exert particular influences on children in contexts of social conflict (Cummings & Davies, 1994). Parental adjustment problems, including maternal depression and paternal alcohol problems, are not only linked with family discord (El-Sheikh & Flanagan, 2001; Zahn-Waxler, Duggal, & Gruber, 2002) but identified as possible pathways for the impact of political and community violence on children (Joshi & O'Donnell, 2003; Lynch, 2003; Shaw, 2003). Marital conflict, parenting, and emotional security may also mediate the effects of parental dysphoria on child adjustment (Du Rocher Schudlich & Cummings, 2007).

Thus multiple levels and aspects of children's social-ecological settings may be related to children's sense of security, with implications for children's adjustment problems (Davies, Harold, et al., 2002; Harold et al., 2004). Moreover, emotional security is closely related to children's experiences of anxiety and fear, which may be especially salient in contexts of political conflict and violence (Campbell et al., 2007). An extension of past research on family processes and emotional security is to hypothesize that emotional security about family and community may mediate relationships between exposure to community and political violence and children's adjustment (Lovell & Cummings, 2001).

CHILDREN AND NORTHERN IRELAND

A Social-Ecological Framework for the "Troubles"

Next, as an illustrative example, we consider the applicability of this approach to understanding children's functioning in a specific context that includes these multiple levels of analysis—that is, Northern Ireland. The advantages of using this context as an example include the fact that it is a rare case in which research has been actively exploring these issues over a significant period of time (e.g., Cairns, 1984); in particular, recent work has been examining these questions with regard to marital conflict and children's emotional security. Thus research in Northern Ireland has begun to address the psychological, community, and familial processes underlying the effects on children of political violence. The hope is that this research, including recent moves to a process-oriented level of analysis (Lovell & Cummings, 2001), will increase our understanding of the role played by marital conflict and emotional security in other contexts of political violence.

The political context for communal conflict in Northern Ireland is often referred to in Great Britain, Ireland, and Northern Ireland as the "Troubles." Figure 9.1 outlines a social-ecological theoretical framework proposed by Lovell and Cummings (2001) for the many different possible effects of the Troubles on children in Northern Ireland. The multiple levels identified in this framework include the macrosystem (e.g., current status of relations between Catholic and Protestant groups); the exosystem (e.g., personal experiences with community conflict [both criminal and politically motivated], as well as the "intensity zone," or historical measure of the politically motivated conflict and violence characterizing the community in which children live); the microsystem (e.g., marital functioning [including marital conflict and violence], quality of parent–child relationships, parental adjustment); and indi-

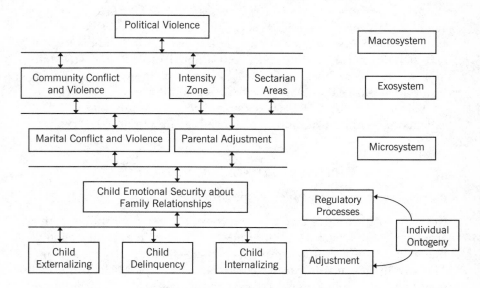

FIGURE 9.1. Theoretical framework for the social ecology of political violence in Northern Ireland. Based on Lovell and Cummings (2001).

vidual ontogeny (children's social attitudes, emotional security). Notably, the specific elements of this social-ecological model most salient to child development are highly likely to vary across cultures. Accordingly, focus groups and other means to explore the characteristics of the political context that affect children are essential to the initial phases of study in any specific culture (Cummings, Goeke-Morey, Schermerhorn, Merrilees, & Cairns, 2009).

In contexts of political violence, different forms of community violence may be distinguished (Cairns & Roe, 2003). As we have noted earlier, community violence derived from dimensions assessed in U.S. studies can be described as nonsectarian, whereas community violence linked with ethnic conflict can be termed sectarian or political violence, which may have multifaceted and overlapping bases (e.g., religious, cultural, historical). With regard to the significance of sectarian community violence, experiences of the Troubles are not uniform across all communities. Recent work suggests that living in "high-intensity zones"—that is, areas of historically high levels of conflict between Catholics and Protestants—substantially increases the impact on family functioning and child development. For example, Smyth and Scott (2000) reported that children living in high-intensity zones in Northern Ireland exhibited more anger, suspicion, and sometimes hatred toward the other group (Catholic or Protestant) than did children living in low-intensity zones. Residential segregation, which is a salient feature of urban life in Northern Ireland, fosters ingroup–outgroup distinctions by children (Cairns, 1987). Jarman and O'Halloran (2000) examined "interface" zones between predominantly Protestant and Catholic areas in Northern Ireland. They noted that much of the violence that has occurred in the course of the Troubles has occurred in these zones—that is, places where highly segregated Catholic and Protestant communities live next to each other. Violence tends to be greatest during the summer parade or "marching" seasons.

Fay, Morrissey, Smyth, and Wong (1999) distinguished among high-, medium-, and low-intensity zones of communal conflict in Northern Ireland. Interviews with residents indicated that respondents in high-intensity areas had the most extreme experiences of various forms of violence (including deaths and being caught up in riots); most often reported significant property damage (e.g., home destruction); had the highest rates of painful memories and experiences of having to conceal things in order to feel safe; and most often reported multiple insecurities and fears, including the feeling that the Troubles had completely changed their lives. A survey by Smyth and Scott (2000) provided much evidence for intergenerational effects of the violence and instability of Northern Ireland. In addition to negative effects on parenting and children's perceptions of security, the survey found that children reported ending friendships, being physically attacked or verbally abused, being victims of home vandalization, witnessing violence, experiencing school disruption, avoiding particular places, and fearing for themselves or their families.

Another psychological process affected by the political violence in Northern Ireland is children's social identity, with implications for children's social cognitions, attributions, and behaviors toward the outgroup (either Protestants or Catholics). Children and adolescents have emotional attachments to their social groups (Cairns & Mercer, 1984), which may serve to heighten hostility toward outgroup adolescents in particular when ingroup adolescents are under threat or stress (Trew, 1981). Children's awareness of these distinct categories in Northern Ireland has long been documented. Cairns (1987) showed that children were aware of these distinctions by at least 5 years of age. The fact that about 90% of children in Northern Ireland attend segregated schools further reminds them of the distinct separation on a daily basis. Thus the world becomes "us" versus "them."

Moreover, children's emotional security and social attitudes may be interrelated in affecting their emotional and behavioral responses to conflict, as well as their self-regulation of how the conflict affects them and how they respond to others in conflict situations. For example, children may be more biased in attributing hostile intentions to others in different social groups, and less likely to generate competent solutions to interpersonal problems (Cairns, 1987; Earls, 2003). In summary, children in high-intensity conflict zones may be more prone to emotional insecurity, with implications for emotional and behavioral dysregulation, and as a result of social identity formation may also be more likely to direct negative cognitions, emotions, and behaviors toward the opposing social group.

There has been relatively little systematic research on the impact of community violence in Northern Ireland as a function of child age, and even less is known about age differences in children's reactions to political violence (Joshi & O'Donnell, 2003). Nonetheless, preliminary studies support the particular urgency of studying these effects in later childhood and adolescence, because of the rates of violence as both perpetrators and victims in these age groups. In particular, recent surveys indicate that preadolescents and adolescents are more likely than younger children to have been directly exposed to the Troubles, as witnesses, victims, and/or perpetrators of sectarian violence (Cairns & Roe, 2003; Fay, Morrissey, Smyth, & Wong, 1999; Smyth & Scott, 2000).

Moreover, although there is considerable interest in gender differences in the effects of social ecologies of violence (Stein et al., 2003), there is little systematic or consistent evidence of such differences in reactions to community violence (Lynch, 2003), and even less is known about the effects of political violence. Recent work on children exposed to war and terrorism suggests that girls may be more prone to anxiety and mood symptoms, and that boys may manifest more behavioral disruptions, but very few studies have systematically examined these issues (Shaw, 2003).

Recent reports also suggest that the effects of different levels of the social ecology of sectarian conflict on children may be interrelated (Fay, Morrissey, Smyth, & Wong, 1999). At the same time, despite the initial progress on these questions, many gaps remain with regard to how the familial, psychological, and community processes affect, and are affected by, the other levels of ecological functioning (Fay, Morrissey, & Smyth, 1999). The merits of an integrated multidisciplinary approach to understanding the effects of the Troubles on children and young adults, as depicted in Figure 9.1, are increasingly recognized (Cairns, 1987, 1996; Cairns & Hewstone, 2002; INCORE, 1995; Niens, Cairns, & Hewstone, 2003; Smyth, 1998). Although much research supports this approach's depiction of relations between marital conflict and violence and child adjustment, including the mediating role of emotional security, little is known about the significance for child development of the relations between broader contexts of political and community violence (macro- and exosystem levels) and family and individual difficulties (microsystem and ontogenic levels). Moreover, there has been little systematic study from an inclusive ecological perspective, including examination of the mediating role of psychological processes such as emotional security.

Postaccord Conflict and Violence

Despite the common wisdom that conflicts end with the signing of peace accords, studies of the social ecologies of political violence continue to remain important in postaccord periods. Thus marital conflict and emotional security about multiple levels of the social ecology remain important issues in understanding reciprocal relations over time between societal conflict and functioning at the levels of communities, families, and children.

There is increasing recognition worldwide that problems do not end with the signing of peace accords. Postaccord ethnic/sectarian violence, and civil and political intransigence in general, often last for years. Furthermore, an ever-present danger exists that war will be renewed or hostilities escalated in postaccord cultures. Therefore, the peace remains imperfect—that is, "no war, no peace" (MacGinty, Muldoon, & Ferguson, 2007)—with the possibility of continuing negative effects on children. Postaccord conflict and violence, and the potential impact upon adolescents and young adults, are continuing concerns in cultures around the world. As of 2006, these cultures included South Africa, Israel–Palestine, Guatemala, Serbia–Montenegro, the Basque country, Mozambique, Angola, Croatia, Ethiopia, and Northern Ireland (Gamba, 2006; Hogland & Zartman, 2006; Murray, 2006; Sisk, 2006; Zahar, 2006).

In Northern Ireland—although seven attempts were made to reach political solutions between 1974 and 1994, and the Good Friday Agreement of 1998 received widespread support (Darby, 2001)—political violence, conflict, and disturbances continue to the present day (Independent Monitoring Commission, 2004, 2007). Although such violence and conflict have declined, substantial rates of multiple forms of sectarian violence and conflict were nevertheless reported in a recent year (Police Service of Northern Ireland, 2007).

In particular, the study of postaccord political conflicts can offer bases for deeper understanding of the risk for renewed conflict in any possible next generation, or, alternatively, better understanding of societal reasons for the stabilization of peace processes (Shirlow & Murtagh, 2006). Thus the study of conflict and violence in postaccord periods may facilitate further development of an ecological, process-oriented model for the effects of both political and community conflict and violence on children, including a better understanding of pathways between and among such violence, family functioning, and adolescents' adjustment.

This level of understanding may be seen as relevant to advances in long-term political conflict resolution. For example, if children maintain historical animosities toward others in their cultures (Cairns & Roe, 2003), including processes that promote expressions of behavioral and emotional dysregulation and hostility, solutions agreed upon only between political leaders may remain short-term and fragile. That is, understanding and resolution of conflicts at multiple levels of societal functioning may be needed to facilitate peace in regions of historical and long-standing political and community conflict and violence.

New Research Directions in Northern Ireland

The viability of these notions is further advanced by empirical analysis. Next, we consider new research directions on political violence and children in Northern Ireland as they pertain to the social-ecological hypothesis. One notion is that sectarian conflict is related to child adjustment, but that community violence mediates this relationship. On the other hand, there is scant basis to rule out direct as well as indirect effects of sectarian conflict, and it may be that broader contexts of political violence affect children in (unknown) ways not reflected in community functioning. Single-parent status may also moderate relations between ecologies of violence and child adjustment problems, amplifying the size of these relations; this would be consistent with findings in the United States that children in single-parent homes are at heightened risk for adjustment problems in high-conflict neighborhoods (e.g., Raudenbush, 2003). Religious affiliation may also be expected to moderate these relations, with children in high-conflict Catholic neighborhoods at greater risk for adjustment problems, due to the historical dominance of Protestants both politically and economically. However, given the narrowing gap between the status of Catholics and Protestants (Osborne, 2004), a prediction might also be made that sectarian status per se will not moderate relations between ecologies of violence and child adjustment. In addition, older children may be at greater risk than younger children for problems, consistent with the earlier-mentioned surveys suggesting that older children are more likely to be exposed to the Troubles as victims, observers, and/or participants (e.g., Fay, Morrissey, Smyth, & Wong, 1999; Smyth & Scott, 2000).

Political and Community Conflict and Children in Derry/Londonderry Northern Ireland

The disputed name (Derry or Londonderry, depending on one's sectarian identity) highlights the division within this city, which witnessed one of the worst examples of violence in Northern Ireland—that is, the "Bloody Sunday" shooting of Catholic civil rights protesters by British troops in 1972. As in many areas of Northern Ireland, Catholic and Protestant residential areas and facilities are highly segregated. Despite the various agreements and ceasefires in recent years, low-level violence occurs on a continuing basis, particularly at the interfaces between Catholic and Protestant working-class districts.

In order to facilitate tests of an ecological model for the effects of conflict on children, a recent study by Goeke-Morey and colleagues (in

press) was concerned with creating ecologically valid and psychometrically sound measures of sectarian (politically motivated) and nonsectarian community-level violence, and with introducing a new measure of
children's emotional security about the community. Toward these ends,
the effects of these different types of violence exposure on children,
and the role of security about community, were examined for a sample
that included 136 mothers recruited through local community centers
in Derry/Londonderry.

In addition to supporting the psychometric properties of these
measures, this study showed that sectarian community violence was correlated with multiple indicators of behavior problems (total difficulties,
emotional symptoms, conduct problems, less prosocial behavior). Moreover, nonsectarian community violence was correlated similarly with
behavior problems (total difficulties, emotional symptoms, and conduct
problems). Both sectarian and nonsectarian community violence were
related to children's insecurity about the community, which in turn was
related to higher levels of emotional symptoms. Supporting the possibly greater impact of sectarian violence was the finding that when both
forms of community violence were entered simultaneously, sectarian
community violence continued to be related to higher-level emotional
symptoms, less prosocial behavior, and greater insecurity about the
community. Thus this study provided initial support for the construct
and predictive validity of the sectarian and nonsectarian community
violence measures, as well as of the new measure of children's security
about the community.

Community Conflict, Marital Conflict, Emotional Security, and Child Adjustment in Belfast

Once psychometric support was obtained for these measures, further
refinements were made to ensure the cultural appropriateness of these
measures and additional measures of family functioning. Then 700
mother–child dyads, with children between 10 and 15 years of age,
from 18 working-class areas in Belfast participated in further research
on the social-ecological model. A study of 304 two-parent families from
this sample (Cummings et al., in press) provided a unique opportunity to examine relations between/among community conflict, marital
conflict, children's emotional security about community and marital
relations, and child adjustment in a context of political conflict and
violence.

The findings supported the mediating roles of marital conflict and
of emotional security about both community and marital relationships

in predicting children's internalizing and externalizing problems. Specifically, sectarian community violence was related to emotional security about the community and to marital conflict. Marital conflict in turn was related to emotional security about interparental relations. Both forms of emotional insecurity were related to both internalizing and externalizing problems. These results thus support the promise of the broader social-ecological model for understanding children's adjustment in contexts of political violence. Moreover, the findings begin to contextualize the role of marital conflict in relation to community conflict, and they support the significance of emotional security processes in understanding these relations. Finally, the results indicate that the level of sectarian community violence in given communities may play a particularly significant role in the effects of political context on marital and child functioning.

Community, Family, Emotional Security, and Child Adjustment: Single- and Two-Parent Families in Belfast

Another direction for exploring these relations emerges from comparisons of community, family, and child functioning, and emotional security, in single-parent and two-parent families across the entire Belfast sample of 700 families (Cummings, Schermerhorn, et al., 2009). For these tests, a measure of familywide conflict was used, and emotional security was based on a composite of assessments of familywide emotional security (Forman & Davies, 2005) and parent–child attachment security (Davies, Harold, et al., 2002). Given the concern with the impact of the Troubles on aggression and behavior problems in youth, the focus was on the prediction of externalizing problems in children.

The results supported pathways between/among sectarian community violence, family conflict, family emotional security, and children's externalizing problems. Next, separate tests were conducted of these relations for single- and two-parent families. Interestingly, although pathways tended to hold at least at the level of trends, relations between sectarian community violence and family conflict were stronger for single-parent families, suggesting that these families may be more vulnerable to community conflict. Moreover, the effects of conflict on children's emotional security about the family also tended to be stronger in single-parent families. These results thus further support the argument that family conflict in single-parent families merits consideration, although the measure of family conflict employed could not distinguish between interadult and other forms of conflict. These findings thus support the importance of further exploring issues surrounding the roles of interadult conflict and children's familywide security in single-parent as well as two-parent families.

CONCLUSIONS AND FUTURE DIRECTIONS

This chapter has explored the potential for marital conflict research, theory, and methodology to contribute to an understanding of child development in the context of a social-ecological model. In some instances (e.g., parental depressive symptoms, parental alcohol problems), research supports the role of marital conflict in contributing to negative effects on child adjustment; nevertheless, there are many remaining questions, with the role of marital conflict sometimes neglected despite the evidence. In other cases (e.g., parent–child attachment, spousal or romantic attachment), the additional contribution made by marital conflict to conceptualization of children's emotional security has long been acknowledged, but is not always fully understood. At the different level of analysis posed by community and societal functioning, there has yet been only limited consideration of marital conflict and emotional security as factors in the adjustment of children. The purpose of this chapter has been to suggest the cogency of the bases for further consideration of marital conflict and emotional security in explanatory or conceptual variables in these broader contexts.

A point we would like to make in closing is that the lessons of marital conflict research for understanding the nature of constructive and destructive conflict processes (see Chapter 3) may be usefully extended to other family systems or family forms, or at least provide initial bases for advancing our understanding of constructive and destructive conflict in these contexts. For example, behaviors classified as constructive or destructive during marital conflict may have a similar meaning or interpretation during parent–adolescent conflicts. Thus researchers can begin to outline how to make these distinctions for parent–adolescent conflicts, using the research on interparental conflicts as a guide.

Another important direction for future research concerns the impact of interparental or interadult conflict on children in families in which the parents are not married (see Chapter 1)—an issue that has been highlighted by the Northern Ireland research. An increasing number of children in Northern Ireland, the United States, and many other nations are being raised in families without stable interparental relationships or with single parents. The bulk of evidence suggests that these children are at enhanced risk for the development of adjustment problems, and interadult conflict may well be an important factor in the childrearing environment in these families. That is, single parents are likely to have partnerships or relationships with other adults, and these relationships are likely to be less stable or continuous than relationships in married or divorced families. Conflict between adults may even be heightened in these unstable or discordant relationships. Children's exposure to conflict in these families may therefore be a source of distress and contribute to risk for adjustment problems. Unfortunately, there has been very little study of these family environments with regard to the role of interadult conflict in affecting child development (see Chapter 1). Thus this is a major potential contributor to the development of children in at-risk families that has been largely undocumented and uninvestigated. Many questions remain, including how to conceptualize the adults in these families from the children's perspective, and how to conceptualize the nature of the conflicts. This topic is another pressing direction for future research; the existing work on marital conflict and children provides possible methodological, empirical, and theoretical starting points for understanding these additional important childrearing environments.

Finally, the positive benefits of constructive conflict have only been studied recently in terms of marital conflict and children, and the study of these benefits remains a gap in these other contexts. For example, the progress made in recent years at the political level in Northern Ireland can be cast in terms of constructive conflict and conflict resolution. Similarly, constructive conflict may be an important domain for understanding progress in sectarian or other politically motivated conflict at the community level, as well as the implications of community conflict for families and children. Conflict is a fact of life, and avoidance of or withdrawal from actual points of contention is far from a positive solution for existing differences. Thus an adequate conceptualization for conflict processes at all levels of analysis—from Bowlby's attachment theory to political violence—requires taking into account the positive as well as the negative ways in which individuals resolve their differences, and the multiple direct and indirect ways in which these different directions in conflict processes affect the adjustment and well-being of the children.

APPENDICES
CODING SYSTEMS AND METHODOLOGY

Conflict in the Interparental System (CIS)— Observational Coding

E. Mark Cummings, Jennifer S. Cummings, Marcie C. Goeke-Morey,
Tina D. Du Rocher Schudlich, and Colleen M. Cummings

I. HISTORY

The Conflict in the Interparental System (CIS) observational coding system was initially developed for (1) diary records of parents' and their children's responses during interparental conflicts in the home, and (2) observational coding of interparental conflict in the laboratory. In comparison to extant coding systems, the CIS provides bases for further capturing forms and continua of constructive conflict, forms and continua of conflict resolution, and continua of emotional responding in conflict—all of which have proven to be significant to the impact of marital conflict on children. More information on the development of the CIS and its psychometric properties can be found in the following sources:

Cummings, E. M., Goeke-Morey, M. C., & Papp, L. M. (2003). Children's responses to everyday marital conflict tactics in the home. *Child Development, 74,* 1918–1929.
Cummings, E. M., Goeke-Morey, M. C., Papp, L. M., & Dukewich, T. L. (2002). Children's responses to mothers' and fathers' emotionality and conflict tactics during marital conflict in the home. *Journal of Family Psychology, 16*(4), 478–492.
Du Rocher Schudlich, T. D., & Cummings, E. M. (2003). Parental dysphoria and children's internalizing symptoms: Marital conflict styles as mediators of risk. *Child Development, 74,* 1663–1681.

Goeke-Morey, M. C., Cummings, E. M., & Papp, L. M. (2007). Children and marital conflict resolution: Implications for emotional security and adjustment. *Journal of Family Psychology, 21*(4), 744–753.

II. Description: Discussion Topics and Behavioral Categories

Topics: Money, work, children, intimacy, habits, relatives, leisure, friends, chores, personality, commitment.

Behaviors during conflicts: Calm discussion, nonverbal anger, withdraw/avoid, defensiveness, humor, support, physical distress, physical affection, verbal affection, verbal anger, threat, pursue, personal insult, problem solving, physical aggression toward a person, physical aggression toward an object.

Behaviors ending conflicts: Agree to discuss later, agree to disagree, withdraw/avoid, compromise, change topic, apologize, verbal anger, give in, support, problem solving.

III. Description: Emotion Coding Scales

Emotion scales: Positivity, Anger, Sadness, Fearfulness. These responses are scored both during and at the end of conflicts.

Anchors for Emotion Codes

0	1	2	3	4	5	6	7	8	9
None	Expressing very little of the particular emotion		Expressing some degree of the particular emotion		Definitely expressing the particular emotion		Expressing the particular emotion more strongly		Expressing the particular emotion intensely or to a marked extent

IV. Description: Scales for Resolution and Constructiveness

The CIS has recently been further adapted to assess the efficacy of prevention programs for improving marital conflict; the adaptation includes scales for Resolution and Constructiveness. These scales are new to the literature and provide bases for objectively assessing key dimensions of positive marital conflict behaviors in ways not adequately covered by any existing coding system. They were first used in the following study:

Cummings, E. M., Faircloth, B. F., Mitchell, P. M., Cummings, J. S., & Schermerhorn, A. C. (2008). Evaluating a brief prevention program for improving marital conflict in community families. *Journal of Family Psychology, 22*, 193–202.

These scales have proven to be especially valuable for assessing parents' adoption of better ways of handling conflicts. By contrast, most available coding systems focus on negative conflict behaviors; a particular gap is the absence of bases for macro-assessment of the positivity level in conflict. We present these two scales in their entirety here, to foster the coverage of positive marital conflict in both family process and translational research studies.

Constructiveness

"Constructiveness" refers to behaviors exhibited and tactics used during disagreements that help to strengthen family relationships—for example, the relationship between the parents and the child's perception of the parents' relationship. Coders mark a value from 0 ("none") to 9 ("high") to denote the degree of constructiveness.

Anchors for Constructiveness Codes

0   *Individual shows a complete absence of any constructiveness*
    The individual may not display any overt destructive behaviors, but also uses no constructive communication skills, techniques, or strategies (e.g., no validation of the partner's statements, no generation of solutions, no discussion that is relevant to the topic and aimed at the goal of resolving the disagreement). For example, the individual gives the partner the silent treatment.

1   *Individual shows very little constructiveness*
    An individual earning a code of 1 *does* discuss, but seems somewhat unengaged and only reacts to the partner's comments, rather than participating proactively. For example, the individual engages in calm discussion minimally.

3   *Individual starts to show a little constructiveness*
    Some definite evidence of constructiveness is displayed, but at a low frequency. The individual may demonstrate a variety of constructive behaviors a limited number of times, or may display one or two constructive behaviors but utilizes them a few times. For example, the individual may paraphrase the partner's statements on a few occasions. As another example, the individual may paraphrase once, make a supportive statement once, and make a problem-solving statement once.

5 *Individual definitely shows some constructiveness*

Use of constructive behaviors characterizes the interaction and is clear and certain. The constructiveness displayed could be considered at an average level, relative to that of all couples who use constructiveness techniques in their interactions. The spouse or a witnessing child would perceive a predominantly positive interaction.

7 *Individual is mostly constructive*

The individual's behaviors are consistent with working toward resolution of the problem being discussed. For example, the individual may display good listening skills, allow the partner to speak, or validate the partner by paraphrasing or making supportive statements. To earn a code of 7, the individual needs to display these positive behaviors throughout the interaction. The individual also still has room for improvement in using each of the skills or one or two in particular.

9 *Individual is completely constructive, not at all destructive*

As in 7 above, but the individual displays more proficiency in use of these positive communication skills and/or demonstrates use of each positive skill to a great extent. Extremely good problem-solving and listening skills, and consistent supportiveness during the interaction. Evidence of positive attempts to resolve disagreement and to work systematically toward resolution.

Resolution

"Resolution" refers to achieving a successful outcome in terms of the discussion's content, as well as the emotional state of each party. Coders mark a value from 0 ("none") to 9 ("high") to denote the degree of resolution.

Anchors for Resolution Codes

0 *No resolution*

Issues are not even discussed.

1 *The issues have been resolved very little*

A problem may have been addressed, but few if any problem-solving strategies have been mentioned. The individual is not confident or personally satisfied.

3 *The issues have been resolved a little*

The problem has been addressed somewhat, and one or two problem-solving strategies have been mentioned/discussed. Few if any areas have been resolved, however. The individual shows hesitation, skepticism, and little confidence that the plan will be implemented and work. Minimal personal satisfaction.

5 *The issues have been somewhat resolved*

The problem has been addressed. Several problem-solving strategies have been mentioned/discussed. The individual is starting to feel personally satisfied and/or confident that the plan will be implemented and will work.

7 *The issues have been mostly resolved*

The problem has been discussed at length. Many and/or very detailed problem-solving strategies have been mentioned/discussed. Almost all aspects of this problem have been resolved. The individual feels personally satisfied and/or confident that the plan will be implemented and will work.

9 *The issues have been completely resolved*

Many and/or very detailed problem-solving strategies have been mentioned/discussed. All aspects have been resolved, and the partners have a clear course of action. The individual expresses complete personal satisfaction and/or complete confidence that the plan will be implemented and will work.

V. CODING MANUAL AND TRAINING RECOMMENDATIONS

A detailed coding manual is available for all CIS coding responses. We recommend following this coding manual for the best use of the complete CIS coding system:

Cummings, E. M., Cummings, J. S., Goeke-Morey, M. C., Du Rocher Schudlich, T. D., & Cummings, C. M. (2006). *Coding manual for behavioral observation of interparental interactions.* Unpublished manuscript, University of Notre Dame.

If research teams are interested in learning about the CIS in more detail, you are welcome to contact Jennifer S. Cummings, PhD, for information on how to do so. We welcome the opportunity to introduce other research teams to our coding system. However, it is important to understand that establishing interrater reliability *prior* to using this coding system is *essential*. It generally takes about 10 weeks of work at 4–6 hours per week to learn to use the CIS reliably. We offer training if you are interested, and you are encouraged to contact us to discuss the possibilities (fees apply). When you are using the coding system in research, we also ask that you keep us informed of your results, and that you cite our system appropriately in reports and manuscripts.

Security in the Interparental Subsystem (SIS) Scale—Child Report

I. OVERVIEW

The Security in the Interparental Subsystem (SIS) scale was developed by Davies, Forman, and colleagues (2002) to obtain children's reports of their reactions to conflicts between their parents. The SIS is specifically designed to capture the three component processes theorized to reflect children's concerns about security: emotional reactivity, regulation of exposure to conflict, and internal representations of the interparental relationship. Information on the development of the measure and an analysis of its psychometric properties (e.g., internal consistency, test–retest reliability, validity) can be found in the original source:

Davies, P. T., Forman, E. M., Rasi, J. A., & Stevens, K. I. (2002). Assessing children's emotional security in the interparental subsystem: The Security in the Interparental Subsystem (SIS) scales. *Child Development, 73*, 544–562.

Note that the version of the SIS presented here is an updated version.

II. DESCRIPTION

Exploratory and confirmatory factor analyses converged to support the existence of seven subscales:

Emotional Reactivity: Frequent, prolonged, and dysregulated experiences of distress.

Behavioral Dysregulation: Behavioral arousal and lack of control.

Avoidance: Strategies used to escape or avoid interparental conflict or its adverse aftermath.

Involvement: Dispositions to become emotionally or behaviorally involved in parental conflicts.

Constructive Family Representations: Appraisals of interparental conflict as benign or constructive for the family.

Destructive Family Representations: Appraisals of destructive consequences of interparental conflict for the family.

Spillover Representations: Children's appraisals that conflicts between parents spill over to affect their own welfare.

III. Scoring Instructions

The items for each of the SIS subscales are simply summed together to obtain measures of the seven dimensions of child reactivity to interparental conflict. The subscales and their items are presented below.

Emotional Reactivity (7 Items)

When my parents argue, I feel . . .

1. Sad.
2. Scared.
3. Angry.
4. Unsafe.

After my parents argue . . .

7. It ruins my whole day.
8. I can't seem to calm myself down.
9. I can't seem to shake off my bad feelings.

Behavioral Dysregulation (3 Items)

When my parents have an argument . . .

13. I yell at, or say unkind things to, people in my family.
14. I hit, kick, slap, or throw things at people in my family.
19. I try to clown around or cause trouble.

Avoidance (7 Items)

When my parents have an argument . . .

12. I try to hide what I'm feeling.
15. I don't know what to do.
22. I try to be really quiet.
23. I end up doing nothing, even though I wish I could do something.
27. I wait and hope things will get better.
29. I feel like staying as far away from them as possible.
31. I try to get away from them (for example, by leaving the room).

Involvement (6 Items)

When my parents have an argument . . .

6. [I feel] Sorry for one or both of my parents.
16. I try to distract them by bringing up other things.
18. I try to be on my best behavior (like doing nice things for them).
26. I try to solve the problem for them.
28. I try to comfort one or both of them.
30. I try to pretend that things are better.

Constructive Family Representations (4 Items)

When my parents have an argument . . .

34. The family is still able to get along with each other.
35. I know they still love each other.
36. I know that everything will be okay.
43. I believe that they can work out their differences.

Destructive Family Representations (4 Items)

When my parents have an argument . . .

38. I worry about my family's future.
39. I worry about what they're going to do next.
40. I know it's because they don't know how to get along.
42. I wonder if they will separate or divorce.

Conflict Spillover Representations (4 Items)

When my parents have an argument . . .

21. I feel caught in the middle.
33. I feel like they are upset with me.
37. I feel like it's my fault.
41. I think they blame me.

IV. THE COMPLETE SIS

Please answer the following questions, based on how true they are for you **during the past year**. Answer each question by circling one answer from the four answer choices below.

1 = Not at all true of me	2 = A little true of me	3 = Somewhat true of me	4 = Very true of me

When my parents argue, I feel . . .

1. Sad.   1   2   3   4
2. Scared.   1   2   3   4
3. Angry.   1   2   3   4
4. Unsafe.   1   2   3   4
5. Happy.   1   2   3   4
6. Sorry for one or both of my parents.   1   2   3   4

After my parents argue . . .

7. It ruins my whole day.   1   2   3   4
8. I can't seem to calm myself down.   1   2   3   4
9. I can't seem to shake off my bad feelings.   1   2   3   4

When my parents have an argument . . .

10. I laugh or smile.   1   2   3   4
11. I keep really still, almost as if I were frozen.   1   2   3   4
12. I try to hide what I'm feeling.   1   2   3   4
13. I yell at, or say unkind things to, people in my family.   1   2   3   4
14. I hit, kick, slap, or throw things at people in my family.   1   2   3   4
15. I don't know what to do.   1   2   3   4
16. I try to distract them by bringing up other things.   1   2   3   4
17. I watch them or listen very closely.   1   2   3   4
18. I try to be on my best behavior
(like doing nice things for them).   1   2   3   4
19. I try to clown around or cause trouble.   1   2   3   4
20. I put it out of my mind.   1   2   3   4
21. I feel caught in the middle.   1   2   3   4
22. I try to be really quiet.   1   2   3   4
23. I end up doing nothing, even though I wish.
I could do something   1   2   3   4
24. I can't stop thinking about their problems.   1   2   3   4
25. I don't worry about it, because it's a waste of time.   1   2   3   4
26. I try to solve the problem for them.   2   3   4
27. I wait and hope things will get better.   1   2   3   4

When my parents have an argument . . .

28. I try to comfort one or both of them.	1	2	3	4
29. I feel like staying as far away from them as possible.	1	2	3	4
30. I try to pretend that things are better.	1	2	3	4
31. I try to get away from them (for example, by leaving the room).	1	2	3	4
32. I end up taking sides with one of them.	1	2	3	4

When my parents have an argument . . .

33. I feel like they are upset with me.	1	2	3	4
34. The family is still able to get along with each other.	1	2	3	4
35. I know they still love each other.	1	2	3	4
36. I know that everything will be okay.	1	2	3	4
37. I feel like it's my fault.	1	2	3	4
38. I worry about my family's future.	1	2	3	4
39. I worry about what they're going to do next.	1	2	3	4
40. I know it's because they don't know how to get along.	1	2	3	4
41. I think they blame me.	1	2	3	4
42. I wonder if they will separate or divorce.	1	2	3	4
43. I believe that they can work out their differences.	1	2	3	4

Security in the Marital Subsystem—
Parent Report (SIMS-PR) Scale

I. OVERVIEW

The Security in the Marital Subsystem—Parent Report (SIMS-PR) scale was initially developed by Davies, Forman, and colleagues (2002) to obtain parents' reports of their children's overt reactions to interparental conflict. The SIMS-PR is specifically designed to assess two component processes of children's insecurity in the interparental relationship: (1) expressions of emotional reactivity and (2) strategies of regulating exposure to conflict. The measure was developed from an earlier diary assessment of children's responses to interparental conflict (Home Data Questionnaire—Adult Version; Garcia O'Hearn, Margolin, & John, 1997). More details on the development of the measure and its psychometric properties can be found in the following sources:

Davies, P. T., & Forman, E. M. (2002). Children's patterns of preserving emotional security in the interparental subsystem. *Child Development,* *73,* 1880–1903.

Davies, P. T., Forman, E. M., Rasi, J. A., & Stevens, K. I. (2002). Assessing children's emotional security in the interparental subsystem: The Security in the Interparental Subsystem (SIS) scales. *Child Development,* *73,* 544–562.

Davies, P. T., Harold, G. T., Goeke-Morey, M. C., & Cummings, E. M. (2002). Child emotional security and interparental conflict. *Monographs of the Society for Research in Child Development, 67*(3, Serial No. 270), 1–115.

Note that the version of the SIMS-PR presented here is an updated version that contains more items per scale than the original instrument.

II. DESCRIPTION

Exploratory and confirmatory factor analyses converged to support the existence of four subscales:

Overt Emotional Reactivity: Expressions of intense, prolonged, and dysregulated bouts of distress.
Behavioral Dysregulation: Behavioral arousal and lack of control.
Overt Avoidance: Strategies used to escape or avoid interparental conflict or its adverse aftermath.
Overt Involvement: Attempts to intervene in interparental conflicts.

III. SCORING INSTRUCTIONS

The items for each of the SIMS-PR subscales are simply summed together to obtain measures of the four dimensions of child reactivity to interparental conflict. The subscales and their items are presented below.

Overt Emotional Reactivity (10 Items)

10. Appears frightened.
11. Appears sad.
12. Watches and listens very closely.
14. Keeps very still (almost as if he or she is frozen).
15. Still seems upset *after* we argue.
16. Can't seem to calm down *after* we argue.
19. Appears to keep feelings inside.
20. Appears upset.
21. Takes a while after the argument to act like him- or herself again.
22. Tries to hide feelings.

Behavioral Dysregulation (5 Items)

6. Yells at family members.
7. Says unkind things to family members.
8. Starts hitting, kicking, slapping, or throwing things at family members.
9. Appears angry.
18. Causes trouble.

Overt Avoidance (4 Items)

5. Tries to get away from us (for example, by leaving the room).
13. Becomes very quiet and withdrawn.
24. Goes off by him- or herself.
25. Tries to stay away from us.

Overt Involvement (9 Items)

1. Tries to distract us by bringing up other things.
2. Tries to help us solve the problem.
3. Tries to comfort one or both of us.
4. Ends up taking sides with one of us.
17. Shows concern and sympathy for one or both of us.
23. Repeatedly brings up questions and concerns about the argument after it's over.
26. Tells us to stop arguing.
27. Gets involved in the argument.
28. Tries to cheer us up after the argument.

IV. The Complete SIMS-PR

Please rate how well each item below describes your child's reactions to **witnessing arguments between you and your partner during the past year.**

1 = Not at all like him or her	2 = A little like him or her	3 = Somewhat like him or her	4 = A lot like him or her	5 = A whole lot like him or her

____ 1. Tries to distract us by bringing up other things.
____ 2. Tries to help us solve the problem.
____ 3. Tries to comfort one or both of us.
____ 4. Ends up taking sides with one of us.
____ 5. Tries to get away from us (for example, by leaving the room).
____ 6. Yells at family members.
____ 7. Says unkind things to family members.
____ 8. Starts hitting, kicking, slapping, or throwing things at family members.
____ 9. Appears angry.
____ 10. Appears frightened.
____ 11. Appears sad.
____ 12. Watches and listens very closely.
____ 13. Becomes very quiet and withdrawn.
____ 14. Keeps very still (almost as if he or she is frozen).

_____ 15. Still seems upset *after* we argue.

_____ 16. Can't seem to calm down *after* we argue.

_____ 17. Shows concern and sympathy for one or both of us.

_____ 18. Causes trouble.

_____ 19. Appears to keep feelings inside.

_____ 20. Appears upset.

_____ 21. Takes a while after the argument to act like him- or herself again.

_____ 22. Tries to hide feelings.

_____ 23. Repeatedly brings up questions and concerns about the argument after it's over.

_____ 24. Goes off by him- or herself.

_____ 25. Tries to stay away from us.

_____ 26. Tells us to stop arguing.

_____ 27. Gets involved in the argument.

_____ 28. Tries to cheer us up after the argument.

Advanced Measurement and Research Design Issues for a Process-Oriented Approach

Understanding the value of methodology is a common objective in undergraduate and graduate training in the social sciences (e.g., Hartmann, 1992; Miller, 1998). Research methodology is integral to refining theory and producing knowledge on the developmental implications of marital conflict.

Recent developments have increased both the value and challenge of understanding methodology, including growth in the availability and accessibility of methodological tools (Cummings et al., 2001; Davies & Cicchetti, 2004; Snyder & Kazak, 2005). Acquiring the ability to use these new tools is imperative to ensure that the methodological revolution will translate into progress in a theoretically informed understanding of children's development in the contexts of marriages and families.

The purpose of this appendix is to provide an overview of the major methodological issues in research on marital conflict. Because some such issues have already been reviewed in the main text of this book, our goal here is to selectively review the most salient additional issues in contemporary marital conflict research. First, we delve into issues of measurement approaches, including questionnaires, structured and semistructured interviews, observations, and daily records. Second, we critique the primary research designs employed in the marital conflict literature (e.g., field study designs, analogue and quasi-analogue and natural experiments). Finally, we extend our treatment of the basic methodological building blocks by outlining future directions—addressing some of the more advanced psychophysiological and neurogenetic techniques likely to be valuable in the next generation of research on marital conflict.

Measurement

Although new statistical software packages have made it progressively easier to test complicated multivariate pathways involving marital conflict and child adjustment, simply understanding how to conduct such testing is not sufficient, because the trustworthiness of the findings largely depends on the quality of the measures employed. The old adage of "garbage in, garbage out" still applies in contemporary quantitative psychology, despite the seductiveness of the new statistical programs. Claims about the ability of advanced statistical analyses to test process-oriented models of family functioning may appear valid, but they can be deceptive and misleading if based on inadequate measurement of the key constructs in these models. Problems with measurement can occur in both (1) the translation of constructs into operational definitions in the form of assessment and quantification, and (2) the selection of specific methods to assess the main constructs. Therefore, we address each of these issues.

Translation of Constructs into Measurement Operations

The failure to effectively capture the conceptual definitions of the main constructs in a measurement battery is one of the more pervasive problems in the family conflict literature. In our experience as journal reviewers, it is one of the biggest reasons for rejecting manuscripts submitted to journal outlets. Likewise, even when some research papers are eventually accepted for publication, the potential impact and implications of the studies are often substantially tempered by discrepancies between the definitions of the constructs in the theory and their operational definitions in the measurement. Thus decisions about measurement must always be made so as to maximize the correspondence between these two types of definitions. In other words, the ultimate goal is to maximize the "construct validity" of the measurement battery, as reflected in the degree to which each scale captures its intended construct.

Achieving construct validity is a multifaceted process that involves an analysis of many specific forms of validity. First, it requires an assessment of the content validity of each measure used. "Content validity" specifically refers to the degree to which the assessment as a whole provides a representative sampling of the target constructs. Thus the key question is this: Does the measure adequately capture the concepts? Mastery of the principles and assumptions of the theory guiding a study is critical in addressing this question. Firm conceptualization of the underlying constructs in marital conflict provides an essential blueprint for building measurement batteries.

Factor-analytic techniques are quantitative tools for evaluating a measure's adequacy in capturing the intended constructs (Floyd & Widaman, 1995; Sabatelli & Bartle, 1995). For example, these techniques allow researchers to determine whether dimensions or components of the assessment "hang together" in a single factor or multiple factors. However, factor analysis is not sufficient in itself, because it does not indicate whether the items constituting each factor provide a comprehensive assessment of a construct. For example, it is entirely possible that the different components of the measurement hang together well but only index a small subset of characteristics of a larger theoretical construct. Complementary qualitative analysis is therefore necessary to determine whether the items adequately sample the construct of interest. Nested within the analysis of the content validity of any measure is also a consideration of the convergent and discriminant validity. "Convergent validity" refers to the degree to which the assessment maps onto the theoretical construct in question. For example, convergent validity might be demonstrated by showing that the measure in question shares empirical overlap with established assessments of the same or a similar construct. Conversely, as one of the most neglected forms of validity, "discriminant validity" refers to the degree to which the assessment is significantly different in its composition from assessments of theoretically distinct constructs.

No study is completely immune to questions and concerns about the validity of measurement. Because validity issues are inextricably intertwined with the selection of specific modes of measurement (e.g., questionnaires, observations) and designs (e.g., field and experimental designs), the analysis of validity must ultimately be evaluated in the broader methodological context. Accordingly, in the next section, we address some of the strengths and weaknesses of different measurement methods.

Any single measurement approach has significant weaknesses that can pose many possible challenges to the interpretation of results. However, because each type of measurement carries its own relatively distinct set of pitfalls and benefits, the use of multiple methods is likely to overcome the disadvantages of any single approach. Put another way, each method is viewed as providing a key piece to the bigger puzzle or picture of understanding process relations between family and child functioning. Accordingly, while it may not always be possible to employ multiple measures of each key construct in a given study, complementing the use of one measurement method with at least one other method within a broader research program is likely to reap considerable benefits.

Strengths and Weaknesses of Different Measurement Methods

Questionnaires and Structured Interviews

If we assume that any given measure has adequate psychometric properties, a key strength of questionnaires or structured interviews lies in their ability to obtain important information on family functioning in a relatively cheap, efficient, and easy way. For models or constructs that have subjective or constructivist elements (Sabatelli & Bartle, 1995), self-report data gathered from questionnaires can be invaluable. Constructivist models of family conflict assume that children are active agents in deciphering the subjective meaning of various family events for matters of significance to them (e.g., Crockenberg & Langrock, 2001a, 2001b; Cummings & Davies, 1996; Grych & Fincham, 1990). The resulting appraisals and attributions of the relational consequences of marital conflict suggest that children are, in many cases, most efficiently and accurately assessed through self-report survey instruments. For example, the cognitive–contextual framework posits that children's tendencies to appraise threat and blame themselves in response to interparental problems are key mechanisms linking their exposure to marital conflict with their psychological problems (Grych & Fincham, 1990).

Moreover, the statistical power necessary to delineate the multiple pathways between/among marital conflict, types of appraisals, and forms of adjustment require large sample sizes. In this context, self-report measures offer a feasible means of assessing subjective appraisals in large samples of children (Grych, Fincham, et al., 2000; Grych et al., 1992, 2003). Finally, administration of questionnaires and standardized interviews provide a basis for comparisons of findings across studies.

This methodology has a number of weaknesses, however. The potential for inaccurate memory or response bias error is one of the better-known limitations, but it is not fully appreciated in the marital conflict literature. For example, although theories commonly conceptualize marital conflict as a multidimensional construct, research designs often fail to discriminate among the specific dimensions of such conflict in models of children's mental health. A primary reason for this gap between theory and research may be rooted in the predominant reliance in the literature on parent questionnaire reports of conflict. The tendencies toward inaccurate recall and response biases in such reports are likely to artificially inflate associations among conflict dimensions (e.g., hostility, disengagement, warmth, resolution) and make it particularly difficult to identify the unique roles of specific dimensions as predictors of child adjustment and coping. In contrast, observational measures have more successfully distinguished among specific conflict dimensions as predictors, correlates, and antecedents of child and family functioning (Davies, Sturge-Apple, et al., 2006; Du Rocher Schudlich, Papp, & Cummings, 2004; Katz & Woodin, 2002; Sturge-Apple et al., 2006a, 2006b).

Inaccuracies in questionnaires may be more broadly evident in parental reports of more subtle forms of child adjustment (see Cummings et al., 2001). For example, parents may have problems with validly reporting on some more subtle forms or patterns of responding to marital conflict (e.g., avoidance, masking), because the competing challenge of engaging in the conflict may prevent them from observing these aspects of their children's behaviors. Likewise, even though parents who are reporting on more trait-like measures of child adjustment can draw to a greater extent on an array of children's behaviors across different contexts, they may be limited in their ability to report on veiled dimensions of children's adaptation (e.g., anxiety, depressive symptoms). Systematic error variance in questionnaires may be further compounded by more insidious problems, including (1) diminished engagement resulting from the sometimes tedious and dull experiences of completing surveys; (2) misunderstanding of the intent of the questions; and (3) the limited language, cognitive, and inferential abilities of some respondents (e.g., children, some at-risk samples of adults).

Although it may be tempting to use existing questionnaires for the sake of ease and expedience, doing so may also constrain and skew the scope of inquiry. To a large extent, questionnaire construction reflects psychometricians' own conceptualizations and operationalizations of key constructs, the significant events or observations that make up the constructs, and the factor structure of the broader theoretical phenomenon (i.e., how the items hang together). Accordingly, utilizing existing questionnaires may be limiting if scientists hope to test their own conceptual models, because such questionnaires reflect the theoretical views and biases of other researchers. In the process of shaping and simplifying complex family processes into a confined set of items and response alternatives, questionnaire development often runs a greater risk than other methods of imposing a narrow, preestablished view of how the world operates. As a result, it may miss or obscure new and exciting ways of conceptualizing and assessing constructs.

Semistructured Interviews

Although the "structured" component of semistructured assessments involves introducing a standard task, problem, or set of questions, the "semi" part of these interviews involves deviating from the more structured protocols by allowing participants to provide more open-ended responses that are not constrained by a set of prefabricated answers. Moreover, on the basis of the often rich narrative responses, experimenters have far greater latitude in formulating follow-up questions and probes, which will prompt participants to elaborate on narrative themes that are pivotal to the assessment of the target constructs. Flexibility in the evolving sequence of questions and responses often yields a richer understanding of marital, family, and child processes than more structured interviews, questionnaires, or even observational methods (see below). Having participants describe family events in their own words can provide considerable insight into the nature, course, and consequences of marital conflict.

For example, the very general nature of questions in many standardized formats is open to multiple inferences, interpretations, and comprehension errors (e.g., "How frequently do you express warmth [or hostility] toward your spouse?"). However, these errors and the resulting biases (e.g., the tendency to underreport hostility and overreport warmth) can often be reduced by eliciting more detailed narratives within a semistructured format. Thus, although frequency questions may still be incorporated within semistructured interviews, the use of open-ended questions (such as "How do you express your warmth [or hostility] toward your spouse when your child is around?") and probes (such as "If I were your child, what would I see [hear] when you and your partner are having a conflict?") can capture richer accounts of relationship processes. In comparison to observational methods, semistructured interviews are more efficient ways to capture relatively rare processes associated with relatively rare family events (e.g., aggressive marital conflicts). For example, Susan Crockenberg's laboratory developed child and parent semistructured interviews to assess the course, nature, and consequences of marital conflict in the family (e.g., Crockenberg & Langrock, 2001b).

Another advantage of the semistructured format is that it often provides answers to qualitatively different types of questions from those addressed in other types of assessments. Rather than simply answering questions about family processes centered on "what," "whether," and "how much," these interviews can also help to generate answers centered on the "how" and "why" of family processes. Put differently, this method is exquisitely designed to capture the underlying subjective meaning making and reasoning of family members, which is often implicit in nature. Semistructured interview techniques have long been considered a methodological staple in the cognitive-developmental literature (e.g., Damon & Hart, 1988; Nucci & Smetana, 1996). However, these methods are only rarely applied to understanding emotional processes in the family. Moreover, despite the valuable knowledge gained in the small body of family studies employing semistructured methods (Kobak et al., 1993; Kobak, Sudler, & Gamble, 1991), it has been largely confined to assessments of parent–child relationship quality rather than broader family or marital processes.

A notable exception to this large methodological gap in the marital conflict literature is the focus on utilizing semistructured, projective story techniques to assess how children actively process the meaning and implications of marital and family adversity (e.g., Davies, Sturge-Apple, et al., 2006; Du Rocher Schudlich, Shamir, & Cummings, 2004; Grych et al., 2002; Shamir et al., 2001). Although some of the specific procedures and stories vary from study to study, a common format is exemplified by the MacArthur Story Stem Battery—a technique that was originally designed to assess parent–child attachment and relationship quality (Bretherton, Ridgeway, & Cassidy, 1990). Experimenters specifically introduce a series of story stems describing various stressors and threats to marital relationships (e.g., a conflict between parents over lost keys). Specific stimuli can be employed to further facilitate engagement in the task, depending on the developmental level of the children being assessed. For example, for preschool and early school-age children, experimenters commonly use dramatic, animated voices, various toy props, and family action figures matching each child's sex and ethnicity. After each story stem, children complete the story with the assistance of the action figures and props, as well as of various probes and prompts by the experimenters. The projective nature of semistructured tasks makes them particularly well suited for capturing the meanings children attach to marital conflicts, which are often implicit, outside their conscious awareness, and skewed by the operation of defensive processing in other forms of assessment (e.g., denial that marital conflict occurs).

The reluctance to develop and use semistructured techniques in the marital conflict literature may be attributable in large part to the misperception that these methods are inherently "less scientific" than other methods. Questions about the validity of the techniques are in many cases predicated on misconceptions about standardization (Ginsburg, 1997; Miller, 1998). If "standardization" is interpreted as ensuring that all procedures, instructions, and questions should be literally equivalent or the same, then, semistructured techniques clearly fall short of this criterion. However, this narrow form of standardization is unnecessary and even detrimental to collecting valid information. Because participants differ in their psychological states, personality characteristics, and intellectual levels, keeping all procedures and instructions constant may maintain or even exacerbate extraneous differences in how individuals understand and respond to each question or problem. To remedy this limitation, valid semistructured techniques strive for *functional equivalence* by adjusting the presentation of problems, probes, and questions to ensure that participants are comparable in their comfort levels; their self-disclosure tendencies; and ultimately the level, details, and quality of the information they provide. The premeditated "informality" of such interviews is often preferred by family members (especially children) over structured techniques, because they are less monotonous, are more engaging, and do not resemble tests as much.

There is a tendency to underestimate the amount of knowledge and training needed to conduct semistructured interviews successfully. In a sense, the experimenter is the testing instrument in semistructured assessments. Thus, as a rule, experimenters need to have excellent communication skills and a much deeper knowledge of the substantive area and the goals of the interview to collect valid data with semistructured techniques than they do for other types of assessment. Due to the considerable training required, semistructured interviews tend to be time-consuming and expensive. Further costs may accrue if transcription of interviews is needed. Because questions often tap implicit or tacit issues, experimenters must exercise patience, be comfortable with long bouts of silence, and refrain from "jumping in" to help participants. Moreover, experimenters must often walk a fine line between asking probing and leading questions. Therefore, even among trained experimenters, there is a risk of committing errors of omission (e.g., failing to obtain information on target constructs, due to tangential questions) and commission (e.g., structuring questions in a way that is unduly weighted toward confirming implicit hypotheses and expectations). In addition, semistructured interviews are often subject to the same retrospective and recall biases as their structured counterparts.

Observational Methods

Flexibility is an overarching advantage of observational methods. First, the "design-free" nature of observations provides a great deal of leeway in implementing them within research designs that run the gamut from experimental to correlational research (Cairns, 1979; Kerig & Baucom, 2004). Second, they can also be feasibly employed in multiple research settings, ranging from structured tasks (e.g., the Strange Situation for assessing attachment) or simulated interactions (e.g., simulations of parental or adult conflict) in the laboratory to unstructured contexts (e.g., playground, home) in the field (Ainsworth et al., 1978; Cummings, 1987; Davies, Sturge-Apple, et al., 2006). Third, researchers have the luxury of choosing among several modes of observational data collection: live observations, audio recordings, or video recordings. Technological advances over the past few decades have resulted in more sensitive, smaller, and more mobile audio-visual equipment, which has increased the economy and practicality of employed observational methods.

If full advantage is taken of the storage capacities of various electronic media, audiovisual records are free of several constraints that are inherent in the use of questionnaires. Although some structure is imparted in the selection of the interaction task and the recording of specific participants, researchers employing observational measures also have the luxury of examining any number of specific parameters within the streams of recorded behavior. As with any assessment procedure, the quantification of key constructs does require the simplification and winnowing of complex data. Thus the coding systems employed must constrain the variables within a manageable scope that is eventually comparable to the scope of questionnaires. However, the luxury of revisiting video or audio recordings provides more flexibility in the development and selection of variables and constructs than other prefabricated methods (e.g., surveys) do. If coders are appropriately trained to implement psychometrically sound ways of assessing and coding observations, it is also true that observations can offset some of the other limitations of questionnaires. For example, observations can reduce or eliminate survey error resulting from memory, subjectivity, and inherent difficulties in sensitively capturing more subtle or complex behaviors (e.g., Kerig, 2001).

The overarching advantage of observational methods—namely, their flexibility—is also a major source of some of their limitations. In our experience, the flexibility and rigor of observations are sometimes so appealing that it is not uncommon for the scientific "eyes" of researchers to be bigger than their scientific "stomachs," as they "bite off more than they can chew" in devising too many observational tasks within a study. In other situations, investigators may be tempted to use observations as a way to hedge against insufficient theory or conceptual structure, which would otherwise effectively tighten the scope of inquiry for a study. In both cases, sifting through the overwhelming amount of data collected in these studies is a formidable task. Coding problems and the ultimate failure to produce knowledge are common consequences.

At the same time, there are also some constraints on the use of observations to capture specific types of processes. Although specific techniques can be used to reduce response biases (see Zahn-Waxler & Radke-Yarrow, 1982), introduction of observational techniques can create reactivity among family members and distort their natural responses. Moreover, rare, private, or illegal behaviors (e.g., incidents of violence, drug use, sexuality) are often not amenable to observations. Finally, although behaviors are core aspects of many theories of marital conflict, the subjective or constructivist components of these models are more effectively captured through self-report assessments.

Decisions also have to be made about the specific types of behaviors to target in coding schemes, as well as the level of the analysis of the coding system along the molar–molecular continuum. Deciding on the level of analysis for coding can be challenging if there is little a priori consideration of how to carve, lump, and split target behaviors. Whereas molar coding systems typically consist of ratings of broad patterns of behavior across relatively large periods of times (i.e., minutes, hours, days) or different settings, molecular ratings reflect observational codes that are bound by smaller conceptual (e.g., changes in eyebrow or lip configurations) or temporal (e.g., milliseconds or seconds) units. Falling between these spans along the continuum are meso-level coding schemes that integrate features of both molar and molecular systems (Lindahl, 2001). Each of these three overarching levels of coding has its own set of pitfalls and advantages. For example, molar ratings offer a collective analysis of the overall organization and pattern of behaviors, but this can often downplay or eliminate variations in behaviors that are due to variations in setting or idiosyncratic events; molecular codes often code behaviors at face value, with little interpretation or weighting of whether the behaviors reflect a combination of child dispositions, states, or the interplay between individuals and contexts. Differences in the composition of the systems make some systems to be better than others for various developmental research questions (e.g., examining stability and change in family and child behavior over time) (see Cairns, 1979, for details).

Even when researchers can eventually overcome these challenges and disseminate knowledge obtained from observational data, poor conceptual and methodological planning can incur considerable costs along the way. We should preface our description of this problem by stating that it is in fact wise to err on the side of increasing precision and splitting (rather than lumping) key coding variables, because analytic techniques can subsequently be used to reduce coded data. But we hasten to add that it is wise to err on the side of greater precision *within the range afforded by one's framework or theory*. An all-too-common problem is taking this rule of thumb to the extreme by implementing a very expensive, complicated, and lengthy microanalytic coding system with little or no conceptual justification. In the end, the specific fruits of the laborious process of coding dozens of specific behaviors on a second-by-second basis are often lumped together into very broad molar composites that often reflect global classes of behavioral negativity or positivity. Much to the chagrin of the poor research assistants who have meticulously coded the data, the final result is a small set of codes that are, in many cases, more general than the more economical molar codes!

Our point here is not to scare researchers away from utilizing observational methods. In fact, when the predominant use of questionnaire research is considered, greater use of observational measures is sorely needed. Moreover, the advances in technology and observational systems designed to capture marital, family, and child functioning make it easier than ever before to capitalize successfully on the strengths of observations (Kerig & Lindahl, 2001). Rather, our point in raising some of the pitfalls is to demonstrate that the strengths of observations do not make these methods inherently better than any other techniques. In particular, the use of powerful and flexible observational methods is only likely to be fruitful if it is balanced by the use of tight conceptual structure and scope, as well as by a full appreciation of the methods' limitations.

Daily Record Measures

Use of daily record measures by spouses has a long history in marital research (e.g., Weiss, Hops, & Patterson, 1973). Although the early procedures focused exclusively on marital functioning, the extension of daily records to research on children's functioning in the context of marital and family conflict testifies to the value of such records for testing process models in this area. In the first application of this method to understanding children's reactions to marital conflict, Cummings and his colleagues (1981, 1984) were able to demonstrate that parents could be feasibly trained to reliably report on key dimensions of marital conflict and their children's reactions to them (see also Repetti, McGrath, & Ishikawa, 1999; Repetti & Wood, 1997). Early versions of spousal diary reports, though valuable, were lengthy and demonstrated low interspousal reliability (e.g., Christensen & Nies, 1980; Margolin, 1987). To address these limitations, Cummings and colleagues specifically trained parents to provide objective narrative records that were as free as possible of inferences about behavior. The eventual result was sufficient reliability (on the order of 85% agreement) between parents and trained research assistants in reporting on parents' own angry expressions and their own children's responses in the home. Although these changes increased the utility and objectivity of daily records, the procedures used by

Cummings and colleagues required parents to dictate highly detailed narratives about family events into a tape recorder as soon as possible after the events occurred. Consequently, several limitations were still evident: (1) the time-consuming nature of the procedure, (2) the risk that observers might not address all the theoretically relevant aspects of the conflict events, and (3) verbal and cognitive demands that were likely to reduce their applicability to the study of diverse or high-risk families.

Further adaptations were undertaken to address these limitations. For example, Garcia O'Hearn and colleagues (1997) created a more practical and simple checklist format for daily record assessments. Parents who were trained by an experimenter to identify children's behaviors indicated within the checklist whether children responded with specific behaviors (e.g., "cried," "became angry," "picked a fight") in response to witnessing a marital conflict. In further refining this methodology, Cummings and colleagues have expanded the checklists to differentiate specific dimensions of marital conflicts (e.g., calm discussion, anger, verbal aggression, physical aggression, withdrawal) and children's reactivity patterns (e.g., specific types of emotions and behaviors), based on prior theory and research (Cummings et al., 2001). Moreover, to increase the objectivity of parental reports, more structured procedures were implemented to train parents to report accurately on conflict events in the home. Consistent with the goal of improving the accuracy of the daily records, agreement between mothers and fathers in identifying dimensions of marital conflict and child reactivity became excellent (for more details, see Cummings, Goeke-Morey, & Papp, 2004; Cummings et al., 2002; Papp, Cummings, & Goeke-Morey, 2002). Thus methodological refinements have resulted in increases in the feasibility, reliability, and validity of daily records.

Daily records also have a number of other strengths. First, because such records are designed to document daily family activities in home, they tend to have high ecological validity; this increases confidence that the processes captured are generalizable to naturalistic family contexts. Second, in providing more immediate accounts of family processes than retrospective reports derived from questionnaires can, daily records have the potential to provide more accurate and valid data, particularly in distinguishing between specific dimensions of marital interactions and children's patterns of responding (Almeida et al., 1999; Laurenceau & Bolger, 2005; Wheeler & Reis, 1991). For example, empirical evidence supports the validity of marital daily records in discriminating between constructive and destructive conflict tactics (e.g., physical aggression, threat, verbal hostility, nonverbal hostility, avoidance, submission, apology, compromise), parental emotions (e.g., anger, sadness, fear), and child reactions to marital conflict (e.g., specific forms of emotion and regulatory behavior) (see Cummings, Goeke-Morey, & Papp, 2004; Cummings et al., 2002; Papp et al., 2002). Third, daily records also constitute a more practical approach than other home-based methods (e.g., observation) to capturing family events such as marital conflict, which are relatively rare and unpredictable in the small spans of time that can be recorded through observations (e.g., minutes or hours).

Finally, the daily record approach affords the opportunity to address a qualitatively different set of questions from those answered by other approaches (Laurenceau & Bolger, 2005). Other measurement strategies capitalize on interindividual or between-subjects approaches. For example, a research question using a between-subjects model might involve examining whether children who witness high levels of marital conflict are more likely to experience distress, involvement, or avoidance during such conflict. In contrast, within-subjects approaches can be utilized to examine whether daily fluctuations in parameters of marital conflict are linked with daily changes in children's forms of reactivity. Furthermore, daily records can allow for the integration of between- and within-subjects approaches. For example, they permit the analysis of whether individual differences *between children* in the experience of contextual and situational conditions might serve to amplify associations between daily changes in marital conflict and children's conflict reactivity.

As with any method, decisions to use daily records must also be informed by their limitations. Although daily record assessments are becoming more and more practical to use, with refinements in formatting and technological advances (e.g., electronic devices such as personal digital assistants), training family members and monitoring rates of participation each day are still very time-intensive endeavors. As a result, the tradeoff for collecting such intensive data is a reduction in the sample size. Although this may not undermine the ability to address some questions (e.g., within-subjects questions) if large numbers of daily records are obtained from each participant, it may reduce the statistical power to address between-subjects questions. Therefore, deciding whether to use a daily record approach requires careful consideration of its match with the study's aims and research questions. In addition, even carefully training parents to report on marital conflict events does not rule out the operation of biases in their observations. For example, the emotionality associated with such events may systematically color parents' evaluations of the characteristics of the interaction and their children's responses. Moreover, engagement in the conflict may undermine parents' ability to detect children's reactions, particularly if these are relatively subtle (e.g., avoidance).

DESIGN

Measurement of any construct or set of constructs is ultimately nested within a broader methodological design. Thus the advantages, disadvantages, and overall meaning of any specific mode of measurement cannot be fully evaluated without an understanding of the broader features of the design. For example, although questionnaires are typically used in the marital conflict literature to assess retrospective reports of family and child functioning in the home, they can be used in a number of different designs, including experimental designs. In turn, use of questionnaires within less common research designs may alter the typical profile of their advantages and disadvantages. As one illustration, problems associated with retrospective recall may be minimized if a questionnaire (e.g., an emotion or mood survey) is employed after a well-defined experimental event (e.g., a conflictual interaction). Because the design defines how the measures are configured together within the broader context of research procedures, it also has important implications for the conclusions that can be drawn about the nature of the relationships among the assessment results.

For the sake of brevity, we focus below on the properties, strengths, and pitfalls of the more basic methodological designs. However, throughout this discussion, it is important to keep in mind that a *multitude* of designs can be derived from crossing three distinct methodological dimensions: (1) the physical setting: the setting in which the study takes place (e.g., laboratory or field); (2) the characteristics of the stimulus (particularly the independent variable); and (3) the social agents (i.e., the participants in each setting). Misunderstanding in the recurrent debates about the relative value of laboratory versus field research commonly stems from the treatment of physical setting and stimulus characteristics as interchangeable labels for the same design dimension. For example, "lab" and "experiment" are often used as synonyms in descriptions of design elements. Yet, in reality, each term describes a distinct dimension—namely, the physical setting and the characteristics of the stimulus, respectively. Interchangeable use of such terms as "field setting" and "nonexperimental design" reflects a similar problem of equating physical setting and stimulus characteristics (Parke, 1979). Thus, in the subsequent sections, we discriminate between these dimensions in our description of the broader research designs.

Field Study Designs

Field studies are designed to examine ongoing relationships among family processes in the naturalistic environment (the physical setting dimension) among family members (the social agent dimension) without any a priori attempts to systematically manipulate the values of the key variables (the stimulus characteristics dimension). As one of the most common types of designs employed in the marital conflict literature, field studies examine naturally occurring relationships between marital conflict and child adjustment. Although field designs can employ any number of measurement strategies, including home observational measures (e.g., Davis et al., 1998; Vuchinich, Emery, & Cassidy, 1988) and daily records (e.g., Cummings, Goeke-Morey, & Papp, 2004; Repetti et al., 1999), questionnaires and interviews are more commonly used in the marital conflict literature (e.g., Davies & Lindsay, 2004; Emery & O'Leary, 1982; Grych et al., 2003;

Jenkins, Smith, & Graham, 1989; Jouriles, Bourg, & Farris, 1991; Jouriles, Murphy, et al., 1991). If the measurement battery of the study is psychometrically sound, field designs often enjoy the advantage of high ecological validity. Thus the findings from field studies are often more readily applicable to actual processes in the family than the findings from other designs are. Moreover, the flexibility of field designs permits the assessment of powerful continuous measures of marital conflict, family processes, and child functioning. In many cases, this results in a richer, more powerful analysis of the main variables than categorical assessments of variables will allow. For example, Jouriles, Bourg, and Farris (1991) and Jouriles, Murphy, and colleagues (1991) were able to demonstrate that a continuous measure of children's exposure to childrearing disagreements between parents was a unique predictor of child adjustment even after their exposure to interparental discord was taken into account. As another illustration, continuous measures of naturally occurring, father-initiated violence in bouts of interparental conflict have been related to child behavior problems, even after statistical controls for general interparental discord (e.g., Fergusson & Horwood, 1998; McDonald, Jouriles, Norwood, Ware, & Ezell, 2000; Yates, Dodds, Sroufe, & Egeland, 2003).

However, there are also significant limitations associated with field designs. Relying on assessments of naturally occurring family processes may not yield sufficient variability in the main predictors (e.g., marital conflict) or outcomes, especially when indices of family and child functioning are relatively rare in the general population (e.g., severe marital violence). As a result, statistical power to identify process relations between/among marital, family, and child functioning may be compromised. Furthermore, in many field designs, internal validity or the ability to infer cause–effect relationships is relatively poor, because there has been no systematic effort to manipulate the proposed cause or to keep potential third variables constant. However, this general rule of thumb has some notable exceptions. For example, daily diary records are often nested within field studies. Yet within-subjects analyses of whether daily fluctuations in family functioning are linked with the day-to-day changes in the adjustment of family members may help to increase internal validity for some research questions (Cummings et al., 2001). Likewise, the use of longitudinal designs may be help to identify the ordering and directionality among family and child variables.

Analogue Designs

In contrast to field designs, analogue studies involve the direct manipulation of the independent variable (the stimulus characteristic dimension), which in most cases is conducted within the context of the laboratory (the physical setting) and involves a mixture of family members and persons outside the family (the social agents). Analogue designs employ simulations of family events that can be presented to family members to obtain their reactions. These simulations can be exhibited in a wide variety of modalities, including live enactments of conflict between two spouses, an adult and child, or a mother and father (Cummings, Hennessy, et al., 1994; Cummings, Iannotti, & Zahn-Waxler, 1989; Davies, Sturge-Apple, et al., 2006; El-Sheikh et al., 1989), and video- or audio-recorded depictions of adult conflict (e.g., E. M. Cummings et al., 1989; Cummings et al., 1993; Davies, Myers, et al., 1999; Goeke-Morey et al., 2003; Grych & Fincham, 1993).

An advantage of this approach is that various dimensions of family events (e.g., marital conflict, parent–child conflict, expression of parental dysphoria) can be precisely specified and presented in the same way across all participants. The precision and control afforded by analogue designs are especially useful in identifying directionality in specific process associations between interparental conflict dimensions and child responses. Full experimental designs, which manipulate specific conflict tactics in the controlled setting of the laboratory and assess their effects on children, provides a useful way of disentangling histories of exposure to interadult conflict in general or specific interadult conflict tactics from the larger matrix of covarying family and interpersonal processes (Cummings & Davies, 1994a). As a result, internal validity is maximized, and more confident conclusions can be drawn about the direct effects of conflict tactics and histories on child functioning (e.g., E. M. Cummings et al., 1989; Davies, Myers, et al., 1999; El-Sheikh & Cheskes, 1995; Grych & Fincham, 1993).

As one illustration, Goeke-Morey and colleagues (2003) sought to identify higher-order categories of conflict behaviors from the children's perspective by classifying their emotional responses to analogue presentations of marital conflict vignettes into destructive and constructive dimensions, based on the balance and organization of the children's positive and negative emotional reactivity to the conflict vignettes. The precise presentation of specific conflict tactics and expressions to children yielded a fine-grained analysis of the destructive and constructive properties of interadult adult conflict. As another example, several theories of interparental conflict (e.g., EST, the cognitive–contextual framework) have postulated that histories of exposure to destructive interparental conflict sensitize children to subsequent conflict, as evidenced by heightened emotional distress, maladaptive coping, and negative appraisals and representations. Although field designs have demonstrated that children from high-conflict homes react more negatively to naturalistic conflicts in the home (e.g., Garcia O'Hearn et al., 1997), these designs alone do not permit researchers to determine whether the negative emotional reactivity is due to the sensitizing effects of distal conflict histories or to the proximal conflict context. Analogue studies, by contrast, can better isolate the effects of conflict history on children's subsequent responses to marital conflict. For example, in one analogue design (Davies, Myers, et al., 1999), children were randomly assigned to view videotapes of the same adult couple engaged in a history of either four hostile, unresolved conflicts (i.e., destructive) or four mild, resolved conflicts (i.e., constructive), to simulate child exposure to conflict histories. Following this manipulation of conflict histories, children were interviewed about their responses to a standard conflict between the same couple. Supporting the sensitization hypothesis, children who witnessed destructive conflict histories generally reported greater negative respond-ing to the standard adult conflict than children exposed to constructive conflict histories did.

One potential limitation of analogue methodology concerns the con-straints in the number of predictors that can be examined in any single study. Whereas researchers have the potential to cast a wide net in examin-ing a multitude of risk and protective factors in naturalistic designs, any single experiment is generally only capable of manipulating one or two independent variables without substantially undermining cell sizes, statisti-cal power, and the necessity of keeping potential third variables constant. Thus analogue designs are generally better suited answering well-defined, circumscribed research questions about specific family process than to exploring questions of a broader scope that incorporate multiple predic-tors. Another common limitation of the experimental design is that the goal of maximizing internal validity can occur at the cost of ecological validity. To return to the Davies, Myers, and colleagues (1999) study, the major con-clusion that can be drawn in support of internal validity is that children's exposure to destructive conflict histories between adults *can* cause them to experience greater distress in subsequent conflicts. However, the simu-lated nature of the design does not authoritatively address the question of whether exposure to destructive conflict histories between adults *does* cause progressively greater distress in response to conflicts in the family.

Quasi-Analogue Designs

The limitations of analogue designs have resulted in a substantial reluctance on the part of scientists to use experimental designs in the study of marital conflict. For example, in a special section of the *Journal of Family Psychol-ogy* devoted to the impact of marital conflict on children, Fincham (1994) stated: "For obvious practical and ethical reasons, experimental manipula-tion is not feasible in this area of inquiry, a factor that may contribute to the paucity of research on causal mechanisms relating marital conflict and child adjustment" (p. 125). Although similar legitimate concerns have been voiced in the literature, we contend that these concerns are often inter-preted in an exaggerated manner that leads to an inappropriate dismissal of the use and value of analogue designs. We argue that a major source of this problem stems from an overinterpretation of the importance of maxi-mizing "mundane realism," or the extent to which the research events in the analogue design actually occur in the lives of participants. As Aronson, Wilson, and Brewer (1998) noted in their analysis of experimental designs, it is not always necessary for an experiment to achieve a high level of mundane realism. Rather, fully evaluating the ecological validity of the design requires a careful analysis of two types of realism: the extent to which the events in the research setting are likely (1) to be engaging and stimulating (i.e., "experimental realism") and (2) to generate psychological processes similar to those that occur in real life (i.e., "psychological realism") (see Cummings, 1995).

As a popular case in point, the assessment of child attachment behavior in the Strange Situation is explicitly designed to consist of a series of "strange" separations and reunions with caregivers in the context of the introduction and departure of an unfamiliar adult. Accordingly, it is explicitly designed to *minimize* mundane realism as a means of evoking two normative forms of anxiety and maximizing engagement of young children (i.e., high experimental realism). The ultimate goal is the activation of the parent–child attachment system and the ability to assess individual differences in children's strategies for increasing the accessibility of their caregivers. Therefore, the ability to capture how children use caregivers as a secure base in times of threat and distress ultimately maximizes psychological realism by eliciting psychological processes that are thought to occur in real life. In a similar vein, simulations of interparental or interadult conflict may not necessarily have a high degree of mundane realism. However, they can still achieve an acceptable degree of ecological validity under conditions when they successfully activate emotional, cognitive, and psychological processes similar to those occurring in the naturalistic context of the interparental relationship or family unit.

In addition, concerns about the narrow scope of predictors and relatively low ecological validity can also be allayed by crafting quasi-analogue designs—that is, hybrids of experimental and naturalistic research procedures. For example, the sensitization hypothesis posits that a history of exposure to interparental conflict intensifies children's distress responses to such conflict. In support of this proposition, field research has demonstrated that children from high-conflict homes do react more negatively to naturalistic conflicts in the home (e.g., Davies, Forman, et al., 2002; Garcia-O'Hearn et al., 1997). Yet the high stability of destructive conflict across time indicates that parents who have a history of such conflict are also disproportionately more likely to exhibit more destructive conflict during the time period of the assessment of children's reactivity to conflict. Thus these designs by themselves cannot determine whether the greater negativity experienced by children is due to the sensitizing effects of distal conflict histories or to the destructive nature of the proximal conflict context that is used to obtain assessments of child reactivity. However, some level of experimental control can be achieved by assessing children's responses to conflicts in standardized, stressful contexts in the laboratory (e.g., audio- or video-recorded conflicts, live simulated conflicts). Because the conflict stimulus is similar or identical across all children in the assessment of their reactivity to conflict, any resulting differences in reactivity between the children cannot be attributed to systematic variation in their concurrent exposure to conflict. As a result, any associations between histories of actual marital conflict through the field component of the design and children's reactivity to conflict in the analogue component of the design cannot be readily attributable to the proximal conflict context. Moreover, recent modifications to analogue tasks provide more viable and appealing options, which in some cases also help to maximize the ecological validity of conflict reactivity measures without substantially sacrificing internal validity. For example, the Simulated Phone Argument Task (SPAT) consists of a simulation of a mild conflict between a mother and father over the phone in a way that maintains some standardization in the emotional expression and content of the conflict. Yet, for all intents and purposes, the conflict between parents depicted in the SPAT is authentic from a child's perspective (see Davies et al., 2007; Davies, Sturge-Apple, et al., 2006, 2008).

Natural Experiments

Another solution to the challenge of maximizing the internal and ecological validity in research designs is to seek out "experiments of nature." As in laboratory experiments, the goal is to understand how the manipulation of a key variable or set of variables may affect a particular process or outcome. Yet the term "natural" reflects the fact that this design capitalizes on change occurring in the real world, rather than change instituted by an experimenter. For example, understanding the developmental implications of exposure to specific types of marital conflict is currently a primary objective in the literature. For ethical reasons, it is obviously not desirable or possible to systematically manipulate children's exposure to specific types of destructive conflict tactics. However, researchers can more precisely isolate specific patterns of child exposure to interparental conflict tactics by taking advantage of naturally occurring differences in children's exposure to dimensions of marital conflict (Cicchetti, 2003).

In these designs (e.g., Fantuzzo et al., 1991; O'Brien et al., 1991), inclusion and exclusion criteria are developed and implemented to identify groups of children who differ in their exposure to specific conflict tactics but are highly similar in sociodemographic characteristics and other family experiences. For example, Fantuzzo and colleagues (1991) compared the psychological adjustment of children in four groups: (1) home residents exposed to verbal interparental aggression, (2) home residents exposed to both verbal and physical interparental aggression, (3) shelter residents exposed to verbal and physical interparental aggression, and (4) a control group of home residents exposed to negligible levels of interparental aggression. By carefully selecting naturally occurring groups of children who differed in their exposure to a well-defined set of family stressors, these researchers disentangled the specific risk posed by the form of aggression and residence (i.e., homelessness) to children's adjustment from a larger constellation of covarying demographic conditions.

Even though categorical risk designs have proven to be excellent strategies for increasing the specificity of conflict assessments, they do have their share of limitations. Classifying groups of children on the basis of their exposure to specific types of conflict tactics in categorical risk designs often involves reducing rich, continuous assessments of conflict into more simple categorical variables based on arbitrary cutoff points. Although this practice is an appropriate step in addressing some research questions, the tradeoff is a substantial loss of information and statistical power. For example, imposing an arbitrary cutoff on a continuous measure of interparental conflict (e.g., verbal aggression) may yield a group of children who exhibit considerable heterogeneity in their exposure to the specific conflict tactic (e.g., moderate vs. no exposure). Thus categorical systems often fail to assess the full quantitative continuum of conflict risk (Seifer, 1995). Moreover, even if theory proposes qualitative shifts in the operation of a risk factor that help to justify a classification scheme, the specific cutoff points used to differentiate categories may not correspond to the threshold at which the change in the nature of the risk occurs. Finally, like its methodological cousin—the experiment—the natural experiment necessitates a commitment to understanding the impact of a small, well-defined set of factors on child or family functioning. Thus, although the precision afforded by natural experiments is an advantage, the relatively narrow focus on a select set of risk or compensatory factors does incur the costs of less flexibility and a greater risk of yielding null findings than field designs have.

In concluding our treatment of design issues, we assert that future research on how children cope with marital conflict will be facilitated by attempts to integrate methodological dimensions of physical setting, stimulus characteristics, and social agents in new ways. Although Ross Parke (1979) meticulously outlined the various advantages of many different designs, research on marital conflict has predominantly relied on a small subset of the broader range of design options. For example, intervention designs not only are designed to directly improve the lives of children and families, but also provide very useful tools for more definitively identifying the directionality of pathways between family processes and child adjustment (see Chapter 8 for more details). However, these designs in themselves can vary widely. For example, field experiments involve deliberate manipulation of the predictor (e.g., a program for helping children cope with divorce, a program designed to help reduce destructive marital conflict), followed by assessments of the dependent measure, all conducted in the field (e.g., reports by teachers about children's adjustment in school) (see Pedro-Carroll, 2005; Pedro-Carroll, Sutton, & Wyman, 1999; Shifflett & Cummings, 1999). Alternatively, other designs attempt to reduce various forms of family adversity (e.g., parent–child relationship disturbances) in high-risk samples and to examine its developmental implications by examining children's adjustment in the context of carefully standardized laboratory assessments (e.g., Toth, Rogosch, Manly, & Cicchetti, 2006). Thus systematically applying these designs to the study of marital conflict is an important methodological direction for future research.

FUTURE DIRECTIONS

Psychophysiological Measures

With the growing influence of developmental psychopathology and its broad interdisciplinary scope, researchers have become increasingly interested in obtaining a more multilevel understanding of children's adaptation to marital conflict (Cicchetti, 2002; Repetti et al., 2002). Although the study of psychophysiology constituted a barely perceptible blip on the scientific radar screen at the time our first book (Cummings & Davies, 1994a) was published, the integration of psychological and physiological processes is emerging as a vibrant, contemporary research direction in the study of marital conflict. However, it is not without its challenges. Despite its potentially informative nature, incorporating physiological measures into psychological research requires scrutiny and consideration of multiple issues. A common myth is that the assessment of physiological processes is the Holy Grail, constituting an inherently better, more objective, and more valid means of assessing child functioning than psychological measurement. Building on the discussion in Chapter 4, we further address psychophysiological assessment issues here.

The sympathetic nervous system (SNS) is the first wave of autonomic response to stressful events that helps to prime the body for fight–flight responses by increasing cardiac output, oxygen flow, and blood glucose levels (Boucsein, 1992). Several dimensions of SNS functioning can be assessed, including (1) preejection period, an index of cardiac sympathetic function (e.g., Oosterman & Schuengel, 2007); (2) skin conductance reactivity (SCR), a measure of the electrical impulses on the surface of the skin that result from activity of the sweat glands innervated by the SNS (e.g., Cummings et al., 2007; El-Sheikh, 2005, 2007; Quigley & Stifter, 2006); and (3) salivary alpha-amylase, an enzyme found in saliva that is regarded as an index of adrenergic activity (Gordis, Granger, Susman, & Trickett, 2006; Granger et al., 2006).

Through its role as a second wave of autonomic responding to stress (Cahill & McGaugh, 1998), the limbic–hypothalamic–pituitary–adrenocortical (LHPA) axis is regarded as a central system for an understanding of children's reactivity to interparental conflict (Saltzman et al., 2005). In response to stressful events, components of the limbic system (e.g., amygdala, hippocampus) involved in processing aversive stimuli modulate the release of corticotropin-releasing factor (CRF) by the hypothalamus. In turn, CRF activates the adrenal gland to secrete cortisol by stimulating the pituitary gland to produce adrenocorticotropic hormone (ACTH) and release it into the bloodstream. Increases in cortisol in response to stress serve to mobilize energy (e.g., glucose, oxygen); increase cardiovascular activity; and modulate the processing, learning, and memory consolidation of emotionally significant events (Cahill & McGaugh, 1998; Gold & Chrousos, 2002; Lupien et al., 2006). Like alpha-amylase, cortisol can be assayed through saliva samples, which are relatively easy to collect. In accordance with the central role the LHPA axis plays in allocating the resources necessary to process and cope with stressful events, children's cortisol reactivity may provide a particularly informative index for understanding how children respond to the stress of witnessing interparental conflict.

Attempts to isolate components of heart rate have also led to the development of surrogate indices of PNS functioning through measures of respiratory sinus arrhythmia (RSA). Two particularly useful components of RSA are vagal tone and suppression of vagal tone in response to challenge or stress (Fox & Card, 1999). High vagal tone is viewed as a marker of greater autonomic system integrity, especially in reflecting its restorative function of regulating homeostasis. Suppression of vagal tone in response to environmental demands is theorized to reflect flexible and efficient engagement and disengagement with stressful events. Vagal suppression, or the "vagal brake," is thought to serve an adaptive function of tamping down the PNS sufficiently to allow individuals to attend to and cope with stressors without having to tax resources through the recruitment of the SNS (El-Sheikh, Harger, & Whitson, 2001; Quigley & Stifter, 2006).

Exploring Neurogenetic Risk

Another future direction in this field will be greater attention to genetic influences. The notion of "neurogenetic risk" is the idea that genetic mechanisms at least partially account for the link between marital conflict and negative child outcomes. This model importantly complements and even challenges the assumption that the stressful nature of witnessing marital conflict is a key environmental cause of children's psychological problems. In particular, it is hypothesized that part (or in some cases all) of the association between marital conflict and children's psychological problems is a spurious artifact resulting from the operation of genetic processes.

A central premise of the neurogenetic risk hypothesis is that parents with genetic vulnerabilities are more likely to experience high levels of interparental conflict. However, this does not mean that parents have a specific set of genes for arguing with their partners. Rather, the adverse genetic makeup of parents may be related to higher conflict in the marital relationship through its expression in phenotypes characterized by overt negative behaviors and personality traits. In other words, the expression of genes in the form of negative personality traits, behaviors, and psychological symptoms is thought to increase the likelihood of strife and discord between partners. At the same time, the underlying genetic liabilities of the parents are also transmitted in some form to their children. By virtue of the shared genetic material, children may exhibit sets of personality traits and symptoms similar to those of their parents. Thus family history reflecting a genetic risk syndrome could be predisposing both the parents and the children to specific forms of maladaptive behavior. It is assumed that marital conflict is largely, if not exclusively, a by-product of the underlying genetic process. As a result, depending on the specific version of this notion that is endorsed, marital conflict is postulated to be a negligible—or, minimally, a more modest—etiological agent in the development of children's problems.

The influence of these genetic pathways may actually be amplified through a process of "selective mating," whereby adults seek out intimate relationships with partners who have similar psychological and behavioral characteristics. The tendency for adults with similar negative traits (e.g., high levels of aggression, negative mood, and impulsivity) to form partnerships and have children is likely to magnify discord and conflict in the interparental relationship. At the same time, the pairing of adults with similar genetic liabilities substantially augments the intergenerational transmission of this unfavorable genetic material to the children. As a result, these children may exhibit a heightened proneness to negative behavioral traits and outcomes.

Few studies relevant to testing the viability of the neurogenetic risk notion have been conducted. The available empirical findings do support some of its elements. For example, in the divorce literature, findings suggest that children's externalizing problems often predate parental separation and divorce. Although part of this link appears to result from children's exposure to caustic family processes (e.g., marital conflict, disrupted parenting) (e.g., Amato & Keith, 1991; Block et al., 1986), a study by Emery, Waldron, Kitzmann, and Aaron (1999) indicated that a maternal history of antisocial behavior was another central mechanism accounting for much of the heightened delinquency of children of divorce. One possible explanation for this pattern of findings is that the heightened risk of externalizing symptoms experienced by children exposed to marital difficulties may result in part from the transmission of a genetic disposition from parents to children. A more systematic empirical test utilizing a large sample of twins provided further support for this explanation: Harden and colleagues (2007) reported that the inheritance of a genetic liability accounted for the association between the frequency of marital conflict and children's externalizing symptoms.

However, it is important to note that these findings do not rule out the operation of the environmental mechanisms central to most existing theories of marital conflict. In fact, there are several reasons to treat prior environmental and genetic models of marital conflict and child psychopathology as complementary and interlocking. For example, genetically based diatheses or vulnerabilities to environmental pathogens (e.g., exposure to family discord) are often counted as part of the genetic influence, in spite of the fact that the psychopathology is dependent on the combination of genetic liability *and* exposure to environmental stress. An adequate explanatory account of genetic influences must account for both genetic and environmental interactions, ideally in terms of longitudinal transactional and bidirectional pathways. Efforts to "claim" dramatic percentages of variance for genetic models by incorporating interaction terms involving the operation of environmental factors as "genetic" influence are ultimately misleading about causality and not very informative to transactional and bidirectional process models of marital conflict and child development. The situation is made more problematic still when environmental influence is poorly measured. For example, frequency of conflict—the index of marital conflict in the Harden and colleagues (2007) study—is widely regarded as a very weak or diluted risk factor in environmental theories of marital conflict. The risk associated with marital conflict is most potent when parents manage their disputes through escalation of hostility, aggression, disengagement, and indifference. The frequency of differences of opinion between parents matters much less to children than the prevalence of their exposure to destructive conflict.

Finally, these data in this line of work to date are essentially correlational, and accordingly provide limited guidance on cause–effect relations. The apparent behavioral genetic stance of ignoring, rather than integrating, powerful lines of evidence generated by other methods and research designs is not consistent with a process-oriented approach. Rigorous measurement of key variables (e.g., marital conflict), and specification and testing of process variables that may account for genetic contributions by multiple methods and research designs, are important next steps. Although future studies of neurogenetic risk will constitute an exciting direction, greater recognition of these and other challenges and alternative explanations is needed, in order for researchers to weigh and fully appreciate their contribution to understanding of relations between marital conflict and children. However, in this case, the most fruitful directions are most likely to involve a molecular genetic approach to identifying how variations in the genetic composition interact with environmental factors (e.g., interparental conflict) in the prediction of children's coping and psychopathology (e.g., Cicchetti, 2007; Rutter, Moffitt, & Caspi, 2006).

References

Ainsworth, M. D. (1969). Object relations, dependency, and attachment: A theoretical review of the infant–mother relationship. *Child Development, 40,* 969–1025.

Ainsworth, M. D. (1985). Patterns of attachment. *Clinical Psychologist, 38,* 27–29.

Ainsworth, M. D. (1989). Attachments beyond infancy. *American Psychologist, 44,* 709–716.

Ainsworth, M. D. S., Blehar, M. C., Waters, E., & Wall, S. (1978). *Patterns of attachment: A psychological study of the strange situation.* Hillsdale, NJ: Erlbaum.

Almeida, D. M., Wethington, E., & Chandler, A. L. (1999). Daily transmission of tensions between marital dyads and parent–child dyads. *Journal of Marriage and the Family, 61,* 49–61.

Anderson, S. A., Russell, C. S., & Schumm, W. R. (1983). Perceived marital quality and family life-cycle categories: A further analysis. *Journal of Marriage and the Family, 45,* 127–139.

Amato, P. R. (2005). The impact of family formation change on the cognitive, social, and emotional well-being of the next generation. *The Future of Children, 15*(2), 75–96.

Amato, P. R. (2007). Studying marriage and commitment with survey data. In L. M. Casper, M. Lynne, & S. L. Hofferth (Eds.), *Handbook of measurement issues in family research* (pp. 53–65). Mahwah, NJ: Erlbaum.

Amato, P. R., & Booth, A. (2001). The legacy of parents' marital discord: Consequences for children's marital quality. *Journal of Personality and Social Psychology, 81,* 627–638.

Amato, P. R., & Keith, B. (1991). Parental divorce and the well-being of children: A meta-analysis. *Psychological Bulletin, 110*(1), 26–46.

Appel, A. E., & Holden, G. W. (1998). The co-occurrence of spouse and physical child abuse: A review and appraisal. *Journal of Family Psychology, 12,* 578–599.

Aronson, E., Wilson, T. D., & Brewer, M. B. (1998). Experimentation in social psychology. In D. T. Gilbert, S. T. Fiske, & G. Lindzey (Eds.), *The handbook of social psychology* (4th ed., pp. 143–179). Boston: McGraw-Hill.

Ashman, S. B., Dawson, G., Panagiotides, H., Yamada, E., & Wilkinson, C. W. (2002) Stress hormone levels of children of depressed mothers. *Development and Psychopathology, 14,* 333–349.

Attar B. K., & Guerra, N. G. (1994, June). *The effects of cumulative violence exposure on children living in urban neighborhoods.* Paper presented at the convention of the American Psychological Society, Washington, DC.

Ballard, M., & Cummings, E. M. (1990). Response to adults' angry behavior in children of alcoholic and non-alcoholic parents. *Journal of Genetic Psychology, 151,* 195–210.

Ballard, M. E., Cummings, E. M., & Larkin, K. (1993). Emotional and cardiovascular responses to adults' angry behavior and challenging tasks in children of hypertensive and normotensive parents. *Child Development, 64,* 500–515.

Bandura, A. (1973). *Aggression: A social learning analysis.* Englewood Cliffs, NJ: Prentice-Hall.

Barber, B. K. (1996). Parental psychological control: Revisiting a neglected construct. *Child Development, 67,* 3296–3319.

Barber, B. K. (2004, March). *Meaning makers: Adolescent soldiers, victims, and freedom fighters.* Invited address presented at the meeting of the Society for Research on Adolescence, Baltimore.

Baron, R. M., & Kenny, D. A. (1986). The moderator–mediator variable distinction in social psychological research: Conceptual, strategic, and statistical considerations. *Journal of Personality and Social Psychology, 51,* 1173–1182.

Barrera, M., Li, S.A., & Chassin, L. (1995). Effects of parental alcoholism and life stress on Hispanic and non-Hispanic Caucasian adolescents: A prospective study. *American Journal of Community Psychology, 23,* 479–507.

Baruch, D. W., & Wilcox, J. A. (1944). A study of sex differences in preschool children's adjustment coexistent with interparental tensions. *Journal of Genetic Psychology, 64,* 281–303.

Basic Behavioral Science Task Force of the National Advisory Mental Health Council. (1996). Basic behavioral science research for mental health: Family processes and social networks. *American Psychologist, 51,* 622–630.

Belsky, J., Campbell, S. B., Cohn, J. F., & Moore, G. (1996). Instability of infant–parent attachment security. *Developmental Psychology, 32,* 921–924.

Belsky, J., & Fearon, R. M. P. (2004). Exploring marriage–parenting typologies: Their contextual antecedents and developmental sequelae. *Development and Psychopathology, 16,* 501–523.

Belsky, J., & Hsieh, K. H. (1998). Patterns of marital change during the early childhood years: Parent personality, coparenting, and division-of-labor correlates. *Journal of Family Psychology, 12,* 511–528.

Belsky, J., & Pensky, E. (1988). Marital change across the transition to parenthood. *Marriage and Family Review, 12,* 133–156.

Belsky, J., Putnam, S., & Crnic, K. (1996). Coparenting, parenting, and early emotional development. *New Directions for Child Development, 74,* 45–55.

Belsky, J., & Rovine, M. (1990). Patterns of marital change across the transition to parenthood: Pregnancy to three years postpartum. *Journal of Marriage and the Family, 52,* 5–19.

Belsky, J., Spanier, G. B., & Rovine, M. (1983). Stability and change in marriage across the transition to parenthood. *Journal of Marriage and the Family, 45,* 567–577.

Belsky, J., Woodworth, S., & Crnic, K. (1996). Troubled family interaction during toddlerhood, *Development and Psychopathology, 8,* 477–495.

Belsky, J., Youngblade, L., Rovine, K., & Volling, B. (1991). Patterns of marital change and parent–child interaction. *Journal of Marriage and the Family, 53,* 487–498.

Berkowitz, S. J. (2003). Children exposed to community violence: The rationale for early intervention. *Clinical Child and Family Psychology Review, 6(4),* 293–302.

Berman, S. L., Kurtines, W. M., Silverman, W. K., & Serafini, L. T. (1996). The impact of exposure to crime and violence on urban youth. *American Journal of Orthopsychiatry, 66(3),* 329–336.

Berton, M. W., & Stabb, S. D. (1996). Exposure to violence and post-traumatic stress disorder in urban adolescents. *Adolescence, 31(122),* 489–498.

Blanchard, V. L., Hawkins, A. J., Baldwin, S. A., & Fawcett, E. B. (2009). Investigating the effects of marriage and relationship education on couples' communication skills: A meta-analytic study. *Journal of Family Psychology, 23(2),* 203–214.

Blatz, W. E. (1966). *Human security: Some reflections.* Toronto: University of Toronto Press.

Block, J. H., Block, J., & Gjerde, P. F. (1986). The personality of children prior to divorce: A prospective study. *Child Development, 57,* 827–840.

Block, J. H., Block, J., & Morrison, A. (1981). Parental agreement–disagreement on child-rearing orientations and gender-related personality correlates in children. *Child Development, 52,* 965–974.

Borkowski, J. G., Smith, L. E., & Akai, C. E. (2007). Designing effective prevention programs: How good science makes good art. *Infants and Young Children, 20,* 229–241.

Boucsein, W. (1992). *Electrodermal activity.* New York: Plenum Press.

Bowlby, J. (1949). The study and reduction of group tensions in the family. *Human Relations, 2,* 123–128.

Bowlby, J. (1969). *Attachment and loss: Vol. 1. Attachment.* New York: Basic Books.

Bowlby, J. (1973). *Attachment and loss: Vol. 2. Separation.* New York: Basic Books.

Bowlby, J. (1980). *Attachment and loss: Vol. 3. Loss: Sadness and depression.* New York: Basic Books.

Bradbury, T. N., Cohan, C. L., & Karney, B. R. (1998). Optimizing longitudinal research for understanding and preventing marital dysfunction. In T. N. Bradbury (Ed.), *The developmental course of marital dysfunction* (pp. 279–311). New York: Cambridge.

Bradbury, T. N., & Karney, B. R. (1993). Longitudinal study of marital interaction and dysfunction: Review and analysis. *Clinical Psychology Review, 13,* 15–27.

Brendgen, M., Vitaro, F., Doyle, A. B., Markiewicz, D., & Bukowski, W. M. (2002). Same-sex peer relations and romantic relationships during early adolescence: Interactive links to emotional, behavioral, and academic adjustment. *Merrill–Palmer Quarterly, 48,* 77–103.

Bretherton, I. (1985). Attachment theory: Retrospect and prospect. In I. Bretherton & E. Waters (Eds.), Growing points of attachment theory and research. *Monographs of the Society for Research in Child Development, 50*(1–2, Serial No. 209), 167–193.

Bretherton, I., Ridgeway, D., & Cassidy, J. (1990). Assessing internal working models of the attachment relationship. In M. T. Greenberg, D. Cicchetti, & E. M. Cummings (Eds.), *Attachment in the preschool years: Theory, research, and intervention* (pp. 273–308). Chicago: University of Chicago Press.

Bronfenbrenner, U. (1979). *The ecology of human development: Experiments by nature and design.* Cambridge, MA: Harvard University Press.

Bronfenbrenner, U. (1986). Ecology of the family as a context for human development: Research perspectives. *Developmental Psychology, 22,* 723–742.

Brown, G. W., & Harris, T. O. (1978). *Social origins of depression: A study of psychiatric disorders in women.* London: Tavistock.

Brown, K., Covell, K., & Abramovitch, R. (1991). Time course and control of emotion: Age differences in understanding and recognition. *Merrill–Palmer Quarterly, 37,* 273–287.

Buchanan, C. M., Maccoby, E. E., & Dornbusch, S. M. (1991). Caught between parents: Adolescents' experience in divorced homes. *Child Development, 62*(5), 1008–1029.

Buehler, C., Anthony, C., Krishnakumar, A., & Stone, G. (1997). Interparental conflict and youth problem behaviors: A meta-analysis. *Journal of Child and Family Studies, 6*(2), 223–247.

Buehler, C., Benson, M. J., & Gerard, J. M. (2006). Interparental hostility and early adolescent problem behavior: The mediating role of specific aspects of parenting. *Journal of Research on Adolescence,* 16, 265–292.

Buehler, C., & Gerard, J. M. (2002). Marital conflict, ineffective parenting, and children's and adolescents' maladjustment. *Journal of Marriage and the Family, 64,* 78–92.

Buehler, C., Krishnakumar, A., Stone, G., Anthony, C., Pemberton, S., Gerard, J., et al. (1998). Interparental conflict styles and youth problem behaviors: A two sample replication study. *Journal of Marriage and the Family, 60,* 119–132.

Buehler, C., Lange, G., & Franck, K. L. (2007). Adolescents' cognitive and emotional responses to marital hostility. *Child Development, 78,* 775–789.

Byng-Hall, J. (1995). Creating a secure family base: Some implications of attachment theory for family therapy. *Family Processes, 34*(1), 45–58.

Byng-Hall, J. (1999). Family couple therapy: Toward greater security. In J. Cassidy & P. R. Shaver (Eds.), *Handbook of attachment: Theory, research, and clinical applications* (pp. 625–645). New York: Guilford Press.

Cabrera, N. J., Shannon, J. D., West, J., & Brooks-Gunn, J. (2006). Parental interactions with Latino infants: Variation by country of origin and English proficiency. *Child Development, 77,* 1190–1207.

Cadoret, R. J., O'Gorman, T. W., Heywood, E., & Troughton, E. (1985). Genetic and environmental factors in major depression. *Journal of Affective Disorders, 9*, 155–164.

Cahill, L., & McGaugh, J. L. (1998). Mechanisms of emotional arousal and lasting declarative memory. *Trends in Neurosciences, 21*(7), 294–299.

Cairns, E. (1984). Television news as a source of knowledge about the violence for children in Ireland: A test of the knowledge-gap hypothesis. *Current Psychological Research and Reviews, 3*(4), 32–38.

Cairns, E. (1987). *Caught in crossfire: Children in Northern Ireland*. Belfast: Appletree Press/Syracuse, NY: Syracuse University Press.

Cairns, E. (1996). *Children and political violence*. Oxford, UK: Blackwell.

Cairns, E., & Hewstone, M. (2002). Northern Ireland: The impact of peacemaking in Northern Ireland on intergroup behaviour. In G. Salomom & B. Neov (Eds.), *Peace education: The concept, principles and practices around the world* (pp. 217–227). Mahwah, NJ: Erlbaum.

Cairns, E., & Mercer, G. W. (1984). Social identity in Northern Ireland. *Human Relations, 37*(12), 1095–1102.

Cairns, E., & Roe, M. D. (2003). *The role of memory in ethnic conflict*. Basingstoke, UK: Palgrave Macmillan.

Cairns, R. B. (Ed.). (1979). *The analysis of social interaction: Methods, issues, and illustrations*. Hillsdale, NJ: Erlbaum.

Caldera, Y. M., & Lindsey, E. W. (2006). Coparenting, mother–infant interaction, and infant–parent attachment relationships in two-parent families. *Journal of Family Psychology, 20*, 275–283.

Campbell, A., Merrilees, C. E., Cummings, E. M., Goeke-Morey, M. C., Schermerhorn A. C., & Cairns, E. (2007). *Inter- and intra-group conflict in post-cease-fire Northern Ireland*. Manuscript submitted for publication.

Campos, J., Mumme, D., Kermoian, R., & Campos, R. (1994). A functionalist perspective on the nature of emotion. In N. Fox (Ed.), The development of emotion regulation: Biological and behavioral considerations. *Monographs of the Society for Research on Child Development, 59*(2–3, Serial No. 240), 284–303.

Carlson, E. A. (1998). A prospective longitudinal study of attachment disorganization/disorientation. *Child Development, 69*, 1107–1128.

Carlson, E. A., Sroufe, L. A., & Egeland, B. (2004). The construction of experience: A longitudinal study of representation and behavior. *Child Development, 75*(1), 66–83.

Caspi, A., & Bem, D. J. (1990). Personality continuity and change across the life course. In L. A. Pervin (Ed.), *Handbook of personality: Theory and research* (pp. 549–575). New York: Guilford Press.

Cassidy, J., & Shaver, P. R. (Eds). (1999). *Handbook of attachment: Theory, research, and clinical applications*. New York: Guilford Press.

Cassidy, J., & Shaver, P. R. (Eds.). (2008). *Handbook of attachment: Theory, research, and clinical applications* (2nd ed.). New York: Guilford Press.

Chase-Lansdale, P. L., Wakschlag, L. S., & Brooks-Gunn, J. (1995). A psychological perspective on the development of caring in children and youth: The role of family. *Journal of Adolescence, 18*, 515–556.

Chassin, L., Curran, P. J., Hussong, A. M., & Colder, C. R. (1996). The relation of parent alcoholism to adolescent substance use: A longitudinal follow-up study. *Journal of Abnormal Psychology, 105*(1), 70–80.

Christensen, A., & Heavey, C. L. (1990). Gender and social structure in the demand/withdraw pattern of marital conflict. *Journal of Personality and Social Psychology, 59*, 73–81.

Christensen, A., & Nies, D. C. (1980). The Spouse Observation Checklist: Empirical analysis and critique. *American Journal of Family Therapy, 8*, 69–79.

Cicchetti, D. (1989). How research on child maltreatment has informed the study of child development: Perspectives from developmental psychopathology. In D. Cicchetti & V. Carlson (Ed.), *Child maltreatment: Theory and research on the causes and consequences of child abuse and neglect* (pp. 377–431). New York: Cambridge University Press.

Cicchetti, D. (1991). Fractures in the crystal: Developmental psychopathology and the emergence of self. *Developmental Review, 11*, 271–287.

Cicchetti, D. (1993). Developmental psychopathology: Reactions, reflections, projections. *Developmental Review, 13*, 471–502.

Cicchetti, D. (2002). The impact of social experience on neurobiological systems: Illustration from a constructivist view of child maltreatment. *Cognitive Development, 17*, 1407–1428.

Cicchetti, D. (2003). Editorial: Experiments of nature: Contributions to developmental theory. *Development and Psychopathology* [Special issue]: *Experiments of Nature: Contributions to Developmental Theory, 15*(4), 833–835.

Cicchetti, D. (2007). Gene–environment interaction. *Development and Psychopathology* [Special issue]: *Gene–Environment Interaction, 19*(4), 957–959.

Cicchetti, D., & Cohen, D. J. (1995). Perspectives on developmental psychopathology. In D. Cicchetti & D. J. Cohen (Eds.), *Developmental psychopathology: Vol. 1. Theory and methods* (pp. 3–20). New York: Wiley.

Cicchetti, D., Cummings, E. M., Greenberg, M. T., & Marvin, R. S. (1990). An organizational perspective on attachment beyond infancy. In M. T. Greenberg, D. Cicchetti, & E. M. Cummings (Eds.), *Attachment in the preschool years: Theory, research, and intervention* (pp. 3–49). Chicago: University of Chicago Press.

Cicchetti, D., & Lynch, M. (1993). Toward an ecological/transactional model of community violence and child maltreatment: Consequences for children's development. *Psychiatry, 56*, 96–118.

Cicchetti, D., & Rogosch, F. A. (1996). Equifinality and multifinality in developmental psychopathology. *Development and Psychopathology, 8*, 597–600.

Cicchetti, D., & Rogosch, F. A. (2001). The impact of child maltreatment and psychopathology upon neuroendocrine functioning. *Development and Psychopathology, 13*, 783–804.

Cicchetti, D., & Toth, S. L. (1995). A developmental psychopathology perspective on child abuse and neglect. *Journal of the American Academy of Child and Adolescent Psychiatry, 34*, 541–565.

Cicchetti, D., & Toth, S. L. (2006). Editorial: Building bridges and crossing them: Translational research in developmental psychopathology. *Development and Psychopathology, 18*, 619–622.

Cicchetti, D., Toth, S. L., & Bush, M. (1988). Developmental psychopathology and incompetence in childhood: Suggestions for intervention. In B. Lahey & A Kazdin (Eds.), *Advances in clinical child psychology* (pp. 1–71). New York: Plenum Press.

Cole, D. A., & Maxwell, S. E. (2003). Testing mediational models with longitudinal data: Questions and tips in the use of structural equation modeling. *Journal of Abnormal Psychology, 112*(4), 558–577.

Connolly, J. A., Furman, W., & Konaski, R. (2000). The role of peers in the emergence of heterosexual romantic relationships in adolescence. *Child Development, 71,* 1395–1408.

Cooley-Quille, M. R., Turner, S. M., & Beidel, D. C. (1995). Emotional impact of children's exposure to community violence: A preliminary study. *Journal of the American Academy of Child and Adolescent Psychiatry, 34*(10), 1362–1368.

Coulton, C. J., Korbin, J. E., & Su, M. (1996). Measuring neighborhood context for young children in an urban area. *American Journal of Community Psychology, 24*(1), 5–32.

Coulton, C. J., Korbin, J. E., & Su, M. (1999). Neighborhoods and child maltreatment: A multi-level study. *Child Abuse and Neglect, 23*(11), 1019–1040.

Covell, K., & Abramovitch, R. (1987). Understanding emotion in the family: Children's and parents' attributions of happiness, sadness, and anger. *Child Development, 58,* 985–991.

Cowan, C. P., Cowan, P. A., & Heming, G. (2005). Two variations of a preventive intervention for couples: Effects on parents and children during the transition to school. In P. A. Cowan, C. P. Cowan, J. C. Ablow, V. K. Johnson, & J. R. Measelle (Eds.). *The family context of parenting in children's adaptation to elementary school* (pp. 277–312). Mahwah, NJ: Erlbaum.

Cowan, C. P., Cowan, P. A., Pruett, M. K., & Pruett, K. (2007). An approach to preventing coparenting conflict and divorce in low-income families: Strengthening couple relationships and fostering fathers' involvement. *Family Process, 46,* 109–121.

Cowan, P. A., Cohn, D. A., Cowan, C. P., & Pearson, J. L. (1996). Parents' attachment histories and children's externalizing and internalizing behaviors: Exploring family systems models of linkage. *Journal of Consulting and Clinical Psychology, 64,* 53–63.

Cowan, P. A., & Cowan, C. P. (2002). Interventions as tests of family systems theories: Marital and family relationships in children's development and psychopathology. *Development and Psychopathology, 14,* 731–759.

Cowan, P. A., Cowan, C. P., & Schulz, M. S. (1996). Thinking about risk and resilience in families. In E. M. Hetherington & E. A. Blechman (Eds.), *Stress, coping, and resiliency in children and families* (pp. 1–38). Mahwah, NJ: Erlbaum.

Cowan, P. A., & McHale, J. P. (1996). Coparenting in a family context: Emerging achievements, current dilemmas, and future directions. *New Directions for Child Development, 74,* 93–106.

Cox, M. J. (1985). Progress and continued challenges in understanding the transition to parenthood. *Journal of Family Issues, 6,* 395–408.

Cox, M. J., & Paley, B. (1997). Families as systems. *Annual Review of Psychology, 48*, 243–267.

Cox, M. J., Paley, B., Burchinal, M., & Payne, C. C. (1999). Marital perceptions and interactions across the transition to parenthood. *Journal of Marriage and the Family, 61*, 611–625.

Cox, M. J., Paley, B., & Harter, K. (2001). Interparental conflict and parent–child relationships. In J. H. Grych & F. D. Fincham (Eds.), *Interparental conflict and child development: Theory, research, and applications* (pp. 249–272). New York: Cambridge University Press.

Crick, M. R., & Dodge, K. A. (1994). A review and reformulation of social information-processing mechanisms in children's social adjustment. *Psychological Bulletin, 115*(1), 74–101.

Crick, M. R., & Dodge, K. A. (1996). Social information-processing mechanisms on reactive and proactive aggression. *Child Development, 67*(3), 993–1002.

Crittenden, P. M. (1992). Quality of attachment in the preschool years. *Development and Psychopathology, 4*, 209–241.

Crockenberg, S., & Langrock, A. (2001a). The role of emotion and emotion regulation in children's responses to Interparental conflict. In J. Grych & F. Fincham (Eds.), *Interparental conflict and child development: Theory, research, and applications* (pp. 129–159). New York: Cambridge University Press.

Crockenberg, S., & Langrock, A. (2001b). The role of specific emotions in children's responses to interparental conflict: A test of the model. *Journal of Family Psychology, 15*(2), 163–182.

Crockenberg, S. B., & Forgays, D. (1996). The role of emotion in children's understanding and emotional reactions to marital conflict. *Merrill–Palmer Quarterly, 42*, 22–47.

Crockenberg, S. C., Leerkes, E. M., & Lekka, S. K. (2007). Pathways from marital aggression to infant emotion regulation: The development of withdrawal in infancy. *Infant Behavior and Development, 30*(1), 97–113.

Crouter, A. C., & Head, M. R. (2002). Parental monitoring and knowledge of children. In M. H. Bornstein (Ed.), *Handbook of parenting: Vol. 3. Being and becoming a parent* (2nd ed., pp. 461–483). Mahwah, NJ: Erlbaum.

Crowell, J. A., Treboux, D., & Waters, E. (2002). Stability of attachment representations: The transition to marriage. *Developmental Psychology, 38*, 467–479.

Cui, M., Conger, R. D., & Lorenz, F. O. (2005). Predicting change in adolescent adjustment from change in marital problems. *Developmental Psychology, 41*, 812–823.

Cui, M., Donnellan, M. B., & Conger, R. D. (2007). Reciprocal influences between parents' marital problems and adolescent internalizing and externalizing behavior. *Developmental Psychology, 43*, 1544–1552.

Cummings, E. M. (1987). Coping with background anger in early childhood. *Child Development, 58*, 976–984.

Cummings, E. M. (1990). Classification of attachment on a continuum of felt-security: Illustrations from the study of children of depressed parents. In M. Greenberg, D. Cicchetti, & E. M. Cummings (Eds.), *Attachment in the preschool years: Theory, research, and intervention* (pp. 311–338). Chicago: University of Chicago Press.

Cummings, E. M. (1994). Marital conflict and children's functioning. *Social Development, 3,* 16–36.

Cummings, E. M. (1995). Usefulness of experiments for the study of the family. *Journal of Family Psychology, 9,* 175–185.

Cummings, E. M. (1998). Stress and coping approaches and research: The impact of marital conflict on children. *Journal of Aggression, Maltreatment, and Trauma, 2,* 31–50.

Cummings, E. M., Ballard, M., & El-Sheikh, M. (1991). Responses of children and adolescents to interadult anger as a function of gender, age, and mode of expression. *Merrill–Palmer Quarterly, 37,* 543–560.

Cummings, E. M., Ballard, M., El-Sheikh, M., & Lake, M. (1991). Resolution and children's responses to interadult anger. *Developmental Psychology, 27,* 462–470.

Cummings, E. M., & Cicchetti, D. (1990). Toward a transactional model of relations between attachment and depression. In M. T. Greenberg, D. Cicchetti, & E. M. Cummings (Eds.), *Attachment in the preschool years: Theory, research, and intervention* (pp. 339–372). Hillsdale, NJ: Erlbaum.

Cummings, E. M., & Cummings, J. S. (1988). A process-oriented approach to children's coping with adults' angry behavior. *Developmental Review, 3,* 296–321.

Cummings, E. M., & Cummings, J. S. (2002). Parenting and attachment. In M. H. Bornstein (Ed.), *Handbook of parenting: Vol. 5. Practical issues in parenting* (pp. 35–58). Mahwah, NJ: Erlbaum.

Cummings, E. M., Cummings, J. S., Goeke-Morey, M. C., Du Rocher Schudlich, T. D., & Cummings, C. M. (2006). *Coding manual for behavioral observation of interparental interactions.* Unpublished manuscript, University of Notre Dame.

Cummings, E. M., & Davies, P. T. (1994a). *Children and marital conflict: The impact of family dispute and resolution.* New York: Guilford Press.

Cummings, E. M., & Davies, P. T. (1994b). Maternal depression and child development. *Journal of Child Psychology and Psychiatry, 35,* 73–112.

Cummings, E. M., & Davies, P. T. (1995). The impact of parents on their children: An emotional security hypothesis. *Annals of Child Development, 10,* 167–208.

Cummings, E. M., & Davies, P. T. (1996). Emotional security as a regulatory process in normal development and the development of psychopathology. *Development and Psychopathology, 8,* 123–139.

Cummings, E. M., & Davies, P. T. (2002). Effects of marital conflict on children: Recent advances and emerging themes in process-oriented research. *Journal of Child Psychology and Psychiatry, 43,* 31–63.

Cummings, E. M., Davies, P. T., & Campbell, S. B. (2000). *Developmental psychopathology and family process: Theory, research, and clinical implications.* New York: Guilford Press.

Cummings, E. M., Davies, P., & Simpson, K. (1994). Marital conflict, gender, and children's appraisal and coping efficacy as mediators of child adjustment. *Journal of Family Psychology, 8,* 141–149.

Cummings, E. M., DeArth-Pendley, G., Du Rocher Schudlich, T., & Smith, D. (2000). Parental depression and family functioning: Towards a process-oriented model of children's adjustment. In S. Beach (Ed.), *Marital and family processes in depression* (pp. 89–110). Washington, DC: American Psychological Association.

Cummings, E. M., El-Sheikh, M., Kouros, C. D., & Buckhalt, J. A. (2009). Children and violence: The role of children's regulation in the marital aggression-child adjustment link. *Clinical Child and Family Psychology Review, 12*(1), 3–15.

Cummings, E. M., El-Sheikh, M., Kouros, C. D., & Keller, P. S. (2007). Children's skin conductance reactivity as a mechanism of risk in the context of parental depressive symptoms. *Journal of Child Psychology and Psychiatry, 48*(5), 436–445.

Cummings, E. M., Faircloth, B. F., Mitchell, P. M., Cummings, J. S., & Schermerhorn, A. C. (2008). Evaluating a brief prevention program for improving marital conflict in community families. *Journal of Family Psychology, 22*(2), 193–202.

Cummings, E. M., Goeke-Morey, M. C., & Dukewich, T. L. (2001). The study of relations between marital conflict and child adjustment: Challenges and new directions for methodology. In J. H. Grych & F. D. Fincham (Eds.), *Interparental conflict and child development: Theory, research, and applications* (pp. 39–63). New York: Cambridge University Press.

Cummings, E. M., Goeke-Morey, M. C., & Papp, L. M. (2003a). Children's responses to everyday marital conflict tactics in the home. *Child Development, 74,* 1918–1929.

Cummings, E. M., Goeke-Morey, M. C., & Papp, L. M. (2003b). A family-wide model for the role of emotion in family functioning. *Marriage and Family Review, 34,* 13–34.

Cummings, E. M., Goeke-Morey, M. C., & Papp, L. M. (2004). Everyday marital conflict and child aggression. *Journal of Abnormal Child Psychology, 32,* 191–202.

Cummings, E. M., Goeke-Morey, M. C., Papp, L. M., & Dukewich, T. L. (2002). Children's responses to mothers' and fathers' emotionality and conflict tactics during marital conflict in the home. *Journal of Family Psychology, 16*(4), 478–492.

Cummings, E. M., Goeke-Morey, M. C., & Raymond, J. (2004). Fathers in family context: Effects of marital quality and marital conflict. In M. Lamb (Ed.), *The role of the father in child development* (4th ed., pp. 196–221). New York: Wiley.

Cummings, E. M., Goeke-Morey, M. C., Schermerhorn, A. C., Merrilees, C. E., & Cairns, E. (2009). Children and political violence from a social ecological perspective: Implications for research on children and family in Northern Ireland. *Clinical Child and Family Psychology Review, 12*(1), 16–38.

Cummings, E. M., Hennessy, K., Rabideau, G., & Cicchetti, D. (1994). Responses of physically abused boys to interadult anger involving their mothers. *Development and Psychopathology, 6,* 31–41.

Cummings, E. M., Iannotti, R., & Zahn-Waxler, C. (1985). The influence of conflict between adults on the emotions and aggression of young children. *Developmental Psychology, 21,* 495–507.

Cummings, E. M., Iannotti, R. J., & Zahn-Waxler, C. (1989). Aggression between peers in early childhood: Individual continuity and developmental change. *Child Development, 60,* 887–895.

Cummings, E. M., & Keller, P. S. (2006). Marital discord and children's emotional self- regulation. In D. K. Snyder, J. Simpson, & J. N. Hughes (Eds.), *Emotion regulation in couples and families: Pathways to dysfunction and health* (pp. 163–182). Washington, DC: American Psychological Association.

Cummings, E. M., Keller, P. S., & Davies, P. T. (2005). Towards a family process model of maternal and paternal depressive symptoms: Exploring multiple relations with child and family functioning. *Journal of Child Psychology and Psychiatry, 46*(5), 479–489.

Cummings. E. M., Merrilees, C. M., Schermerhorn, A. C., Goeke-Morey, M. C., Shirlow, P., & Cairns, E. (in press). Political violence and child adjustment in Northern Ireland: Testing pathways in a social ecological model for families and children. *Development and Psychopathology.*

Cummings, E. M., & O'Reilly, A. (1997). Fathers in family context: Effects of marital quality on child adjustment. In M. E. Lamb (Ed.), *The role of the father in child development* (3rd ed., pp. 49–65). New York: Wiley.

Cummings, E. M., & Schermerhorn, A. C. (2003). A developmental perspective on children as agents in the family. In L. Kuczynski (Ed.), *Handbook of dynamics of parent–child relations* (pp. 91–108). Newbury Park, CA: Sage.

Cummings, E. M., Schermerhorn, A. C., Davies, P. T., Goeke-Morey, M. C., & Cummings, J. S. (2006). Interparental discord and child adjustment: Prospective investigations of emotional security as an explanatory mechanism. *Child Development, 77*(1), 132–152.

Cummings, E. M., Schermerhorn, A. C., Keller, P. S., & Davies, P. T. (2008). Parental depressive symptoms, children's representations of family relationships, and child adjustment. *Social Development, 17,* 278–305.

Cummings, E. M., Schermerhorn, A. C., Merrilees, C. M., Goeke-Morey, M. C., & Cairns, E. (2009). *Political violence and child adjustment in Northern Ireland: Testing pathways in a social ecological model for families and children.* Manuscript submitted for publication.

Cummings, E. M., Simpson, K. S., & Wilson, A. (1993). Children's responses to interadult anger as a function of information about resolution. *Developmental Psychology, 29,* 978–985.

Cummings, E. M., Vogel, D., Cummings, J. S., & El-Sheikh, M. (1989). Children's responses to different forms of expression of anger between adults. *Child Development, 60,* 1392–1404.

Cummings, E. M., & Wilson, A. G. (1999). Contexts of marital conflict and children's emotional security: Exploring the distinction between constructive and destructive conflict from the children's perspective. In M.

Cox & J. Brooks-Gunn (Eds.), *Formation, functioning, and stability of families* (pp. 105–129). Mahwah, NJ: Erlbaum.

Cummings, E. M., Wilson, J., & Shamir, H. (2003). Reactions of Chilean and American children to marital discord. *International Journal of Behavioral Development, 27*(5), 437–444.

Cummings, E. M., Zahn-Waxler, C., & Radke-Yarrow, M. (1981). Young children's responses to expressions of anger and affection by others in the family. *Child Development, 52,* 1274–1282.

Cummings, E. M., Zahn-Waxler, C., & Radke-Yarrow, M. (1984). Developmental changes in children's reactions to anger in the home. *Journal of Child Psychology and Psychiatry, 25,* 63–74.

Cummings, J. S., Pellegrini, D., Notarius, C., & Cummings, E. M. (1989). Children's responses to angry adult behavior as a function of marital distress and history of interparental hostility. *Child Development, 60,* 1035–1043.

Curran, M., Hazen, N., Jacobvitz, D., & Sasaki, T. (2006). How representations of the parental marriage predict marital emotional attunement during the transition to parenthood. *Journal of Family Psychology, 20,* 477–484.

Curtis, W. J., & Cicchetti, D. (2007). Emotion and resilience: A multilevel investigation of hemispheric electroencephalogram asymmetry and emotion regulation in maltreated and nonmaltreated children. *Development and Psychopathology, 19,* 811–840.

Dadds, M. R., Atkinson, E., Turner, C., Blums, G. J., & Lendich, B. (1999). Family conflict and child adjustment: Evidence for a cognitive-contextual model of intergenerational transmission. *Journal of Family Psychology, 13,* 194–208.

Damon, W., & Hart, D. (1988). *Self-understanding in childhood and adolescence.* New York: Cambridge University Press.

Darby, J. (2001). *The effects of violence on peace processes.* Washington, DC: U.S. Institute of Peace Press.

David, K. M., & Murphy, B. C. (2004). Interparental conflict and late adolescents' sensitization to conflict: The moderating effects of emotional functioning and gender. *Journal of Youth and Adolescence, 33,* 187–200.

David, K. M., & Murphy, B. C. (2007). Interparental conflict and preschoolers' peer relations: The moderating roles of temperament and gender. *Social Development, 16,* 1–23.

Davidov, M., & Grusec, J. E. (2006). Multiple pathways to compliance: Mothers' willingness to cooperate and knowledge of their children's reactions to discipline. *Journal of Family Psychology, 20,* 705–708.

Davies, P. T., & Cicchetti, D. (2004). Editorial: Toward an integration of family systems and developmental psychopathology approaches. *Development and Psychopathology, 16,* 477–481.

Davies, P. T., & Cummings, E. M. (1994). Marital conflict and child adjustment: An emotional security hypothesis. *Psychological Bulletin, 116,* 387–411.

Davies, P. T., & Cummings, E. M. (1998). Exploring children's emotional security as a mediator of the link between marital relations and child adjustment. *Child Development, 69,* 124–139.

Davies, P. T., & Cummings, E. M. (2006). Interparental discord, family process, and developmental psychopathology. In D. Cicchetti & D. Cohen (Eds.), *Developmental psychopathology: Vol. 3. Risk, disorder, and adaptation* (2nd ed., pp. 86–128). Hoboken, NJ: Wiley.

Davies, P. T., Cummings, E. M., & Winter, M. A. (2004). Pathways between profiles of family functioning, child security in the interparental subsystem, and child psychological probems. *Development and Psychopathology, 16,* 525–550.

Davies, P. T., Dumenci, L., & Windle, M. (1999). The interplay between maternal depressive symptoms and marital distress in the prediction of adolescent adjustment. *Journal of Marriage and the Family, 61(1),* 238–254.

Davies, P. T., & Forman, E. M. (2002). Children's patterns of preserving emotional security in the interparental subsystem. *Child Development, 73,* 1880–1903.

Davies, P. T., Forman, E. M., Rasi, J. A., & Stevens, K. I. (2002). Assessing children's emotional security in the interparental relationship: The Security in the Interparental Subsystem scales. *Child Development, 73*(2), 544–562.

Davies, P. T., Harold, G. T., Goeke-Morey, M. C., & Cummings, E. M. (2002). Child emotional security and interparental conflict. *Monographs of the Society for Research in Child Development, 67*(3, Serial No. 270), 1–115.

Davies, P. T., & Lindsay, L. (2001). Does gender moderate the effects of conflict on children? In J. Grych & F. Fincham (Eds.), *Interparental conflict and child development: Theory, research, and applications* (pp. 64–97). New York: Cambridge University Press.

Davies, P. T., & Lindsay, L. L. (2004). Interparental conflict and adolescent adjustment: Why does gender moderate early adolescent vulnerability? *Journal of Family Psychology, 18,* 170–180.

Davies, P. T., Myers, R. L., & Cummings, E. M. (1996). Responses of children and adolescents to marital conflict scenarios as a function of the emotionality of conflict endings. *Merrill–Palmer Quarterly, 42,* 1–21.

Davies, P. T., Myers, R. L., Cummings, E. M., & Heindel, S. (1999). Adult conflict history and children's subsequent responses to conflict. *Journal of Family Psychology, 13,* 610–628.

Davies, P. T., & Sturge-Apple, M. L. (2006). The impact of domestic violence on children's development. In T. L. Nicholls & J. Hamel (Eds.), *Family interventions in domestic violence: A handbook of gender-inclusive theory and treatment* (pp. 165–189). New York: Springer.

Davies, P. T., & Sturge-Apple, M. L. (2007). Advances in the formulation of emotional security theory: An ethologically based perspective. *Advances in Child Development and Behavior, 35,* 87–137.

Davies, P. T., Sturge-Apple, M. L., Cicchetti, D., & Cummings, E. M. (2007). The role of child adrenocortical functioning in pathways between interparental conflict and child maladjustment. *Developmental Psychology, 43(4),* 918–930.

Davies, P. T., Sturge-Apple, M. L., Cicchetti, D., & Cummings, E. M. (2008). Adrenocortical underpinnings of children's psychological reactivity to interparental conflict. *Child Development, 79*(6), 1693–1706.

Davies, P. T., Sturge-Apple, M. L., & Cummings, E. M. (2004). Interdependencies among interparental discord and parenting styles: The role of adult attributes and relationship characteristics. *Development and Psychopathology, 16*(3), 773–797.

Davies, P. T., Sturge-Apple, M. L., Winter, M. A., Cummings, E. M., & Farrell, D. (2006). Child adaptational development in contexts of interparental conflict over time. *Child Development, 77*(1), 218–233.

Davies, P. T., Sturge-Apple, M. L., Woitach, M. J., & Cummings, E. M. (in press). A process analysis of the transmission of distress from interparental conflict to parenting: Adult relationship security as an explanatory mechanism. *Developmental Psychology.*

Davies, P. T., & Windle, M. (1997). Gender-specific pathways between maternal depressive symptoms, family discord, and adolescent adjustment. *Developmental Psychology, 33*(4), 657–668.

Davies, P. T., & Windle, M. (2001). Interparental discord and adolescent adjustment trajectories: The potentiating and protective role of intrapersonal attributes. *Child Development, 72*; 1163–1178.

Davies, P. T., Winter, M. A., & Cicchetti, D. (2006). The implications of emotional security theory for understanding and treating childhood psychopathology. *Development and Psychopathology, 18*, 707–735.

Davies, P. T., & Woitach, M. J. (2008). Children's emotional security in the interparental relationship. *Current Directions in Psychological Science, 17*(4), 269–274.

Davies, P. T., Woitach, M. J., Winter, M. A., & Cummings, E. M. (2008). Children's insecure representations of the interparental relationship and their school adjustment: The mediating role of attention difficulties. *Child Development, 79*(5), 1570–1582.

Davis, B. T., Hops, H., Alpert, A., & Sheeber, L. (1998). Child responses to parental conflict and their effect on adjustment. *Journal of Family Psychology, 12*, 163–177.

DeArth-Pendley, G., & Cummings, E. M. (2002). Children's emotional reactivity to interadult nonverbal conflict expressions. *Journal of Genetic Psychology, 163*(1), 97–111.

Denham, S. A. (1998). *Emotional development in young children.* New York: Guilford Press.

DeWolff, M., & van IJzendoorn, M. H. (1997). Sensitivity and attachment: A meta-analysis on parental antecedents of infant attachment. *Child Development, 68*, 571–591.

Dickerson, S. S., & Kemeny, M. E. (2004). Acute stressors and cortisol responses: A theoretical integration and synthesis of laboratory research. *Psychological Bulletin, 130*, 355–391.

Dingfelder, S. F. (2004, February). A shift in priorities at NIMH. *APA Monitor,* p. 58.

Dion, R., Avellar, S., Zaveri, H., & Hershey, A. (2006). *Implementing healthy marriage programs for unmarried couples with children: Early lessons from the Building Strong Families Project, final report.* Washington, DC: Mathematica Policy Research.

Dix, T. (1991). The affective organization of parenting: Adaptive and maladaptive processes. *Psychological Bulletin, 110,* 3–25.

Doumas, D., Margolin, G., & John, R. S. (1994). The intergenerational transmission of aggression across three generations. *Journal of Family Violence, 9(2),* 157–175.

Downey, G., & Coyne, J. C. (1990). Children of depressed parents: An integrative review. *Psychological Bulletin, 108,* 50–76.

Dunn, J., & Davies, L. (2001). Sibling relationships and interparental conflict. In J. H. Grych & F. D. Fincham (Eds.), *Interparental conflict and child development: Theory, research, and applications* (pp. 273–290). New York: Cambridge University Press.

DuRant, R. H., Getts, A. G., Cadenhead, C., & Woods, E. R. (1995). The association between weapon-carrying and the use of violence among adolescents living in or around public housing. *Journal of Adolescence, 18(5),* 579–592.

Du Rocher Schudlich, T., & Cummings, E. M. (2003). Parental dysphoria and children's internalizing symptoms: Marital conflict styles as mediators of risk. *Child Development, 74,* 1663–1681.

Du Rocher Schudlich, T., & Cummings, E. M. (2007). Parental dysphoria and children's adjustment: Marital conflict styles, children's emotional security, and parenting as mediators of risk. *Journal of Abnormal Child Psychology, 35,* 627–639.

Du Rocher Schudlich, T., Papp, L., & Cummings, E. M. (2004). Relations of husbands' and wives' dysphoria to marital conflict resolution strategies. *Journal of Family Psychology, 18,* 171–183.

Du Rocher Schudlich, T., Shamir, H., & Cummings, E. M. (2004). Children's representations of parent–child relations as mediators between marital conflict and children's peer relations. *Social Development, 13(2),* 171–192.

Earls, M. (2003). Advertising to the herd: How understanding our true nature challenges the ways we think about advertising and market research. *International Journal of Market Research, 45(3),* 311–336.

Easterbrooks, M. A., Cummings, E. M., & Emde, R. N. (1994). Young children's responses to constructive marital disputes. *Journal of Family Psychology, 8,* 160–169.

Edwards, E. P., Eiden, R. D., & Leonard, K. E. (2004). Impact of fathers' alcoholism and associated risk factors on parent–infant attachment stability from 12 to 18 months. *Infant Mental Health Journal, 25,* 556–579.

Egeland, B., Carlson, E., & Sroufe, L. A. (1993). Resilience as process. *Development and Psychopathology, 5,* 517–528.

Eisenberg, N., Fabes, R. A., Guthrie, I. K., Murphy, B. C., Maszk, P., Holmgren, R., et al. (1996). The relations of regulation and emotionality to problem behavior in elementary school children. *Development and Psychopathology, 8,* 141–162.

Elbedour, S., ten-Bensel, R., & Bastien, D. T. (1993). Ecological integrated model of children in war: Individual and social psychology. *Child Abuse and Neglect, 17(6),* 805–819.

Ellis, B. J., & Garber, J. (2000). Psychosocial antecedents of variation in girls' pubertal timing: Maternal depression, stepfather presence, and marital and family stress. *Child Development, 71*, 485–501.

El-Sheikh, M. (1994). Children's emotional and physiological responses to interadult angry behavior: The role of history of interparental hostility. *Journal of Abnormal Child Psychology, 22*, 661–678.

El-Sheikh, M. (2005). The role of emotional responses and physiological reactivity in the marital conflict–child functioning link. *Journal of Child Psychology and Psychiatry, 46*(11), 1191–1199.

El-Sheikh, M. (2007). Children's skin conductance level and reactivity: Are these measures stable over time and across tasks? *Developmental Psychobiology, 49*(2), 180–186.

El-Sheikh, M., Buckhalt, J. A., Cummings, E. M., & Keller, P. (2007). Sleep disruptions and emotional insecurity are pathways of risk for children. *Journal of Child Psychology and Psychiatry, 48*(1), 88–96.

El-Sheikh, M., Buckhalt, J. A., Keller, P., Cummings, E. M., & Acebo, C. (2007). Child emotional insecurity and academic achievement: The role of sleep disruptions. *Journal of Family Psychology, 21*(1), 29–38.

El-Sheikh, M., Buckhalt, J. A., Mize, J., & Acebo, C. (2006). Marital conflict and disruption of children's sleep. *Child Development, 77*(1), 31–43.

El-Sheikh, M., & Cheskes, J. (1995). Background verbal and physical anger: A comparison of children's responses to adult–adult and adult–child arguments. *Child Development, 66*, 446–458.

El-Sheikh, M., & Cummings, E. M. (1995). Children's responses to angry adult behavior as a function of experimentally manipulated exposure to resolved and unresolved conflict. *Social Development, 4*, 75–91.

El-Sheikh, M., Cummings, E. M., Buckhalt, J., & Keller, P. S. (2007). Sleep disruptions and emotional insecurity are pathways of risk for children. *Journal of Child Psychology and Psychiatry, 48*(1), 88–96.

El-Sheikh, M., Cummings, E. M., & Goetsch, V. (1989). Coping with adults' angry behavior: Behavioral, physiological, and self-reported responding in preschoolers. *Developmental Psychology, 25*, 490–498.

El-Sheikh, M., Cummings, E. M., Kouros, C. D., Elmore-Staton, L., & Buckhalt, J. A. (2008). Marital psychological and physical aggression and children's mental and physical health: Direct, mediated, and moderated effects. *Journal of Consulting and Clinical Psychology, 78*(1), 138–148.

El-Sheikh, M., Cummings, E. M., & Reiter, S. (1996). Preschoolers' responses to ongoing interadult conflict: The role of prior exposure to resolved versus unresolved arguments. *Journal of Abnormal Child Psychology, 24*(5), 665–679.

El-Sheikh, M., & Flanagan, E. (2001). Parental problem drinking and children's adjustment: Family conflict and parental depression as mediators and moderators of risk. *Journal of Abnormal Child Psychology, 29*(5), 417–432.

El-Sheikh, M., Harger, J., & Whitson, S. M. (2001). Exposure to interparental conflict and children's adjustment and physical health: The moderating role of vagal tone. *Child Development, 72*, 1617–1636.

El-Sheikh, M., Keller, P. S., & Erath, S. A. (2007). Marital conflict and risk for child maladjustment over time: Skin conductance level reactivity as a vulnerability factor. *Journal of Abnormal Child Psychology, 35*, 715–727.

El-Sheikh, M., Kouros, C. D., Erath, S., Cummings, E. M., Keller, P., & Staton, L. (2009). Marital conflict and children's externalizing behavior: Interactions between parasympathetic and sympathetic nervous system activity. *Monographs of the Society for Research in Child Development, 74*(1, Serial No. 292), 1–79.

El-Sheikh, M., & Whitson, S. A. (2006). Longitudinal relations between marital conflict and child adjustment: Vagal regulation as a protective factor. *Journal of Family Psychology, 20*(1), 30–39.

Emery, R. E. (1982). Interparental conflict and the children of discord and divorce. *Psychological Bulletin, 92*, 310–330.

Emery, R. E. (1988). *Marriage, divorce, and children's adjustment.* Beverly Hills, CA: Sage.

Emery, R. E. (1989). Family violence. *American Psychologist, 44*, 321–328.

Emery, R. E. (1999). *Marriage, divorce, and children's adjustment* (2nd ed.). Thousand Oaks, CA: Sage.

Emery, R. E. (2004). *The truth about children and divorce: Dealing with the emotions so you and your children can thrive.* New York: Viking.

Emery, R. E., Fincham, F. D., & Cummings, E. M. (1992). Parenting in context: Systemic thinking about parental conflict and its influence on children. *Journal of Consulting and Clinical Psychology, 60*, 909–912.

Emery, R. E., & O'Leary, K .D. (1982). Children's perceptions of marital discord and behavior problems of boys and girls. *Journal of Abnormal Child Psychology, 10*, 11–24.

Emery, R. E., & O'Leary, K .D. (1984). Marital discord and child behavior problems in a nonclinic sample. *Journal of Abnormal Child Psychology, 12*, 411–420.

Emery, R. E., Waldron, M., Kitzmann, K. M., & Aaron, J. (1999). Delinquent behavior, future divorce or nonmarital childbearing, and externalizing behavior among offspring: A 14-year prospective study. *Journal of Family Psychology, 13*(4), 568–579.

Emery, R. E., Weintraub, S., & Neale, J. M. (1982). Effects of marital discord on the school behavior of children of schizophrenic, affectively disordered and normal parents. *Journal of Abnormal Child Psychology, 10*(2), 215–228.

Engfer, A. (1988). The interrelatedness of marriage and the mother–child relationship. In R. Hinde & J. Stevenson-Hinde (Eds.), *Relationships within families: Mutual influences* (pp. 83–103). New York: Oxford University Press.

Erath, S. A., Bierman, K. L., & the Conduct Problems Prevention Research Group. (2006). Aggressive marital conflict, maternal harsh punishment, and child aggressive–disruptive behavior: Evidence for direct and mediated relations. *Journal of Family Psychology, 20*, 217–226.

Erath, S. A., El-Sheikh, M., & Cummings, E. M. (2009). Harsh parenting and child externalizing behavior: skin conductance level reactivity as a moderator. *Child Development, 80*(2), 578–592.

Erel, O., & Burman, B. (1995). Interrelatedness of marital relations and parent–child relations: A meta-analytic review. *Psychological Bulletin, 118,* 108–132.

Erel, O., Margolin, G., & John, R. S. (1998). Observed sibling interactions: Links with the marital and the mother–child relationship. *Developmental Psychology, 34,* 288–298.

Essex, M. J., Klein, M. H., Cho, E., & Kalin, N. H. (2002). Maternal stress beginning in infancy may sensitize children to later stress exposure: Effects of cortisol on behavior. *Biological Psychiatry, 52,* 776–784.

Evans, J. (2003). In two minds: Dual-process accounts of reasoning. *Trends in Cognitive Sciences, 7*(10), 454–459.

Fabes, R. A., Leonard, S. A., Kupanoff, K., & Martin, C. L. (2001). Parental coping with children's negative emotions: Relations with children's emotional and social responding. *Child Development, 72*(3), 907–920.

Faircloth, B. F., & Cummings, E. M. (2008). Evaluating a parent education program for preventing the negative effects of marital conflict. *Journal of Applied Developmental Psychology, 29*(2), 141–156.

Faircloth, W. B., Schermerhorn, A. C., Mitchell, P. M., Cummings, J. S., & Cummings, E. M. (2009). *Testing the long-term efficacy of a prevention program for improving marital conflict in community families.* Manuscript submitted for publication.

Fantuzzo, J. W., DePaola, L. M., Lambert, L., Martino, T., Anderson, G., & Sutton, S. (1991). Effects of interparental violence on the psychological adjustment and competencies of young children. *Journal of Consulting and Clinical Psychology, 59*(2), 258–265.

Farver, J. M., Natera, L. X., & Frosch, D. L. (1999). Effects of community violence on inner-city preschoolers and their families. *Journal of Applied Developmental Psychology, 20*(1), 143–158.

Fauber, R., Forehand, R., Thomas, A. M., & Wierson, M. (1990). A meditational model of the impact of marital conflict on adolescent adjustment in intact and divorced families: The role of disrupted parenting. *Child Development, 61,* 1112–1123.

Fauber, R. L., & Long, N. (1991). Children in context: The role of the family in child psychotherapy. *Journal of Consulting and Clinical Psychology, 59,* 813–820.

Fay, M.T., Morrissey, M., & Smyth, M. (1999). *Northern Ireland's Troubles: The human costs.* London: Pluto Press.

Fay, M.T., Morrissey, M., Smyth, M., & Wong, T. (1999). *The Cost of the Troubles study. Report on the Northern Ireland survey: The experience and impact of the Troubles.* Derry/Londonderry, North Ireland: Initiative on Conflict Resolution and Ethnicity (INCORE).

Feerick, M. M., & Prinz, R. J. (2003). Next steps in research on children exposed to community violence or war/terrorism. *Clinical Child and Family Psychology Review, 6*(4), 303–305.

Feiring, C. (1996). Concepts of romance in 15-year-old adolescents. *Journal of Research on Adolescence, 6,* 181–200.

Fergusson, D. M., & Horwood, L. J. (1998). Exposure to interparental violence in childhood and psychosocial adjustment in young adulthood. *Child Abuse and Neglect, 22,* 339–357.

Field, T., Diego, M. A., Dieter, J., Hernandez-Reif, M., Schanberg, S., Kuhn, C., et al. (2001). Depressed withdrawn and intrusive mothers' effects on their fetuses and neonates. *Infant Behavior and Development, 24,* 27–39.

Fincham, F. D. (1994). Understanding the association between marital conflict and child adjustment: Overview. *Journal of Family Psychology, 8*(2), 123–127.

Fincham, F. D. (1998). Child development and marital relations. *Child Development, 69,* 543–574.

Fincham, F. D., Grych, J. H., & Osborne, L. N. (1994). Does marital conflict cause child maladjustment?: Directions and challenges for longitudinal research. *Journal of Family Psychology, 8,* 128–140.

Flowers, A., Lanclos, N. F., & Kelley, M. L. (2002). Validation of a screening instrument for exposure to violence in African American children. *Journal of Pediatric Psychology, 27*(4), 351–361.

Floyd, F., Gilliom, L. A., & Costigan, C. L. (1998). Marriage and the parenting alliance: Longitudinal prediction of change in parenting perceptions and behaviors. *Child Development, 69,* 1461–1479.

Floyd, F. J., & Widaman, K. F. (1995). Factor analysis in the development and refinement of clinical assessment instruments. *Psychological Assessment* [Special issue]: *Methodological Issues in Psychological Assessment Research, 7*(3), 286–299.

Floyd, F. J., & Zmich, D. E. (1991). Marriage and the parenting partnership: Perceptions and interactions of parents with mentally retarded and typically developing children. *Child Development, 62,* 1434–1448.

Forman, E. M., & Davies, P. T. (2003). Family instability and adolescent maladjustment: The mediating effects of parenting quality and adolescent appraisals of family security. *Journal of Clinical Child and Adolescent Psychology, 32,* 94–105.

Forman, E. M., & Davies, P. T. (2005). Assessing children's appraisals of security in the family system: The development of the Security in the Family System (SIFS) scales. *Journal of Child Psychology and Psychiatry, 46*(8), 900–916.

Fosco, G. M., & Grych, J. H. (2007). Emotional expression in the family as a context for children's appraisals of interparental conflict. *Journal of Family Psychology, 21,* 248–258.

Fox, N. A., & Card, J. A. (1999). Psychophysiological measures in the study of attachment. In J. Cassidy & P. R. Shaver (Eds.), *Handbook of attachment: Theory, research, and clinical applications* (pp. 226–245). New York: Guilford Press.

Fox, N. A., Hane, A. A., & Perez-Edgar, K. (2006). Psychophysiological methods for the study of developmental psychopathology. In D. Cicchetti & D. J. Cohen (Eds.), *Developmental psychopathology: Vol. 2. Developmental neuroscience* (2nd ed., pp. 381–426). Hoboken, NJ: Wiley.

Frosch, C. A., & Mangelsdorf, S. C. (2001). Marital behavior, parenting behavior, and multiple reports of preschoolers' behavior problems: Mediation or moderation? *Developmental Psychology, 37,* 502–519.

Frosch, C. A., Mangelsdorf, S. C., & McHale, J. L. (1998). Correlates of marital behavior at 6 months postpartum. *Developmental Psychology, 34*(6), 1438–1449.

Frosch, C. A., Mangelsdorf, S. C., & McHale, J. L. (2000). Marital behavior and the security of preschooler-parent attachment relationships. *Journal of Family Psychology, 14*(1), 144–161.

Furman, W., & Wehner, E. A. (1994). Romantic views: Toward a theory of adolescent romantic relationships. In R. Montemayor, G. R. Adams, & T. P. Gullotta (Eds.), *Personal relationships during adolescence* (pp. 168–195). Thousand Oaks, CA: Sage.

Gamba, V. (2006). Post-agreement demobilization, disarmament, and reintegration: Toward a new approach. In J. Darby (Ed.), *Violence and reconstruction* (pp. 53–77). Notre Dame, IN: University of Notre Dame Press.

Garbarino, J., Dubrow, N., Koselny, K., & Pardo, C. (1992). *Children in danger: Coping with the consequences of community violence.* San Francisco: Jossey-Bass.

Garcia Coll, C. (2005). Editorial. *Developmental Psychology, 41,* 299–300.

Garcia-O'Hearn, C., Margolin, G., & John, R. (1997). Mothers' and fathers' reports of children's reactions to naturalistic marital conflict. *Journal of the American Academy of Child and Adolescent Psychiatry, 36,* 1366–1373.

Garmezy, N. (1985). Stress-resistant children: The search for protective factors. In J. E. Stevenson (Ed.), *Recent research in developmental psychopathology* (*Journal of Child Psychology and Psychiatry* Book Suppl. 4, pp. 213–233). Oxford, UK: Pergamon Press.

Gassner, S., & Murray, E. J. (1969). Dominance and conflict in the interactions between parents of normal and neurotic children. *Journal of Abnormal Psychology, 74*(1), 33–41.

Gelles, R. J. (1987). *Family violence.* Newbury Park, CA: Sage.

Gerard, J. G., & Buehler, C. (1999). Multiple family risk factors and youth problem behaviors. *Journal of Marriage and the Family, 61,* 343–361.

Gerard, J. G., Krishnakumar, A., & Buehler, C. (2006). Marital conflict, parent–child relations, and youth maladjustment: A longitudinal investigation of spillover effects. *Journal of Family Issues, 27,* 951–975.

Gest, S. D., Reed, M. J., & Masten, A. S. (1999). Measuring developmental changes in exposure to adversity: A life chart and rating scale approach. *Development and Psychopathology, 11,* 171–192.

Gibson, K. (1989). Children in political violence. *Social Science and Medicine, 28,* 659–667.

Glenn, N. (1990). Quantitative research on marital quality in the 1980's: A critical review. *Journal of Marriage and the Family, 52,* 818–831.

Goeke-Morey, M. C., & Cummings, E. M. (2007). Impact of father involvement: A closer look at indirect effects models involving marriage and child adjustment. *Applied Developmental Science, 11*(4), 1–5.

Goeke-Morey, M. C., Cummings, E. M., Ellis, K., Merrilees, C. E., Schermerhonrn, A. C., Shirlow, P., et al. (in press). The differential impact on children of inter- and intra-community violence in Northern Ireland. *Peace and Conflict: Journal of Peace Psychology.*

Goeke-Morey, M. C., Cummings, E. M., Harold, G. T., & Shelton, K. H. (2003). Categories and continua of destructive and constructive marital conflict tactics from the perspective of U.S. and Welsh children. *Journal of Family Psychology, 17,* 327–338.

Goeke-Morey, M. C., Cummings, E. M., & Papp, L. M. (2007). Children and marital conflict resolution: Implications for emotional security and adjustment. *Journal of Family Psychology, 21*(4), 744–753.

Gold, P. W., & Chrousos, G. P. (2002). Organization of the stress system and its dysregulation in melancholic and atypical depression: High vs. low CRH/NE states. *Molecular Psychiatry, 7*(3), 254–275.

Goldberg, S., Grusec, J. E., & Jenkins, J. M. (1999). Confidence in protection: Arguments for a narrow definition of attachment. *Journal of Family Psychology, 13,* 475–483.

Gomulak-Cavicchio, B. M., Davies, P. T., & Cummings, E. M. (2006). The role of maternal communication patterns about interparental disputes in associations between interparental conflict and child psychological maladjustment. *Journal of Abnormal Child Psychology, 34,* 757–771.

Gonzales, N. A., Pitts, S. C., Hill, N. E., & Roosa, M. W. (2000). A mediational model of the impact of interparental conflict on child adjustment in a multiethnic, low-income sample. *Journal of Family Psychology, 14,* 365–379.

Goodman, S. H., & Gotlib, I. H. (1999). Risk for psychopathology in the children of depressed mothers: A developmental model for understanding mechanisms of transmission. *Psychological Review, 106*(3), 458–490.

Goodman, S. H., & Gotlib, I. H. (Eds.). (2002). *Children of depressed parents: Mechanisms of risk and implications for treatment.* Washington, DC: American Psychological Association.

Goodyer, I. M. (1990). *Life experiences, development, and childhood psychopathology.* Chichester, UK: Wiley.

Gordis, E. B., Granger, D. A., Susman, E. J., & Trickett, P. K. (2006). Asymmetry between salivary cortisol and a-amylase reactivity to stress: Relation to aggressive behavior in adolescents. *Psychoneuroendocrinology, 31*(8), 976–987.

Gorman-Smith, D., & Tolan, P. (1998). The role of exposure to community violence and developmental problems among inner-city youth. *Development and Psychopathology, 10*(1), 101–116.

Gordis, E. B., Margolin, G., & John, R. (1997). Marital aggression, observed parental hostility, and child behavior during triadic family interaction. *Journal of Family Psychology, 11,* 76–89.

Gottman, J. M. (1994). *Why marriages succeed or fail.* New York: Simon & Schuster.

Gottman, J. M., & Katz, L. F. (1989). Effects of marital discord on young children's peer interactions and health. *Developmental Psychology, 25,* 273–281.

Gottman, J. M., & Gottman, J. S. (1999). The marriage survival kit: A research-based marital therapy. In R. Berger & M. T. Hannah (Eds.), *Preventive approaches in couples therapy* (pp. 304–330). Philadelphia: Brunner/Mazel.

Graber, J. A., & Brooks-Gunn, J. (1996). Transitions and turning points: Navigating the passage from childhood through adolescence. *Developmental Psychology, 32*, 768–776.

Granger, D. A., Kivlighan, K. T., Blair, C., Mize, J., Buckhalt, J. A., Handwerger, K., et al. (2006). Integrating the measurement of salivary a-amylase into studies of child health, development, and social relationships. *Journal of Social and Personal Relationships* [Special issue]: *Physiology and Human Relationships, 23*(2), 267–290.

Granger, D. A., Weisz, J. R., & Kauneckis, D. (1994). Neuroendocrine reactivity, internalizing behavior problems, and control-related cognitions in clinic-referred children and adolescents. *Journal of Abnormal Psychology, 103*, 267–276.

Granic, I., & Hollenstein, T. (2003). Dynamic systems methods for models of developmental psychopathology. *Development and Psychopathology, 15*, 641–669.

Gray, M. R., & Steinberg, L. (1999). Unpacking authoritative parenting: Reassessing a multidimensional construct. *Journal of Marriage and the Family, 61*, 574–587.

Greenberg, M. T. (1999). Attachment and psychopathology in childhood. In J. Cassidy & P. R. Shaver (Eds.), *Handbook of attachment: Theory, research, and clinical applications* (pp. 469–496). New York: Guilford Press.

Greenberg, M. T., & Speltz, M. L. (1988). Attachment and the ontogeny of conduct problems. In J. Belsky & T. Nezworski (Eds.), *Clinical implications of attachment* (pp. 177–218). Hillsdale, NJ: Erlbaum.

Greenberg, M. T., Speltz, M. L., & DeKlyen, M. (1993). The role of attachment in the early development of disruptive behavior problems. *Development and Psychopathology, 5*, 191–214.

Grolnick, W. S., & Slowiaczek, M. L. (1994). Parents' involvement in children's schooling: A multidimensional conceptualization and motivational model. *Child Development, 65*, 237–252.

Grusec, J. E., & Goodnow, J. J. (1994). Impact of parental discipline methods on the child's internalization of values: A reconceptualization of current points of view. *Developmental Psychology, 30*, 4–19.

Grych, J. H. (1998). Children's appraisals of interparental conflict: Situational and contextual influences. *Journal of Family Psychology, 12*, 437–453.

Grych, J. H. (2002). Marital relationships and parenting. In M. H. Bornstein (Ed.), *Handbook of parenting: Vol. 4. Social conditions and applied parenting* (2nd ed., pp. 203–225). Mahwah, NJ: Erlbaum.

Grych, J. H., & Fincham, F. D. (1990). Marital conflict and children's adjustment: A cognitive–contextual framework. *Psychological Bulletin, 108*, 267–290.

Grych, J. H., & Fincham, F. D. (1992). Interventions for children of divorce: Towards greater integration of research and action. *Psychological Bulletin, 111*, 434–454.

Grych, J. H., & Fincham, F. D. (1993). Children's appraisals of marital conflict: Initial investigations of the cognitive–contextual framework. *Child Development, 64*, 215–230.

Grych, J. H., & Fincham, F. D. (2001a). Interparental conflict and child adjustment: An overview. In J. H. Grych & F. D. Fincham (Eds.), *Interparental conflict and child development: Theory, research, and applications* (pp. 1–6). New York: Cambridge University Press.

Grych, J. H., & Fincham, F. D. (Eds.). (2001b). *Interparental conflict and child development: Theory, research, and applications*. New York: Cambridge University Press.

Grych, J. H., Fincham, F. D., Jouriles, E. N., & McDonald, R. (2000). Interparental conflict and child adjustment: Testing the mediational role of appraisals in the cognitive-contextual framework. *Child Development, 71*, 1648–1661.

Grych, J. H., Harold, G. T., & Miles, C. J. (2003). A prospective investigation of appraisals as mediators of the link between interparental conflict and child adjustment. *Child Development, 74*(4), 1176–1193.

Grych, J. H., Jouriles, E. N., Swank, P. R., McDonald, R., & Norwood, W. D. (2000). Patterns of adjustment among children of battered women. *Journal of Consulting and Clinical Psychology, 68*(1), 84–94.

Grych, J. H., Raynor, S. R., & Fosco, G. M. (2004). Family processes that shape the impact of interparental conflict on adolescents. *Development and Psychopathology, 16*, 649–665.

Grych, J. H., Seid, M., & Fincham, F. D. (1992). Assessing marital conflict from the child's perspective. *Child Development, 63*, 558–572.

Grych, J. H., Wachsmuth-Schlaefer, T., & Klockow, L. L. (2002). Interparental aggression and young children's representations of family relationships. *Journal of Family Psychology, 16*, 259–272.

Gunnar, M. R., & Vazquez, D. M. (2001). Low cortisol and a flattening of expected daytime rhythm: Potential indices of risk in human development. *Development and Psychopathology, 13*, 515–538.

Guterman, N. B., Cameron, M., & Staller, K. (2000). Definitional and measurement issues in the study of community violence among children and youths. *Journal of Community Psychology, 28*(6), 571–587.

Halgunseth, L. C., Ispa, J. M., & Rudy, D. (2006). Parental control in Latino families: An integrated review of the literature. *Child Development, 77*, 1282–1297

Halpern, E. (2001). Family psychology from an Israeli perspective. *American Psychologist, 56*, 58–64.

Harden, K. P., Turkheimer, E., Emery, R. E., D'Onofrio, B., Slutske, W. S., Heath, A. C., et al. (2007). Marital conflict and conduct problems in children of twins. *Child Development, 78*, 1–18.

Harold, G. T., Aitken, J. J., & Shelton, K. H. (2007). Inter-parental conflict and children's academic attainment: A longitudinal analysis. *Journal of Child Psychology and Psychiatry, 48*(12), 1223–1232.

Harold, G. T., & Conger, R. D. (1997). Marital conflict and adolescent distress: The role of adolescent awareness. *Child Development, 68*, 330–350.

Harold, G. T., Fincham, F. D., Osborne, L. N., & Conger, R. D. (1997). Mom and Dad are at it again: Adolescent perceptions of marital conflict and adolescent psychological distress. *Developmental Psychology, 33*, 333–350.

Harold, G. T., Shelton, K. H., Goeke-Morey, M. C., & Cummings, E. M. (2004).

Marital conflict and child adjustment: Prospective longitudinal tests of the mediating role of children's emotional security about family relationships. *Social Development, 13*(3), 350–376.

Hartmann, D. P. (1992). Design, measurement, and analysis: Technical issues in developmental research. In M. H. Bornstein & M. E. Lamb (Eds.), *Developmental psychology: An advanced textbook* (3rd ed., pp. 59–151). Hillsdale, NJ: Erlbaum.

Heatherington, L., Friedlander, M., & Greenberg, L. (2005). Change process research in couple and family therapy: Methodological challenges and opportunities. *Journal of Family Psychology, 19,* 18–27.

Heim, C., Ehlert, U., & Hellhammer, D. (2000). The potential role of hypocortisolism in the pathophysiology of stress-related bodily disorders. *Psychoneuroendocrinology, 25,* 1–35.

Helgeson, V. S. (1994). Relation of agency and communion to well-being: Evidence and potential explanations. *Psychological Bulletin, 116,* 412–428.

Hennessy, K. D., Rabideau, G. J., Cicchetti, D., & Cummings, E. M. (1994). Responses of physically abused children to different forms of interadult anger. *Child Development, 65,* 815–828.

Hetherington, E. M., & Clingempeel, W. G. (1992). Coping with marital transitions: A family systems perspective. *Monographs of the Society for Research in Child Development, 57*(2–3, Serial No. 227), 1–242.

Hilburn-Cobb, C. (2004). Adolescent psychopathology in terms of multiple behavioral systems: The role of attachment and controlling strategies and frankly cisorganized behavior. In L. Atkinson & S. Goldberg (Eds.), *Attachment issues in psychopathology and intervention.* (pp. 95–135). Mahwah, NJ: Erlbaum.

Hill, J. P., & Lynch, M. E. (1983). The intensification of gender-related role expectations during early adolescence. In J. Brooks-Gunn & A. C. Petersen (Eds.), *Girls at puberty: Biological and psychosocial perspectives.* New York: Plenum Press.

Hoffman, M. L. (1994). Discipline and internalization. *Developmental Psychology, 30,* 26–28.

Hogland, K., & Zartman, I. W. (2006). Violence by the state: Official spoilers and their allies. In J. Darby (Ed.), *Violence and reconstruction* (pp. 11–32). Notre Dame, IN: University of Notre Dame Press.

Holden, G. W. (1998). Introduction: The development of research into another consequence of family violence. In E. N. Jouriles, G. W. Holden, & R. Geffner (Eds.), *Children exposed to marital violence: Theory, research, and applied issues* (pp. 1–18). Washington DC: American Psychological Association.

Holden, G. W., Stein, J. D., Ritchie, K. L., Harris, S. D., & Jouriles, E. N. (1998). Parenting behaviors and beliefs of battered women. In G. W. Holden, R. A., Geffner, & E. N. Jouriles (Eds.), *Children exposed to marital violence: theory, research, and applied issues* (pp. 289–334). Washington, DC: American Psychological Association.

Holmbeck, G. N. (1997). Toward terminology, conceptual, and statistical clarity in the study of mediators and moderators: Examples from the child clinical and pediatric psychology literatures. *Journal of Consulting and Clinical Psychology, 65,* 599–610.

Holmbeck, G. N. (2002). Post-hoc probing of significant moderational and mediational effects in studies of pediatric populations. *Journal of Pediatric Psychology, 27,* 87–96.

Hotaling, G. T., Straus, M. A., & Lincoln, A. J. (1990). Intrafamily violence, and crime and violence outside the family. In M. Straus & R. J. Gelles (Eds.), *Physical violence in American families* (pp. 315–375). New Brunswick, NJ: Transaction.

Hotaling, G. T., & Sugarman, D. B. (1990). A risk marker analysis of assaulted wives. *Journal of Family Violence, 5*(1), 1–13.

Hubbard, R. M., & Adams, C. F. (1936). Factors affecting the success of child guidance clinic treatment. *American Journal of Orthopsychiatry, 6,* 81–102.

Hughes, H. M. (1988). Psychological and behavioral correlates of family violence in child witness and victims. *American Journal of Orthopsychiatry, 58,* 77–90.

Hughes, H. M. (1997). Research concerning children of battered women: Clinical implications. In R. Geffner, S. B. Sorenson, & P. K. Lundberg-Love (Eds.), *Violence and sexual abuse at home: Current issues, interventions, and research in spousal battering and child maltreatment* (pp. 225–244). Binghamton, NY: Haworth Press.

Hughes, H. M., Graham-Bermann, S. A., & Gruber, G. (2001). Resilience in children exposed to domestic violence. In S. A. Graham-Bermann & J. L. Edleson (Eds.), *Domestic violence in the lives of children: The future of research, intervention, and social policy* (pp. 67–90). Washington, DC: American Psychological Association.

Hughes, H. M., Parkinson, D., & Vargo, M. (1989). Witnessing spouse abuse and experiencing physical abuse: A "double whammy"? *Journal of Family Violence, 4*(2), 197–209.

Independent Monitoring Commission. (2004). *First report of the Independent Monitoring Commission.* London: The Stationery Office. Retrieved from *cain. ulst.ac.uk/issues/politics/docs/imc/imc200404.pdf*

Independent Monitoring Commission. (2007, November). *Seventeenth report of the Independent Monitoring Commission.* London: The Stationery Office. Retrieved from *cain.ulst.ac.uk/issues/politics/docs/imc/imc071107.pdf*

Initiative on Conflict Resolution and Ethnicity (INCORE). (1995). *Coming out of violence: Peace dividends.* Derry/Londonderry, Northern Ireland: Author.

Ingoldsby, E. M., Shaw, D. S., Owens, E. B., & Winslow, E. B. (1999). A longitudinal study of interparental conflict, emotional and behavioral reactivity, and preschoolers' adjustment problems among low-income families. *Journal of Abnormal Child Psychology, 27,* 343–356.

Institute of Medicine. (1994). *Reducing risks for mental disorders: Frontiers for preventive intervention research.* Washington, DC: National Academy Press.

Isabella, R. A., & Belsky, J. (1985). Marital change during the transition to parenthood and security of infant–parent attachment. *Journal of Family Issues, 6*(4), 505–522.

Jarman, N., & O'Halloran, C. (2000). *Peacelines or battlefields?: Responding to violence in interface areas.* Belfast: Community Development Centre.

Jaycox, L. H., Stein, B. D., Kataoka, S. H., Wong, M., Fink, A., Escudero, P., et al. (2002). Violence exposure, posttraumatic stress disorder, and depressive symptoms among recent immigrant schoolchildren. *Journal of the American Academy of Child and Adolescent Psychiatry, 41*(9), 1104–1110.

Jenkins, E. J., & Bell, C. C. (1994). Violence among inner city high school students and post-traumatic stress disorder. In S. Friedman (Ed.), *Anxiety disorders in African Americans* (pp. 76–88). New York: Springer.

Jenkins, J., Simpson, A., Dunn, J., Rasbash, J., & O'Connor, T.G. (2005). Mutual influence of marital conflict and children's behavior problems: Shared and nonshared family risks. *Child Development, 76,* 24–39.

Jenkins, J. M., & Smith, M. A. (1990). Factors protecting children living in disharmonious homes: Maternal reports. *Journal of the American Academy of Child and Adolescent Psychiatry, 29,* 60–69.

Jenkins, J. M., & Smith, M. A. (1991). Marital disharmony and children's behavior problems: Aspects of poor marriage that affect children adversely. *Journal of Child Psychology and Psychiatry, 32,* 793–810.

Jenkins, J. M., Smith, M. A., & Graham, P. J. (1989). Coping with parental quarrels. *Journal of the American Academy of Child and Adolescent Psychiatry, 28*(2), 182–189.

Johnson, P. L., & O'Leary, K. D. (1987). Parental behavior patterns and conduct disorders in girls. *Journal of Abnormal Child Psychology, 15,* 573–581.

Johnston, J. R. (1994). High-conflict divorce. *The Future of Children, 4(1),* 165–182.

Johnston, J. R., Gonzalez, R., & Campbell, L. E. (1987). Ongoing post-divorce conflict and child disturbance. *Journal of Abnormal Child Psychology, 15,* 497–509.

Johnston, J. R., & Roseby, V. (1997). *In the name of the child: A developmental approach to understanding and helping children of conflicted and violent divorce.* New York: Free Press.

Johnston, J. R., Roseby, V., & Kuehnle, K. (2005). *In the name of the child: A developmental approach to understanding and helping children of conflict and violent divorce.* New York: Springer.

Joshi, P. T., & O'Donnell, D. A. (2003). Consequences of child exposure to war and terrorism. *Clinical Child and Family Psychology Review, 6(4),* 275–292.

Jouriles, E. N., Barling, J., & O'Leary, K. D. (1987). Predicting child behavior problems in maritally violent families. *Journal of Abnormal Child Psychology, 15,* 165–173.

Jouriles, E. N., Bourg, W., & Farris, A. (1991). Marital adjustment and child conduct problems: A comparison of the correlation across samples. *Journal of Consulting and Clinical Psychology, 59,* 354–357.

Jouriles, E. N., & Farris, A. M. (1992). Effects of marital conflict on subsequent parent–son interactions. *Behavior Therapy, 23,* 355–374.

Jouriles, E. N., McDonald, R., Norwood, W. D., & Ezell, E. (2001). Issues and controversies in documenting the prevalence of children's exposure to domestic violence. In S. A. Graham-Bermann & J. L. Edleson (Eds.),

Domestic violence in the lives of children: The future of research, intervention, and social policy (pp. 12–34). Washington, DC: American Psychological Association.

Jouriles, E. N., Murphy, C., Farris, A. M., Smith, D.A., Richters, J. E., & Waters, E. (1991). Marital adjustment, childrearing disagreements, and child behavior problems: Increasing the specificity of the marital assessment. *Child Development, 62,* 1424–1433.

Jouriles, E. N., Murphy, C. M., & O'Leary, K. D. (1989). Interspousal aggression, marital discord, and child problems. *Journal of Consulting and Clinical Psychology, 57,* 453–455.

Jouriles, E. N., Norwood, W. D., McDonald, R., Vincent, J. P., & Mahoney, A. (1996). Physical violence and other forms of marital aggression: Links with children's behaviour problems. *Journal of Family Psychology, 10(2),* 223–234.

Jouriles, E. N., Spiller, L. C., Stephens, N., McDonald, R., & Swank, P. (2000). Variability in adjustment of children of battered women: The role of child appraisals of interparent conflict. *Cognitive Therapy and Research, 24,* 233–249.

Kagan, J. (1980). Four questions in psychological development. *International Journal of Behavioral Development, 3,* 231–241.

Karney, B. R., & Bradbury, T. N. (1995). The longitudinal course of marital quality and stability: A review of theory, methods, and research. *Psychological Bulletin, 118(1),* 3–34.

Kaslow, F. W. (2001). Families and family psychology at the millennium: Intersecting crossroads. *American Psychologist, 56,* 37–46.

Katz, L. F. (2001). Physiological processes and mediators of the impact of marital conflict on children. In J. H. Grych & F. D. Fincham (Eds.), *Interparental conflict and child development: Theory, research, and applications* (pp. 188–212). New York: Cambridge University Press.

Katz, L. F., & Gottman, J. M. (1995). Vagal tone protects children from marital conflict. *Development and Psychopathology, 7,* 83–92.

Katz, L. F., & Gottman, J. M. (1996). Spillover effects of marital conflict: In search of parenting and coparenting mechanisms. *New Directions for Child Development, 74,* 57–76.

Katz, L. F., & Gottman, J. M. (1997a). Buffering children from marital conflict and dissolution. *Journal of Clinical Child Psychology, 26,* 157–171.

Katz, L. F., & Gottman, J. M. (1997b, April). *Positive parenting and regulatory physiology as buffers from marital conflict and dissolution.* Paper presented at the biennial meeting of the Society for Research in Child Development, Washington, DC.

Katz, L. F., & Windecker-Nelson, B. (2006). Domestic violence, emotion coaching, and child adjustment. *Journal of Family Psychology, 20,* 56–67.

Katz, L. F., & Woodin, E. M. (2002). Hostility, hostile detachment, and conflict engagement in marriages: Effects on child and family functioning. *Child Development, 73,* 636–651.

Kazak, A. E. (2004). Editorial: Context, collaboration, and care. *Journal of Family Psychology, 18,* 3–4.

Keller, P. S., Cummings, E. M., Davies, P. T., & Mitchell, P. M. (2008). Longitudinal relations between parental drinking problems, family functioning,
and child adjustment. *Development and Psychopathology, 20,* 195–212.

Kempton, T., Thomas, A. M., & Forehand, R. (1989). Dimensions of interparental conflict and adolescent functioning. *Journal of Family Violence, 4(4),*
297–307.

Kerig, P. (1996). Assessing the links between interparental conflict and child
adjustment: The conflicts and problem-solving scales. *Journal of Family Psychology, 10,* 454–473.

Kerig, P. K. (1998). Moderators and mediators of the effects of interparental
conflict on children's adjustment. *Journal of Family Violence, 15,* 345–363.

Kerig, P. K. (2001). Children's coping with interparental conflict. In J. H. Grych
& F. D. Fincham (Eds.), *Interparental conflict and child development: Theory,
research, and application* (pp. 213–245). Cambridge, UK: Cambridge University Press.

Kerig, P. K., & Baucom, D. H. (Eds.). (2004). *Couple observational coding systems.*
Mahwah, NJ: Erlbaum.

Kinsfogel, K. M., & Grych, J. H. (2004). Interparental conflict and adolescent
dating relationships: Integrating cognitive, emotional, and peer influences. *Journal of Family Psychology, 18,* 505–515.

Kitzmann, B. C. (2000). The effects of the type of service interaction on the relationship between employee and customer attitudes. *Dissertation Abstracts
International, 60,* 4944B.

Kitzmann, K. M., Gaylord, N. K., Holt, A. R., & Kenny, E. D. (2003). Child witnesses to domestic violence: A meta-analytic review. *Journal of Consulting
and Clinical Psychology, 71,* 339–352.

Klimes-Dougan, B., Hastings, P. D., Granger, D. A., Usher, B. A., & Zahn-Waxler,
C. (2001). Adrenocortical activity in at-risk and normally developing adolescents: Individual differences in salivary cortisol levels, diurnal variation, and responses to social challenges. *Development and Psychopathology,
13,* 695–719.

Kobak, R. R., Cole, H. E., Ferenz-Gillies, R., Fleming, W. S., & Gamble, W.
(1993). Attachment and emotion regulation during mother–teen problem
solving: A control theory analysis. *Child Development., 64,* 231–245.

Kobak, R. R., Sudler, N., & Gamble, W. (1991). Attachment and depressive symptoms during adolescence: A developmental pathways analysis. *Development
and Psychopathology* [Special issue]: *Attachment and Developmental Psychopathology, 3(4),* 461–474.

Kouros, C. D., Merrilees, C. E., & Cummings, E. M. (2008). Marital conflict and
children's emotional security in the context of parental depression. *Journal
of Marriage and the Family, 70(3),* 684–697.

Kretchmar, M. D., & Jacobvitz, D. B. (2002). Observing mother–child relationships across generations: Boundary patterns, attachment, and the transmission of caregiving. *Family Process, 41,* 351–374.

Krishnakumar, A., & Buehler, C. (2000). Interparental conflict and parenting
behaviors: A meta-analytic review. *Family Relations, 49(1),* 25–44.

Krishnakumar, A., Buehler, C., & Barber, B. K. (2003). Youth perceptions of interpersonal conflict, ineffective parenting, and youth problem behaviors in European-American and African-American families. *Journal of Social and Personal Relationships, 20,* 239–260.

Kuther, T. L. (1999). A developmental–contextual perspective on youth covictimization by community violence. *Adolescence, 34,* 699–714.

Lamb, M. (1984). Fathers, mothers and childcare in the 1980s: Family influences on child development. In K. Borman, D. Quarm, & S. Gideouse (Eds.), *Women in the workplace* (pp. 61–88). Norwood, NJ: Ablex.

Laumakis, M., Margolin, G., & John, R. (1998). The emotional, cognitive, and coping responses of preadolescent children to different dimensions of marital conflict. In G. Holden, B. Geffner, & E. Jouriles (Eds.), *Children and family violence* (pp. 257–288). Washington, DC: American Psychological Association.

Laurenceau, J.-P., & Bolger, N. (2005). Using diary methods to study marital and family processes. *Journal of Family Psychology, 19,* 86–97.

Laurenceau, J.-P., Stanley, S. M., Olmos-Gallo, A., Baucom, B., & Markman, H. J. (2004). Community-based prevention of marital dysfunction: Multilevel modeling of a randomized effectiveness study. *Journal of Consulting and Clinical Psychology, 72*(6), 933–943.

Leary, A., & Katz, L. F. (2004). Coparenting, family-level processes, and peer outcomes: The moderating role of vagal tone. *Development and Psychopathology, 16,* 593–608.

LeBlanc, M. M., Self-Brown, S., & Kelley, M. L. (2003, April). *Family violence exposure and family relationship skills in adolescents exposed to community violence.* Poster session presented at the biennial meeting of the Society for Research in Child Development, Tampa, FL.

Lee, C. M., & Gotlib, I. H. (1991). Family disruption, parental availability, and child adjustment. *Advances in Behavioral Assessment of Children and Families, 5,* 171–199.

Levendosky, A. A., & Graham-Bermann, S. A. (2000). Behavioral observations of parenting in battered women. *Journal of Family Psychology, 14,* 80–94.

Levendosky, A. A., Huth-Bocks, A. C., Shapiro, D. L., & Semel, M. A. (2003). The impact of domestic violence on the maternal–child relationship and preschool-age children's functioning. *Journal of Family Psychology, 17,* 275–287.

Levendosky, A. A., Leahy, K. L., Bogat, G. A., Davidson, W. S., & von Eye, A. (2006). Domestic violence, maternal parenting, maternal mental health, and infant externalizing behavior. *Journal of Family Psychology, 20,* 544–552.

Liberman, A. F., Van Horn, P., & Ippen, C. G. (2005). Toward evidence-based treatment: Child–parent psychotherapy with preschoolers exposed to marital violence. *Journal of the American Academy of Child and Adolescent Psychiatry, 44*(12), 1241–1248.

Linares, L. O., Hereen, T., Bronfman, E., Zuckerman, B., Augustyn, M., & Tronick, E. (2001). A mediational model for the impact of exposure to community violence on early child behavior problems. *Child Development, 72*(2), 639–652.

Lindahl, K. M. (2001). Methodological issues in family observational research. In P. K. Kerig & K. M. Lindahl (Eds.), *Family observational coding systems: Resources for systemic research* (pp. 23–32). Mahwah, NJ: Erlbaum.

Lindahl, K. M., & Malik, N. M. (1999). Marital conflict, family processes, and boys' externalizing behavior in Hispanic American and European American families. *Journal of Clinical Child Psychology, 28,* 12–24.

Lindahl, K. M., Malik, N. M., Kaczynski, K., & Simons, J. S. (2004). Couple power dynamics, systemic family functioning, and child adjustment: A test of a mediational model in a multiethnic sample. *Development and Psychopathology, 16,* 609–630.

Lindsey, E. W., Colwell, M. J., Frabutt, J. M., & MacKinnon-Lewis, C. (2006). Family conflict in divorced and non-divorced families: Potential consequences for boys' friendship status and friendship quality. *Journal of Social and Personal Relationships, 23,* 45–63.

Lindsey, E. W., MacKinnon-Lewis, C., Campbell, J., Frabutt, J. M., & Lamb, M. E. (2002). Marital conflict and boys' peer relationships: The mediating role of mother–son emotional reciprocity. *Journal of Family Psychology, 16,* 466–477.

Long, N. J., & Forehand, R. L. (1987). The effects of parental divorce and parental conflict on children: An overview. *Journal of Developmental and Behavioral Pediatrics, 8,* 292–296.

Long, N. J., & Forehand, R. L. (2002). *Parenting the strong-willed child: The clinically proven five-week program for parents of two- to six-year-olds.* New York: McGraw-Hill.

Long, N. J., Slater, E., Forehand, R. L., & Fauber, R. (1988). Continued high or reduced interparental conflict following divorce: Relation to young adolescent adjustment. *Journal of Consulting and Clinical Psychology, 56,* 467–469.

Lovell, E. L., & Cummings, E. M. (2001). *Conflict, conflict resolution, and the children of Northern Ireland: Towards understanding the impact on children and families* (Joan B. Kroc Institute Occasional Paper Series, Vol. 21, OP No. 1). Notre Dame, IN: Joan B. Kroc Institute for International Peace Studies.

Low, S. M., & Stocker, C. (2005). Family functioning and children's adjustment: Associations among parents' depressed mood, marital hostility, parent–child hostility, and children's adjustment. *Journal of Family Psychology, 19,* 394–403.

Lupien, S. J., Fiocco, A., Wan, N., Lord, C., Tu, M. T., Schramek, T., et al. (2006). Of chickens and men: Reply to the letter to the editor of Gallagher, JP et al., CRF is the "egg and chicken," whereas ACTH and corticosteroids are only "chickens" in response to stress. *Psychoneuroendocrinology, 31*(1), 144–145.

Lupien, S. J., King, S., Meaney, M. J., & McEwen, B. S. (2001). Can poverty get under your skin?: Basal cortisol levels and cognitive function in children from low and high socioeconomic status. *Development and Psychopathology, 13,* 653–676.

Luthar, S. S. (1993). Annotation: Methodological and conceptual issues in research on childhood resilience. *Journal of Child Psychology and Psychiatry, 34,* 441–453.

Luthar, S. S., & Cicchetti, D. (2000). The construct of resilience: Implications for interventions and social policies. *Development and Psychopathology, 12,* 857–885.

Luthar, S. S., Cicchetti, D., & Becker, B. (2000). The construct of resilience: A critical evaluation and guidelines for future work. *Child Development, 71,* 543–562.

Luthar, S. S., Doernberger, C. H., & Zigler, E. (1993). Vulnerability and competence: A review of research on resilience in childhood. In M. E. Hertzig & E. A. Farber (Eds.), *Annual progress in child psychiatry and child development (1992)* (pp. 232–255). New York: Brunner/Mazel.

Lynch, M. (2003). Consequences of children's exposure to community violence. *Clinical Child and Family Psychology Review, 6*(4), 265–274.

Lynch, M., & Cicchetti, D. (1998). An ecological–transactional analysis of children and contexts: The longitudinal interplay among child maltreatment, community violence, and children's symptomatology. *Development and Psychopathology, 10,* 235–257.

Lynch, M., & Cicchetti, D. (2002). Links between community violence and the family system: Evidence from children's feelings of relatedness and perceptions of parent behavior. *Family Processes, 41*(3), 519–532.

Lyons-Ruth, K. (1995). Broadening our conceptual frameworks: Can we reintroduce relational strategies and implicit representational systems to the study of psychopathoogy? *Developmental Psychology, 31,* 432–436.

Mabanglo, M. A. G. (2002). Trauma and the effects of violence exposure and abuse on children: A review of the literature. *Smith College Studies in Social Work, 72*(2), 231–251.

Maccoby, E. E., & Martin, J. (1983). Socialization in contexts of the family: Parent–child interaction. In P. H. Mussen (Series Ed.) & E. M. Hetherington (Vol. Ed.), *Handbook of child psychology: Vol. 4. Socialization, personality, and social development* (4th ed., pp. 1–101). New York: Wiley.

MacGinty, R. Muldoon, O. T., & Ferguson, N. (2007). No war, no peace: Northern Ireland after the agreement. *Poiltical Psychology, 28*(1), 1–11.

MacKinnon, D. P., Lockwood, C. M., Hoffman, J. M., West, S. G., & Sheets, V. (2002). A comparison of methods to test mediation and other intervening variable effects. *Psychological Methods, 7,* 83–104.

Madigan, S., Moran, G., Schuengel, C., Pederson, D. R., & Otten, R. (2007). Unresolved maternal attachment representations, disrupted maternal behavior and disorganized attachment in infancy: Links to toddler behavior problems. *Journal of Child Psychology and Psychiatry, 48,* 1042–1050.

Mahoney, A., Jouriles, E. N., & Scavone, J. (1997). Marital adjustment, marital discord over childrearing, and child behavior problems: Moderating effects of child age. *Journal of Clinical Child Psychology, 26,* 415–423.

Mahoney, A., Lape, L. M., Query, L., & Wieber, J. (1997, April). *Mothers' and fathers' reliance on overt and covert strategies to manage marital conflict: Links with child behavior problems.* Paper presented at the biennial meeting of the Society for Research in Child Development, Washington, DC.

Mann, B. J., & MacKenzie, E. P. (1996). Pathways among marital functioning, parental behaviors, and child behavior problems in school-age boys. *Journal of Clinical Child Psychology, 25,* 183–191.

Marcus, N. E., Lindahl, K. M., & Malik, N. M. (2001). Interparental conflict, children's social cognitions, and child aggression: A test of a mediational model. *Journal of Family Psychology, 15,* 315–333.

Margolin, G. (1987). Participant observation procedures in marital and family assessment. In T. Jacob (Ed.), *Family interaction and psychopathology: Theories, methods, and findings* (pp. 391–426). New York: Plenum Press.

Margolin, G., & Gordis, E. B. (2000). The effects of family and community violence on children. *Annual Review of Psychology, 51,* 445–479.

Margolin, G., & Gordis, E. B. (2003). Co-occurrence between marital aggression and parents' child abuse potential: The impact of cumulative stress. *Violence and Victims, 18,* 243–258.

Margolin, G., Gordis, E. B., & Oliver, P. H. (2004). Links between marital and parent–child interactions: Moderating role of husband-to-wife aggression. *Development and Psychopathology, 16,* 753–771.

Margolin, G., John, R. S., & O'Brien, M. (1989). Sequential affective patterns as a function of marital conflict style. *Journal of Social and Clinical Psychology, 8,* 45–61.

Markman, H. J., & Floyd, F. (1980). Possibilities for the prevention of marital discord: A behavioral perspective. *American Journal of Family Therapy, 8*(2), 29–48.

Markman, H. J., Floyd, F. J., Stanley, S. M., & Storaasli, R. D. (1988). Prevention of marital distress: A longitudinal investigation. *Journal of Consulting and Clinical Psychology, 56,* 210–217.

Markman, H. J., & Kraft, S. A. (1989). Men and women in marriage: Dealing with gender differences in marital therapy. *The Behavior Therapist, 12,* 51–56.

Martinez, P., & Richters, J. E. (1993). The NIMH Community Violence Project: II. Children's distress symptoms associated with violence exposure. *Psychiatry: Interpersonal and Biological Processes, 56*(1), 22–35.

Marvin, R. S., & Stewart, R. B. (1990). A family systems framework for the study of attachment. In M. Greenberg, D. Cicchetti, & E. M. Cummings (Eds.), *Attachment in the preschool years: Theory, research, and intervention* (pp. 51–86). Chicago: University of Chicago Press.

Masten, A. S., Best, K., & Garmezy, N. (1990). Resilience and development: Contributions from the study of children who overcome adversity. *Development and Psychopathology, 2,* 425–444.

Matthews, K. A., Gump, B. B., & Owens, J. F. (2001). Chronic stress influences cardiovascular and neuroendocrine responses during acute stress and recovery, especially for men. *Health Psychology, 20,* 403–410.

Maughan, A., & Cicchetti, D. (2002). Impact of child maltreatment and inter-adult violence on children's emotion regulation abilities and socioemotional adjustment. *Child Development, 73*(5), 1525–1542.

McCoy, K., Cummings, E. M., & Davies, P. T. (2009). Constructive and destructive marital conflict, emotional security, and children's prosocial behavior. *Journal of Child Psychology and Psychiatry, 50*(3), 270–279.

McDonald, R., & Jouriles, E. N. (1991). Marital aggression and child behavior problems: Research findings, mechanisms, and intervention strategies. *The Behavior Therapist, 14,* 189–192.

McDonald, R., Jouriles, E. N., Norwood, E., Ware, H. S., & Ezell E. (2000). Husbands' marital violence and the adjustment problems of clinic-referred children. *Behavior Therapy, 31*(4), 649–655.

McElwain, N. L., & Booth-LaForce, C. (2006). Maternal sensitivity to infant distress and nondistress as predictors of infant–mother attachment security. *Journal of Family Psychology, 20*, 247–255.

McHale, J. P. (1995). Coparenting and triadic interactions during infancy: The roles of marital distress and child gender. *Developmental Psychology, 31*, 985–996.

McHale, J. P. (1997). Overt and covert coparenting processes in the family. *Family Process, 36*, 183–201.

McHale, J. P. (2007). When infants grow up in multiperson relationship systems. *Infant Mental Health Journal, 28*, 370–392.

McHale, J. P., Kazali, C., Rotman, T., Talbot, J., Carleton, M., & Lieberson, R. (2004). The transition to coparenthood: Parents' prebirth expectations and early coparental adjustment at 3 months postpartum. *Development and Psychopathology, 16*, 711–733.

McHale, J. P., & Rasmussen, J. L. (1998). Coparental and family group-level dynamics during infancy: Early family precursors of child and family functioning during preschool. *Development and Psychopathology, 10*, 39–59.

McLanahan, S., Garfinkel, I., Reichman, N., Teitler, J., Carlson, M., & Audigier, C. (2003). *Baseline national report: Fragile Families and Child Wellbeing Study.* Retrieved from *www.fragilefamilies.princeton.edu/documents/nationalreport. pdf*

McLanahan, S., & Sandefur, G. (1994). *Growing up with a single parent: What hurts, what helps.* Cambridge, MA: Harvard University Press.

McLoyd, V. C., Harper, C. I., & Copeland, N. L. (2001). Ethnic minority status, interparental conflict, and child adjustment. In J. H. Grych & F. D. Fincham (Eds.), *Interparental conflict and child development: Theory, research, and applications* (pp. 98–125). New York: Cambridge University Press.

Mikulincer, M., Florian, V., Cowan, P. A., & Cowan, C. P. (2002). Attachment security in couple relationships: A systemic model and its implications for family dynamics. *Family Process, 41*, 405–434.

Mikulincer, M., & Goodman, G. S. (Eds.). (2006). *Dynamics of romantic love: Attachment, caregiving, and sex.* New York: Guilford Press.

Miller, S. A. (1998). *Developmental research methods* (2nd ed.). Englewood Cliffs, NJ: Prentice-Hall.

Minuchin, P. (1985). Families and individual development: Provocations from the field of family therapy. *Child Development, 56*, 289–302.

Mitchell, P. M., McCoy, K. P., Cummings, E. M., Faircloth, W. B., & Cummings, J. S. (in press). *Prevention of the negative effects of conflict on children: A component for children.* Hauppauge, NY: Nova Science.

Morgan, J. R., Nu'Man-Sheppard, J., & Allin, D. W. (1990). Prevention through parent training: Three preventive parent education programs. *Journal of Primary Prevention, 10*, 321–332.

Muller, R. T., Goebel-Fabbri, A. E., Diamond, T., & Dinklage, D. (2000). Social support and the relationship between family and community violence exposure and psychopathology among high risk adolescents. *Child Abuse and Neglect, 24*(4), 449–464.

Murray, D. (2006). Post-accord police reform. In J. Darby (Ed.), *Violence and reconstruction* (pp. 77–100). Notre Dame, IN: University of Notre Dame Press.

Muthen, B., & Muthen, L. K. (2000). Integrating person-centered and variable-centered analyses: Growth mixture modeling with latent trajectory classes. *Alcoholism: Clinical and Experimental Research, 24,* 882–891.

Nation, M., Crusto, C., Wanderman, A., Kumofer, K. L., Sevbolt, D., & Morrissey, K. E. et al. (2003). What works in prevention?: Principles of effective prevention programs. *American Psychologist, 58,* 229–456.

National Advisory Mental Health Council Behavioral Science Workgroup. (2000). *Translating behavioral science into action: Report of the National Advisory Mental Health Counsel Workgroup* (NIH Publication No. 00–4699). Bethesda, MD: National Institute of Mental Health.

Nicolotti, L., El-Sheikh, M., & Whitson, S. M. (2003). Children's coping with marital conflict and their adjustment and physical health: Vulnerability and protective functions. *Journal of Family Psychology, 17,* 315–326.

Niens, U., Cairns, E., & Hewstone, M. (2003). Contact and conflict in Northern Ireland. In O. Hargie & D. Dickson (Eds.), *Researching the Troubles: Social science perspectives on the Northern Ireland conflict* (pp. 123–140). Edinburgh, UK: Mainstream.

Nock, S. (2005). Marriage as a public issue. *The Future of Children, 15*(2), 13–32.

Notarius, C., & Markman, H. (1993). *We can work it out: Making sense of marital conflict.* New York: Putnam.

Nucci, L., & Smetana, J. G. (1996). Mothers' concept of young children's areas of personal freedom. *Child Development, 67*(4), 1870–1886.

O'Brien, M., Margolin, G., John, R. S., & Krueger, L. (1991). Mothers' and sons' cognitive and emotional reactions to simulated marital and family conflict. *Journal of Consulting and Clinical Psychology, 59,* 692–703.

O'Connor, T. G., Hetherington, E. M., & Clingempeel, W. G. (1997). Systems and bidirectional influences in families. *Journal of Social and Personal Relationships, 14,* 491–504.

O'Connor, T. G., Hetherington, E. M., & Reiss, D. (1998). Family systems and adolescent development: Shared and nonshared risk and protective factors in nondivorced and remarried families. *Development and Psychopathology, 10,* 353–375.

O'Connor, T. G., & Insabella, G. M. (1999). Adolescent siblings in stepfamilies: Functioning and adolescent adjustment. Marital satisfaction, relationships, and roles. *Monographs of the Society for Research on Child Development, 64*(4, Serial No. 259), 50–78.

O'Keefe, M. (1997). Adolescents' exposure to community and school violence: Prevalence and behavioral correlates. *Journal of Adolescent Health, 20*(5), 368–376.

Okun, A., Parker, J. G., & Levendosky, A. A. (1994). Distinct and interactive contributions of physical abuse, socioeconomic disadvantage, and negative life events to children's social, cognitive, and affective adjustment. *Development and Psychopathology, 6,* 77–98.

Oosterman, M., & Schuengel, C. (2007). Physiological effects of separation and reunion in relation to attachment and temperament in young children. *Developmental Psychobiology, 49*(2), 119–128.

Oppenheim, D., Emde, R. N., & Warren, S. (1997). Children's narrative representations of mothers: Their development and associations with child and mother adaptation. *Child Development, 68,* 127–138.

Osborne, B. (Ed.). (2004). Fair employment in Northern Ireland: A generation on. Belfast: Blackstaff Press.

Owen, M. T., & Cox, M. J. (1997). Marital conflict and the development of infant–parent attachment relationships. *Journal of Family Psychology, 11,* 152–164.

Papp, L. M., Cummings, E. M., & Goeke-Morey, M. C. (2002). Marital conflict in the home when children are present versus absent. *Developmental Psychology, 38,* 774–783.

Papp, L. M., Cummings, E. M., & Schermerhorn, A. (2004). The impact of marital adjustment on mothers' and fathers' symptomatology: Implications for children's functioning. *Journal of Marriage and Family, 66,* 368–384.

Papp, L. M., Goeke-Morey, M. C., & Cummings, E. M. (2007). Linkages between spouses' psychological distress and marital conflict in the home. *Journal of Family Psychology, 21,* 533–537.

Parke, R. D. (1979). Interactional designs. In R. B. Cairns (Ed.), *The analysis of social interaction: Methods, issues, and illustrations* (pp. 15–39). New York: Wiley.

Parke, R. D. (1998). Editorial. *Journal of Family Psychology, 12,* 3–6.

Parke, R. D. (2000). Beyond white and middle class: Cultural variations in families—assessments, processes, and policies. *Journal of Family Psychology, 14,* 331–333.

Parke, R.D., Kim, M., Flyr, M., McDowell, D. J., Simpkins, S. D., Killian, C. M., et al. (2001). Managing marital conflict: Links with children's peer relationships. In J. H. Grych & F. D. Fincham (Eds.), *Interparental conflict and child development: Theory, research, and applications* (pp. 291–314). New York: Cambridge University Press.

Patterson, G. R., DeBaryshe, B., & Ramsey, E. (1989). A developmental perspective on antisocial behavior. *American Psychologist, 44,* 329–335.

Patterson, G. R., & Yoerger, K. (1997). A developmental model for late-onset delinquency. In D. W. Osgood (Ed.), *Nebraska Symposium on Motivation: Vol. 44. Motivation and delinquency* (pp. 119–177). Lincoln: University of Nebraska Press.

Pauli-Pott, U., & Beckmann, D. (2007). On the association of interparental conflict with developing behavioral inhibition and behavior problems in early childhood. *Journal of Family Psychology, 21*(3), 529–532.

Pedro-Carroll, J. L. (2005). Fostering resilience in the aftermath of divorce: The role of evidence-based programs for children. *Family Court Review* [Special issue]: *Prevention: Research, Policy, and Evidence-Based Practice, 43*(1), 52–64.

Pedro-Carroll, J. L., Sutton, S. E., & Wyman, P. A. (1999). A two-year follow-up evaluation of a preventive intervention for young children of divorce. *School Psychology Review* [Special issue]: *Beginning School Ready to Learn: Parental Involvement and Effective Educational Programs, 28*(3), 467–476.

Pehrson, K.L., & Robinson, C.C. (1990). Parent education: Does it make a difference? *Child Study Journal, 20,* 221–236.

Pendry, P., & Adam, E. K. (2007). Associations between parents' marital functioning, maternal parenting quality, maternal emotion and child cortisol levels. *International Journal of Behavioral Development, 31,* 218–231.

Peris, T. S., Goeke-Morey, M. C., Cummings, E. M., & Emery, R. E. (2008). Marital conflict and support-seeking by parents in adolescence: Empirical support for the parentification construct. *Journal of Family Psychology, 22*(4), 633–642.

Phares, V., Fields, S., Kamboukis, D., & Lopez, E. (2005). Still looking for Poppa. *American Psychologist, 60(7),* 735–736.

Pine, D., & Charney, D. (2002). Children, stress, and sensitization: An integration of basic and clinical research on emotion. *Biological Psychiatry, 52,* 773–775.

Police Service of Northern Ireland. (2007). *Summary of statistics relating to the security situation: 1st April 2006–31st March 2007.* Retrieved from *www.psni. police.uk/6._statistics_relating_to_the_security_situation.pdf*

Pollak, S. D. (2005). Early adversity and mechanisms of plasticity: Integrating affective neuroscience with developmental approaches to psychopathology. *Development and Psychopathology, 17,* 735–752.

Pollak, S. D., & Tolley-Schell, S. A. (2003). Selective attention to facial emotion in physically abused children. *Journal of Abnormal Psychology, 112,* 323–338.

Porges, S. W., Doussard-Roosevelt, J. A., Portales, A. L., & Greenspan, S. I. (1996). Infant regulation of the vagal "brake" predicts child behavior problems: A psychobiological model of social behavior. *Developmental Psychobiology, 29,* 697–712.

Porges, S.W., Doussard-Roosevelt, J. A., Portales, L. A., & Suess, P. E. (1994). Cardiac vagal tone: Stability and relation to difficultness in infants and 3–year-olds. *Developmental Psychobiology, 27,* 289–300.

Porter, B., & O'Leary, K.D. (1980). Marital discord and childhood behavior problems. *Journal of Abnormal Child Psychology, 8,* 287–295.

Prinz, R. J., & Feerick, M. M. (2003). Next steps in research on children exposed to domestic violence. *Clinical Child and Family Psychology Review, 6*(3), 215–219.

Punamaki, R. L. (2001). From childhood trauma to adult well-being through psychosocial assistance of Chilean families. *Journal of Community Psychology, 29*(3), 281–303.

Quigley, B. M., & Leonard, K. E. (2000). Alcohol and the continuation of early marital aggression. *Alcoholism: Clinical and Experimental Research, 24*(7), 1003–1010.

Quigley, K., & Stifter, C. A. (2006). A comparative validation of sympathetic reactivity in children and adults. *Psychophysiology, 43,* 357–365.

Raikes, H. A., & Thompson, R. A. (2005). Links between risk and attachment security: Models of influence. *Journal of Applied Developmental Psychology, 26*, 440–455.

Raudenbush, S. W. (2003). Comments on "Measurement, objectivity, and trust" by Theodore M. Porter. *Measurement: Interdisciplinary Research Perspectives, 1*(4), 274–278.

Reiss, D., Plomin, R., & Hetherington, E. M. (1991). Genetics and psychiatry: An underalded window on the environment. *American Journal of Psychiatry, 148*, 283–291.

Repetti, R. L., McGrath, E. P., & Ishikawa, S. S. (1999). Daily stress and coping in childhood and adolescence. In A. J. Goreczny & M. Hersen (Eds.), *Handbook of pediatric and adolescent health psychology* (pp. 343–360). Needham Heights, MA: Allyn & Bacon.

Repetti, R. L., Taylor, S. E., & Saxbe, D. (2007). The influence of early socialization experiences on the development of biological systems. In J. Grusec & P. Hastings (Eds.), *Handbook of socialization* (pp. 124–152). New York: Guilford Press.

Repetti, R. L., Taylor, S. E., & Seeman, T. E. (2002). Risky families: Family social environments and the mental and physical health of offspring. *Psychological Bulletin, 128*, 330–366.

Repetti, R. L., & Wood, J. (1997). Effects of daily stress at work on mothers' interactions with preschoolers. *Journal of Family Psychology, 11*, 90–108.

Rhoades, K. A. (2008). Children's responses to interparental conflict: A meta-analysis of their associations with child adjustment. *Child Development, 75*(6), 1942–1956.

Rholes, W. S., Simpson, J. A., & Friedman, M. (2006). Avoidant attachment and the experience of parenting. *Personality and Social Psychology Bulletin, 32*, 275–285.

Richters, J. E. (1997). Toward a developmental perspective on conduct disorder. *Development and Psychopathology, 9*, 193–229.

Richters, J. E., & Martinez, P. (1993a). Children as victims of and witnesses to violence in a Washington, D.C. neighborhood. In N. A. Fox & L. A. Leavitt (Eds.), *The psychological effects of war and violence on children* (pp. 243–278). Hillsdale, NJ: Erlbaum.

Richters, J. E., & Martinez, P. (1993b). Violent communities, family choices, and children's chances: An algorithm for improving the odds. *Development and Psychopathology, 5*(4), 609–627.

Rogers, C. R. (1965). A humanistic conception of man. In R. E. Farson (Ed.), *Science and human affairs* (pp. 18–31). Palo Alto, CA: Science & Behavior Books.

Rogers, M. J., & Holmbeck, G. N. (1997). Effects of interparental aggression on children's adjustment: The moderating role of cognitive appraisal and coping. *Journal of Family Psychology, 11*, 125–130.

Rossman, B. B. R., & Rea, J. G. (2005). The relation of parenting styles and inconsistencies to adaptive functioning for children in conflictual and violent families. *Journal of Family Violence, 20*, 261–277.

Rutter, M. (1970). Sex differences in response to family stress. In E. J. Anthony

& C. Koupernik (Eds.), *The child and his family* (pp. 165–196). New York: Wiley.

Rutter, M. (1983). Statistical and personal interactions: Facets and perspectives. In D. Magnusson & V. Allen (Eds.), *Human development: An interactional perspective* (pp. 295–319). New York: Academic Press.

Rutter, M., Moffitt, T. E., & Caspi, A. (2006). Gene-environment interplay and psychopathology: Multiple varieties but real effects. *Journal of Child Psychology and Psychiatry, 47*(3–4), 226–261.

Rutter, M., Yule, B., Quinton, D., Rowlands, O., Yule, W., & Berger, M. (1974). Attainment and adjustment in two geographical areas: III. Some factors accounting for area differences. *British Journal of Psychiatry, 125,* 520–533.

Sabatelli, R. M., & Bartle, S. E. (1995). Survey approaches to the assessment of family functioning: Conceptual, operational, and analytical issues. *Journal of Marriage and the Family, 57*(4), 1025–1039.

Saltzman, K. M., Holden, G. W., & Holahan, C. J. (2005). The psychobiology of children exposed to marital violence. *Journal of Clinical Child and Adolescent Psychology, 34,* 129–139.

Schacht, P. M., Cummings, E. M., & Davies, P. T. (in press). Fathering in family context and child adjustment: A longitudinal analysis. *Journal of Family Psychology.*

Schermerhorn, A. C., & Cummings, E. M. (2008). Transactional family dynamics: A new framework for conceptualizing family influence processes. *Advances in Child Development and Behavior, 36,* 187–250.

Schermerhorn, A. C., Cummings, E. M., & Davies, P. T. (2005). Children's perceived agency in the context of marital conflict: Relations with marital conflict over time. *Merrill–Palmer Quarterly, 51*(2), 121–144.

Schermerhorn, A. C., Cummings, E. M., & Davies, P. T. (2008). Children's representations of multiple family relationships: Organizational structure and development in early childhood. *Journal of Family Psychology, 22,* 89–101.

Schermerhorn, A. C., Cummings, E. M., DeCarlo, C. A., & Davies, P. T. (2007). Children's influence in the marital relationship. *Journal of Family Psychology, 21*(2), 259–269.

Schoppe-Sullivan, S. J., Mangelsdorf, S. C., & Frosch, C. A. (2001). Coparenting, family process, and family structure: Implications for preschoolers' externalizing behavior problems. *Journal of Family Psychology, 15,* 526–545.

Schoppe-Sullivan, S. J., Mangelsdorf, S. C., Frosch, C. A., & McHale, J. L. (2004). Associations between coparenting and marital behavior from infancy to the preschool years. *Journal of Family Psychology, 18,* 194–207.

Schoppe-Sullivan, S. J., Schermerhorn, A. C., & Cummings, E. M. (2007). Marital conflict and children's adjustment: Evaluation of the parenting process model. *Journal of Marriage and Family, 69*(5), 1118–1134.

Schwartz, D., & Gorman, A. H. (2003). Community violence exposure and children's academic functioning. *Journal of Educational Psychology, 95*(1), 163–173.

Schwartz, D., & Proctor, L. J. (2000). Community violence exposure and children's social adjustment in the school peer group: The mediating roles of emotion regulation and social cognition. *Journal of Consulting and Clinical Psychology, 68*(4), 670–683.

Seifer, R. (1995). Perils and pitfalls of high-risk research. *Developmental Psychology, 31*(3), 420–424.

Selner-O'Hagan, M. B., Kindlon, D. J., Buka, S. I., Raudenbush, S. W., & Earls, F. J. (1998). Assessing exposure to violence in urban youth. *Journal of Child Psychology and Psychiatry, 39*(2), 215–224.

Shamir, H., Du Rocher Schudlich, T., & Cummings, E. M. (2001). Marital conflict, parenting styles, and children's representations of family relationships. *Parenting: Science and Practice, 1*(1–2), 123–151.

Shaw, J.A. (2003). Children exposed to war/terrorism. *Clinical Child and Family Psychology Review, 6*, 237–246.

Shaw, D. S., Gilliom, M., Ingoldsby, E. M., & Nagin, D. S. (2003). Trajectories leading to school-age conduct problems. *Developmental Psychology, 39*, 189–200.

Shelton, K. H., Harold, G. T., Goeke-Morey, M. C., & Cummings, E. M. (2006). Children's coping with marital conflict: The role of conflict expression and gender. *Social Development, 15*, 232–247.

Shields, A., Ryan, R. M., & Cicchetti, D. (2001). Narrative representations of caregivers and emotion dysregulation as predictors of maltreated children's rejection by peers. *Developmental Psychology, 37*, 321–337.

Shifflett, K., & Cummings, E. M. (1999). A program for educating parents about the effects of divorce and conflict on children. *Family Relations, 48*(1), 79–98.

Shifflett-Simpson, K., & Cummings, E. M. (1996). Mixed message resolution and children's responses to interadult conflict. *Child Development, 67*(2), 437–448.

Shirlow, P., & Murtagh, B. (2006). *Belfast: Segregation, violence and the city.* London: Pluto Press.

Shrout, P. E., & Bolger, N. (2002). Mediation in experimental and nonexperimental studies: New procedures and recommendations. *Psychological Methods, 7*, 422–445.

Sibley, C. G., & Overall, N. C. (2007). The boundaries between attachment and personality: Associations across three levels of the attachment network. *Journal of Research in Personality, 41*, 960–967.

Sim, H., & Vuchinich, S. (1996). The declining effects of family stressors on antisocial behavior from childhood to adolescence and early adulthood. *Journal of Family Issues, 17*, 408–427.

Singer, M. I., Anglin, T. M., Song, L., & Lunghofer, L. (1995). Adolescents' exposure to violence and associated symptoms of psychological trauma. *Journal of the American Medical Association, 273*(6), 477–482.

Singer, M. I., Miller, D. B., Guo, S., Flannery, D. J., Frierson, T., & Slovak, K. (1999). Contributions to violent behavior among elementary and middle school children. *Pediatrics, 104*, 878–884.

Sisk, T. D. (2006). Political violence and peace accords: Searching for the silver lining. In J. Darby (Ed.), *Violence and reconstruction* (pp. 121–142). Notre Dame, IN: University of Notre Dame Press.

Skopp, N. A., McDonald, R., Jouriles, E. N., & Rosenfield, D. (2007). Partner aggression and children's externalizing problems: Maternal and partner warmth as protective factors. *Journal of Family Psychology, 21,* 459–467.

Slater, E. J., & Haber, J. D. (1984). Adolescent adjustment following divorce as a function of familial conflict. *Journal of Consulting and Clinical Psychology, 52,* 920–921.

Smyth, J. M. (1998). Written emotional expression: Effect sizes, outcome types, and moderating variables. *Journal of Consulting and Clinical Psychology, 66*(1), 174–184.

Smyth, M., & Scott, M. (2000). *The Youthquest 2000 Survey: A report on young people's views and experiences in Northern Ireland.* Derry/Londonderry, Northern Ireland: Initiative on Conflict Resolution and Ethnicity (INCORE).

Snyder, D. K., & Kazak, A. E. (2005). Methodology in family science: Introduction to the special issue. *Journal of Family Psychology, 19*(1), 3–5.

Snyder, D. K., Klein, M, A., Gdowski, C. L., Faulstich, C., & LaCombe, J. (1988). Generalized dysfunction in clinic and nonclinic families: A comparative analysis. *Journal of Abnormal Child Psychology, 16,* 97–109.

Snyder, J., Cramer, A., Afrank, J., & Patterson, G. R. (2005). The contributions of ineffective discipline and parental hostile attributions of child misbehavior to the development of conduct problems at home and school. *Developmental Psychology, 41,* 30–41.

Snyder, J. R. (1998). Marital conflict and child adjustment: What about gender? *Developmental Review, 18(3),* 390–420.

Sroufe, L. A. (1990). Considering normal and abnormal together: The essence of developmental psychopathology. *Development and Psychopathology, 2,* 335–347.

Sroufe, L. A. (1997). Psychopathology as an outcome of development. *Development and Psychopathology, 9,* 251–268.

Sroufe, L. A., Egeland, B., & Kreutzer, T. (1990). The face of early experience following developmental change: Longitudinal approaches to individual adaptation in childhood. *Child Development, 61,* 1363–1373.

Sroufe, L. A., & Rutter, M. (1984). The domain of developmental psychopathology. *Child Development, 55,* 17–29.

Stein, B. D., Jaycox, L. H., Kataoka, S., Rhodes, H. J., & Vestal, K. D. (2003). Prevalence of child and adolescent exposure to community violence. *Clinical Child and Family Psychology Review, 6*(4), 247–264.

Steinberg, L., & Avenevoli, S. (2000). The role of context in the development of psychopathology: A conceptual framework and some speculative propositions. *Child Development, 71*(1), 66–74.

Steinberg, L., Lamborn, S. D., Dornbusch, S. M., & Darling, N. (1992). Impact of parenting practices on adolescent achievement: Authoritative parenting, school involvement, and encouragement to succeed. *Child Development, 63,* 1266–1281.

Sternberg, K. J., Lamb, M. E., Greenbaum, C., Cicchetti, D., Dawud, S., Cortes, R. M., et al. (1993). Effects of domestic violence on children's behavior problems and depression. *Developmental Psychology, 29,* 44–52.

Stevenson-Hinde, J. (1990). Attachment within family systems: An overview. *Infant Mental Health Journal, 11,* 218–227.

Stocker, C. M., & Richmond, M. K. (2007). Longitudinal associations between hostility in adolescents' family relationships and friendships and hostility in their romantic relationships. *Journal of Family Psychology, 21,* 490–497.

Stocker, C. M., & Youngblade, L. (1999). Marital conflict and parental hostility: Links with children's sibling and peer relationships. *Journal of Family Psychology, 13,* 598–609.

Stolz, H. E., Barber, B. K., & Olsen, J. A. (2005). Toward disentangling fathering and mothering: An assessment of relative importance. *Journal of Marriage and the Family, 67,* 1076–1092.

Straus, M. A., Gelles, R. J., & Steinmetz, S. K. (1980). *Behind closed doors: Violence in the American family.* Garden City, NY: Anchor/Doubleday.

Sturge-Apple, M. L., Davies, P. T., & Cummings, E. M. (2006a). Hostility and withdrawal in marital conflict: Effects on parental emotional unavailability and inconsistent discipline. *Journal of Family Psychology, 20*(2), 227–238.

Sturge-Apple, M. L., Davies, P. T., & Cummings, E. M. (2006b). The impact of hostility and withdrawal in interparental conflict on parental emotional unavailability and children's adjustment difficulties. *Child Development, 77*(6), 1623–1641.

Sturge-Apple, M., Davies, P. T., Winter, M. A., Cummings, E. M., & Schermerhorn, A. C. (2008). Interparental conflict and children's school performance: The explanatory role of children's internal representations of interparental and parent–child relationships. *Developmental Psychology, 44*(6), 1678–1690.

Susman, E. J. (2006). Psychobiology of persistent antisocial behavior: Stress, early vulnerabilities, and the attenuation hypothesis. *Neuroscience and Biobehavioral Reviews, 30,* 376–389.

Thompson, R. A. (1997). Sensitivity and security: New questions to ponder. *Child Development, 68,* 595–597.

Thompson, R. A. (1998). Early sociopersonality development. In W. Damon (Series Ed.) & N. Eisenberg (Vol. Ed.), *Handbook of child psychology: Vol 3. Social, emotional, and personality development* (5th ed., pp. 25–104). New York: Wiley.

Toth, S. L., & Cicchetti, D. (2006). Promises and possibilities: The application of research in the area of child maltreatment to policies and practices. *Journal of Social Issues, 62,* 863–880.

Toth, S. L., Rogosch, F. A., Manly, J. T., & Cicchetti, D. (2006). The efficacy of toddler-parent psychotherapy to reorganize attachment in the young offspring of mothers with major depressive disorder: A randomized preventive trial. *Journal of Consulting and Clinical Psychology, 74*(6), 1006–1016.

Towle, C. (1931). The evaluation and management of marital status in foster homes. *American Journal of Orthopsychiatry, 1,* 271–284.

Treboux, D., Crowell, J. A., & Waters, E. (2004). When "new" meets "old": Configurations of adult attachment representations and their implications for marital functioning. *Developmental Psychology, 40,* 295–314.

Trew, K. (1981). Sectarianism in Northern Ireland: A research perspective. *Bulletin of the British Psychological Society, 34,* 390.

Trickett, P. K., Aber, J. L., Carlson, V., & Cicchetti, D. (1991). Relationship of socioeconomic status to the etiology and developmental sequelae of physical child abuse. *Developmental Psychology, 27,* 148–158.

Trickett, P. K., Duran, L., & Horn, J. L. (2003). Community violence as it affects child development: Issues of definition. *Clinical Child and Family Psychology Review, 6*(4), 223–236.

Trickett, P. K., & Susman, E. J. (1989). Perceived similarities and disagreements about childrearing practices in abusive and nonabusive families: Intergenerational and concurrent family processes. In D. Cicchetti & V. Carlson (Eds.), *Child maltreatment: Theory and research on the causes and consequences of child abuse and neglect* (pp. 280–301). Cambridge, UK: Cambridge University Press.

Tschann, J. M., Flores, E., Pasch, L., & Marin, B. V. (1999). Assessing interparental conflict: Reports of parents and adolescents in European and Mexican American families. *Journal of Marriage and the Family, 61,* 269–283.

Turner, C. M., & Dadds, M. R. (2001). Clinical prevention and remediation of child adjustment problems. In J. H. Grych & F. D. Fincham (Eds.), *Interparental conflict and child development: Theory, research, and applications* (pp. 387–416). New York: Cambridge University Press.

Van IJzendoorn, M. H., Bakermans-Kranenburg, M. J., & Sagi-Schwartz, A. (2003). Are children of Holocaust survivors less well-adapted?: A meta-analytic investigation of secondary traumatization. *Journal of Traumatic Stress, 16*(5), 459–469.

Vuchinich, S., Emery, R. E., & Cassidy, J. (1988). Family members and third parties in dyadic family conflict: Strategies, alliances, and outcomes. *Child Development, 59*(5), 1293–1302.

Wachs, T. D. (1991). Environmental considerations in studies with nonextreme groups. In T. D. Wachs & R. Plomin (Eds.), *Conceptualization and measurement of organism–environment interaction* (pp. 162–182). Washington, DC: American Psychological Association.

Wallace, R. (1935). A study of relationship between emotional tone in the home and adjustment status in cases referred to a traveling child guidance clinic. *Journal of Juvenile Research, 19,* 205–220.

Wallerstein, J. S., & Blakeslee, S. (1989). *Second chances: Men, women, and children a decade after divorce.* New York: Ticknor & Fields.

Wampler, K. S., Riggs, B., & Kimball, T. G. (2004). Observing attachment behavior in couples: The Adult Attachment Behavior Q-Set (AABQ). *Family Process, 43,* 315–335.

Wasserstein, S. B., & La Greca, A. M. (1996). Can peer support buffer against behavioral consequences of parental discord? *Journal of Clinical Child Psychology, 25,* 177–182.

Waters, E., & Cummings, E. M. (2000). A secure base from which to explore close relationships. *Child Development, 49,* 164–172.

Webster-Stratton, C. (1994). Advancing videotape parent training: A comparison study. *Journal of Consulting and Clinical Psychology, 62*(3), 583–593.

Webster-Stratton, C., & Hammond, M. (1999). Marital conflict management skills, parenting style, and early-onset conduct problems: Processes and pathways. *Journal of Child Psychology and Psychology, 40,* 917–927.

Weiss, R. L., Hops, H., & Patterson, G. R. (1973). A framework for conceptualizing marital conflict, a technology for altering it, some data for evaluating it. In L. A. Hamerlynck, L. C. Handy, & E. J. Mash (Eds.), *Behavior change: Methodology, concepts, and practice* (pp. 309–342). Champaign, IL: Research Press.

Weissman, M. M., Warner, V., Wickramaratne, P., Moreau, D., & Olfson, M. (1997). Offspring of depressed parents: 10 years later. *Archives of General Psychiatry, 54(10)*, 932–940.

Werner, H. (1957). The concept of development from a comparative and organismic point of view. In D. B. Harris (Ed.), *The concept of development* (pp. 125–148). Minneapolis: University of Minnesota Press.

West, M. O., & Prinz, R. J. (1987). Parental alcoholism and childhood psychopathology. *Psychological Bulletin, 102*, 204–218.

Westerman, M. A. (1987). "Triangulation," marital discord, and child behavior problems. *Journal of Social and Personality Relationships, 4*, 87–106.

Wheeler, L., & Reis, H. T. (1991). Self-recording of everyday life events: Origins, types, and uses. *Journal of Personality, 59*, 339–354.

Whisman, M. A. (2001). The association between depression and marital dissatisfaction. In S. R. H. Beach (Ed.), *Marital and family processes in depression: A scientific foundation for clinical practice* (pp. 3–24). Washington, DC: American Psychological Association.

Wierson, M., Forehand, R., & McCombs, A. (1988). The relationship of early adolescent functioning to parent-reported and adolescent-perceived interparental conflict. *Journal of Abnormal Child Psychology, 16*, 707–718.

Willett, J. B., Singer, J. D., & Martin, N. C. (1998). The design and analysis of longitudinal studies of development and psychopathology in context: Statistical models and methodological recommendations. *Development and Psychopathology, 10*, 395–426.

Wilson, B. J., & Gottman, J. M. (1995). Marital interaction and parenting. In M. H. Bornstein (Ed.), *Handbook of parenting: Vol. 4. Applied and practical parenting* (pp. 33–55). Hillsdale, NJ: Erlbaum.

Windle, M. (2000). A latent growth curve model of delinquent activity among adolescents. *Applied Developmental Science, 4*, 193–207.

Windle, M., & Davies, P. T. (1999). Developmental theory and research. In K. E. Leonard & H. T. Blane (Eds.), *Psychological theories of drinking and alcoholism* (2nd ed., pp. 164–202). New York: Guilford Press.

Windle, M., & Tubman, J. G. (1999). Children of alcoholics. In W. K. Silverman & T. H. Ollendick (Eds.), *Developmental issues in the clinical treatment of children* (pp. 393–414). Needham Heights, MA: Allyn & Bacon.

Winter, M. A., Davies, P. T., Hightower, A. D., & Meyer, S. (2006). Relations among family adversity, caregiver communications, and children's family representations. *Journal of Family Psychology, 20*, 348–351.

Wolchik, S. A., West, S. G. Sandler, I. N., Tein, J.-Y., Coatsworth, D., Lengua, L. et al. (2000). An experimental evaluation of theory-based mother and mother–child programs for children of divorce. *Journal of Consulting and Clinical Psychology, 68*, 843–856.

Wolfe, D. A., Jaffe, P., Wilson, S. K., & Zak, L. (1985). Children of battered women: The relation of child behavior to family violence and maternal stress. *Journal of Consulting and Clinical Psychology, 53*(5), 657–665.

Wood, B. L., Klebba, K. B., & Miller, B. D. (2000). Evolving the biobehavioral family model: The fit of attachment. *Family Process, 39*, 319–344.

Yates, T. M., Dodds, M. F., Sroufe, L. A., & Egeland, B. (2003). Exposure to partner violence and child behavior problems: A prospective study controlling for child physical abuse and neglect, child cognitive ability, socioeconomic status, and life stress. *Development and Psychopathology, 15*(1), 199–218.

Zahar, M. J. (2006). Political violence in peace processes: Voice, exit, and loyalty in the post-accord period. In J. Darby (Ed.), *Violence and reconstruction* (pp. 33–52). Notre Dame, IN: University of Notre Dame Press.

Zahn-Waxler, C., Duggal, S., & Gruber, R. (2002). Parental psychopathology. In M. H. Bornstein (Ed.), *Handbook of parenting: Vol. 4. Social conditions and applied parenting* (2nd ed., pp. 295–327). Mahwah, NJ: Erlbaum.

Zahn-Waxler, C., & Radke-Yarrow, M. (1982). The development of altruism: alternative research strategies. In N. Eisenberg-Berg (Ed.), *The development of prosocial behavior* (pp. 109–317). New York: Academic Press.

Index

Page numbers followed by *f* indicate figure, *t* indicate table